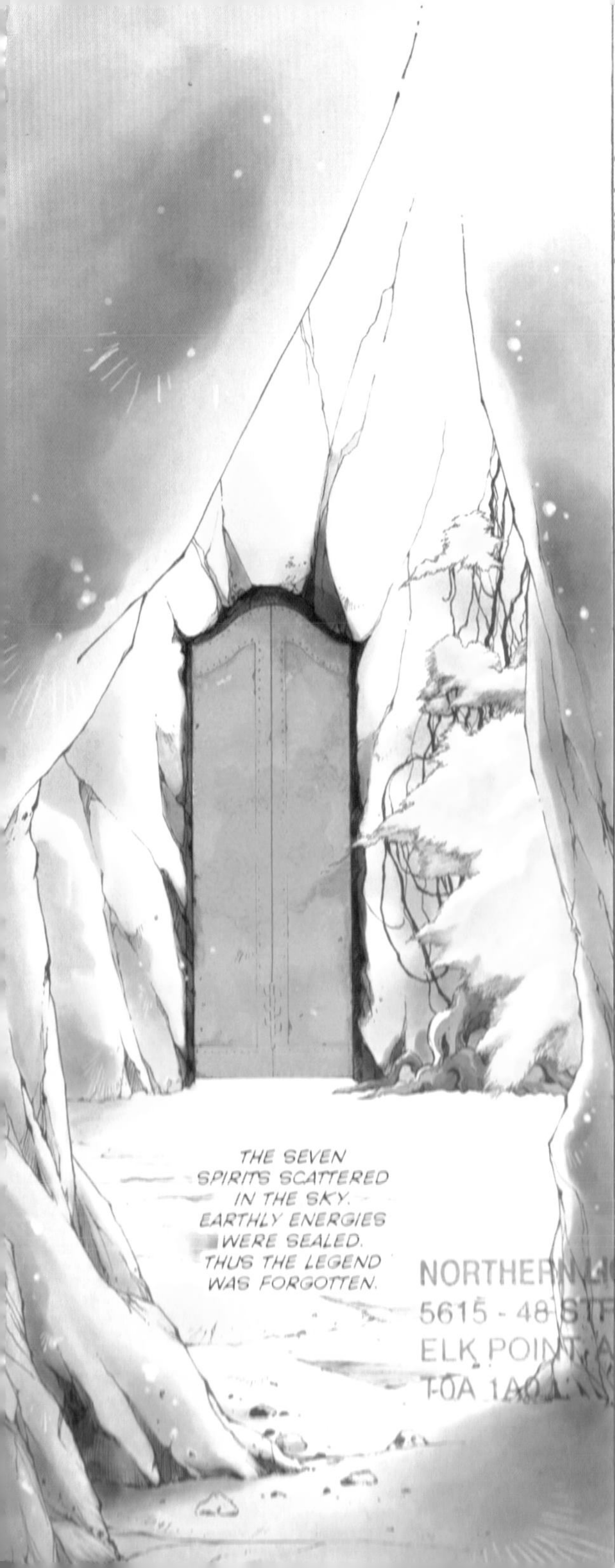
THE SEVEN SPIRITS SCATTERED IN THE SKY. EARTHLY ENERGIES WERE SEALED. THUS THE LEGEND WAS FORGOTTEN.

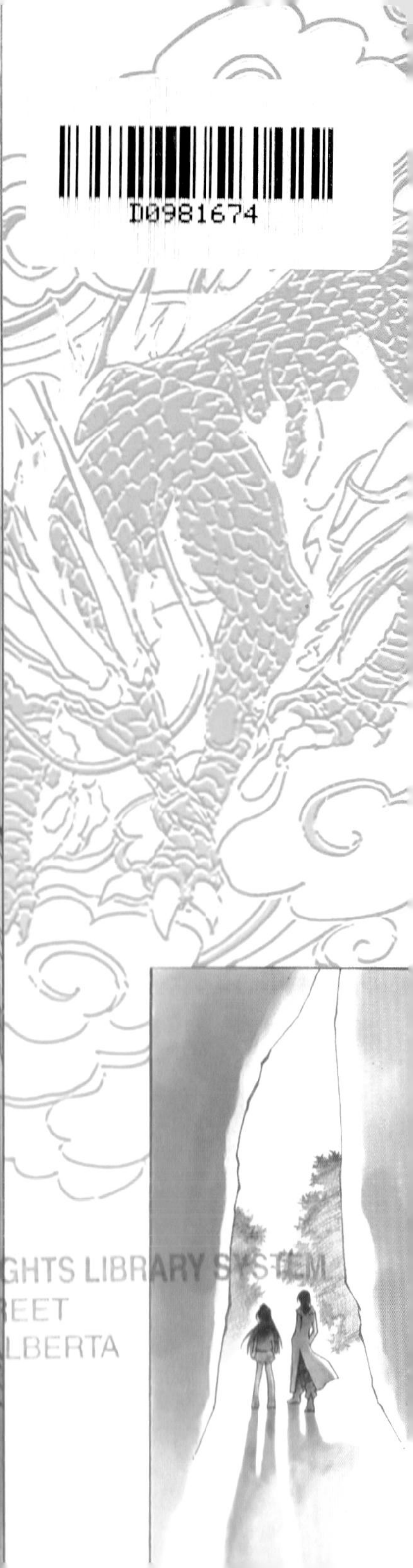

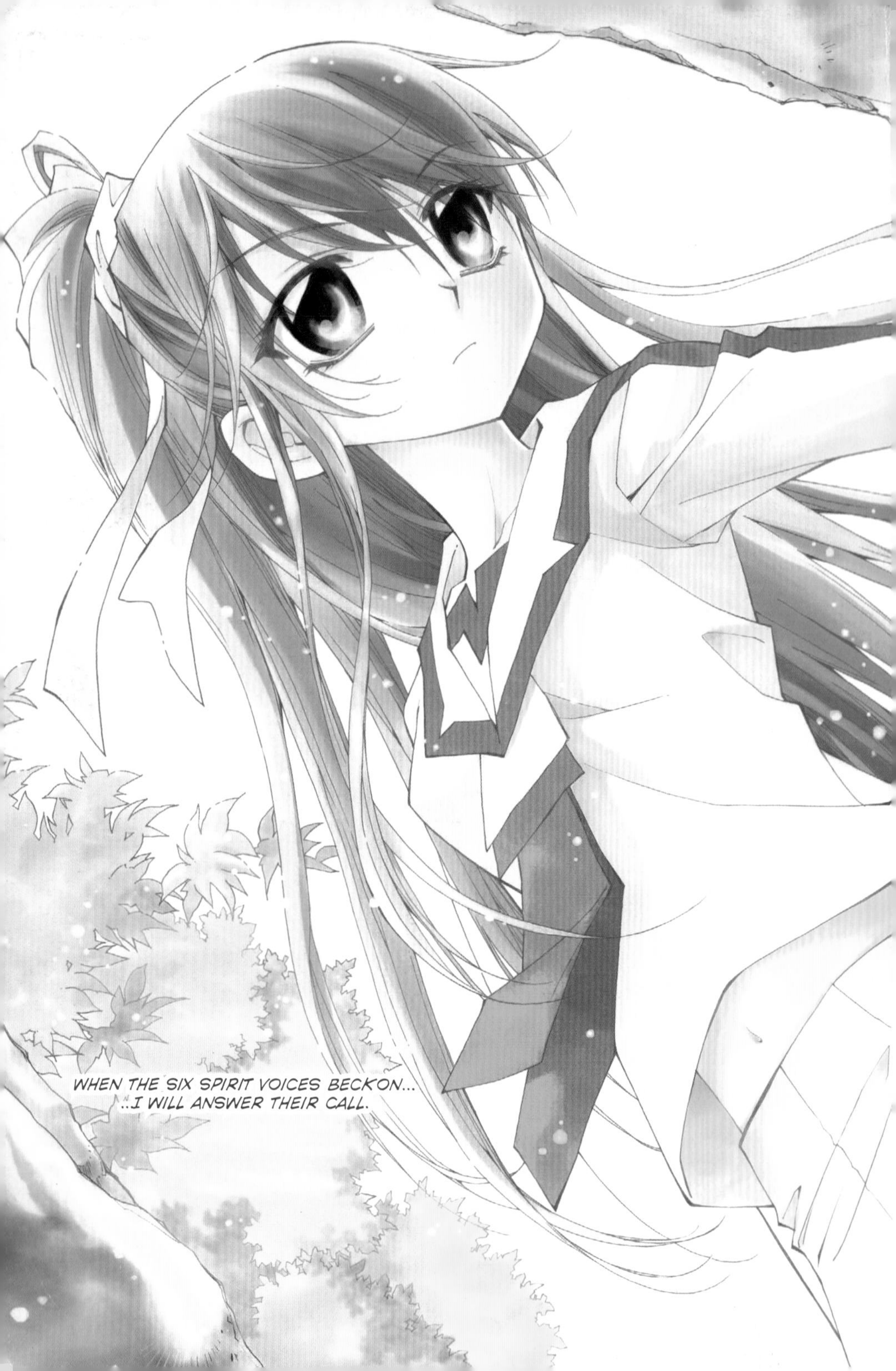
WHEN THE SIX SPIRIT VOICES BECKON...
...I WILL ANSWER THEIR CALL.

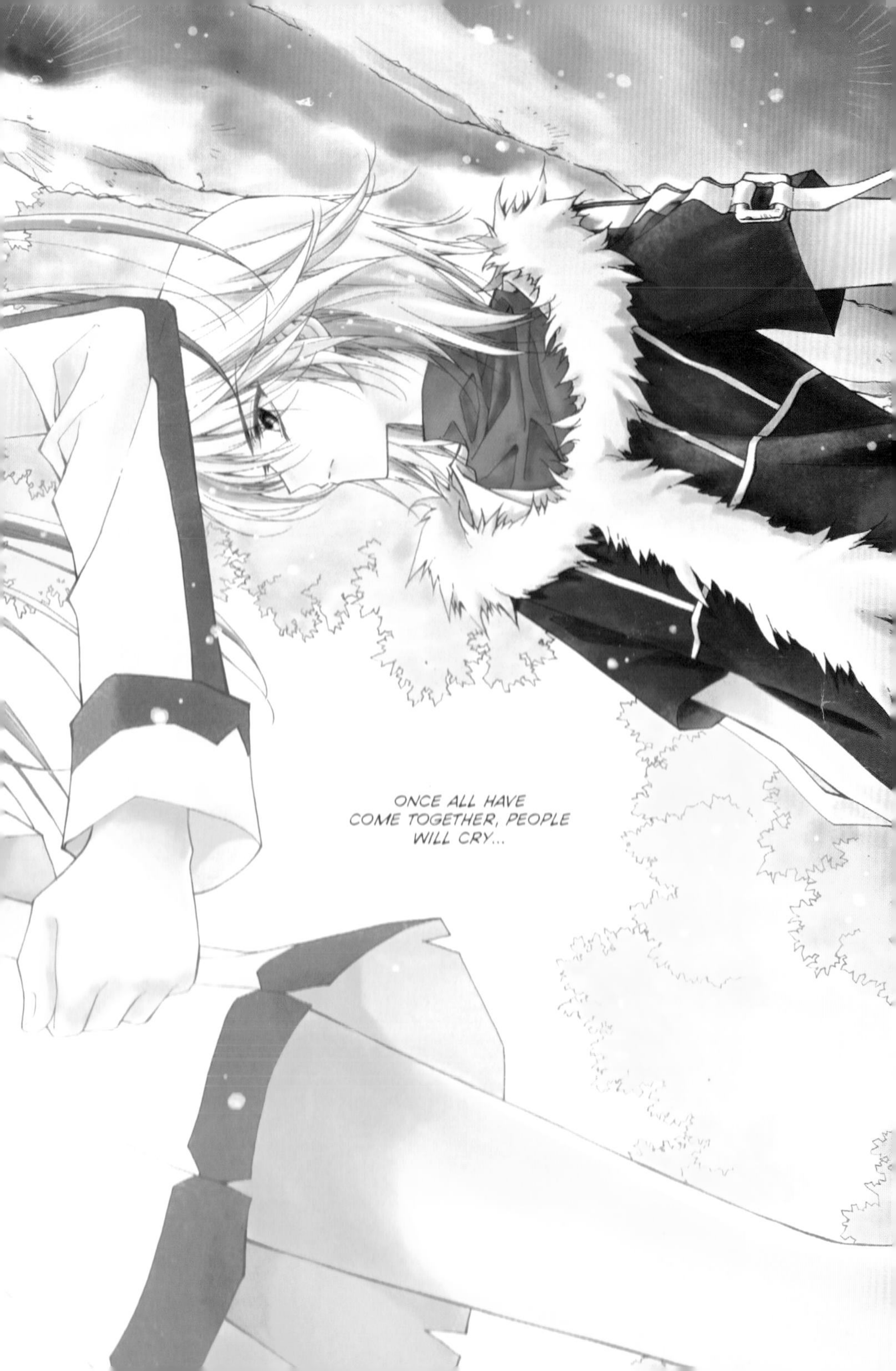
ONCE ALL HAVE
COME TOGETHER, PEOPLE
WILL CRY...

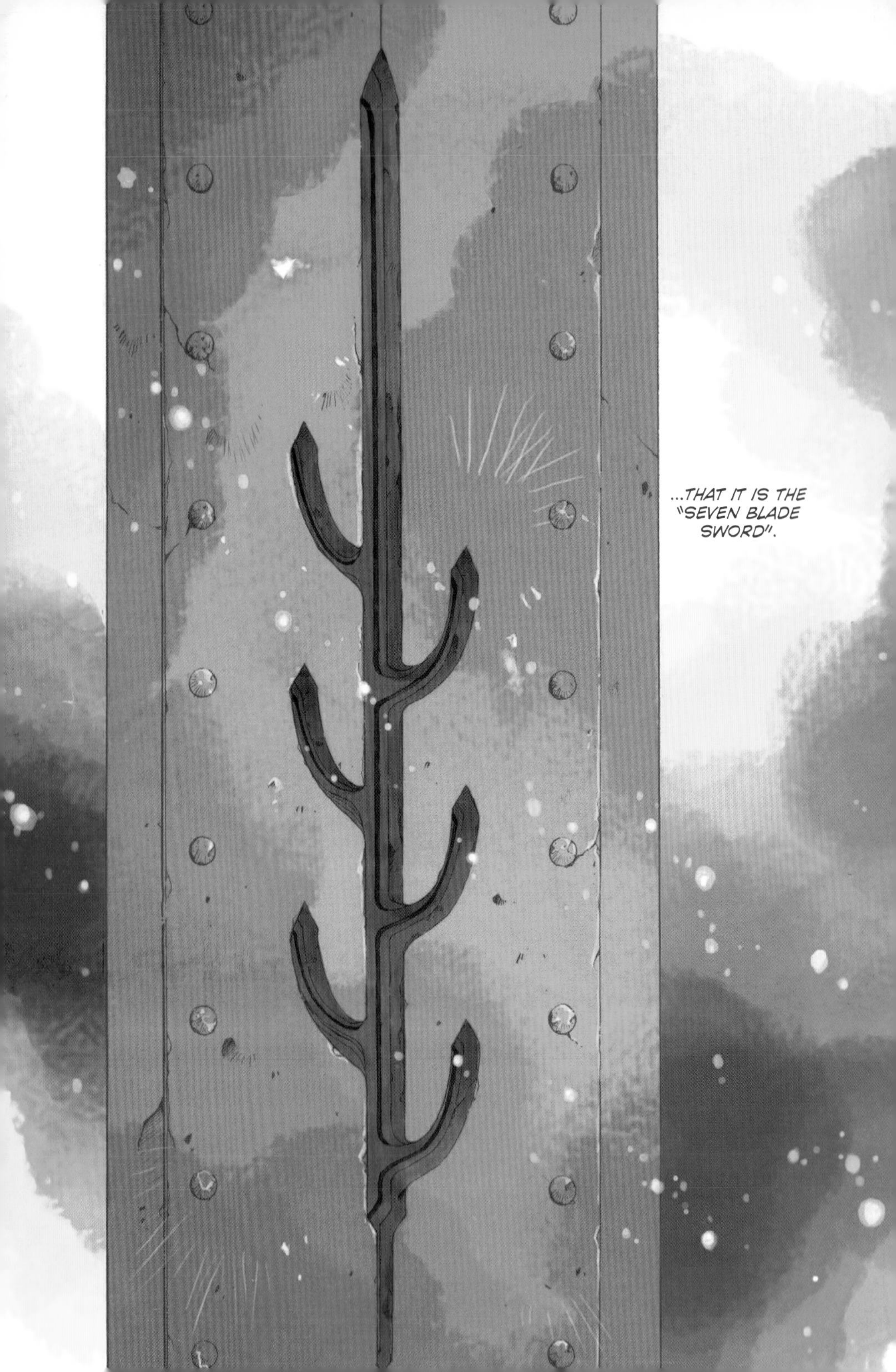
...THAT IT IS THE "SEVEN BLADE SWORD".

ginal · Danbi Original · Danbi Original · Danbi Original · Danbi Original · Danbi Original · Da

Legend

vol.1

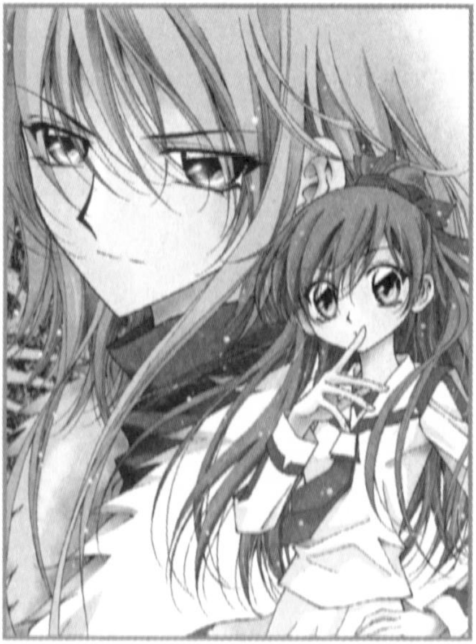

Kara ·Woo SooJung

ice
Kunion

CONTENTS

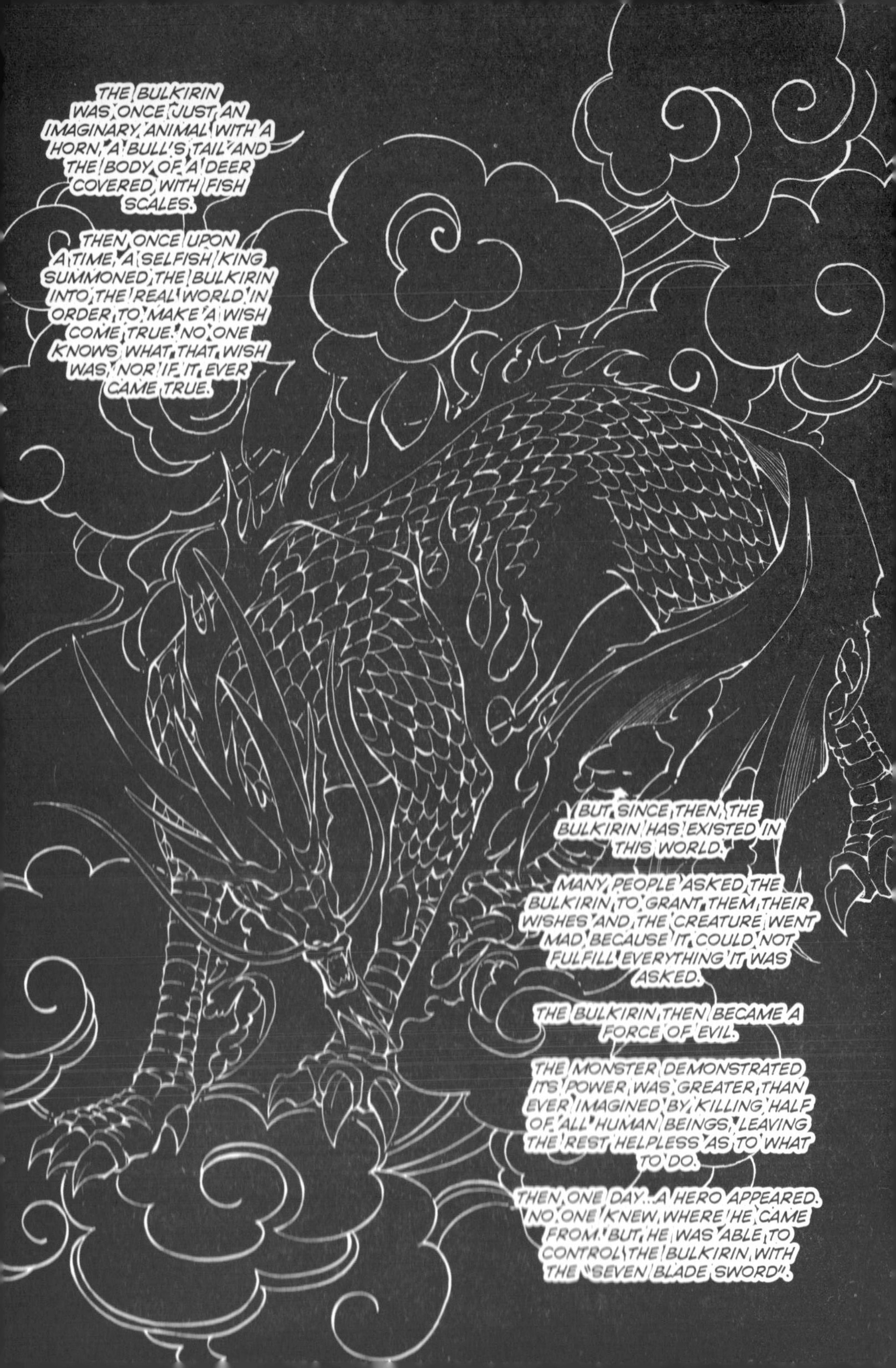
THE BULKIRIN WAS ONCE JUST AN IMAGINARY ANIMAL WITH A HORN, A BULL'S TAIL AND THE BODY OF A DEER COVERED WITH FISH SCALES.
THEN ONCE UPON A TIME, A SELFISH KING SUMMONED THE BULKIRIN INTO THE REAL WORLD IN ORDER TO MAKE A WISH COME TRUE. NO ONE KNOWS WHAT THAT WISH WAS, NOR IF IT EVER CAME TRUE.
BUT SINCE THEN, THE BULKIRIN HAS EXISTED IN THIS WORLD.
MANY PEOPLE ASKED THE BULKIRIN TO GRANT THEM THEIR WISHES AND THE CREATURE WENT MAD BECAUSE IT COULD NOT FULFILL EVERYTHING IT WAS ASKED.
THE BULKIRIN THEN BECAME A FORCE OF EVIL.
THE MONSTER DEMONSTRATED ITS POWER WAS GREATER THAN EVER IMAGINED BY KILLING HALF OF ALL HUMAN BEINGS, LEAVING THE REST HELPLESS AS TO WHAT TO DO.
THEN, ONE DAY...A HERO APPEARED. NO ONE KNEW WHERE HE CAME FROM. BUT HE WAS ABLE TO CONTROL THE BULKIRIN WITH THE "SEVEN BLADE SWORD".

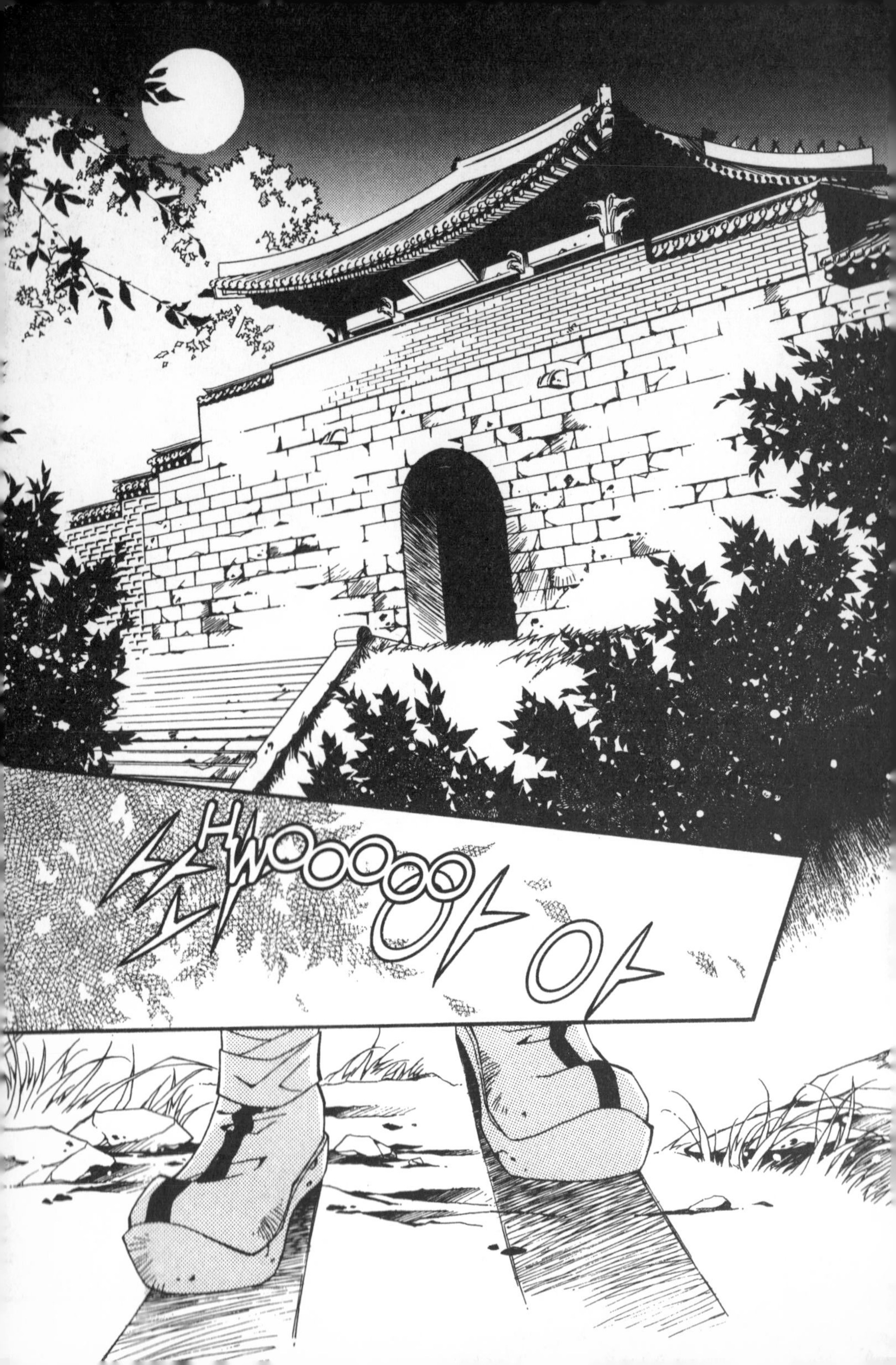
HWOOOOO

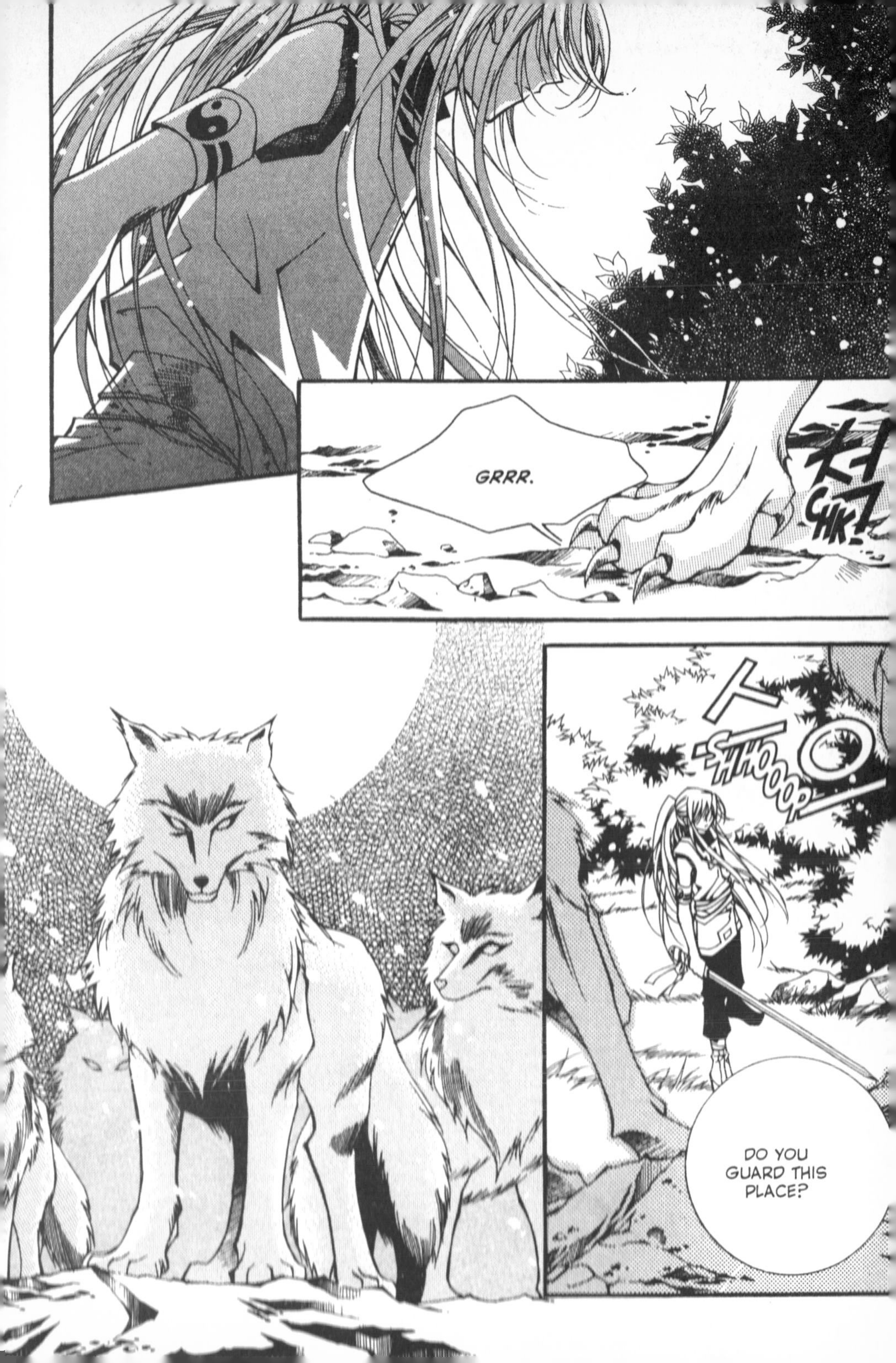
GRRR.
척
CHK!
SHOOOP
DO YOU GUARD THIS PLACE?

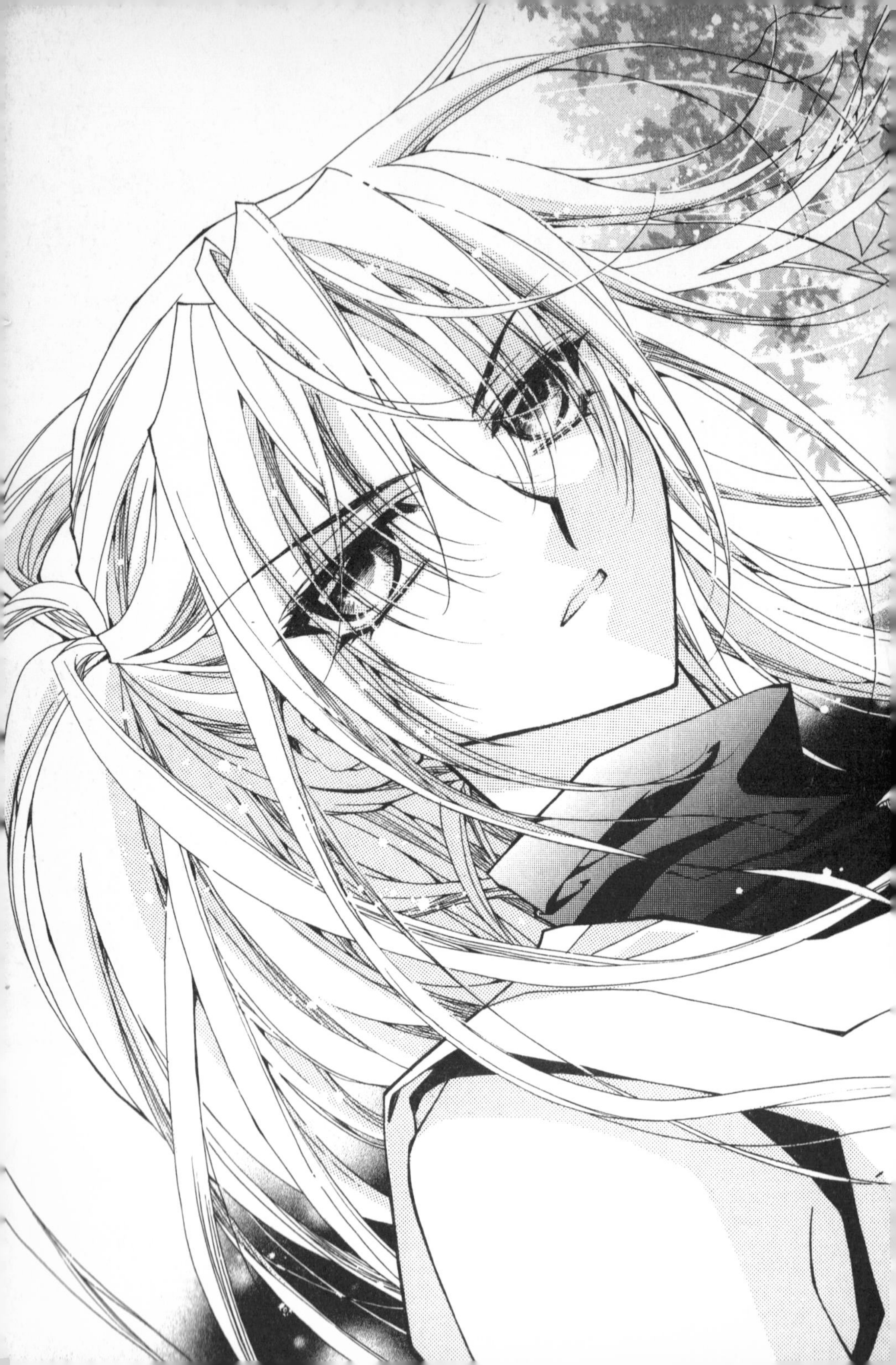

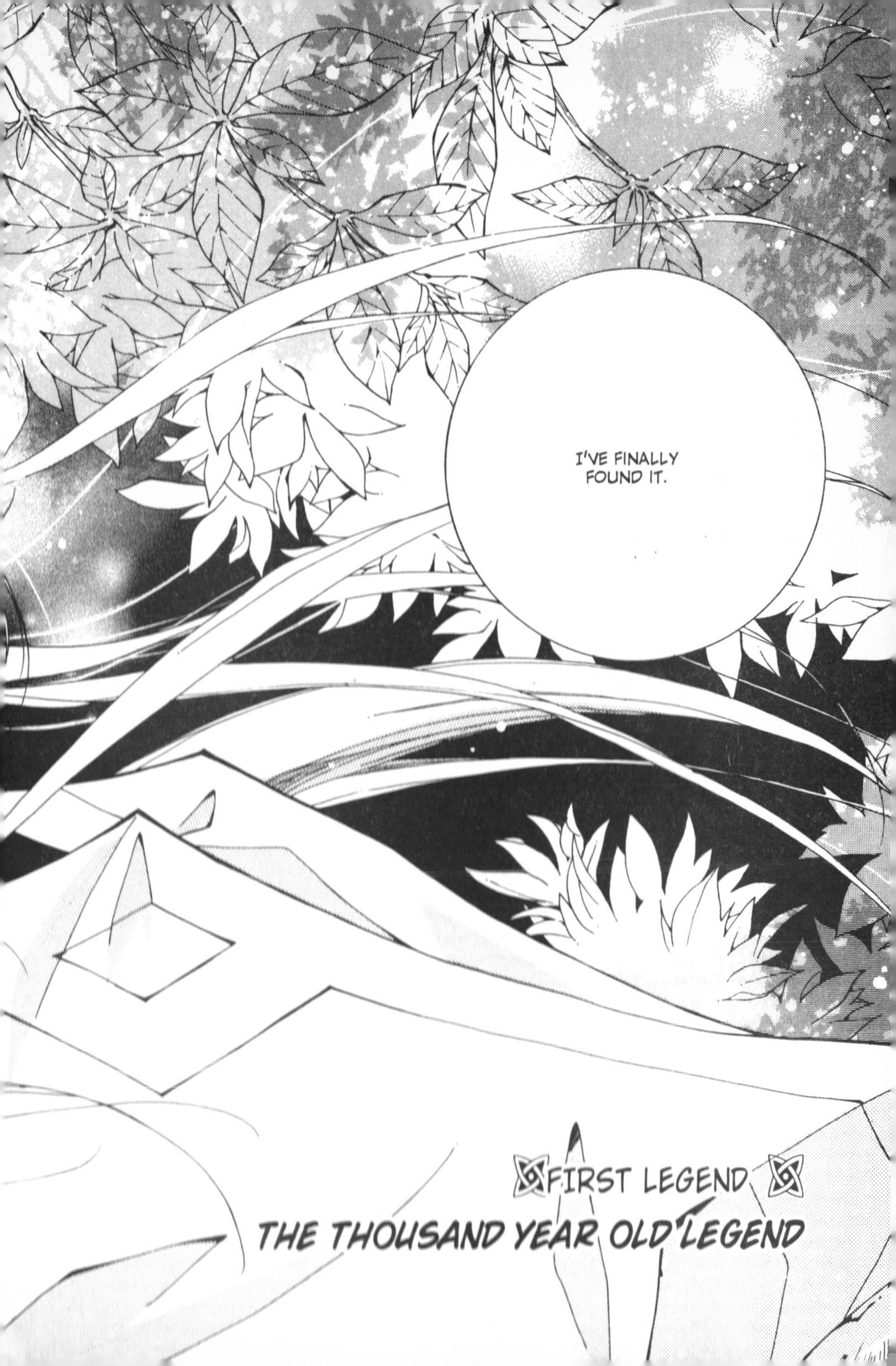
I'VE FINALLY FOUND IT.
FIRST LEGEND
THE THOUSAND YEAR OLD LEGEND

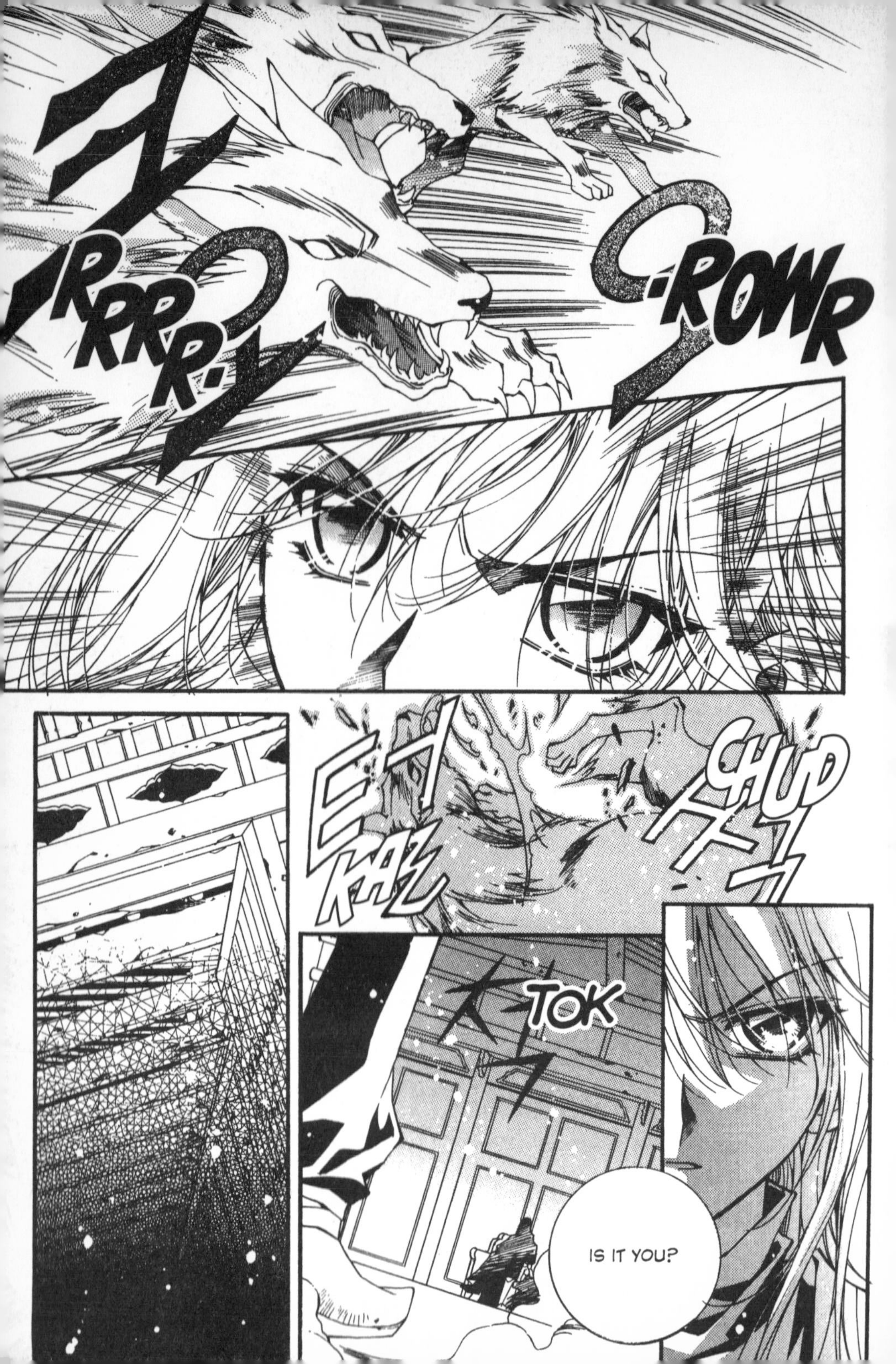
RRRR-Y
-ROWR
KAZ
CHUD
TOK
IS IT YOU?

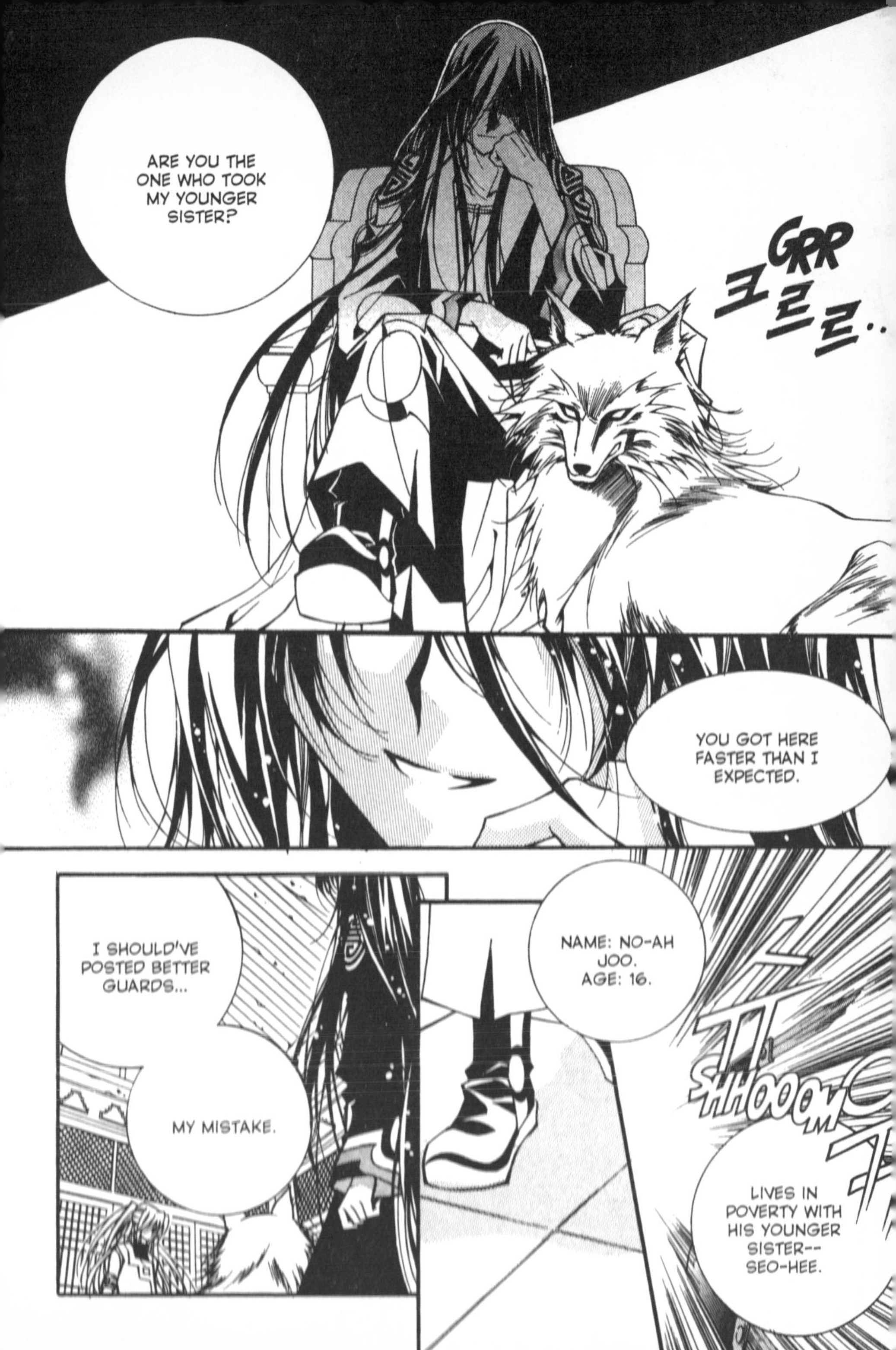
ARE YOU THE ONE WHO TOOK MY YOUNGER SISTER?
GRR
크르르..
YOU GOT HERE FASTER THAN I EXPECTED.
I SHOULD'VE POSTED BETTER GUARDS...
MY MISTAKE.
NAME: NO-AH JOO. AGE: 16.
SHHOOOM
LIVES IN POVERTY WITH HIS YOUNGER SISTER-- SEO-HEE.

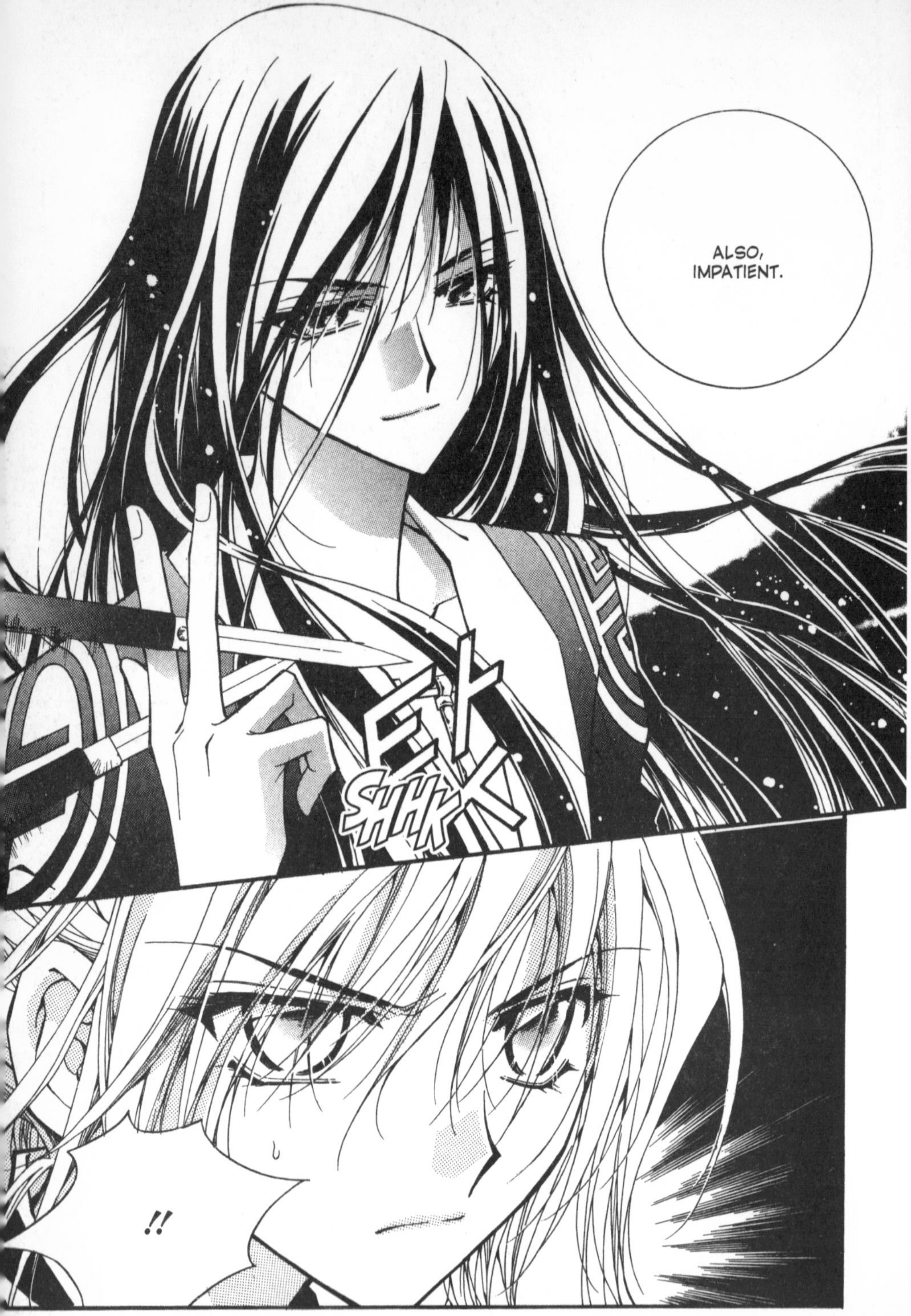

ALSO, IMPATIENT.
SHHK
!!

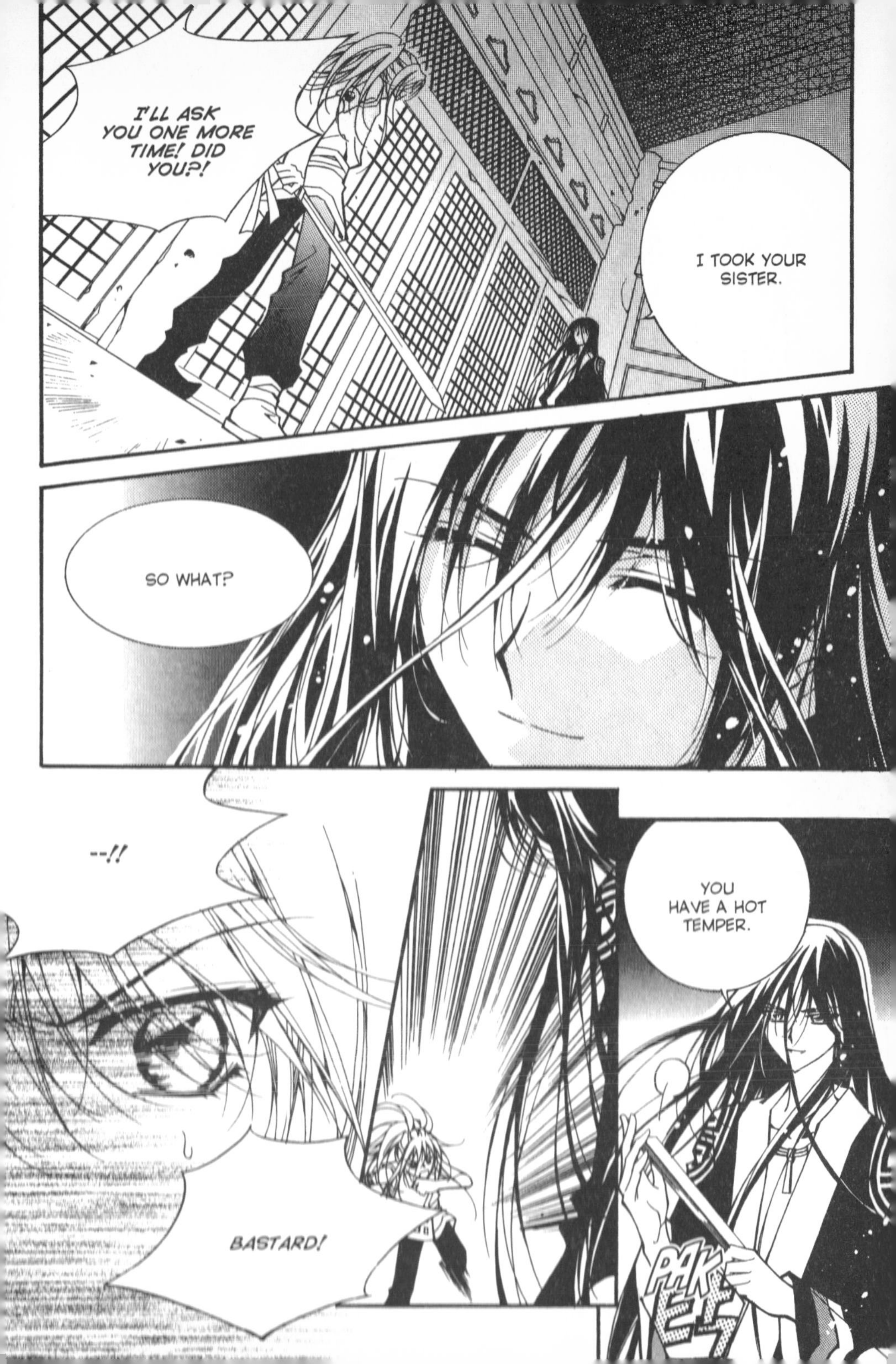
I'LL ASK YOU ONE MORE TIME! DID YOU?!
I TOOK YOUR SISTER.
SO WHAT?
--!!
BASTARD!
YOU HAVE A HOT TEMPER.
PAK

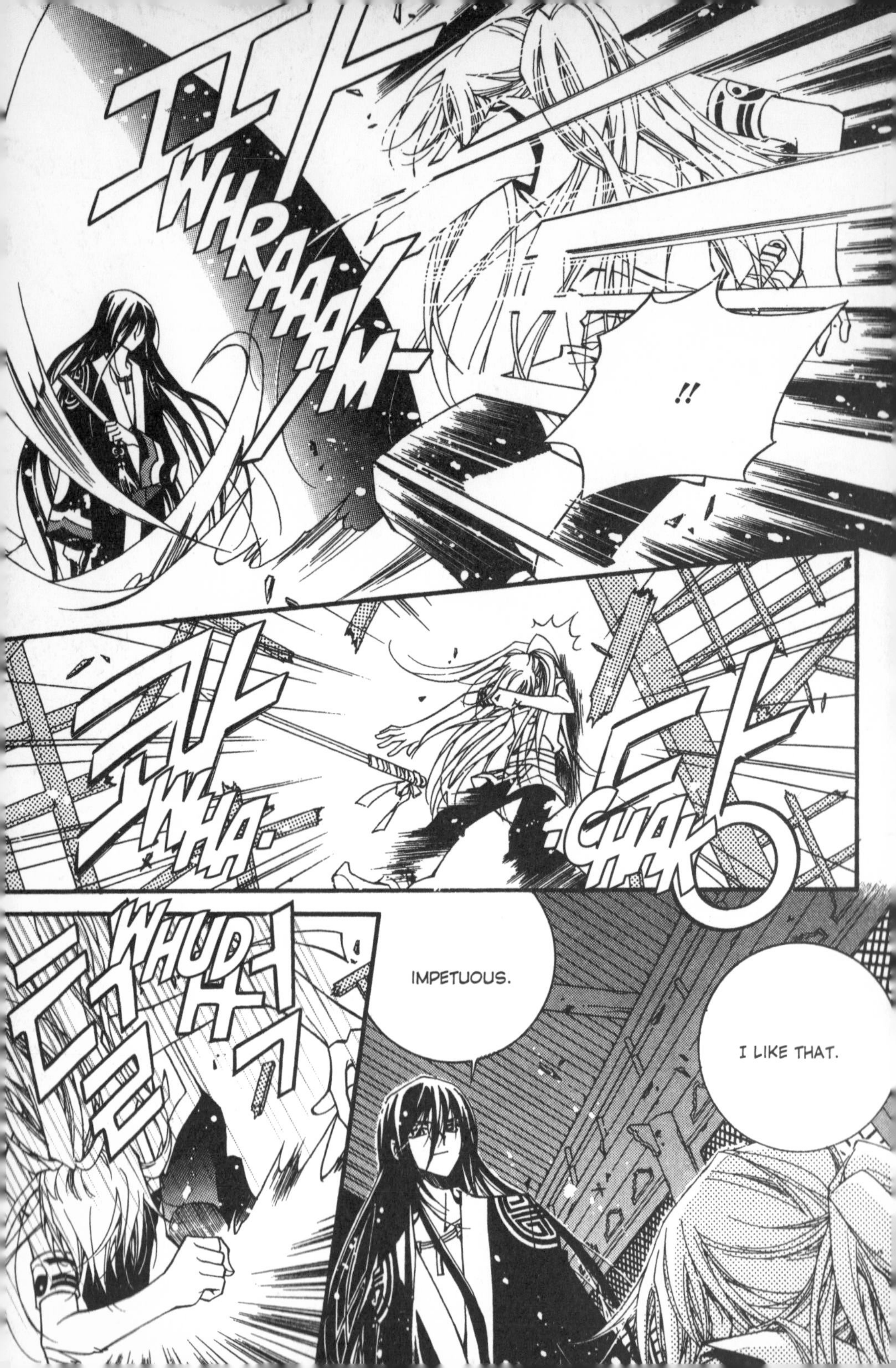
WHRAAAAM-
!!
WHA-
-CHAK
WHUD
IMPETUOUS.
I LIKE THAT.

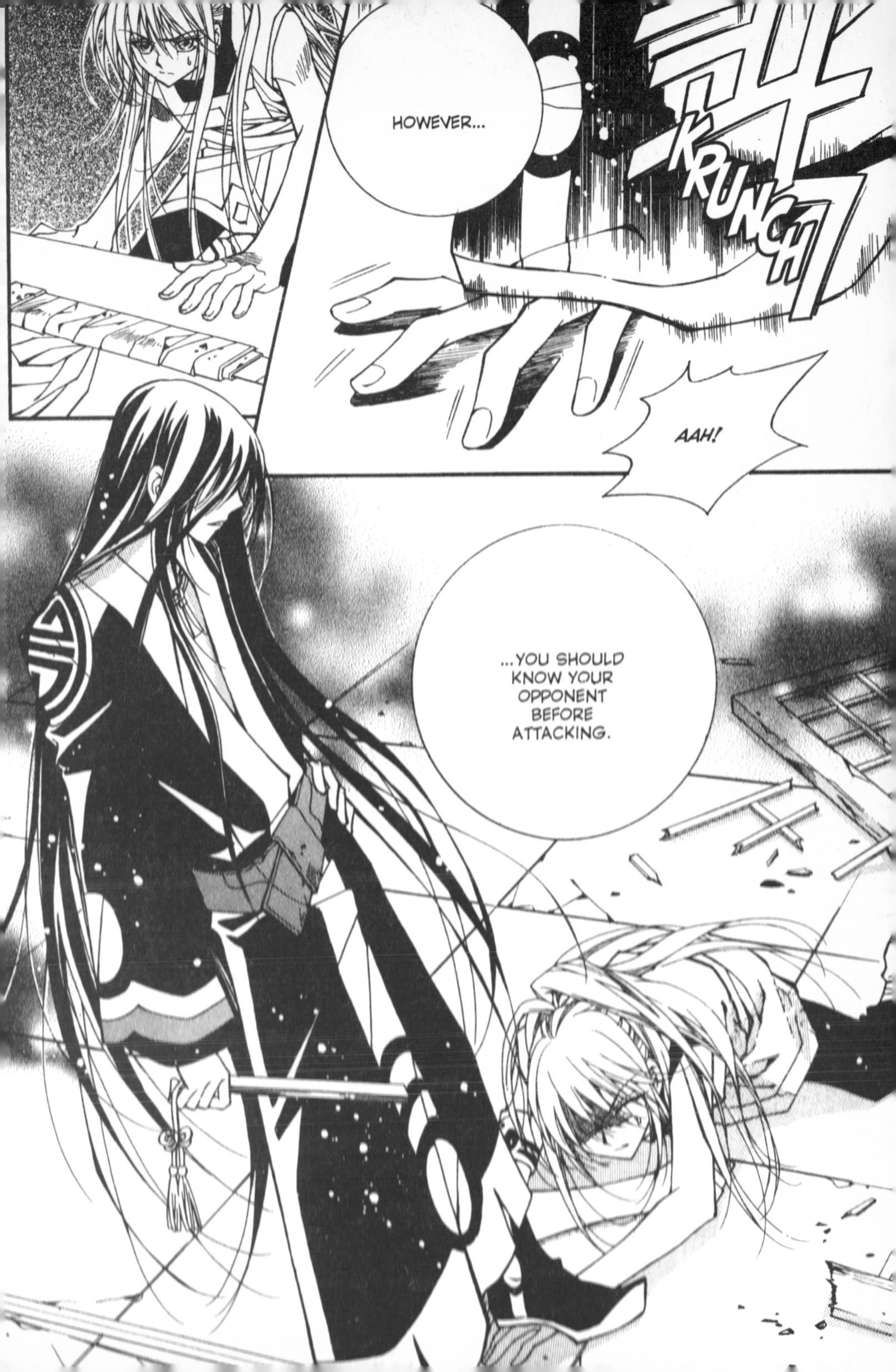
HOWEVER...
KRUNCH
AAH!
...YOU SHOULD KNOW YOUR OPPONENT BEFORE ATTACKING.

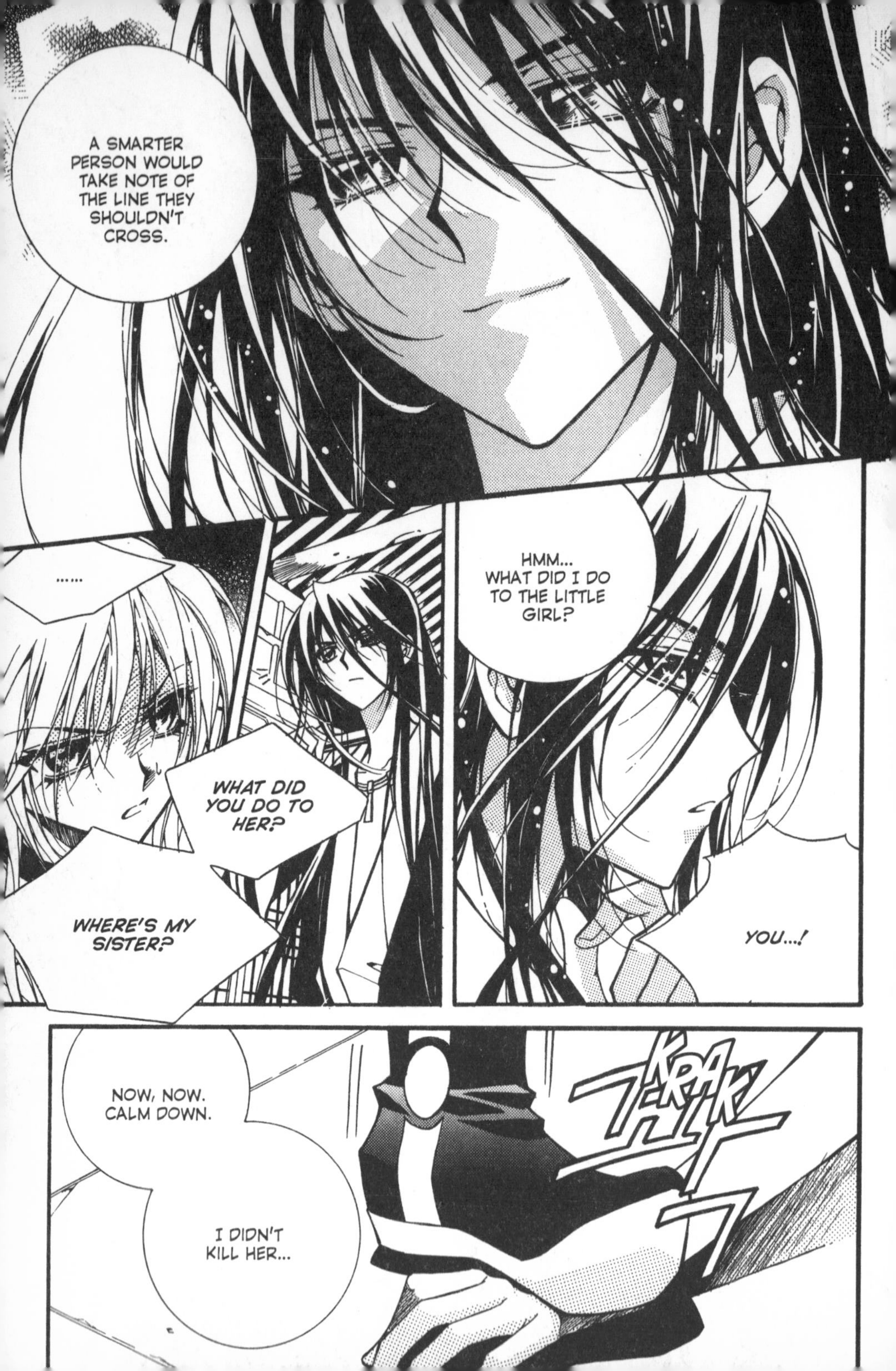
A SMARTER PERSON WOULD TAKE NOTE OF THE LINE THEY SHOULDN'T CROSS.
......
WHAT DID YOU DO TO HER?
WHERE'S MY SISTER?
HMM... WHAT DID I DO TO THE LITTLE GIRL?
YOU...!
NOW, NOW. CALM DOWN.
I DIDN'T KILL HER...
KRAK

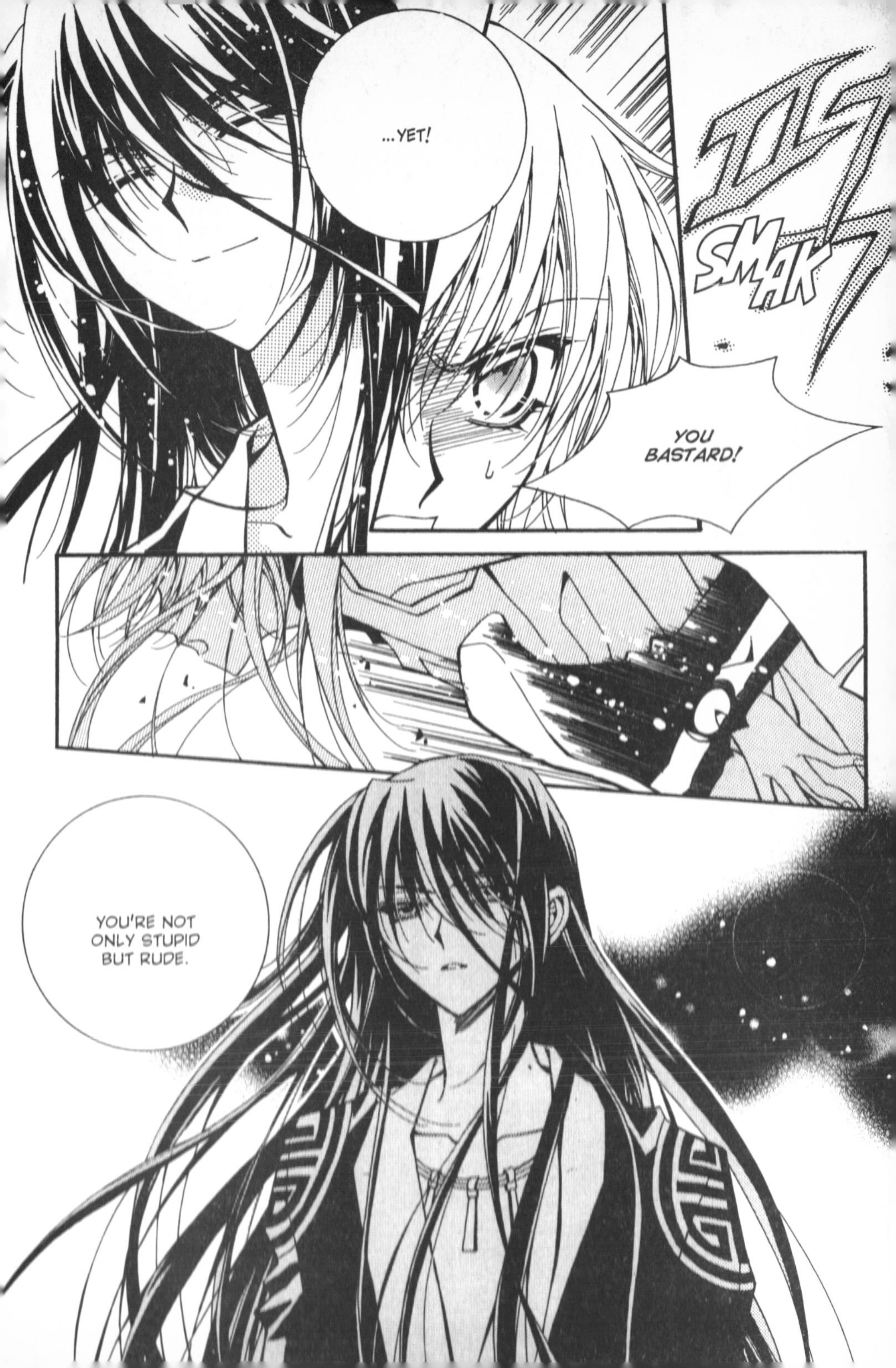
...YET!
ZOS
SMAK
YOU BASTARD!
YOU'RE NOT ONLY STUPID BUT RUDE.

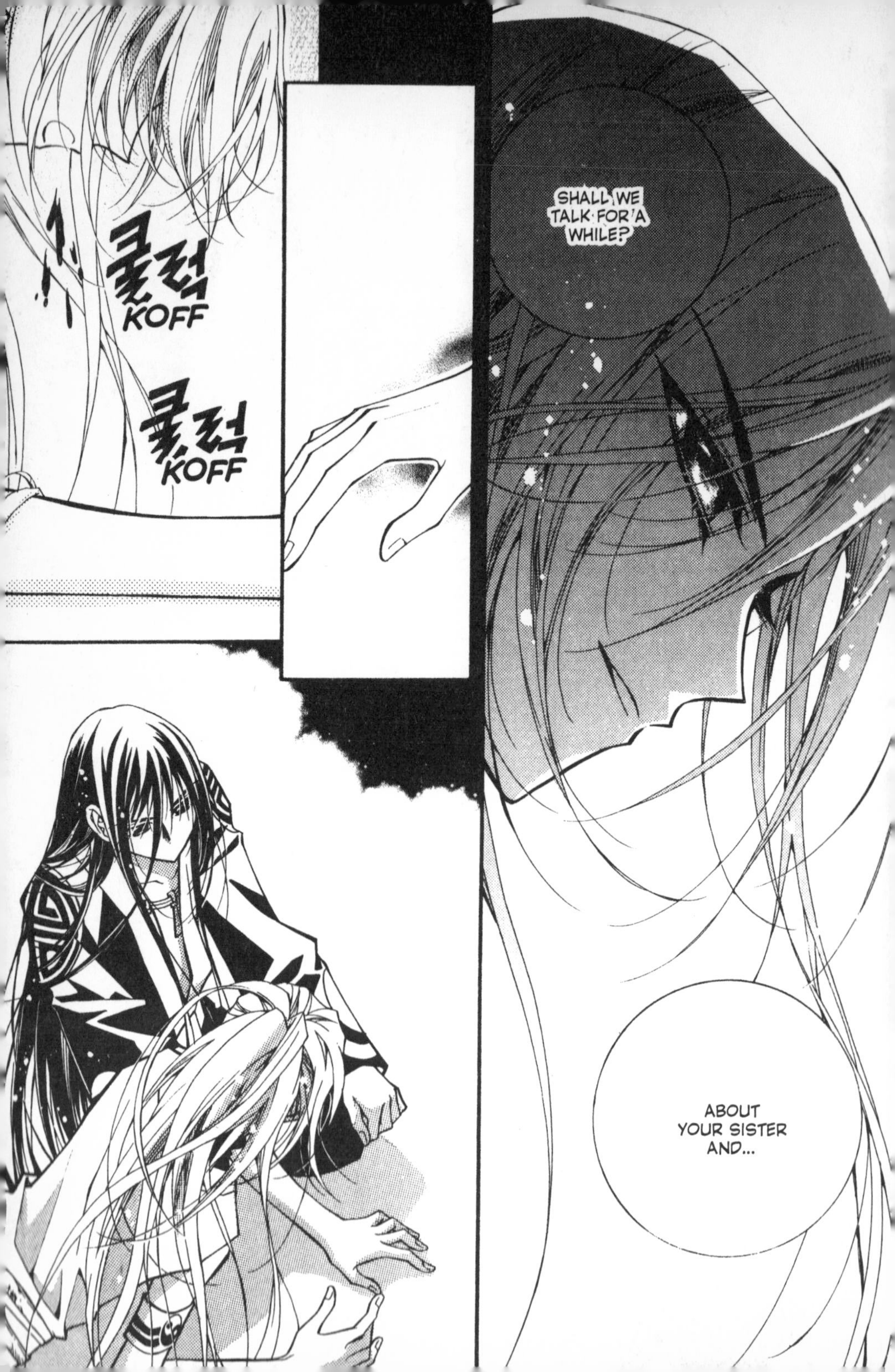
쿨럭
KOFF
쿨럭
KOFF
SHALL WE TALK FOR A WHILE?
ABOUT YOUR SISTER AND...

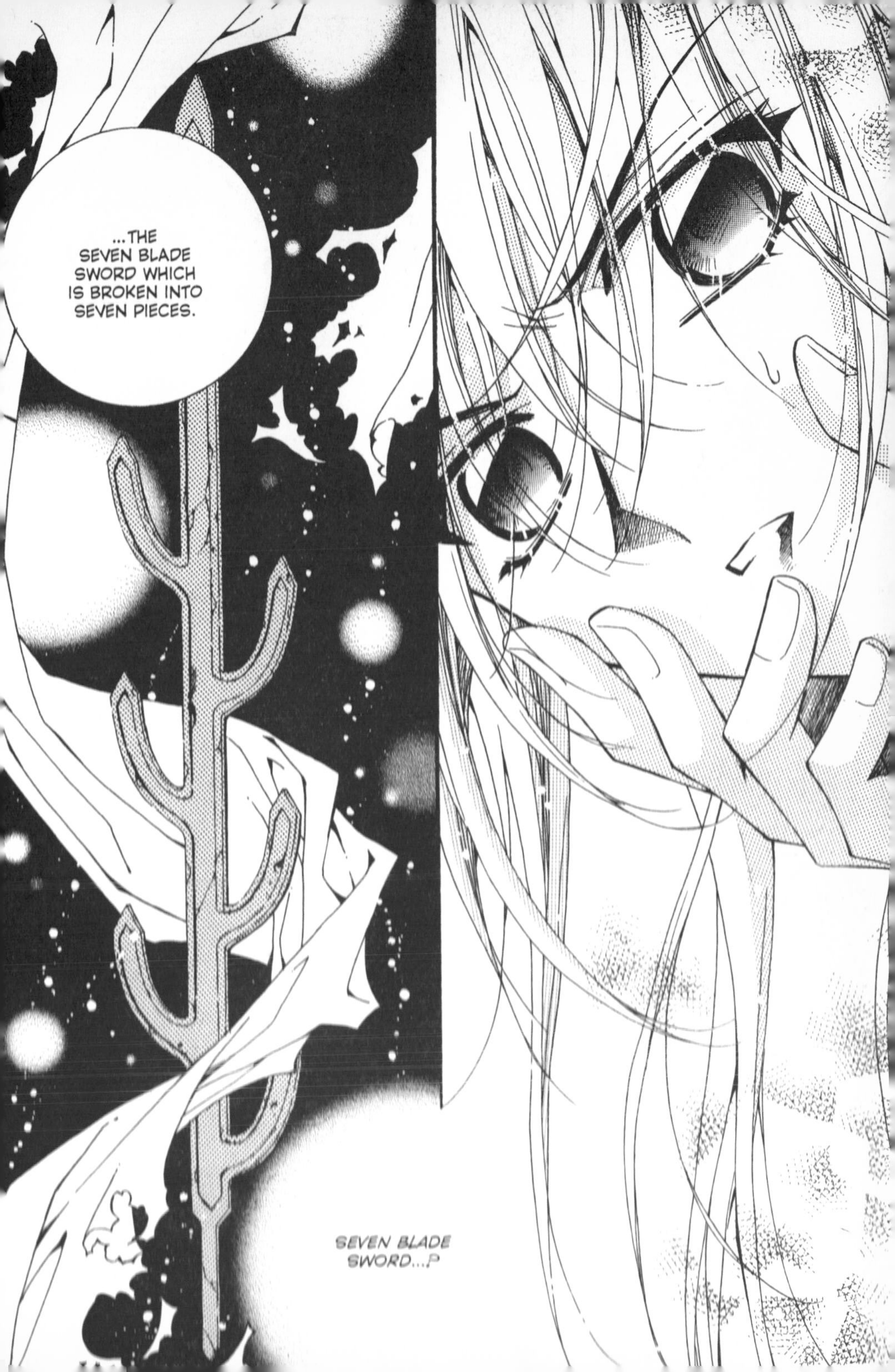
...THE SEVEN BLADE SWORD WHICH IS BROKEN INTO SEVEN PIECES.
SEVEN BLADE SWORD...?

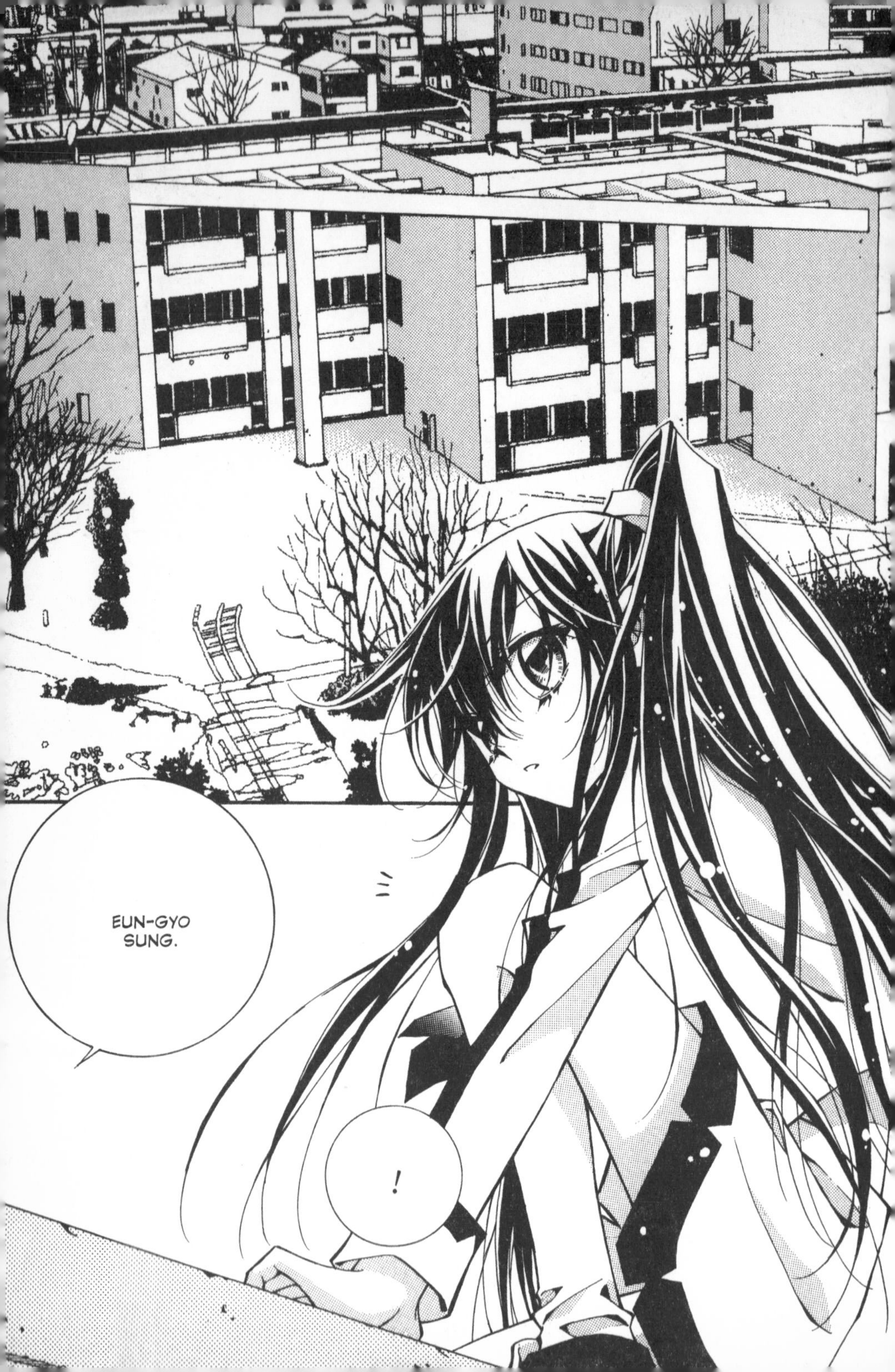
EUN-GYO SUNG.
!

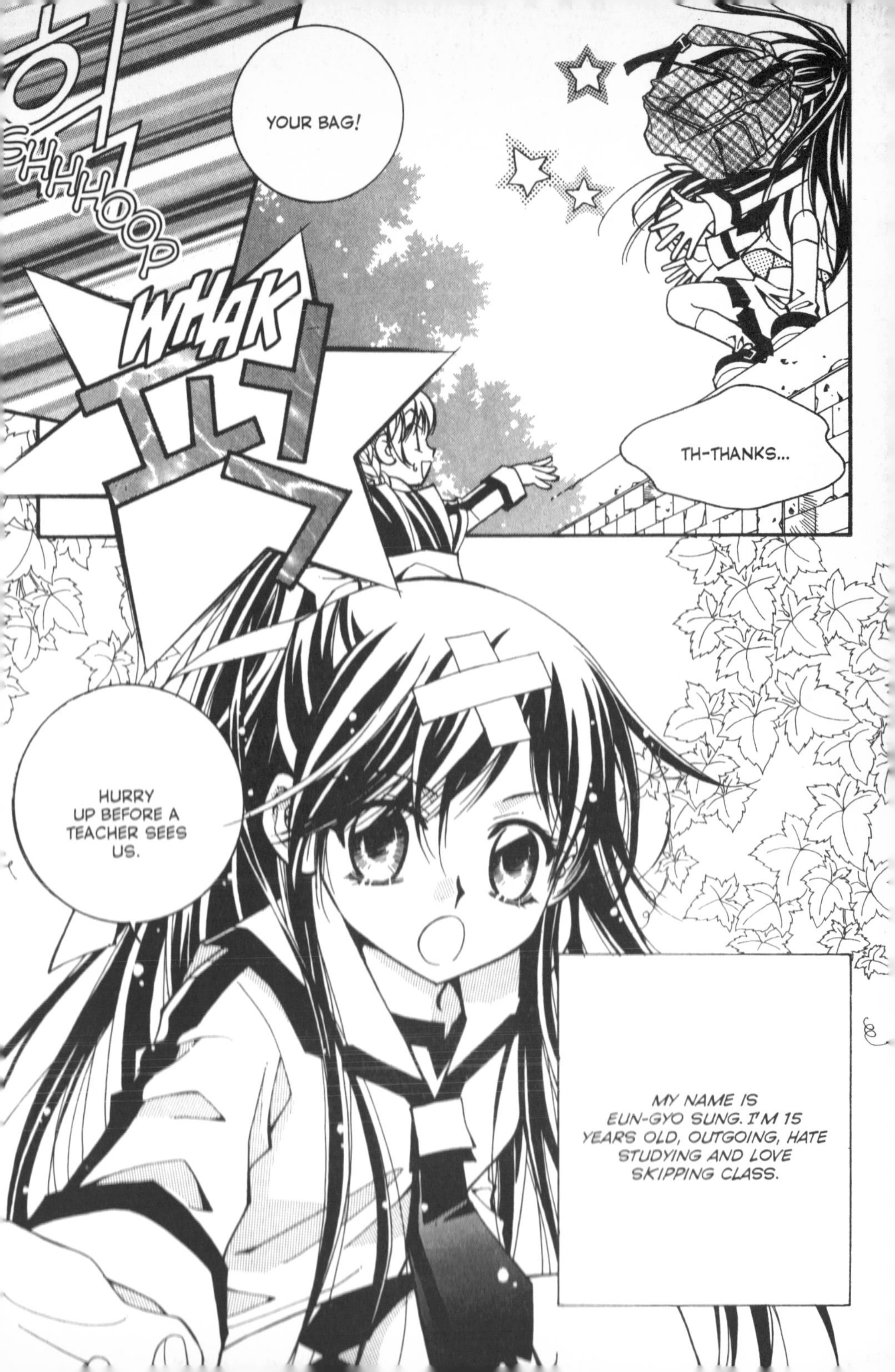
SHHHOOP
YOUR BAG!
WHAK
TH-THANKS...
HURRY UP BEFORE A TEACHER SEES US.
MY NAME IS EUN-GYO SUNG. I'M 15 YEARS OLD, OUTGOING, HATE STUDYING AND LOVE SKIPPING CLASS.

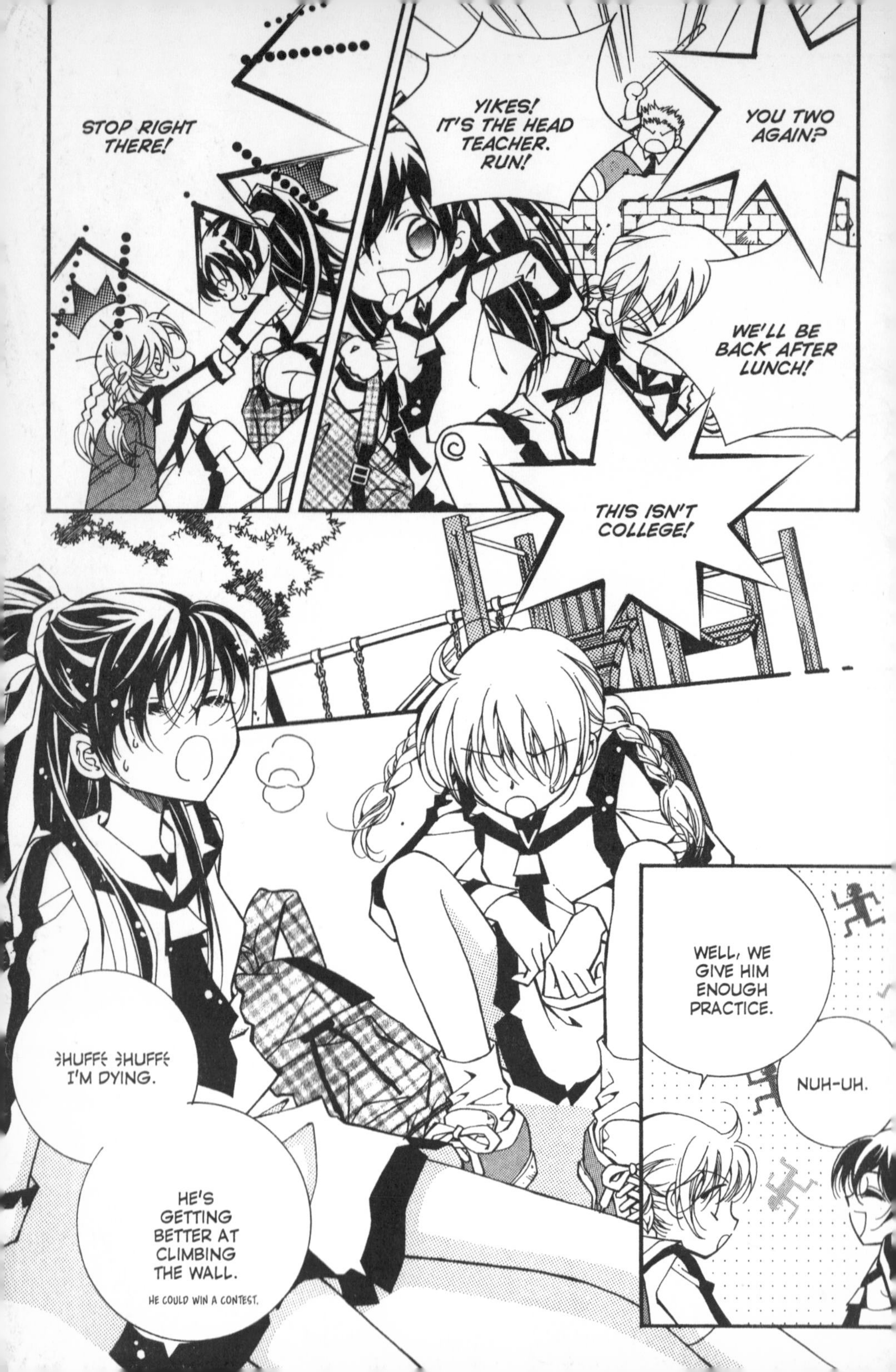

STOP RIGHT THERE!
YIKES! IT'S THE HEAD TEACHER. RUN!
YOU TWO AGAIN?
WE'LL BE BACK AFTER LUNCH!
THIS ISN'T COLLEGE!
HUFF HUFF I'M DYING.
HE'S GETTING BETTER AT CLIMBING THE WALL.
HE COULD WIN A CONTEST.
WELL, WE GIVE HIM ENOUGH PRACTICE.
NUH-UH.

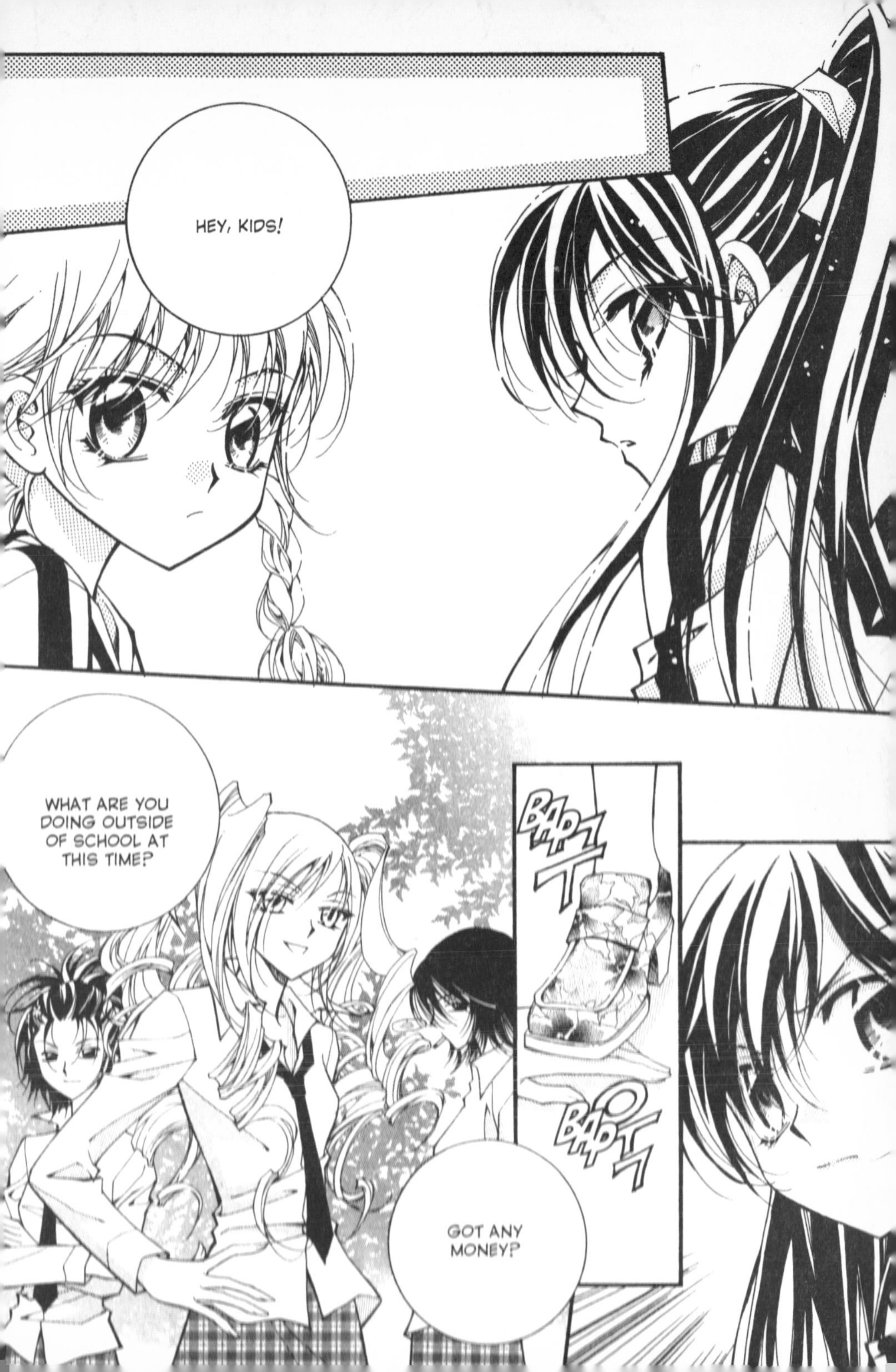
HEY, KIDS!
WHAT ARE YOU DOING OUTSIDE OF SCHOOL AT THIS TIME?
BAP
BAP
GOT ANY MONEY?

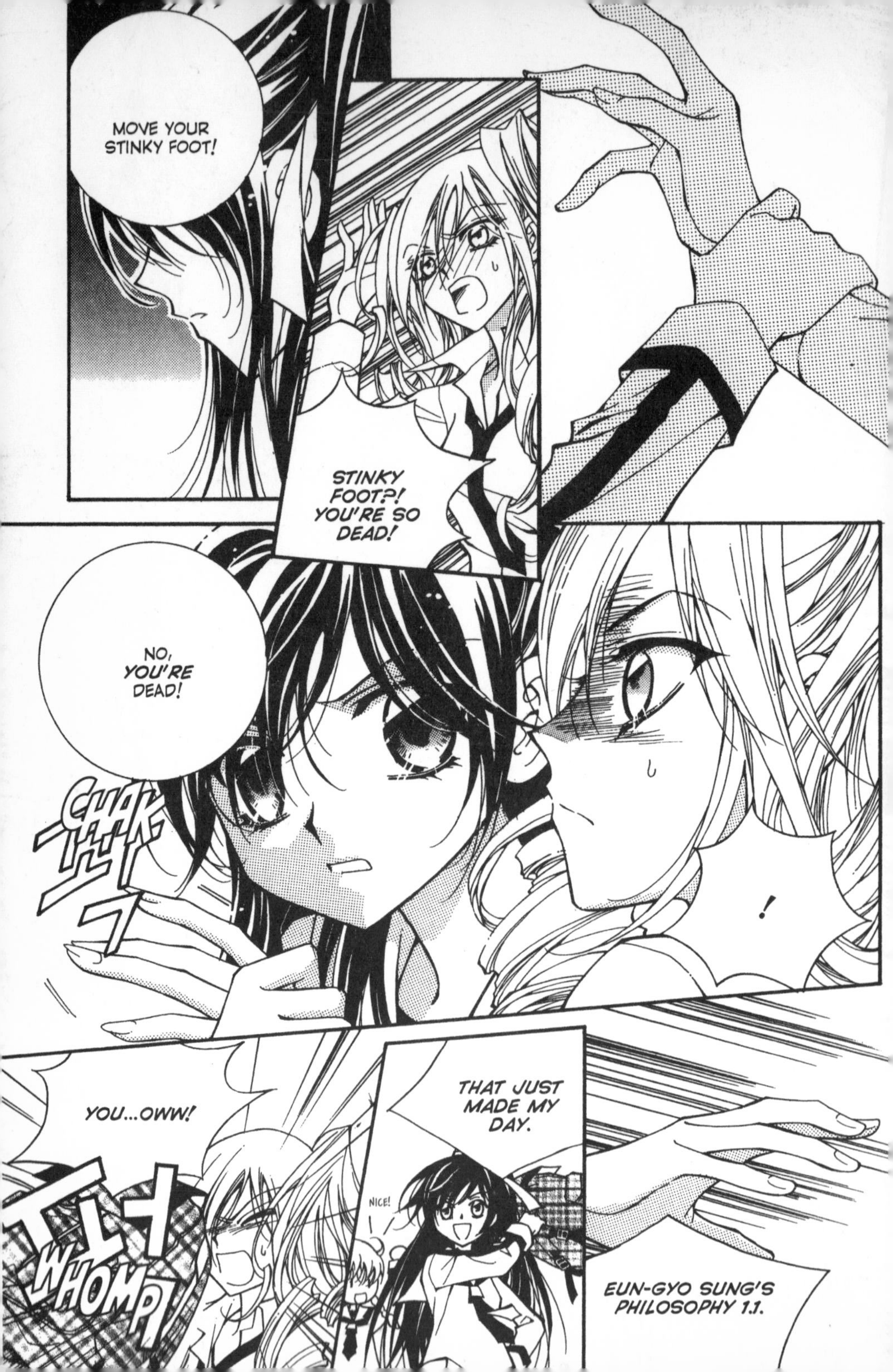
MOVE YOUR STINKY FOOT!
STINKY FOOT?! YOU'RE SO DEAD!
NO, YOU'RE DEAD!
CHAK
!
YOU...OWW!
WHOMP
THAT JUST MADE MY DAY.
NICE!
EUN-GYO SUNG'S PHILOSOPHY 1.1.

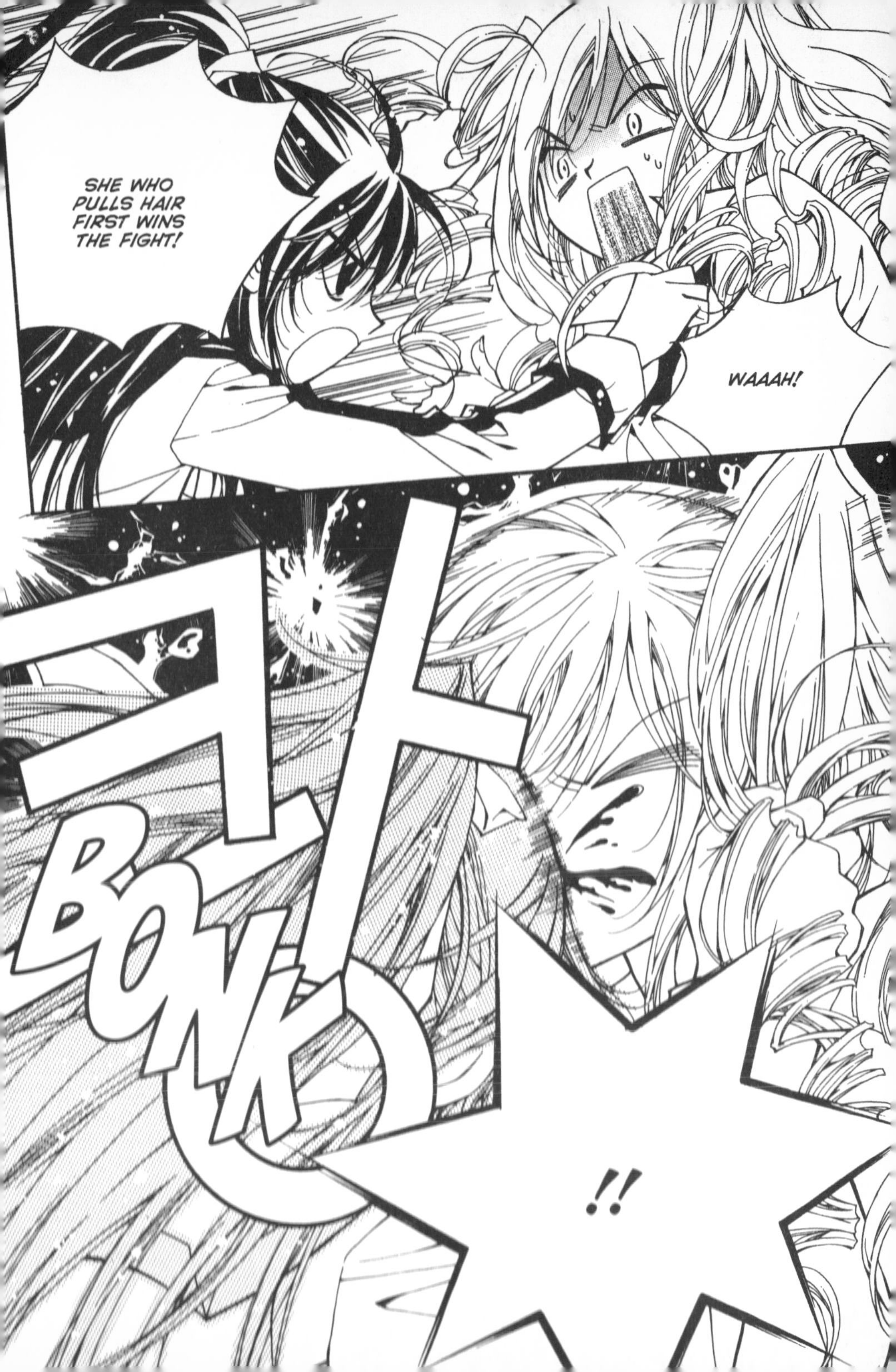
SHE WHO PULLS HAIR FIRST WINS THE FIGHT!
WAAAH!
BONK
!!

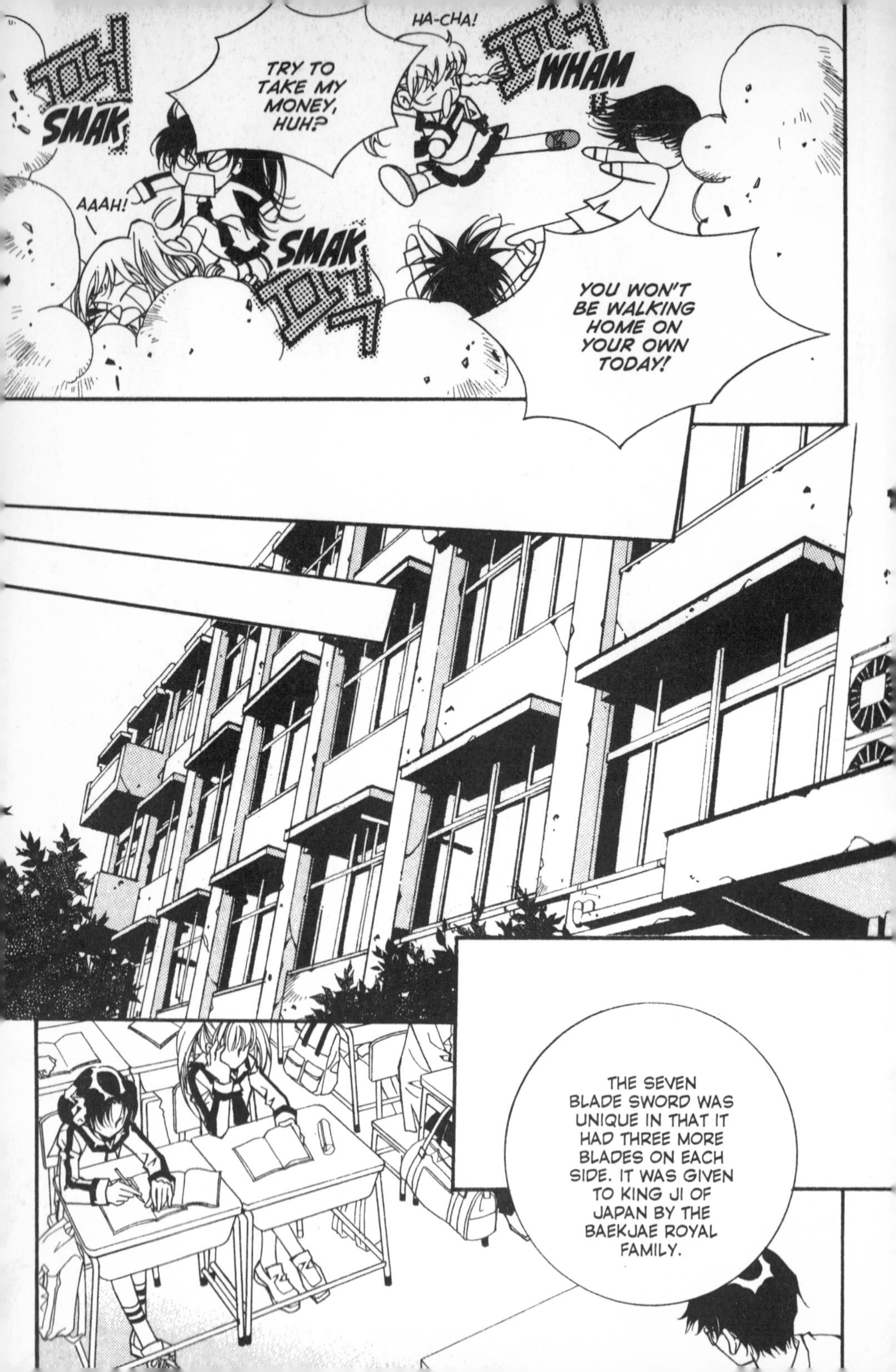
SMAK
AAAH!
TRY TO TAKE MY MONEY, HUH?
HA-CHA!
WHAM
SMAK
YOU WON'T BE WALKING HOME ON YOUR OWN TODAY!
THE SEVEN BLADE SWORD WAS UNIQUE IN THAT IT HAD THREE MORE BLADES ON EACH SIDE. IT WAS GIVEN TO KING JI OF JAPAN BY THE BAEKJAE ROYAL FAMILY.

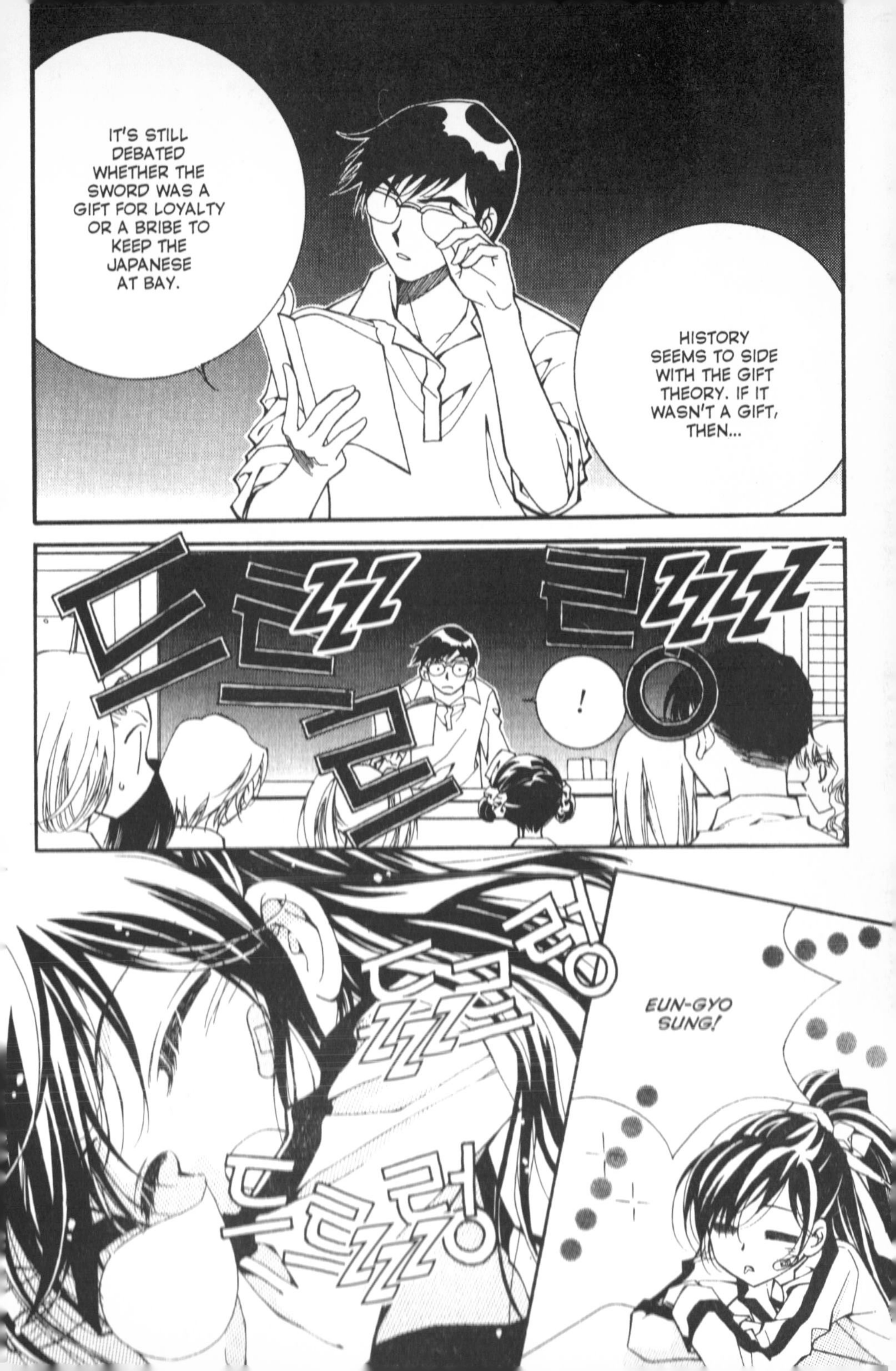
IT'S STILL DEBATED WHETHER THE SWORD WAS A GIFT FOR LOYALTY OR A BRIBE TO KEEP THE JAPANESE AT BAY.
HISTORY SEEMS TO SIDE WITH THE GIFT THEORY. IF IT WASN'T A GIFT, THEN...
!
EUN-GYO SUNG!

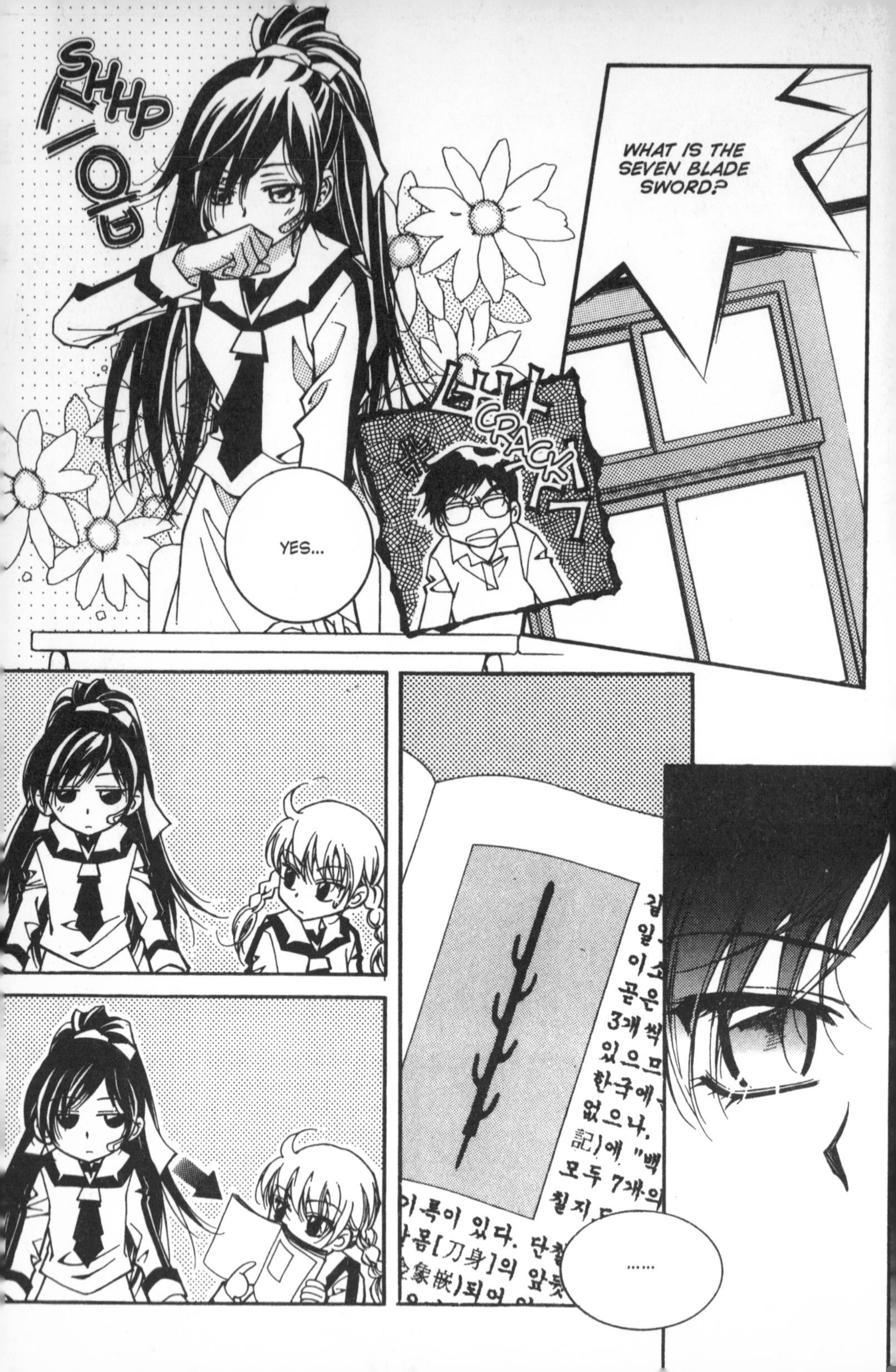

SHHP
YES...
CRACK
WHAT IS THE SEVEN BLADE SWORD?
......

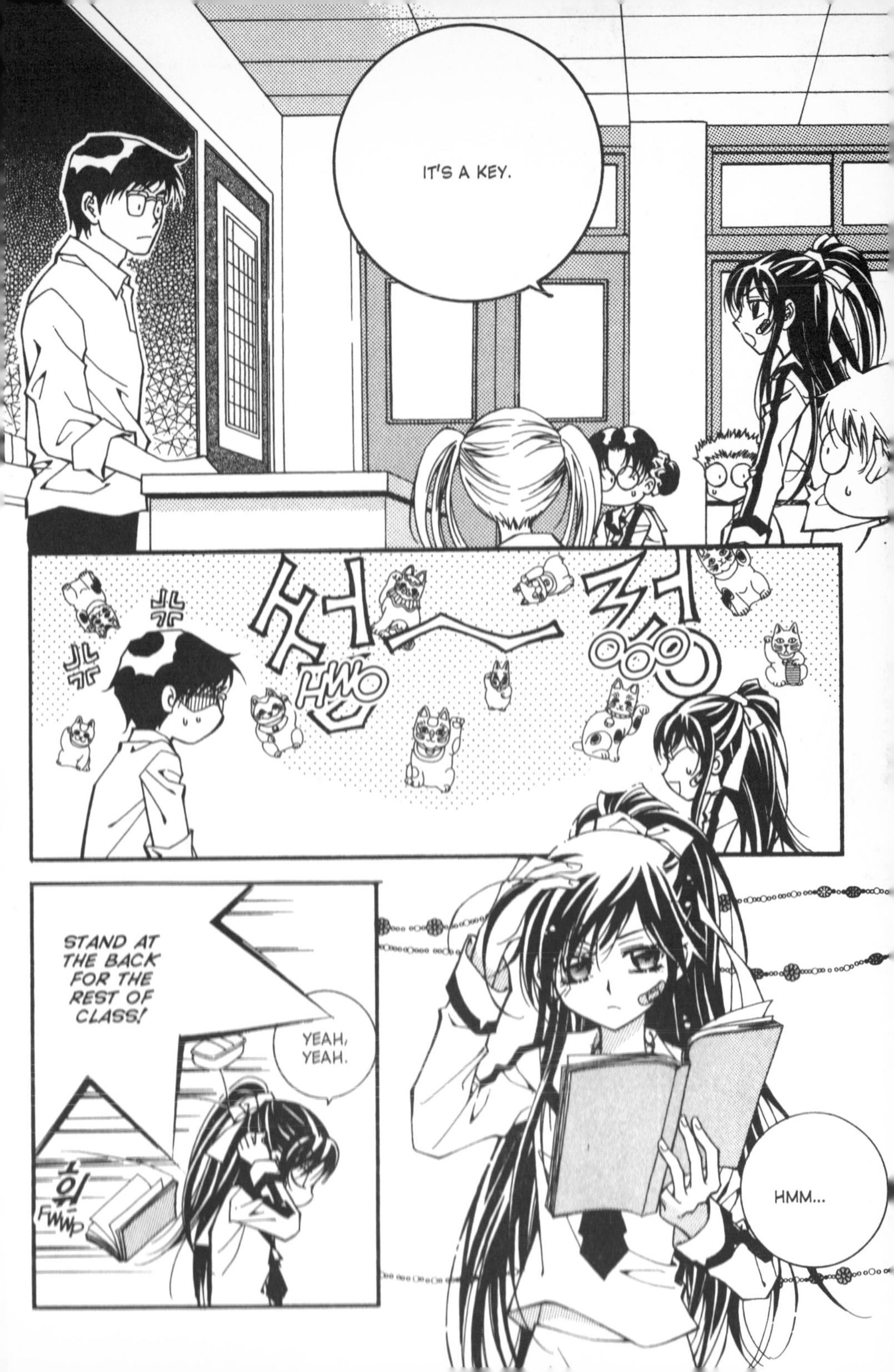

IT'S A KEY.
STAND AT THE BACK FOR THE REST OF CLASS!
YEAH, YEAH.
FWMP
HMM...

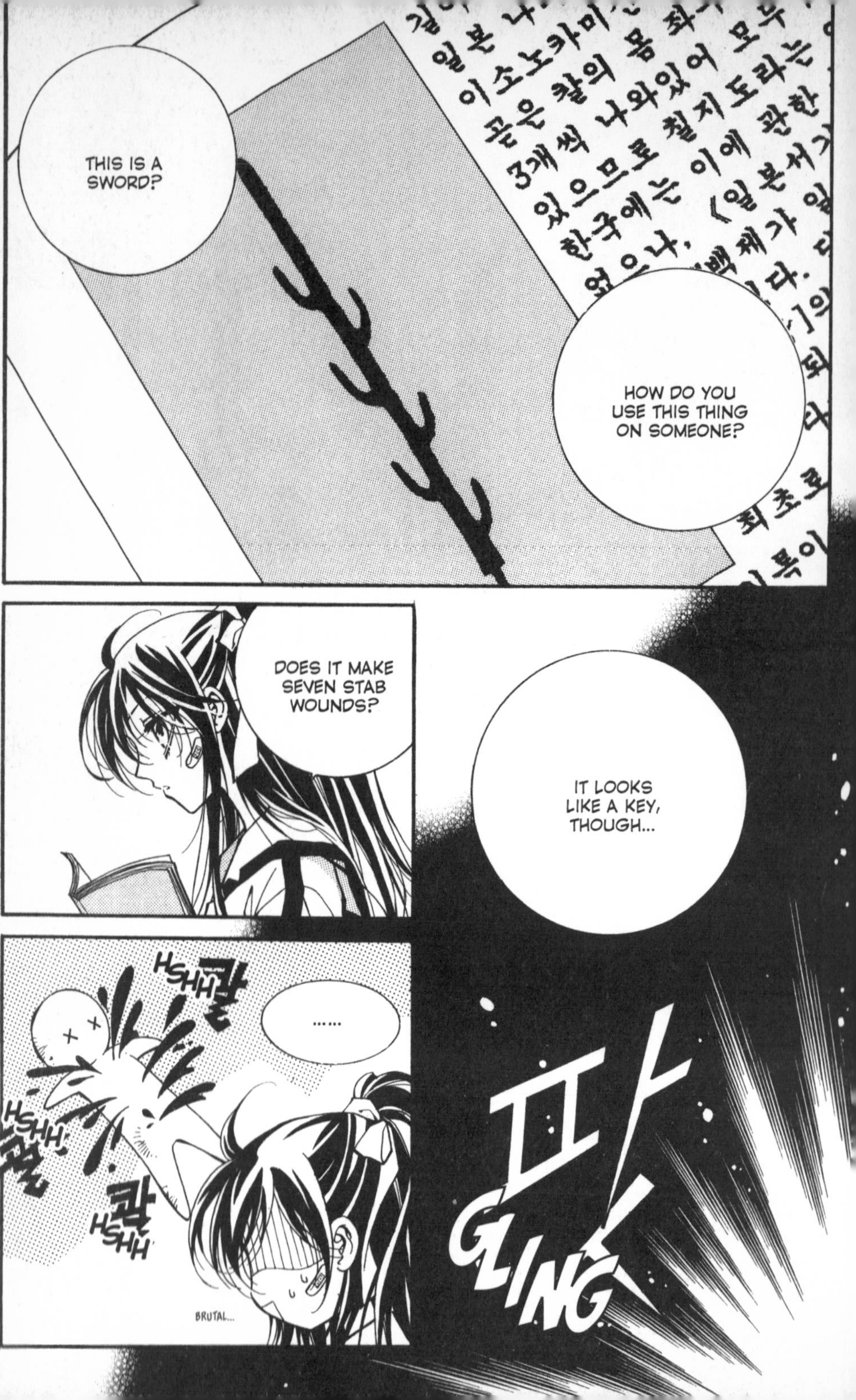
THIS IS A SWORD?
HOW DO YOU USE THIS THING ON SOMEONE?
DOES IT MAKE SEVEN STAB WOUNDS?
IT LOOKS LIKE A KEY, THOUGH...
......
HSHH 콱
HSHH! 콱
콱 HSHH
BRUTAL...
띠! GLING!

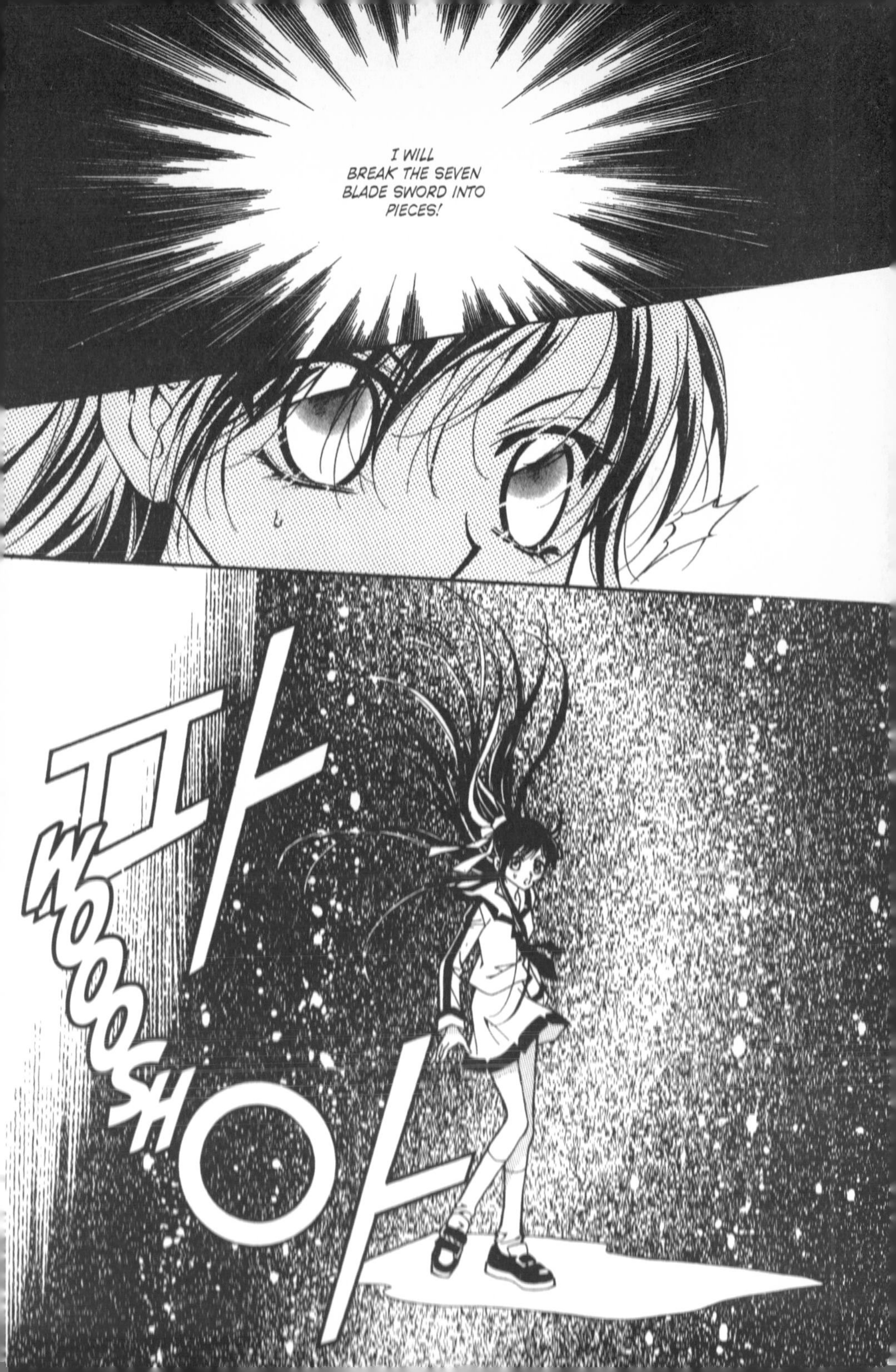
I WILL BREAK THE SEVEN BLADE SWORD INTO PIECES!
WHOOOSH

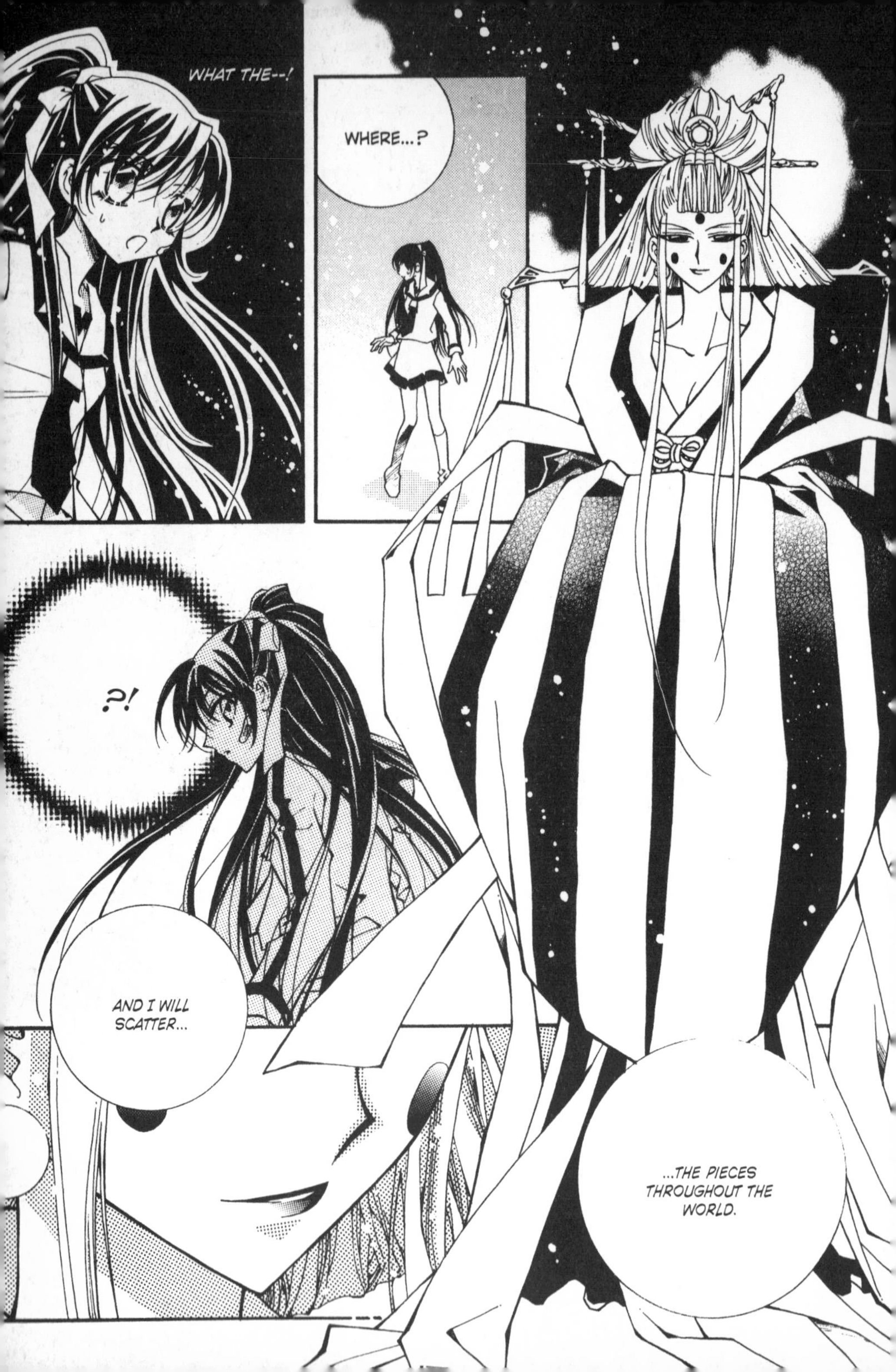

WHAT THE--!
WHERE...?
?!
AND I WILL SCATTER...
...THE PIECES THROUGHOUT THE WORLD.

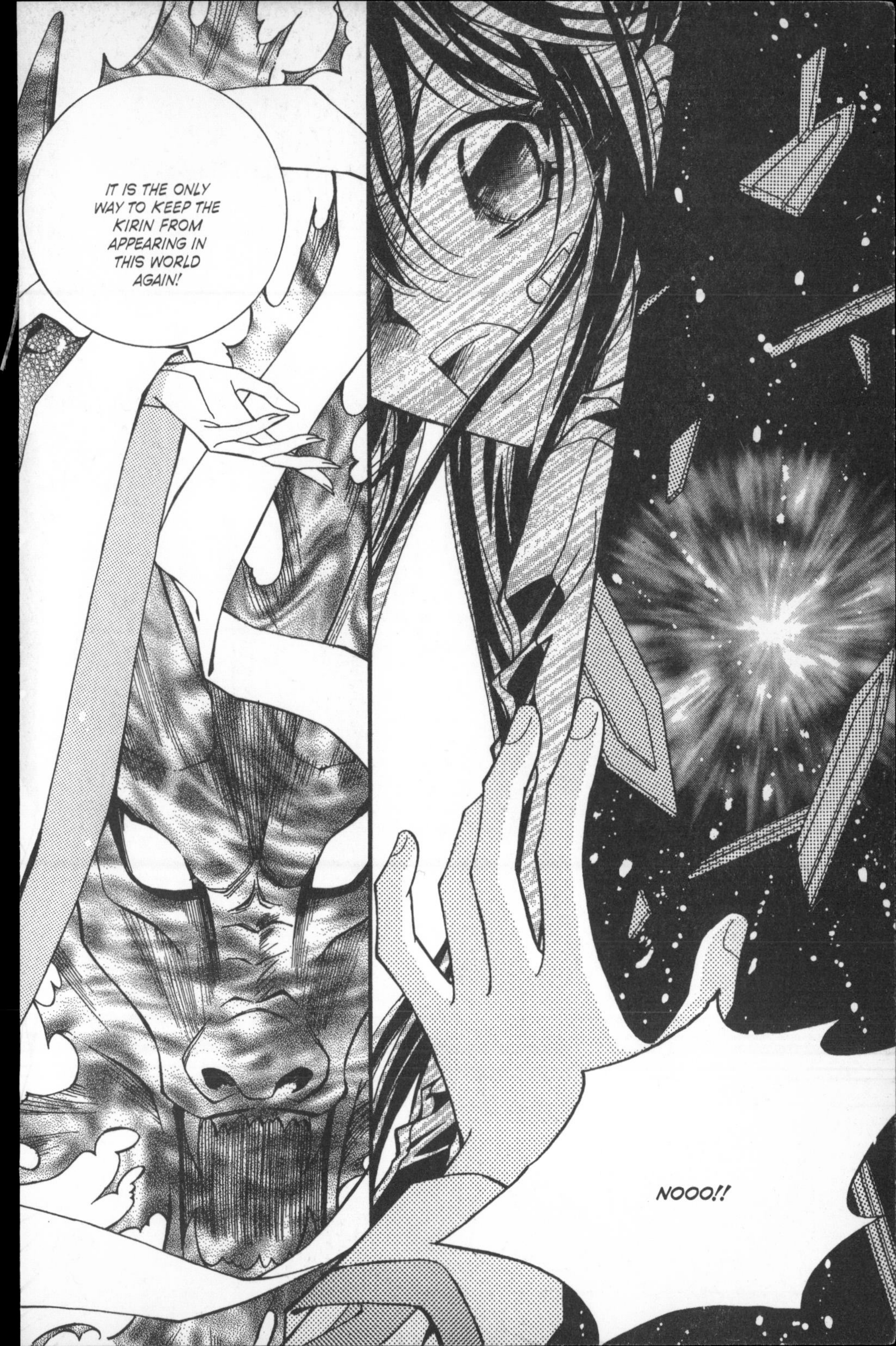
IT IS THE ONLY WAY TO KEEP THE KIRIN FROM APPEARING IN THIS WORLD AGAIN!
NOOO!!

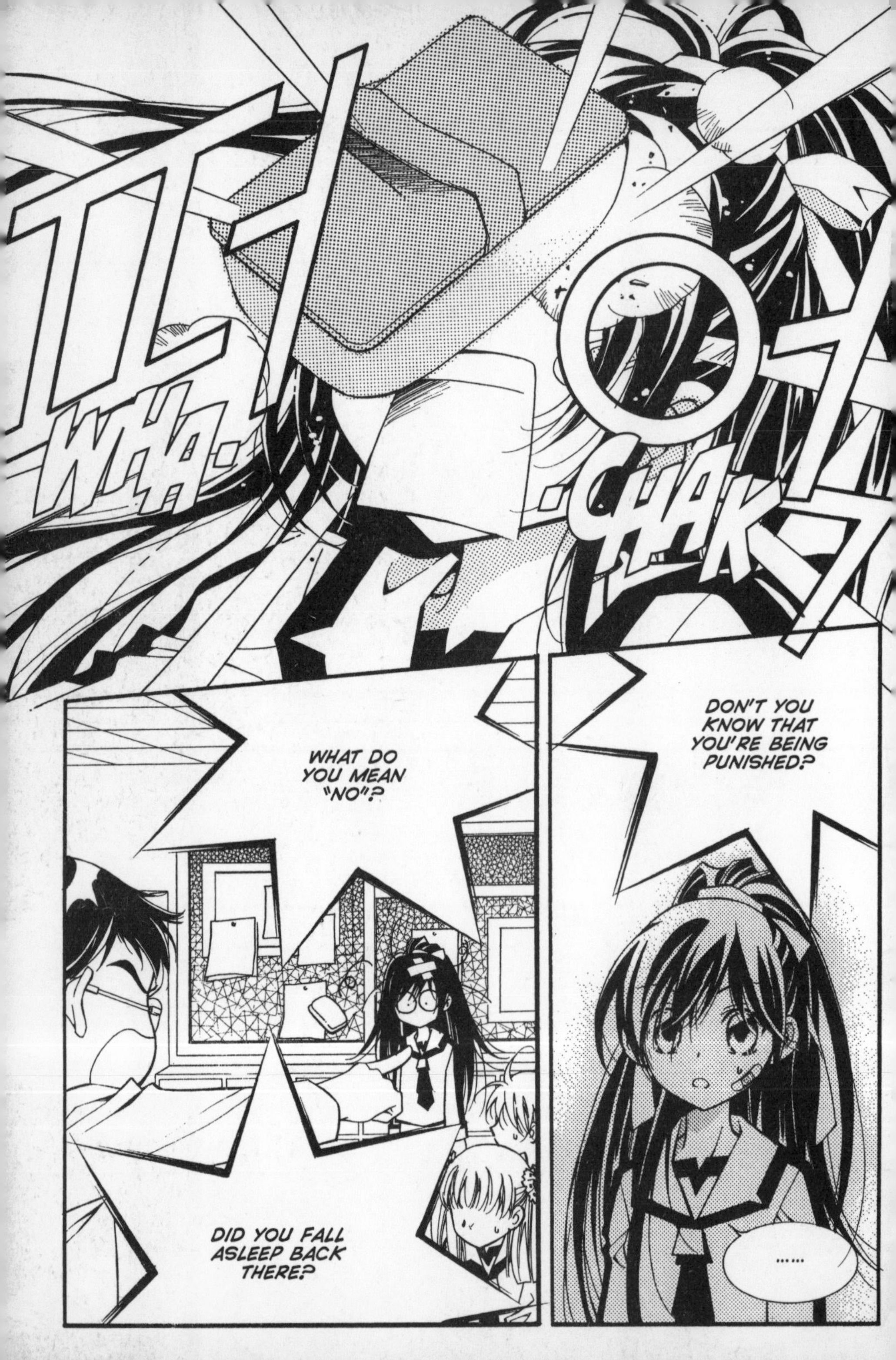
WHA..
.CHAK
WHAT DO YOU MEAN "NO"?
DID YOU FALL ASLEEP BACK THERE?
DON'T YOU KNOW THAT YOU'RE BEING PUNISHED?
......

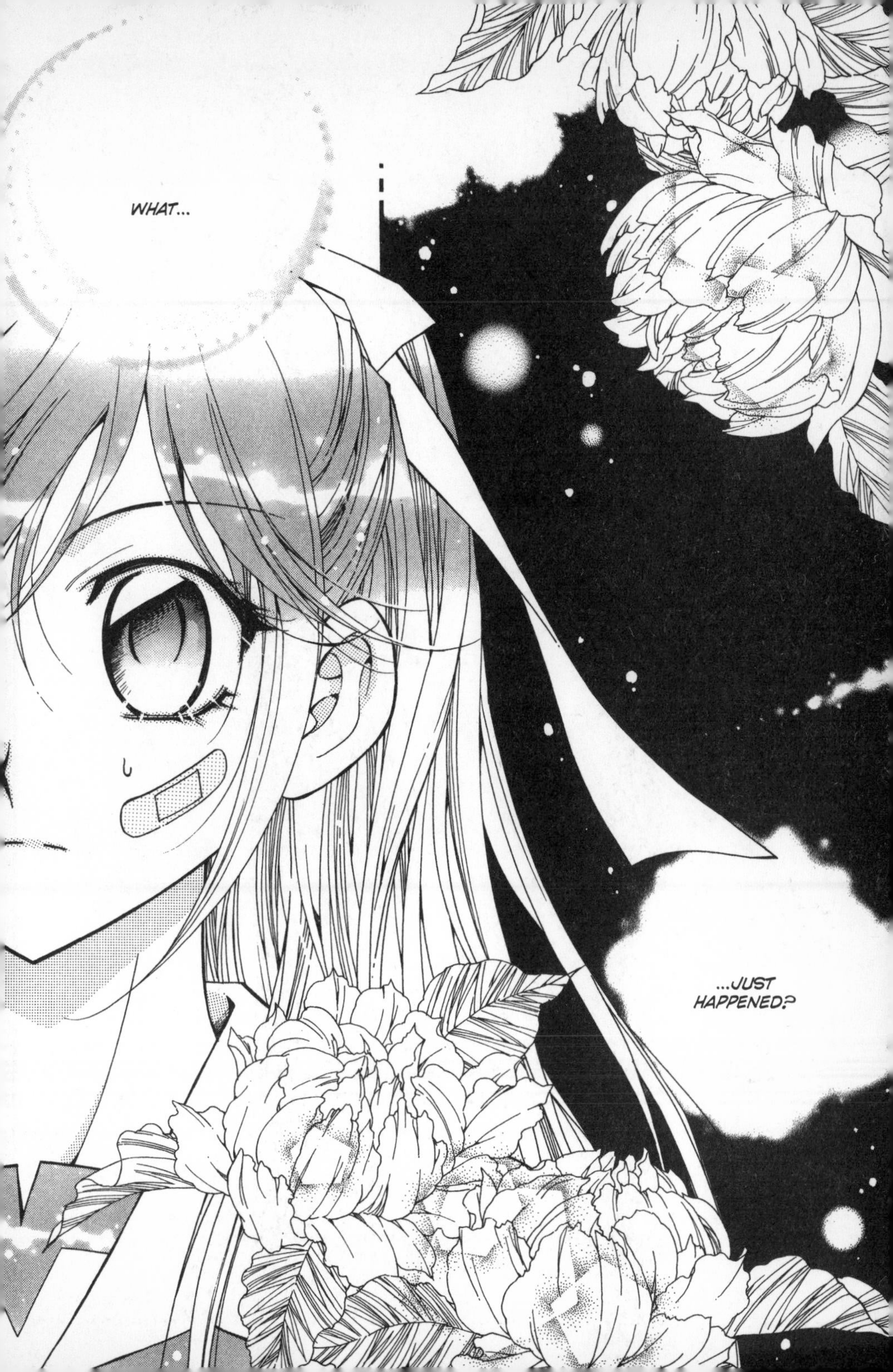
WHAT...
...JUST HAPPENED?

MINI INTERVIEW

NAME: EUN-GYO SUNG
AGE: 15
BLOOD TYPE: O
SIGN: SAGITTARIUS
HEIGHT: 152 CM
WEIGHT: WHY DO YOU WANT TO KNOW?

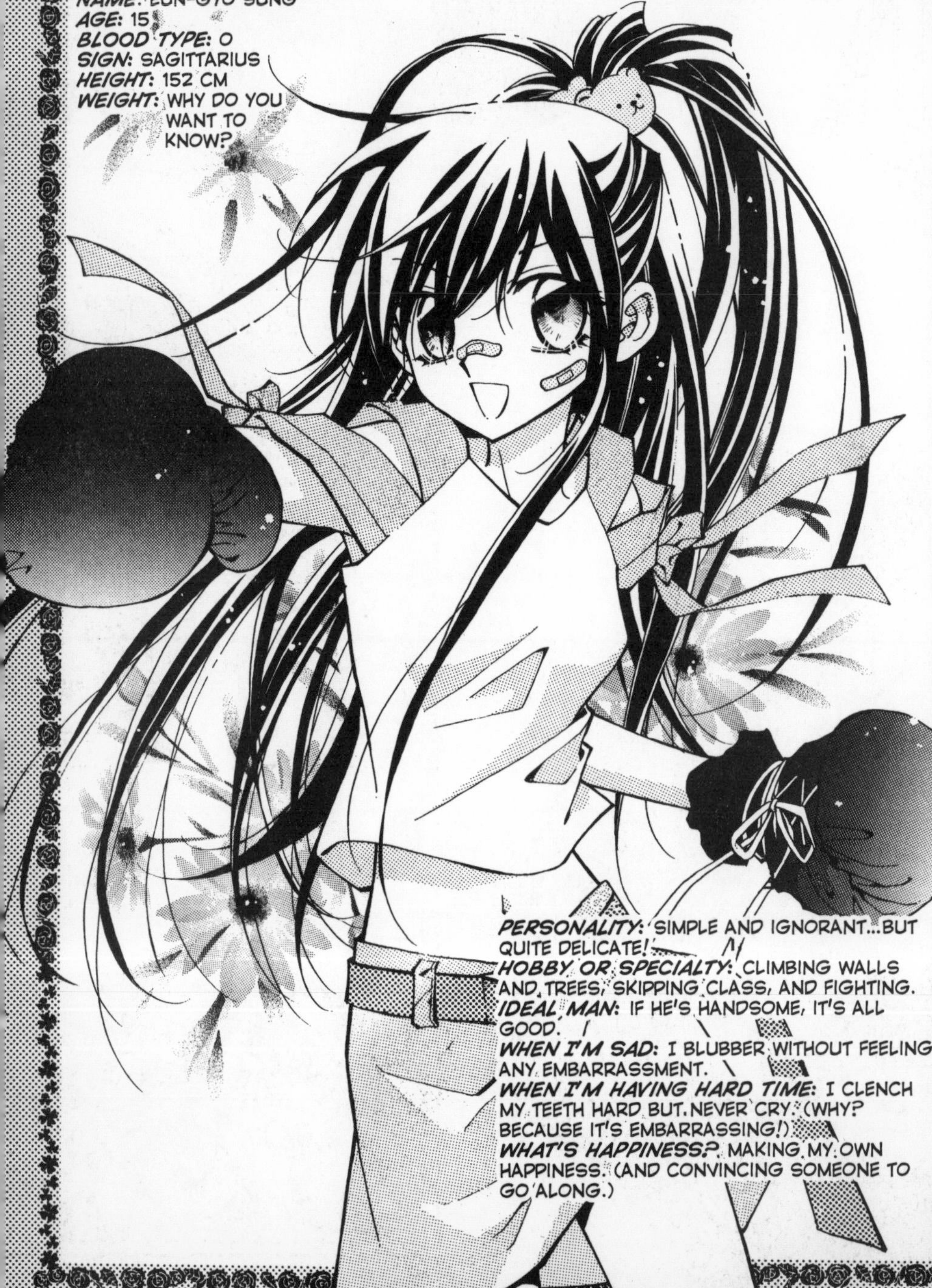

PERSONALITY: SIMPLE AND IGNORANT...BUT QUITE DELICATE!
HOBBY OR SPECIALTY: CLIMBING WALLS AND TREES, SKIPPING CLASS, AND FIGHTING.
IDEAL MAN: IF HE'S HANDSOME, IT'S ALL GOOD.
WHEN I'M SAD: I BLUBBER WITHOUT FEELING ANY EMBARRASSMENT.
WHEN I'M HAVING HARD TIME: I CLENCH MY TEETH HARD BUT NEVER CRY. (WHY? BECAUSE IT'S EMBARRASSING!)
WHAT'S HAPPINESS?: MAKING MY OWN HAPPINESS. (AND CONVINCING SOMEONE TO GO ALONG.)

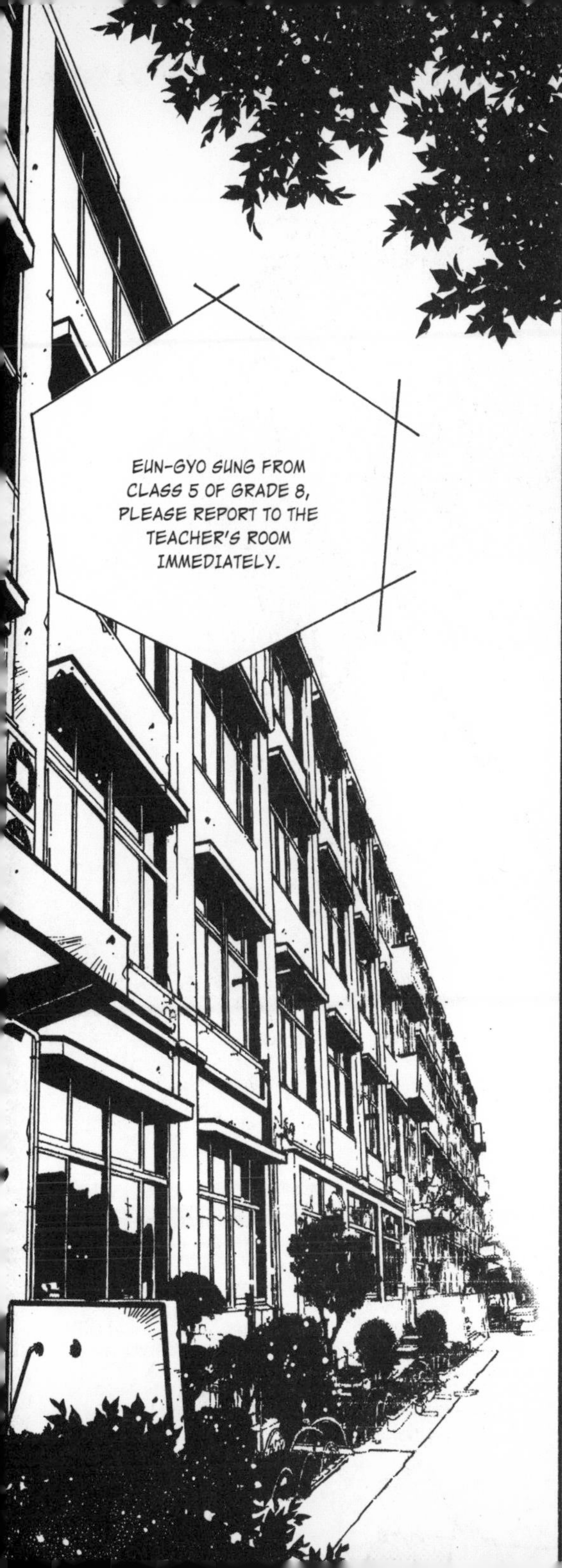

EUN-GYO SUNG FROM CLASS 5 OF GRADE 8, PLEASE REPORT TO THE TEACHER'S ROOM IMMEDIATELY.

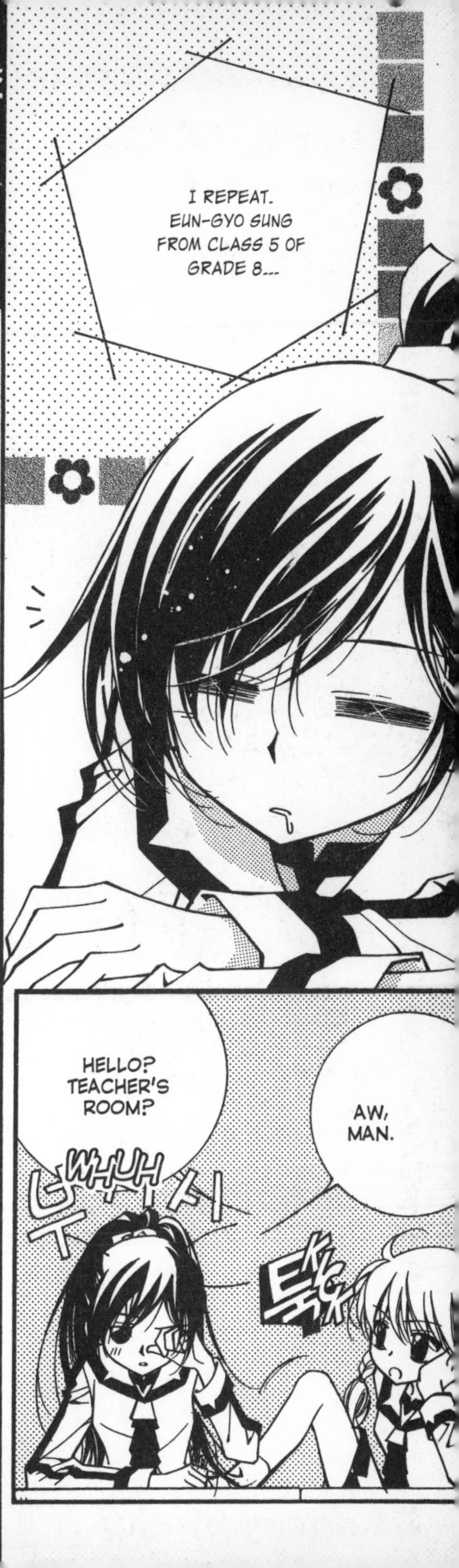

I REPEAT. EUN-GYO SUNG FROM CLASS 5 OF GRADE 8...
HELLO? TEACHER'S ROOM?
AW, MAN.
WHUH
KICK

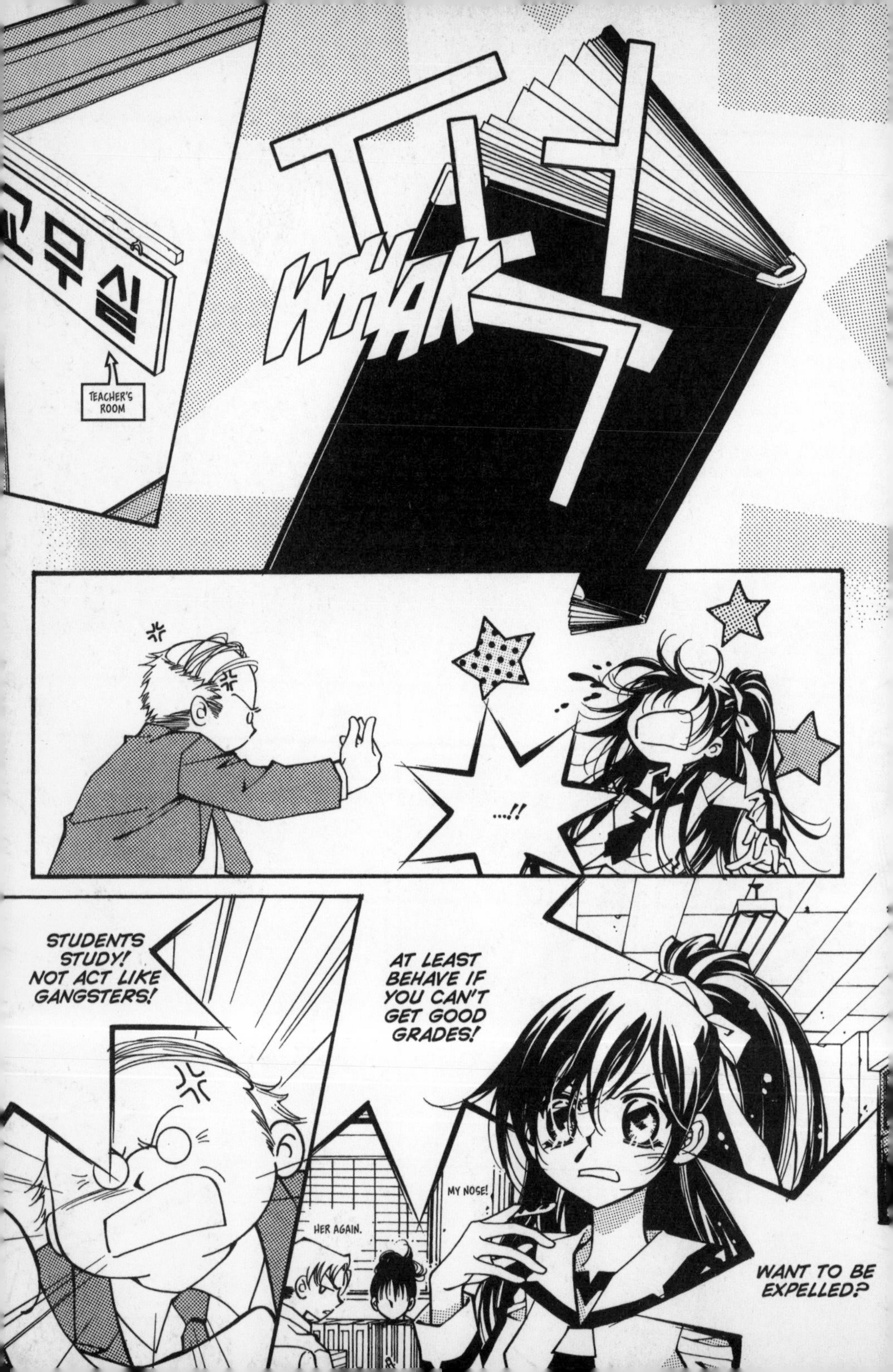
교무실
TEACHER'S ROOM
WHAK
...!!
STUDENTS STUDY! NOT ACT LIKE GANGSTERS!
AT LEAST BEHAVE IF YOU CAN'T GET GOOD GRADES!
MY NOSE!
HER AGAIN.
WANT TO BE EXPELLED?

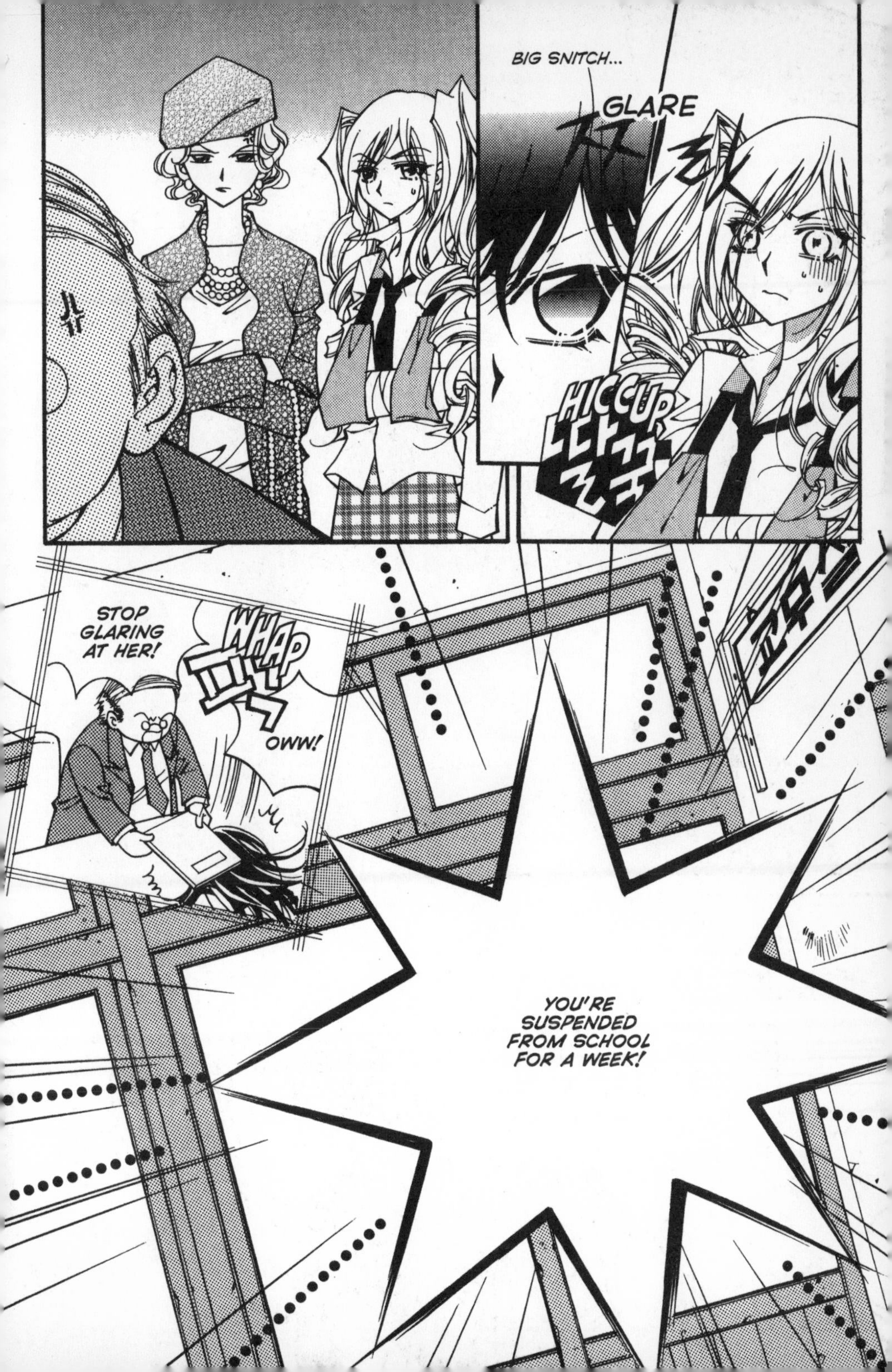
BIG SNITCH...
GLARE
HICCUP
STOP GLARING AT HER!
WHAP
OWW!
YOU'RE SUSPENDED FROM SCHOOL FOR A WEEK!

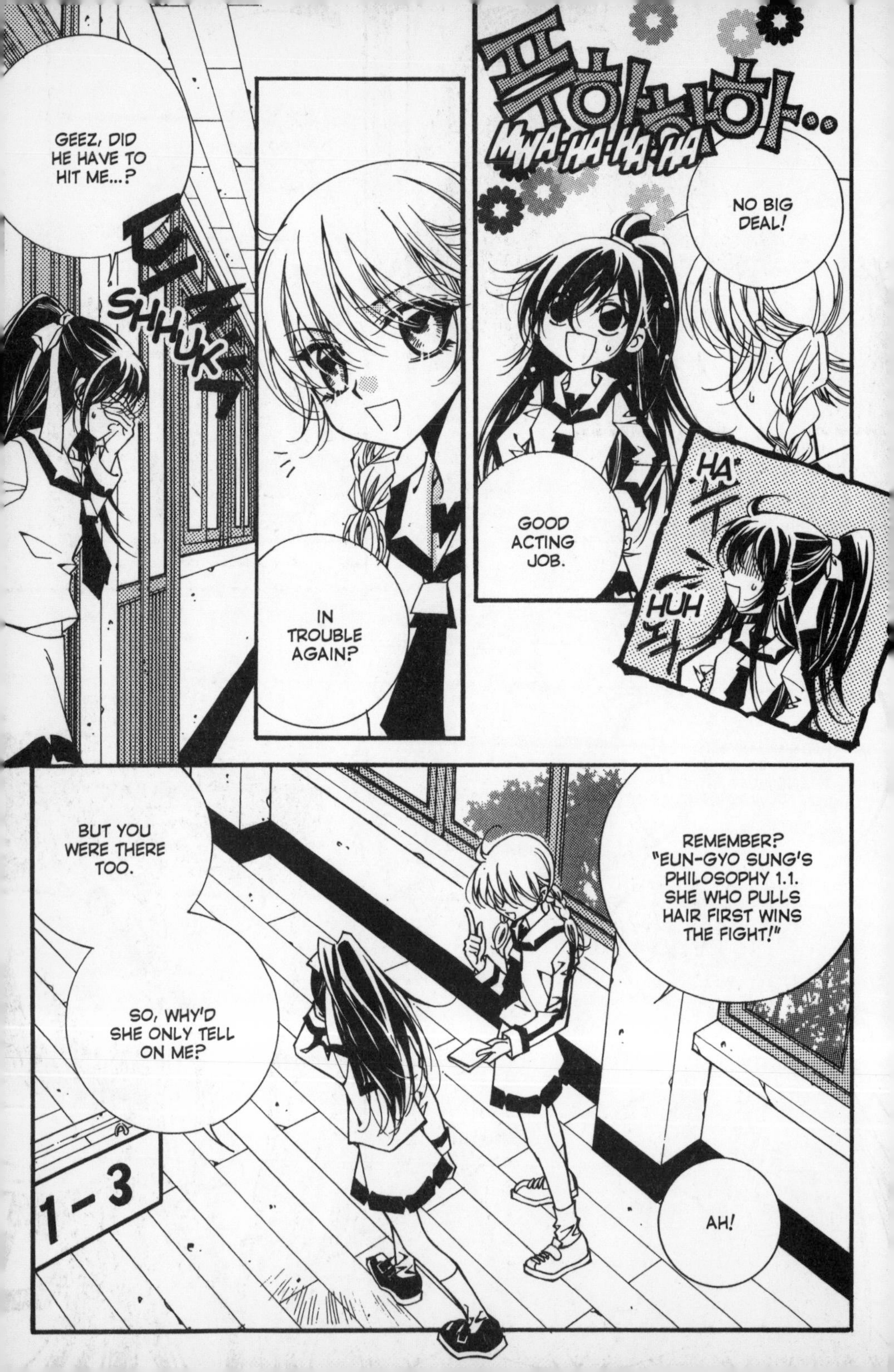
GEEZ, DID HE HAVE TO HIT ME...?
SHHUK
IN TROUBLE AGAIN?
MWA-HA-HA-HA
NO BIG DEAL!
GOOD ACTING JOB.
HA
HUH
BUT YOU WERE THERE TOO.
SO, WHY'D SHE ONLY TELL ON ME?
1-3
REMEMBER? "EUN-GYO SUNG'S PHILOSOPHY 1.1. SHE WHO PULLS HAIR FIRST WINS THE FIGHT!"
AH!

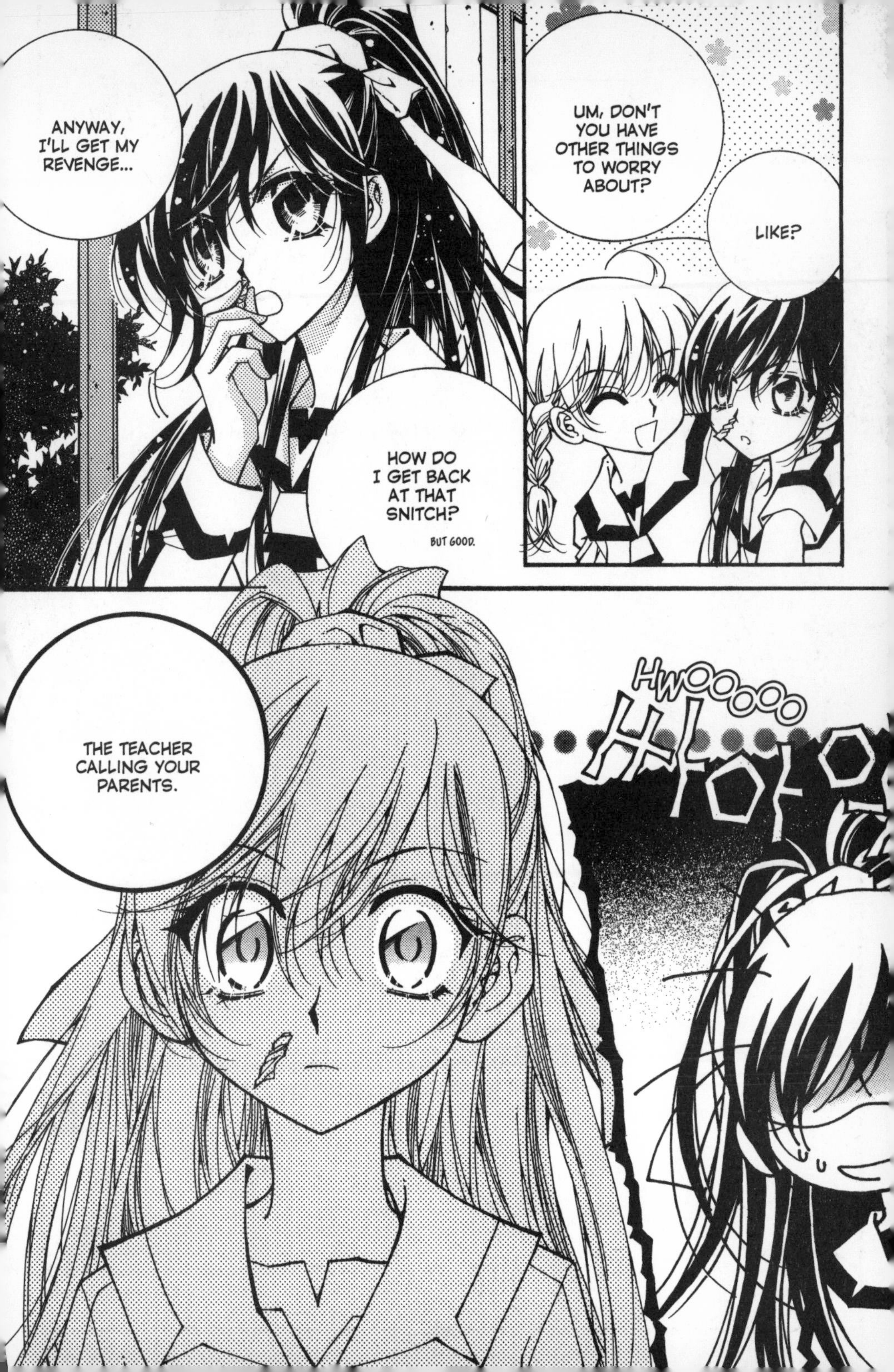
ANYWAY, I'LL GET MY REVENGE...
HOW DO I GET BACK AT THAT SNITCH?
BUT GOOD.
UM, DON'T YOU HAVE OTHER THINGS TO WORRY ABOUT?
LIKE?
THE TEACHER CALLING YOUR PARENTS.
HWOOOOO

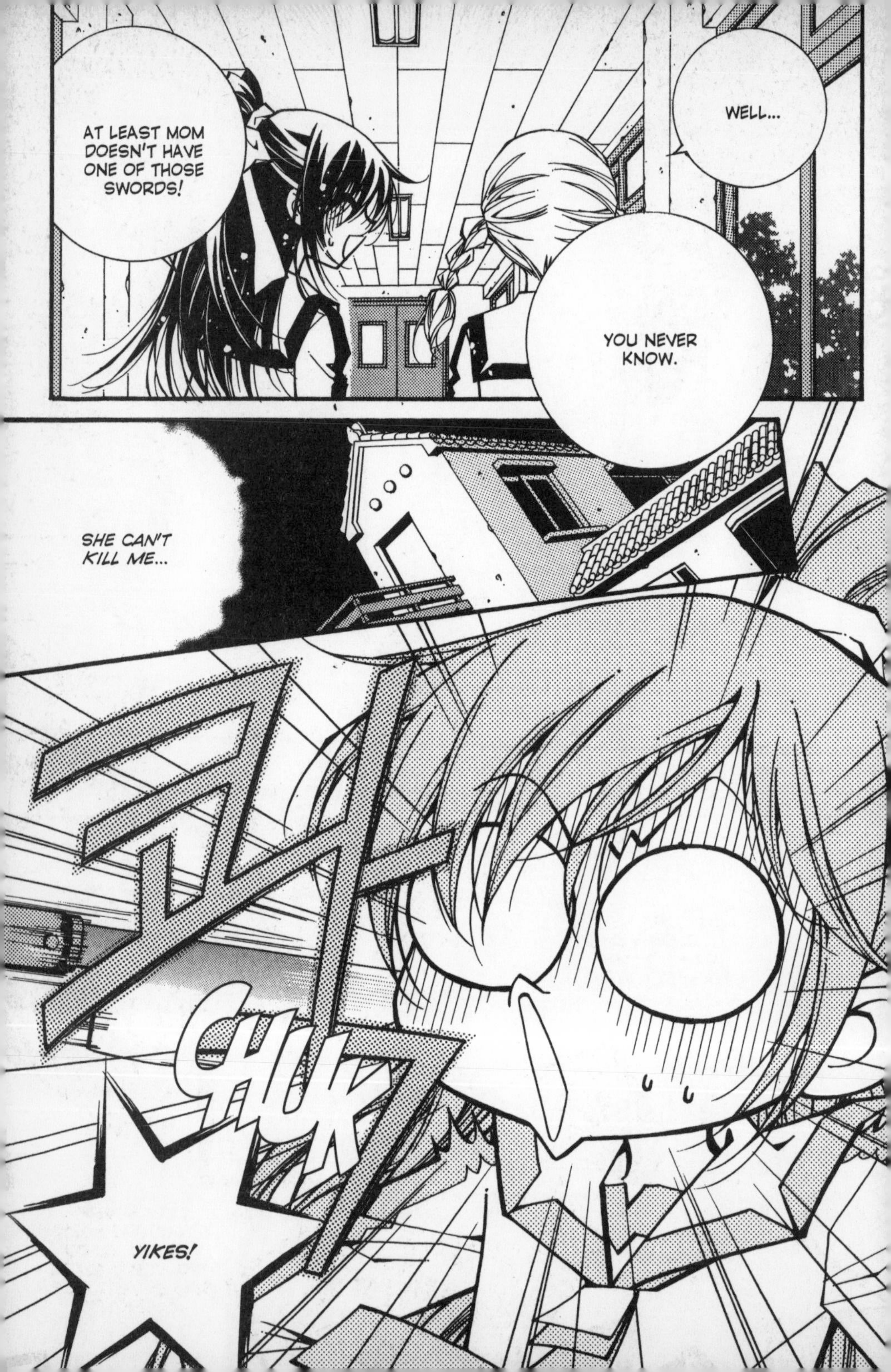
AT LEAST MOM DOESN'T HAVE ONE OF THOSE SWORDS!
WELL...
YOU NEVER KNOW.
SHE CAN'T KILL ME...
CHUK
YIKES!

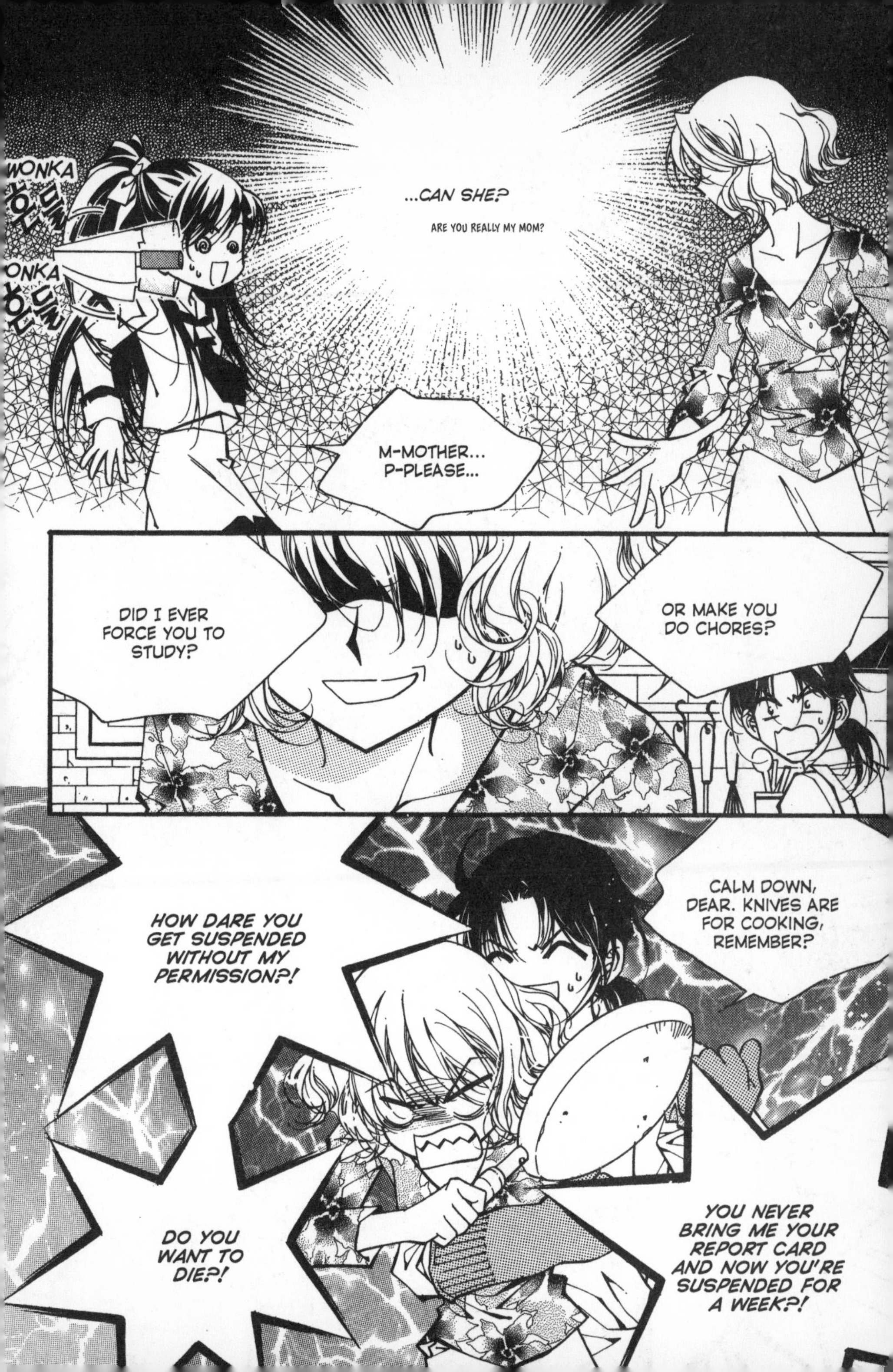

WONKA
WONKA
...CAN SHE?
ARE YOU REALLY MY MOM?
M-MOTHER... P-PLEASE...
DID I EVER FORCE YOU TO STUDY?
OR MAKE YOU DO CHORES?
HOW DARE YOU GET SUSPENDED WITHOUT MY PERMISSION?!
CALM DOWN, DEAR. KNIVES ARE FOR COOKING, REMEMBER?
DO YOU WANT TO DIE?!
YOU NEVER BRING ME YOUR REPORT CARD AND NOW YOU'RE SUSPENDED FOR A WEEK?!

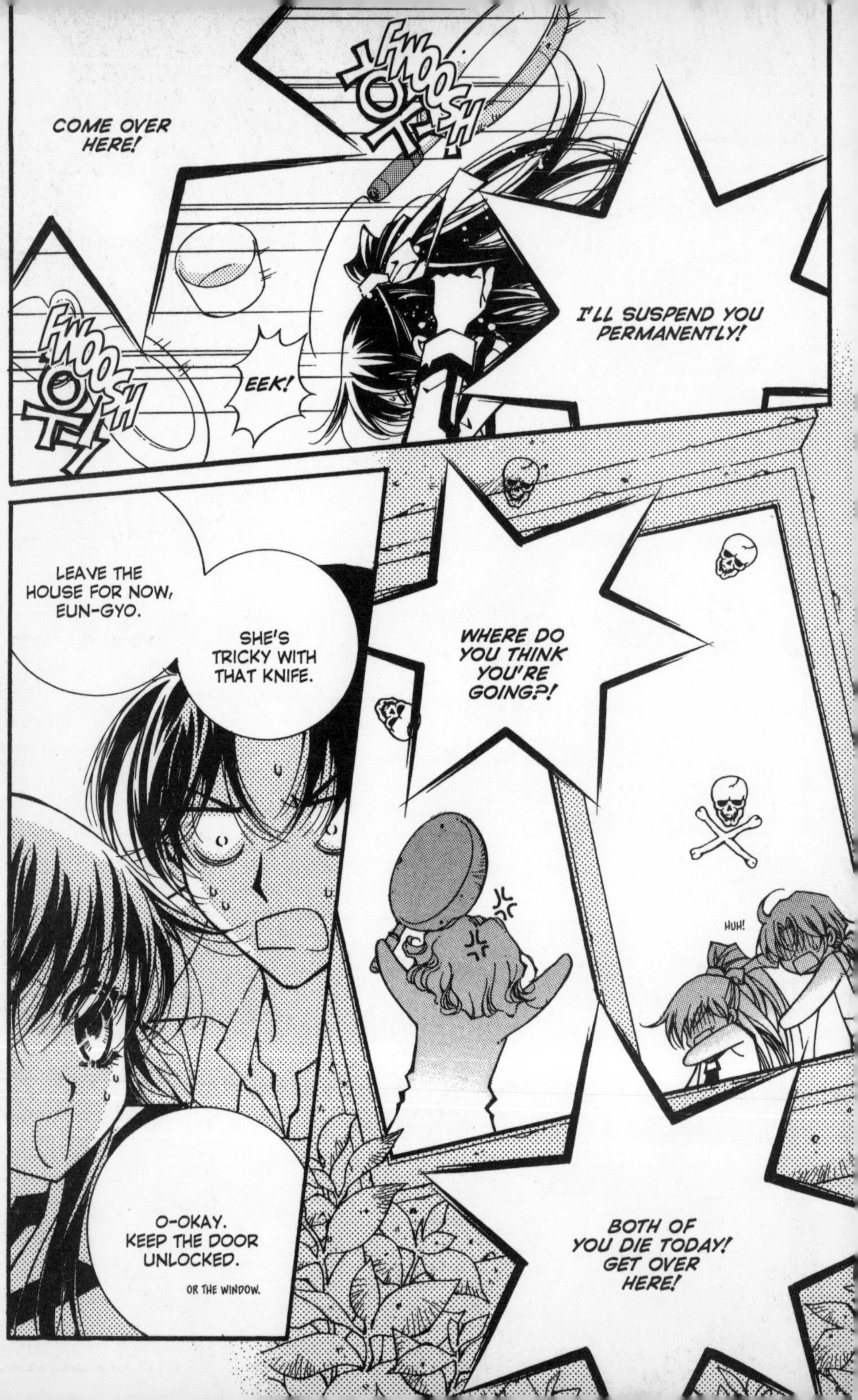
COME OVER HERE!
FWOOSH
FWOOSH
EEK!
I'LL SUSPEND YOU PERMANENTLY!
LEAVE THE HOUSE FOR NOW, EUN-GYO.
SHE'S TRICKY WITH THAT KNIFE.
O-OKAY. KEEP THE DOOR UNLOCKED.
OR THE WINDOW.
WHERE DO YOU THINK YOU'RE GOING?!
HUH!
BOTH OF YOU DIE TODAY! GET OVER HERE!

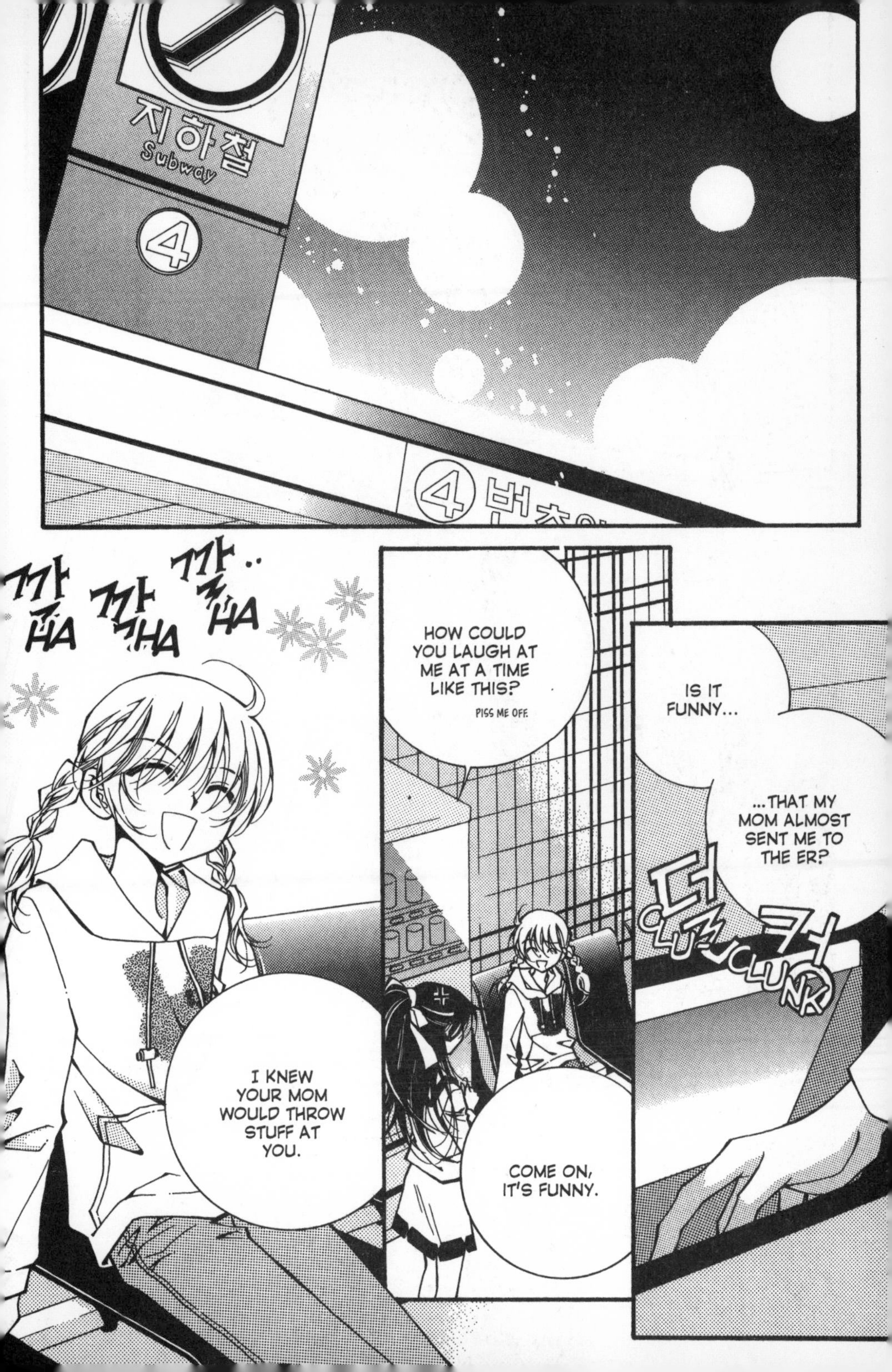

지하철
Subway
4
HA HA HA
I KNEW YOUR MOM WOULD THROW STUFF AT YOU.
HOW COULD YOU LAUGH AT ME AT A TIME LIKE THIS?
PISS ME OFF.
COME ON, IT'S FUNNY.
IS IT FUNNY...
...THAT MY MOM ALMOST SENT ME TO THE ER?
CLUNK CLUNK

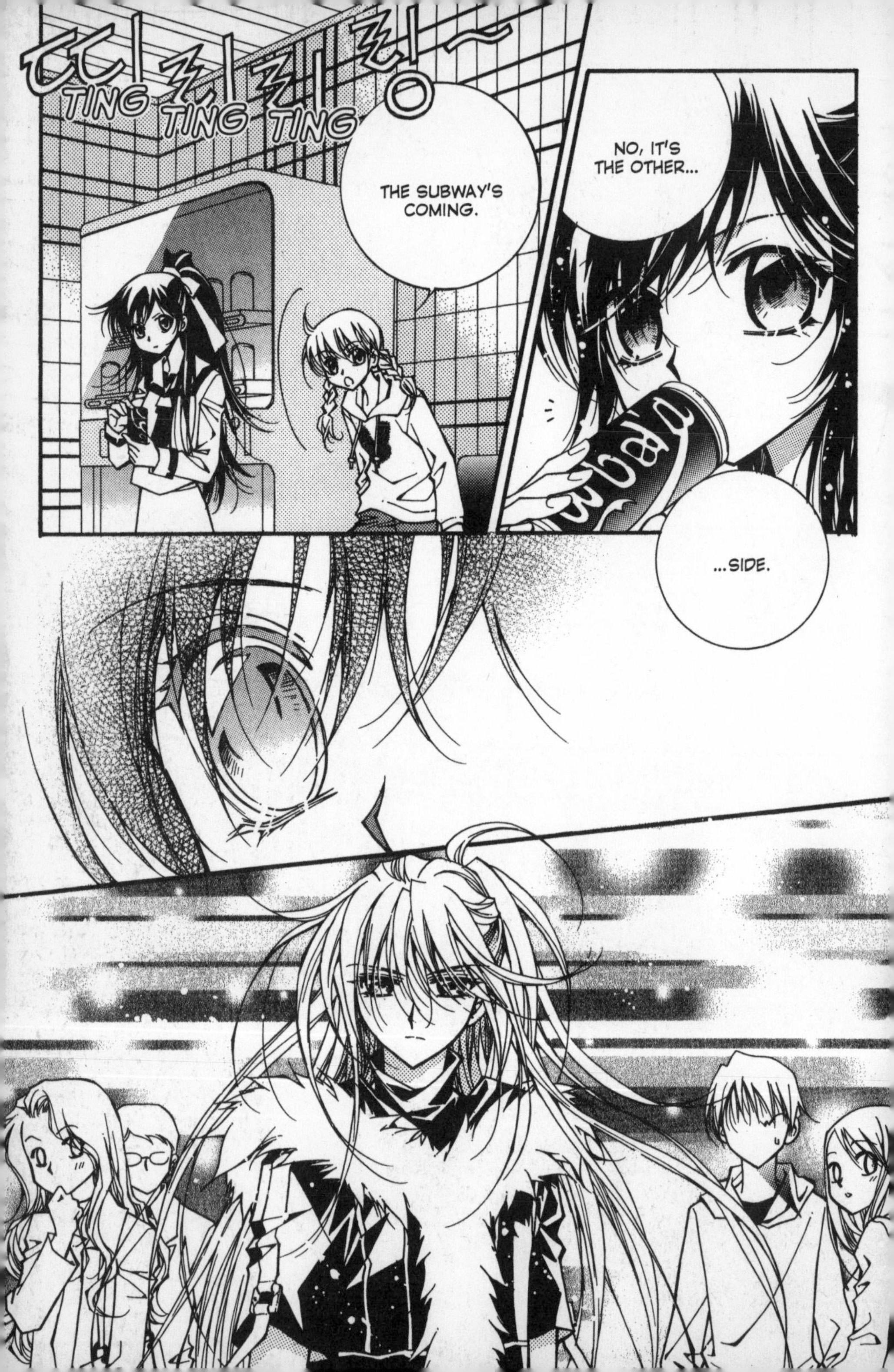
TING TING TING
THE SUBWAY'S COMING.
NO, IT'S THE OTHER...
...SIDE.

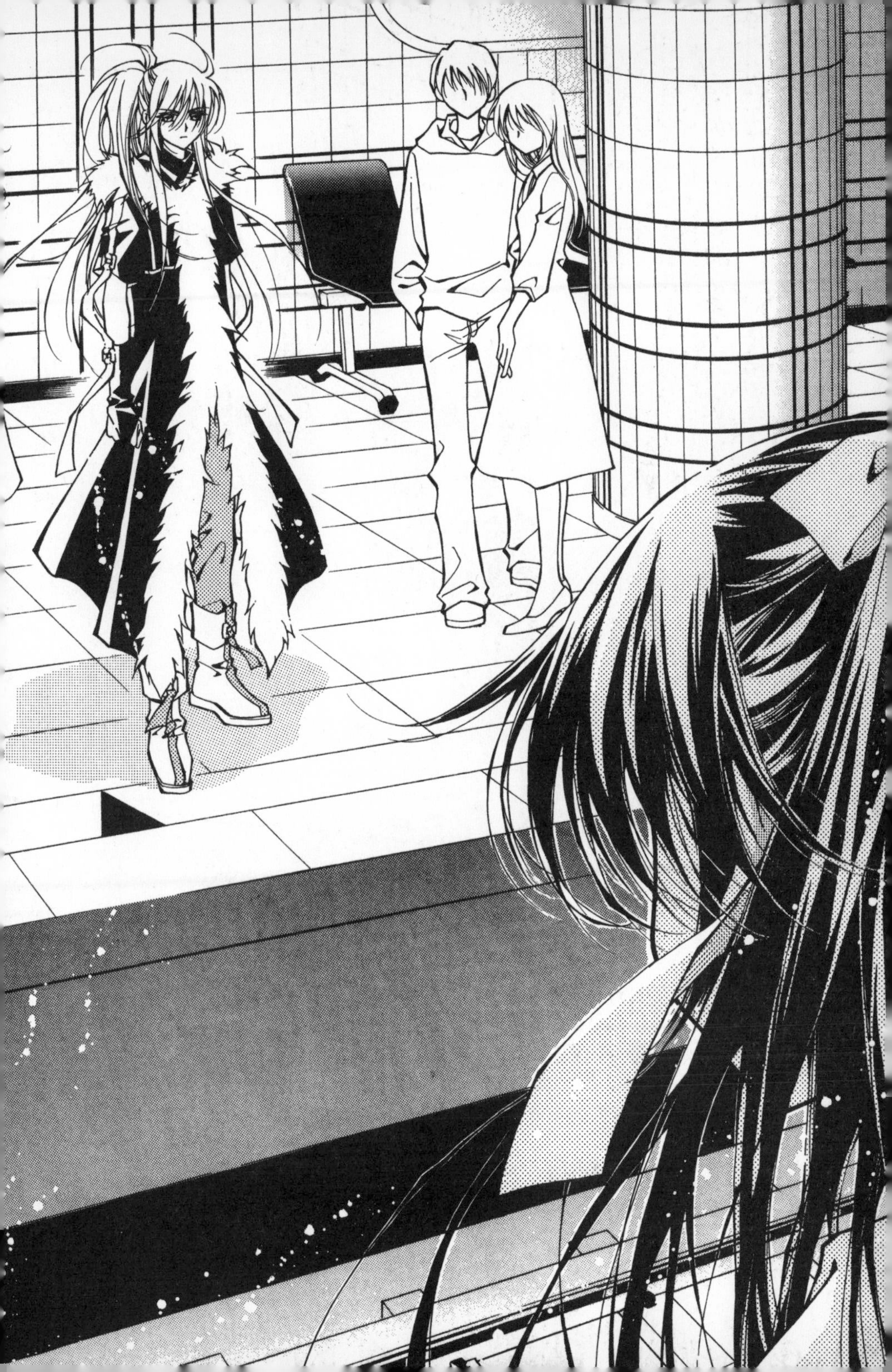

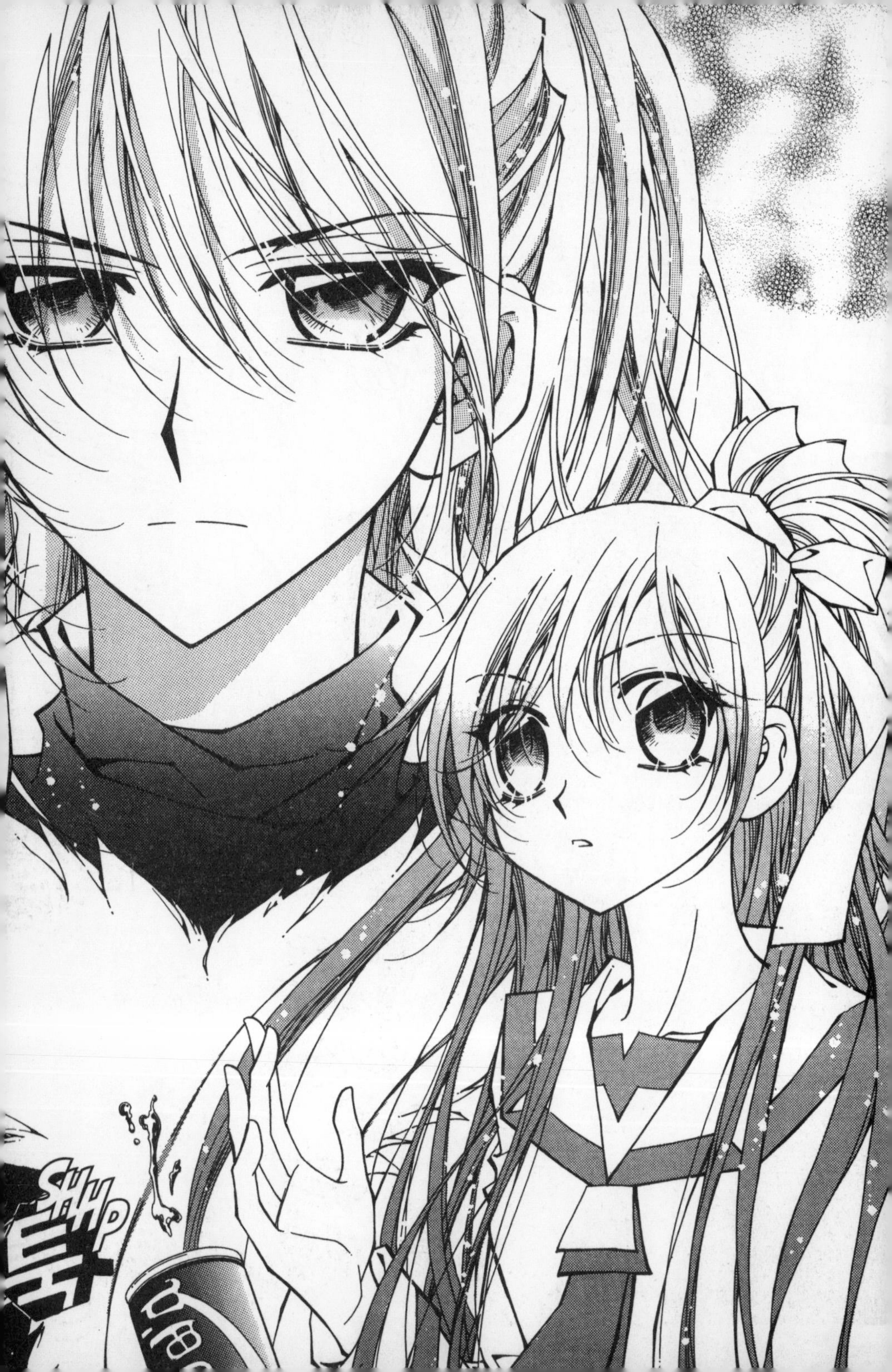
SHHP
탁

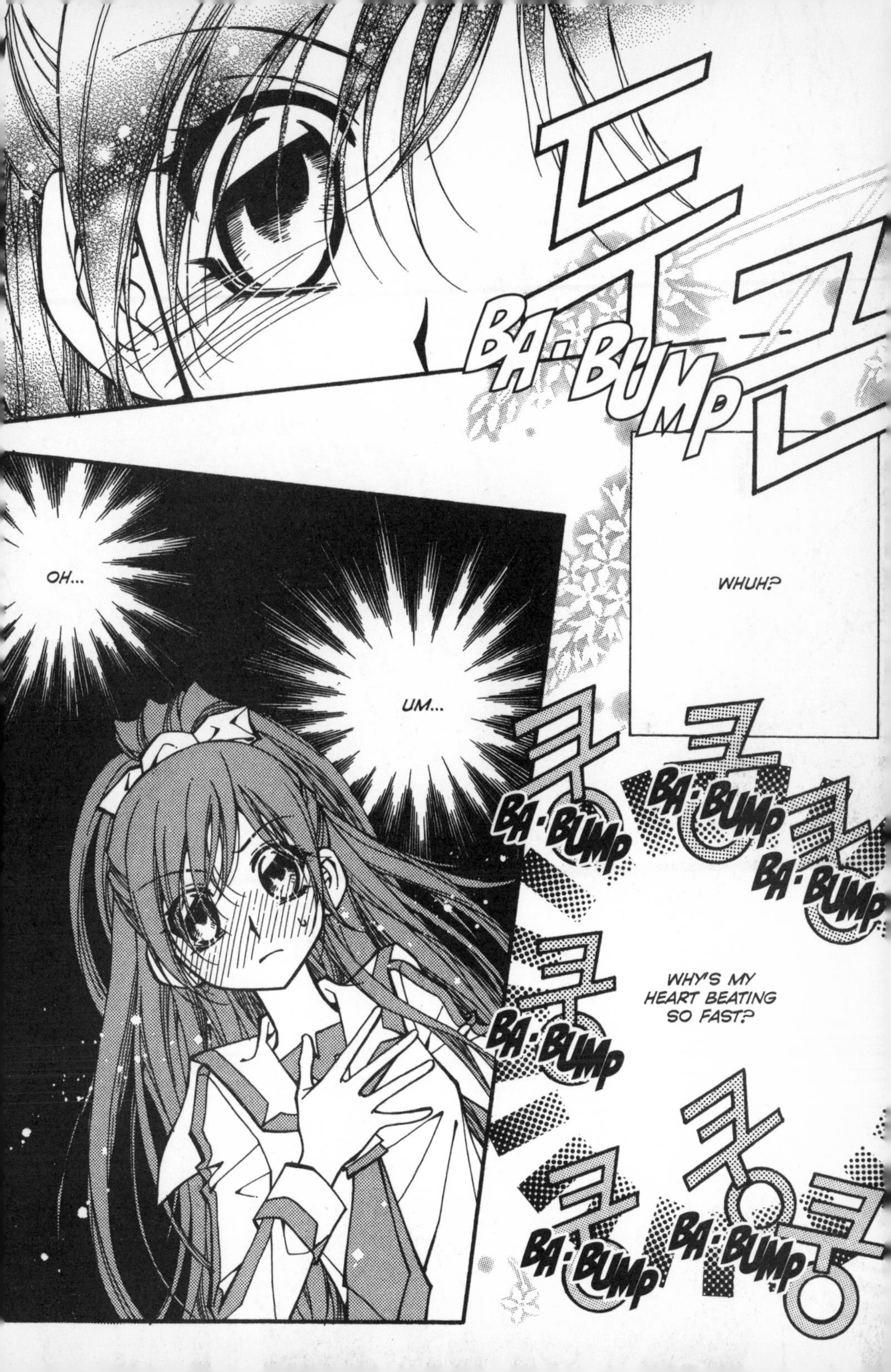

BA-BUMP
OH...
UM...
WHUH?
BA-BUMP
BA-BUMP
BA-BUMP
WHY'S MY HEART BEATING SO FAST?
BA-BUMP
BA-BUMP
BA-BUMP

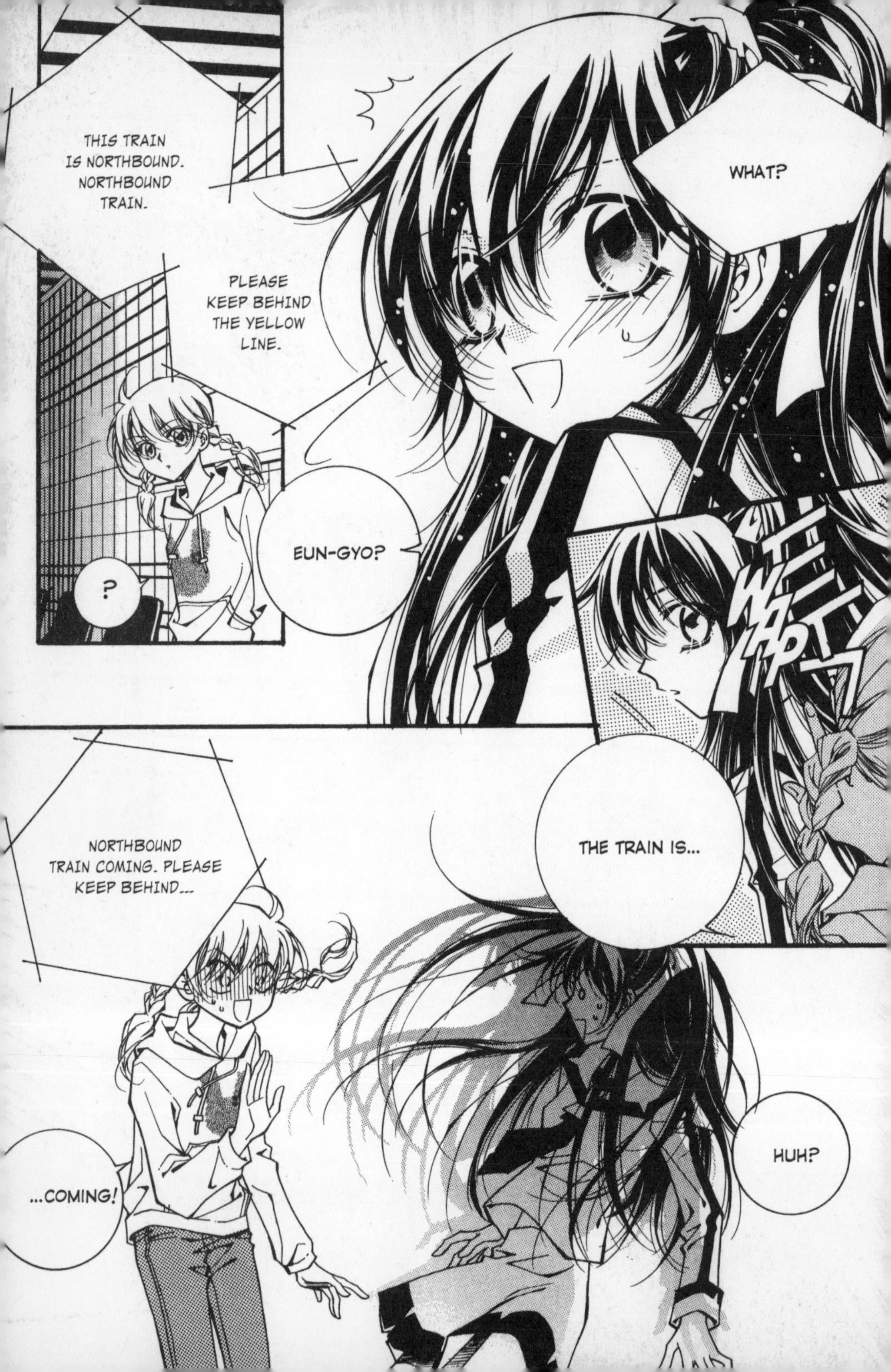
THIS TRAIN IS NORTHBOUND. NORTHBOUND TRAIN.
PLEASE KEEP BEHIND THE YELLOW LINE.
?
WHAT?
EUN-GYO?
WHAP
THE TRAIN IS...
NORTHBOUND TRAIN COMING. PLEASE KEEP BEHIND...
...COMING!
HUH?

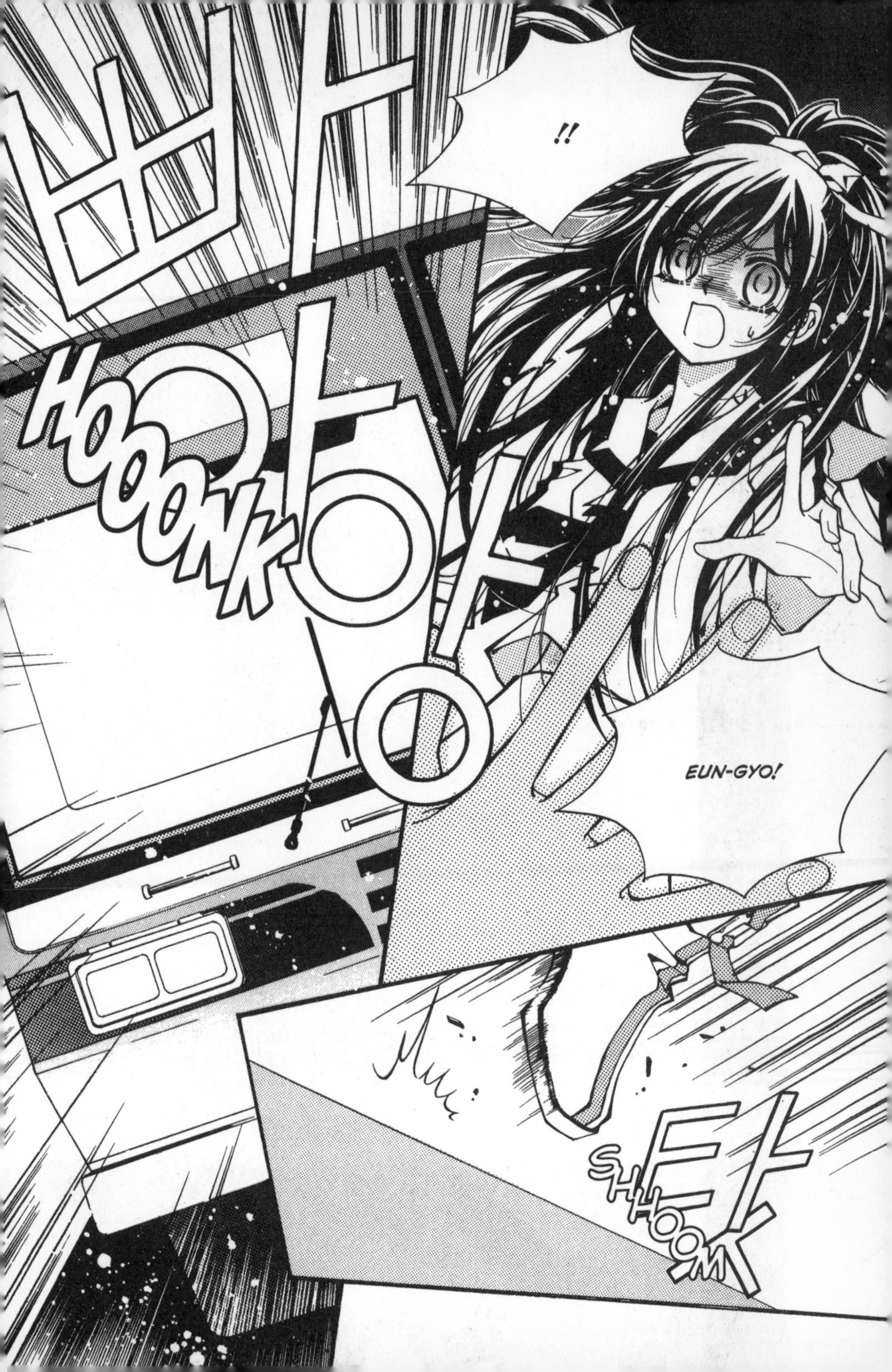
!!
HOOONK
EUN-GYO!
SHHOOM

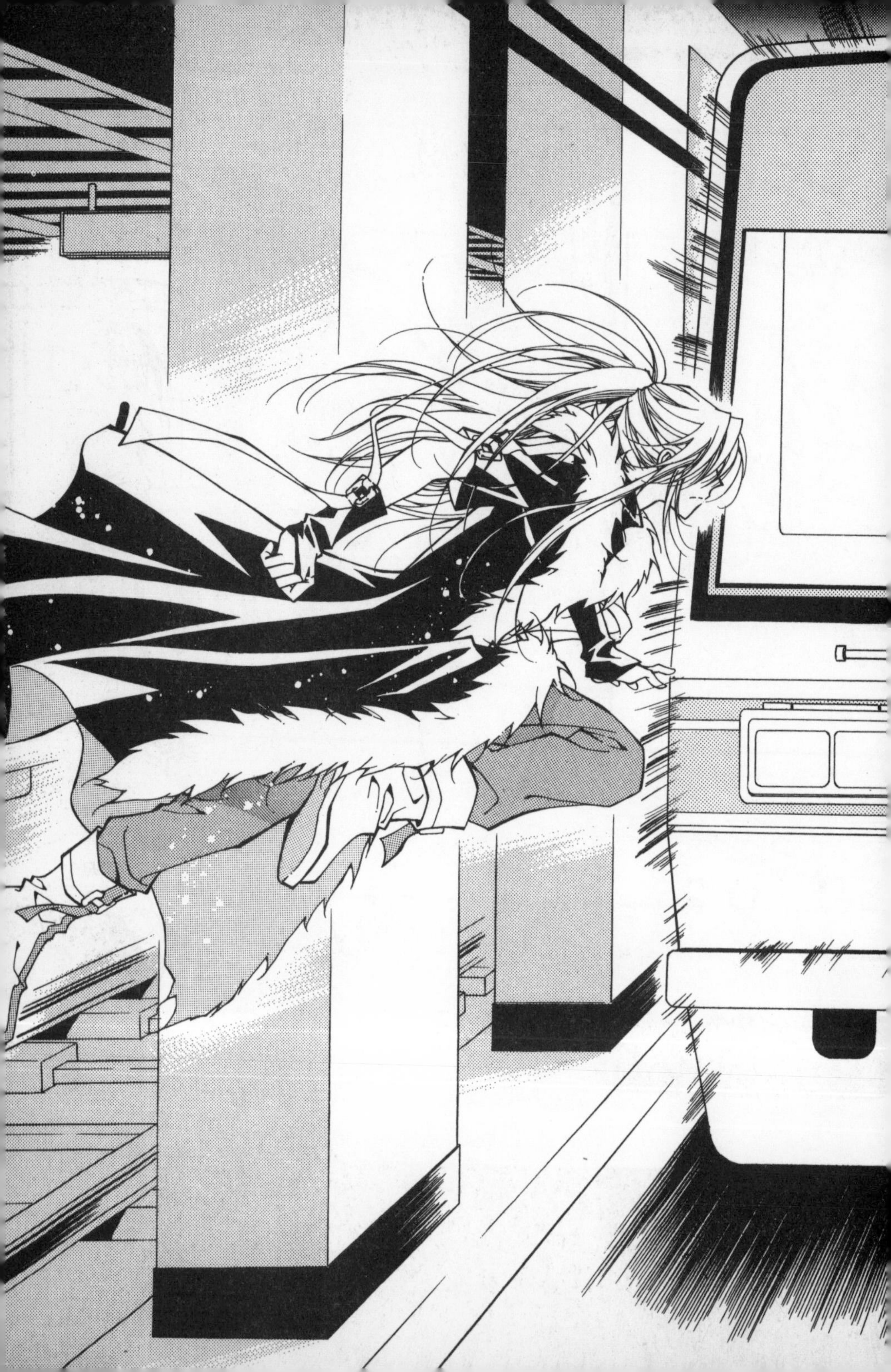

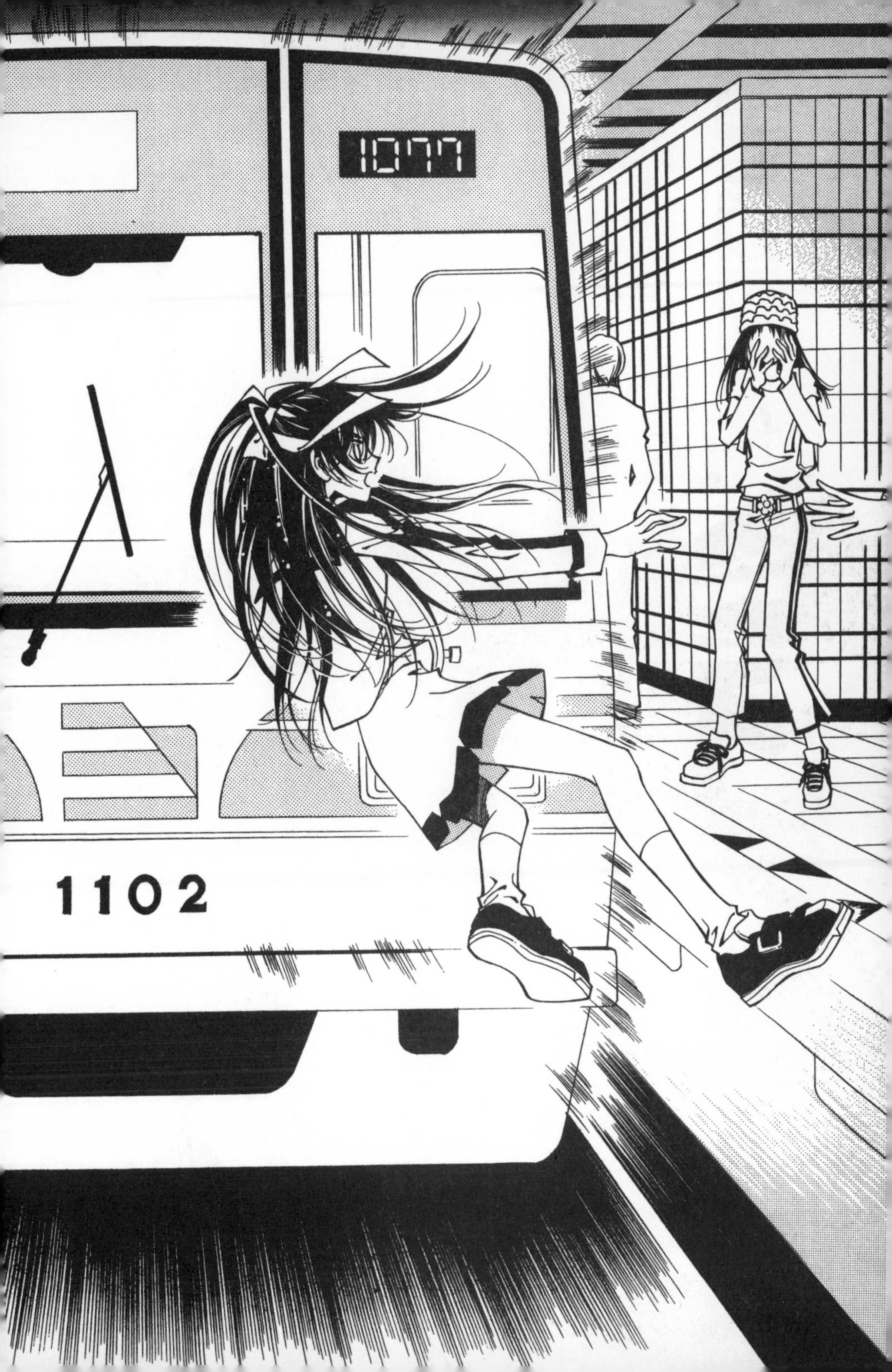
1077
1102

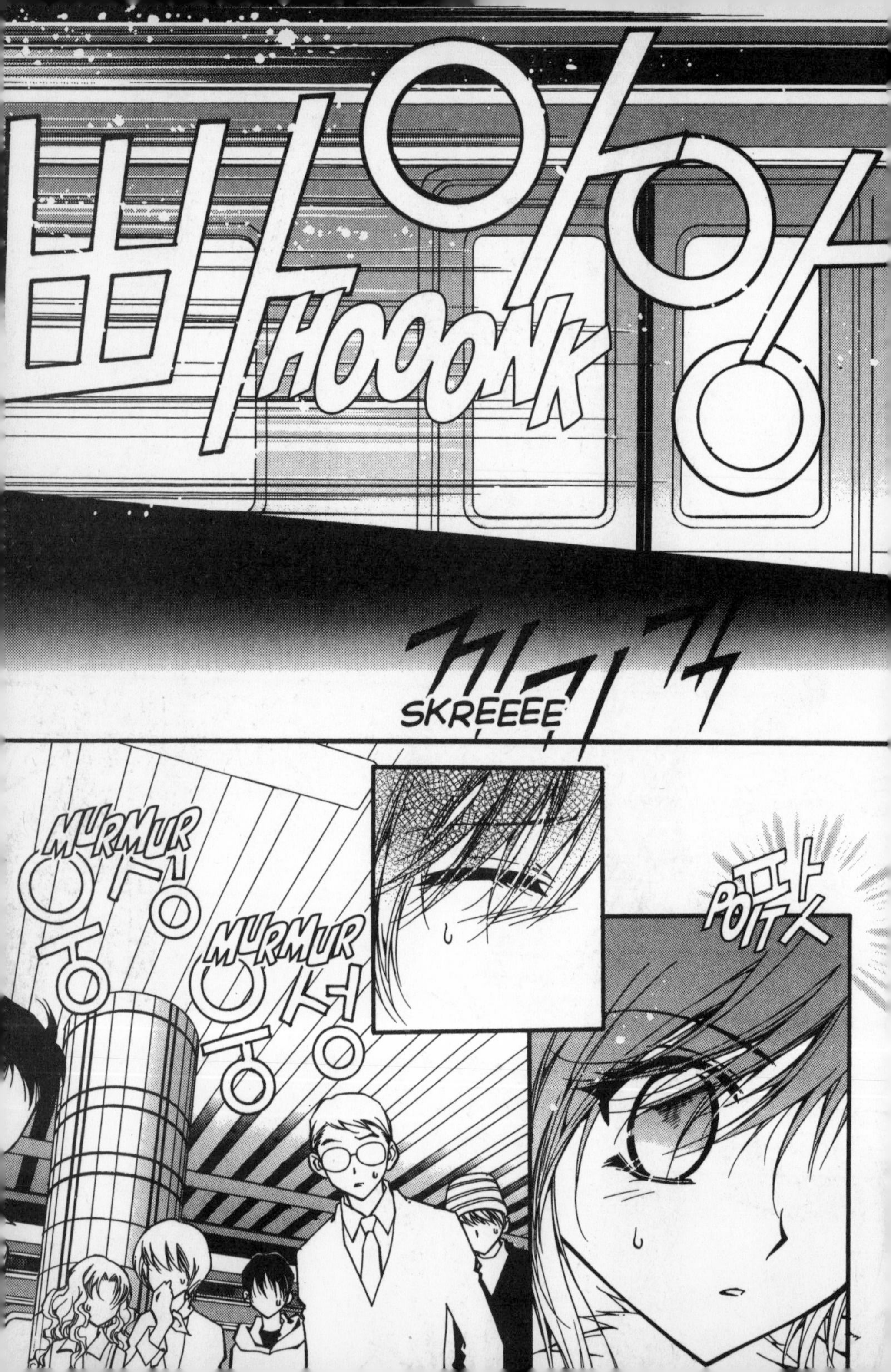
HOOONK
SKREEEE
MURMUR
MURMUR
POIT

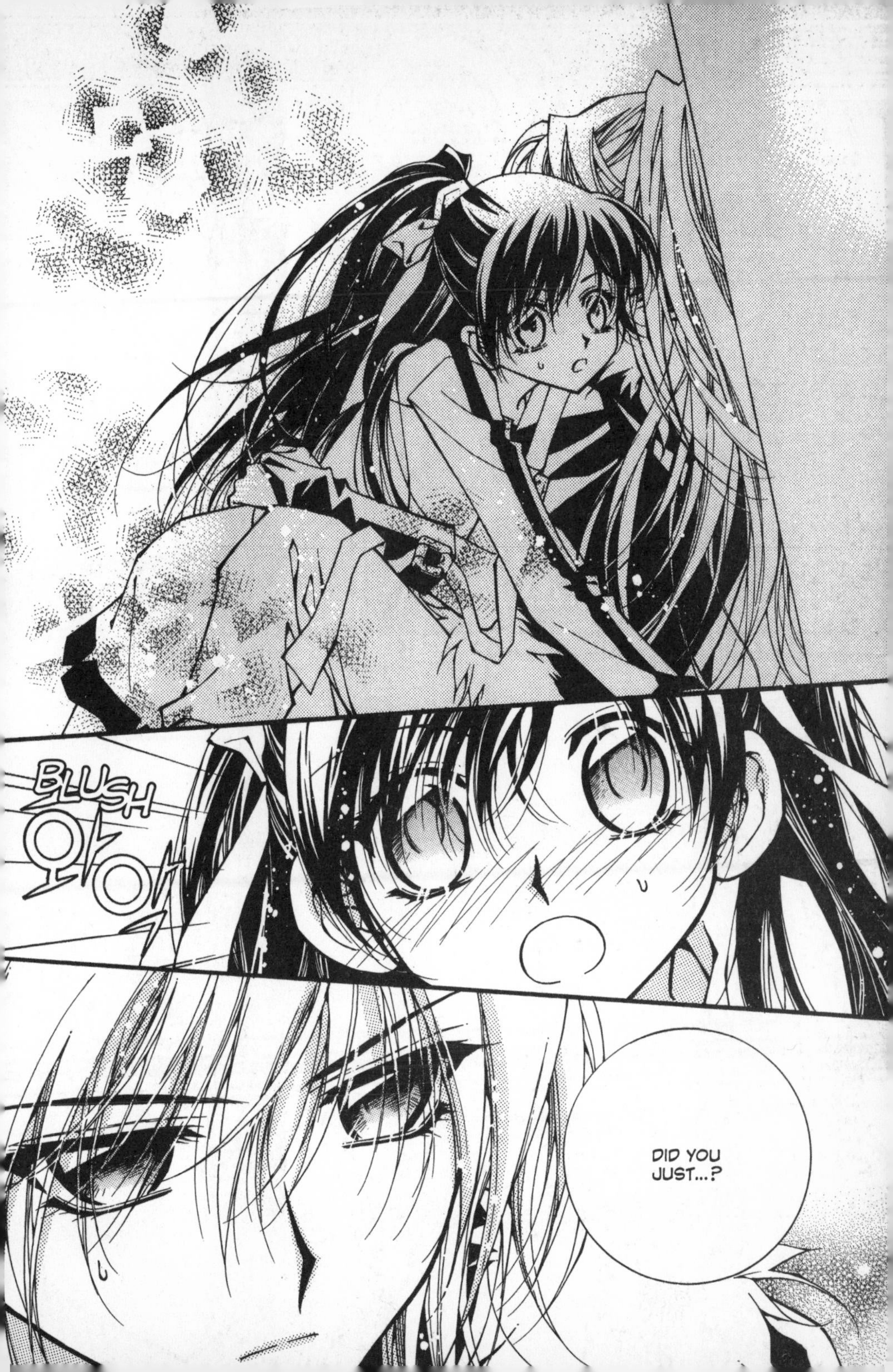
BLUSH
DID YOU JUST...?

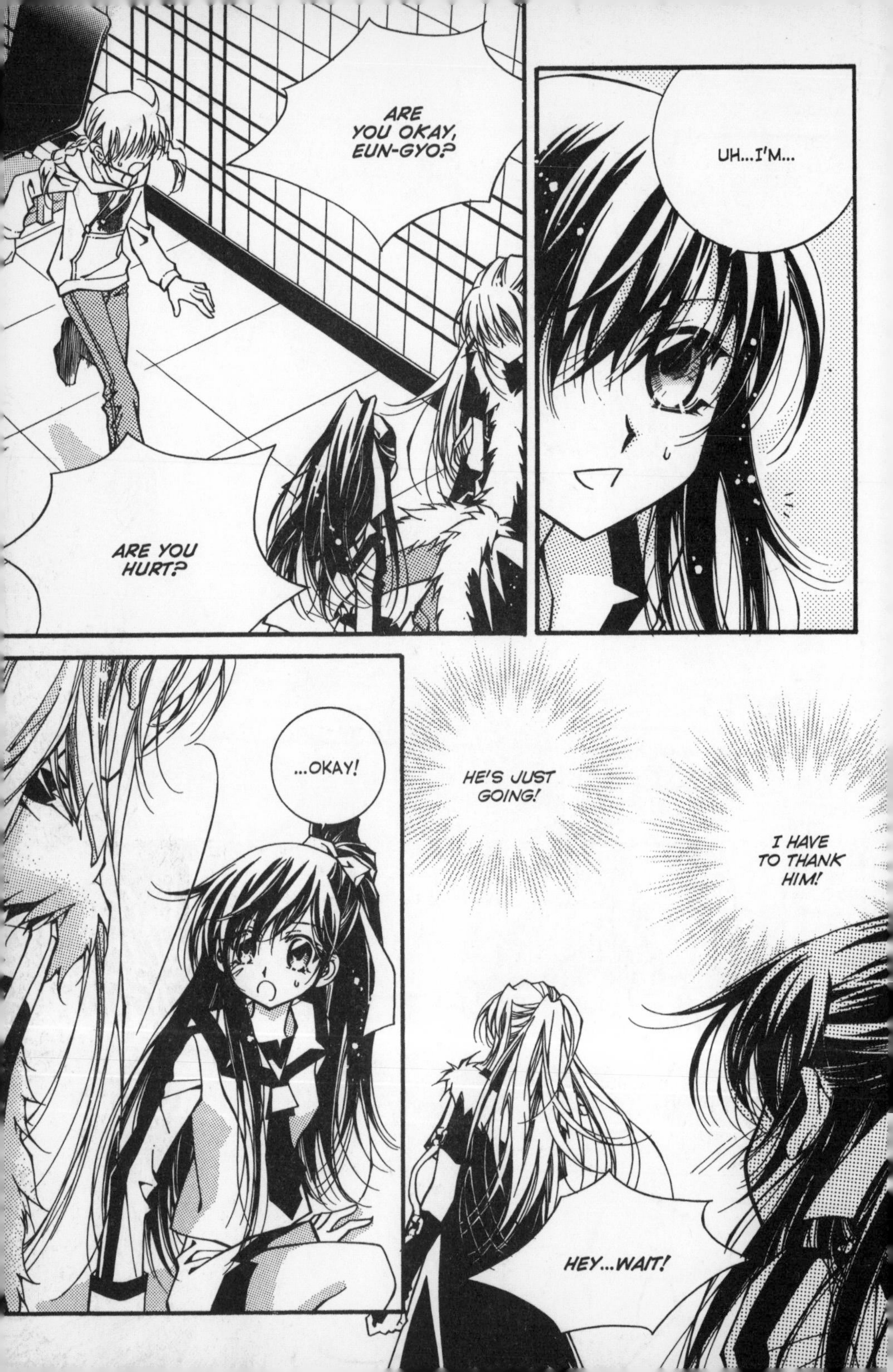
ARE YOU OKAY, EUN-GYO?
ARE YOU HURT?
UH...I'M...
...OKAY!
HE'S JUST GOING!
I HAVE TO THANK HIM!
HEY...WAIT!

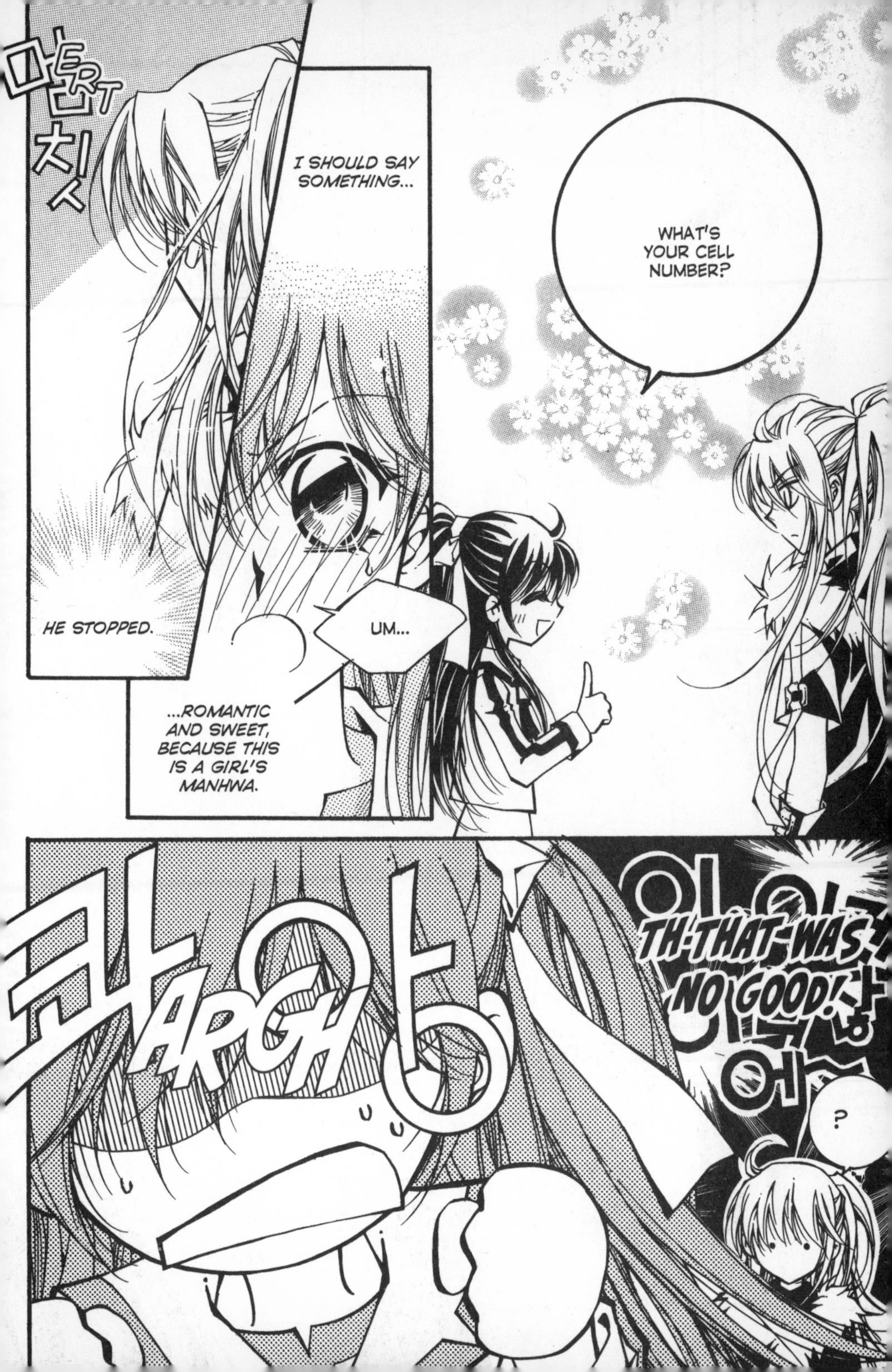
멈칫
ERT
HE STOPPED.
I SHOULD SAY SOMETHING...
UM...
...ROMANTIC AND SWEET, BECAUSE THIS IS A GIRL'S MANHWA.
WHAT'S YOUR CELL NUMBER?
ARGH
TH-THAT WAS NO GOOD!
?

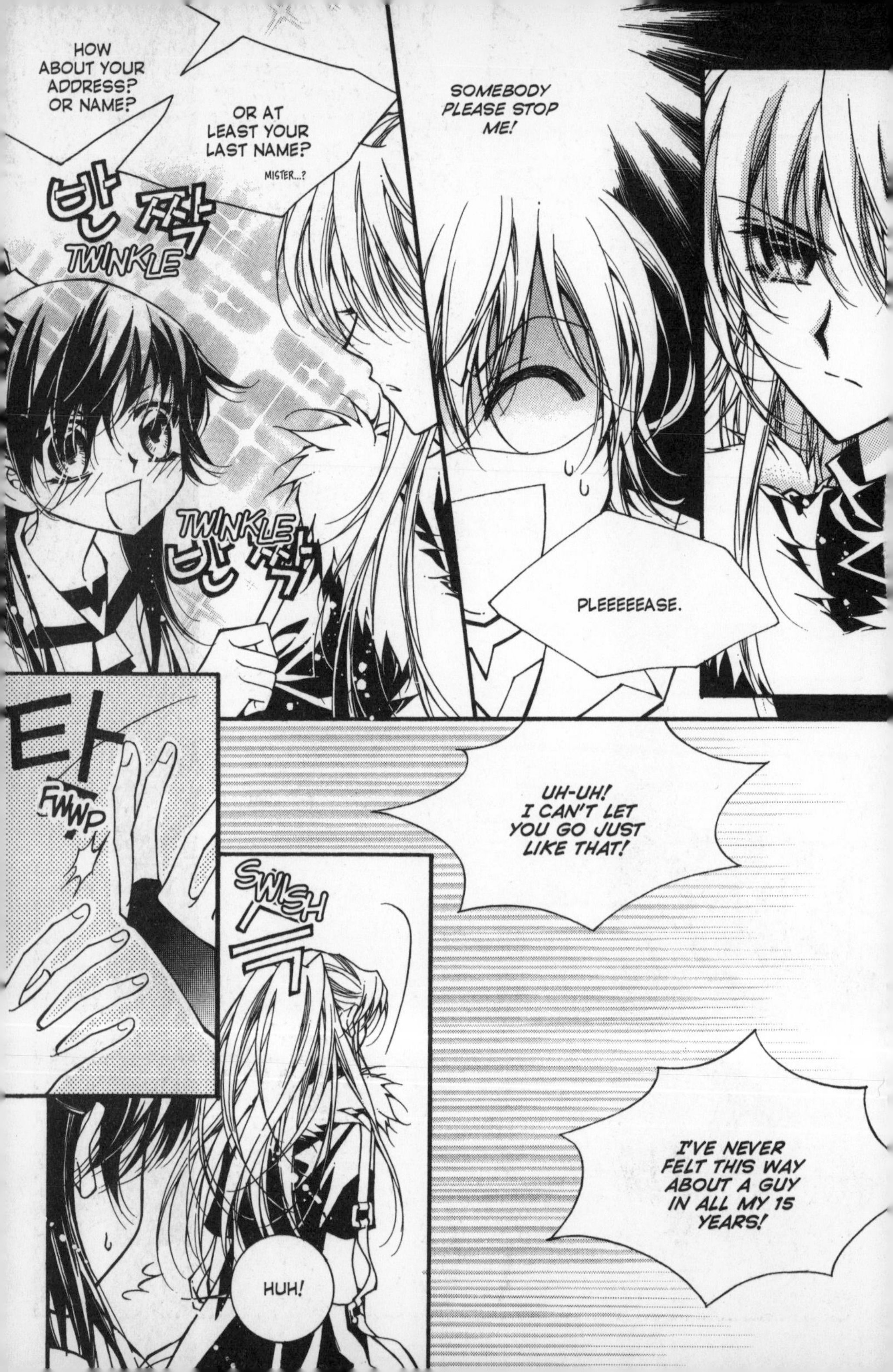
HOW ABOUT YOUR ADDRESS? OR NAME?
OR AT LEAST YOUR LAST NAME?
MISTER...?
반짝
TWINKLE
TWINKLE
반짝
SOMEBODY PLEASE STOP ME!
PLEEEEEASE.
타
FWWP
SWISH
HUH!
UH-UH! I CAN'T LET YOU GO JUST LIKE THAT!
I'VE NEVER FELT THIS WAY ABOUT A GUY IN ALL MY 15 YEARS!

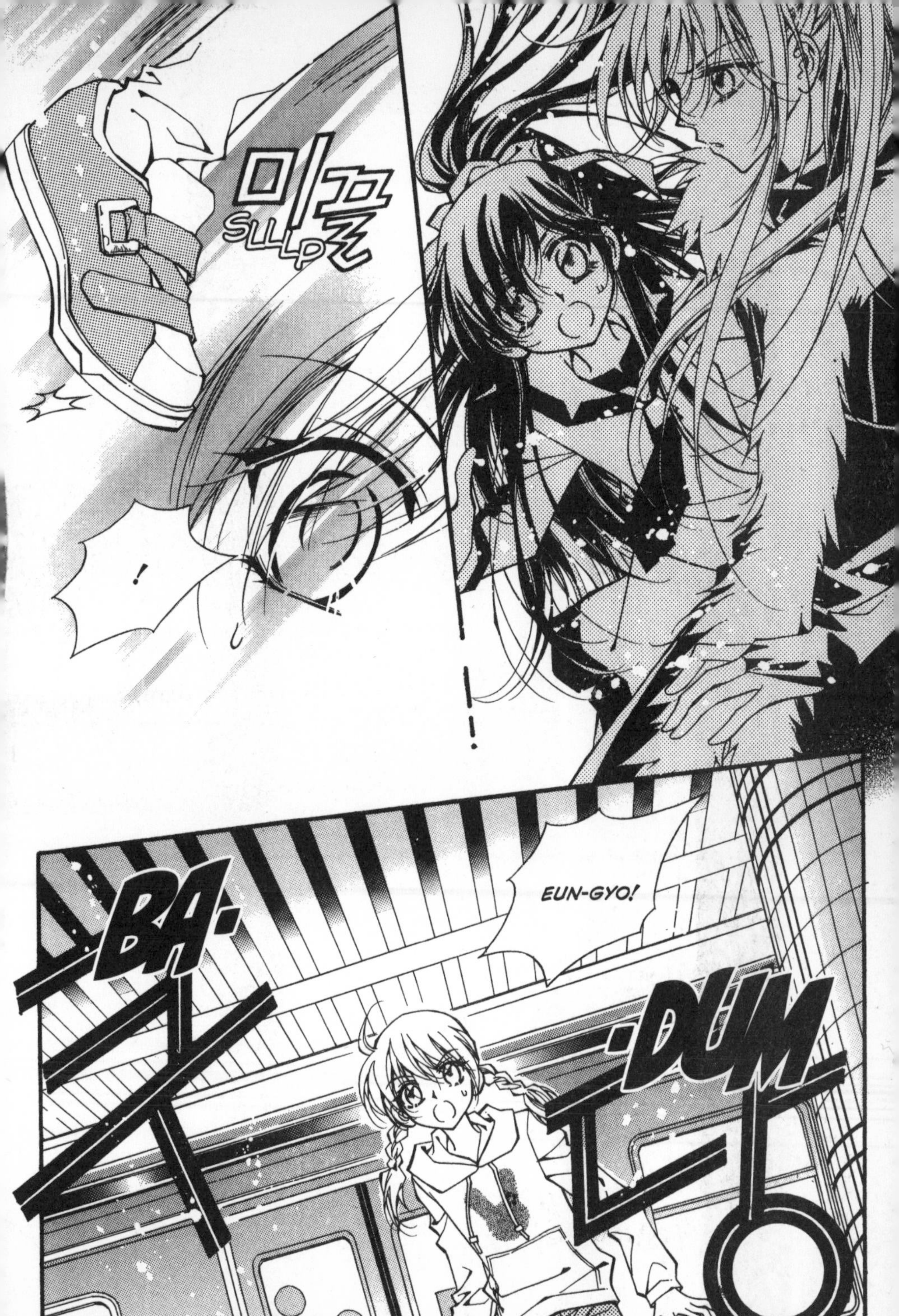
SLLLP
!
BA-
EUN-GYO!
-DUM

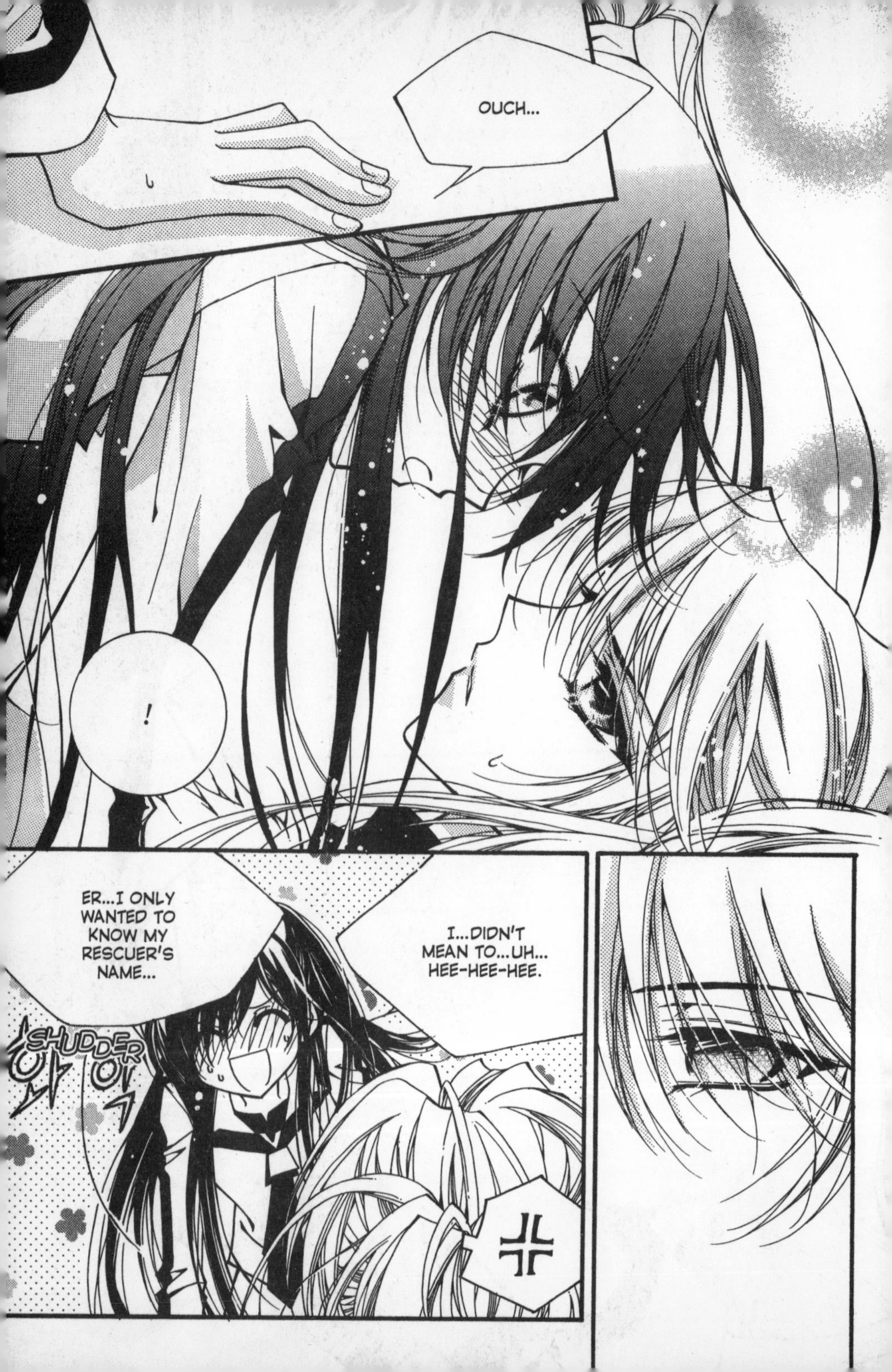
OUCH...
!
ER...I ONLY WANTED TO KNOW MY RESCUER'S NAME...
I...DIDN'T MEAN TO...UH... HEE-HEE-HEE.
SHUDDER

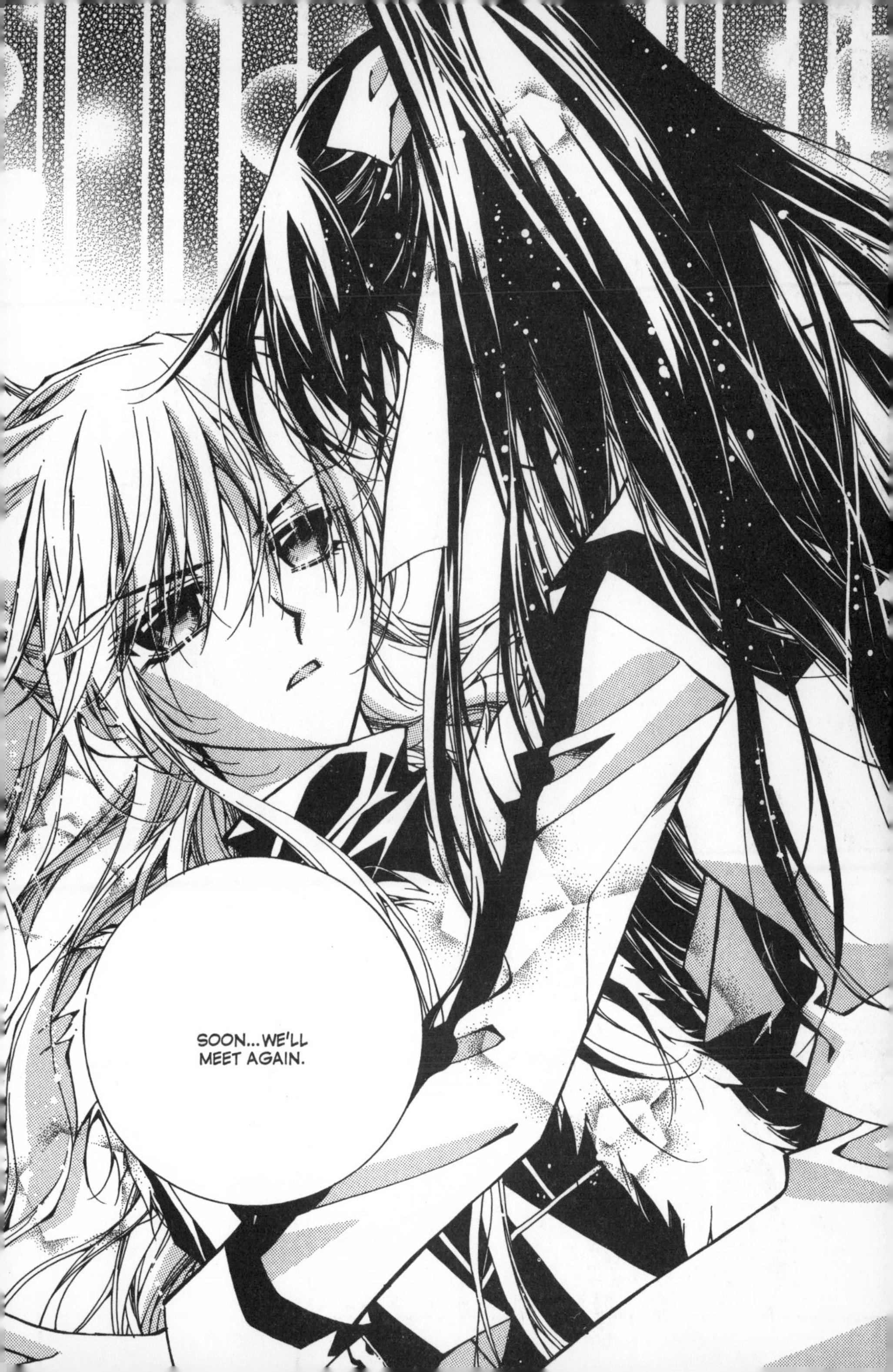
SOON...WE'LL MEET AGAIN.

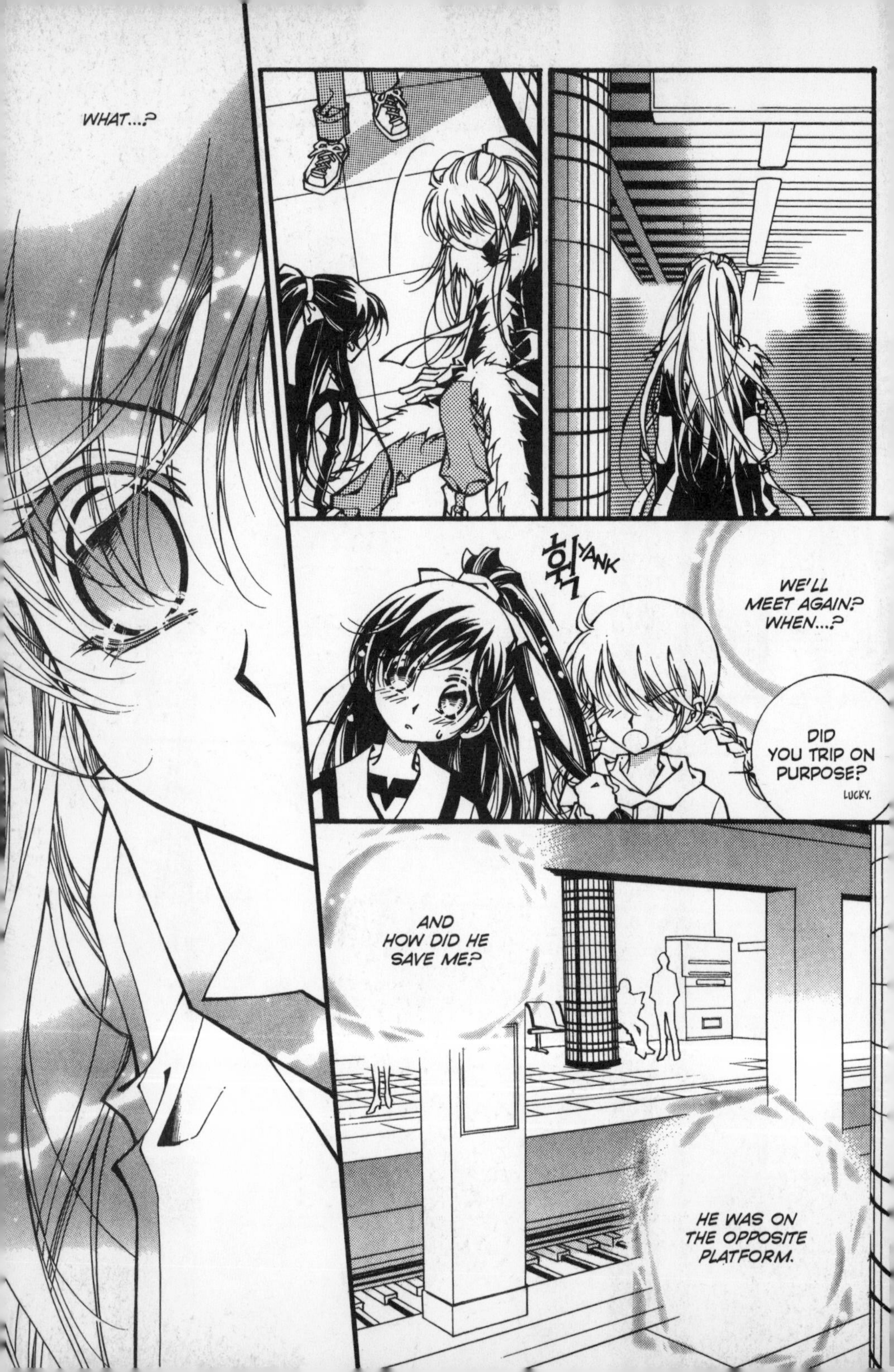
WHAT...?
휙 YANK
WE'LL MEET AGAIN? WHEN...?
DID YOU TRIP ON PURPOSE?
LUCKY.
AND HOW DID HE SAVE ME?
HE WAS ON THE OPPOSITE PLATFORM.

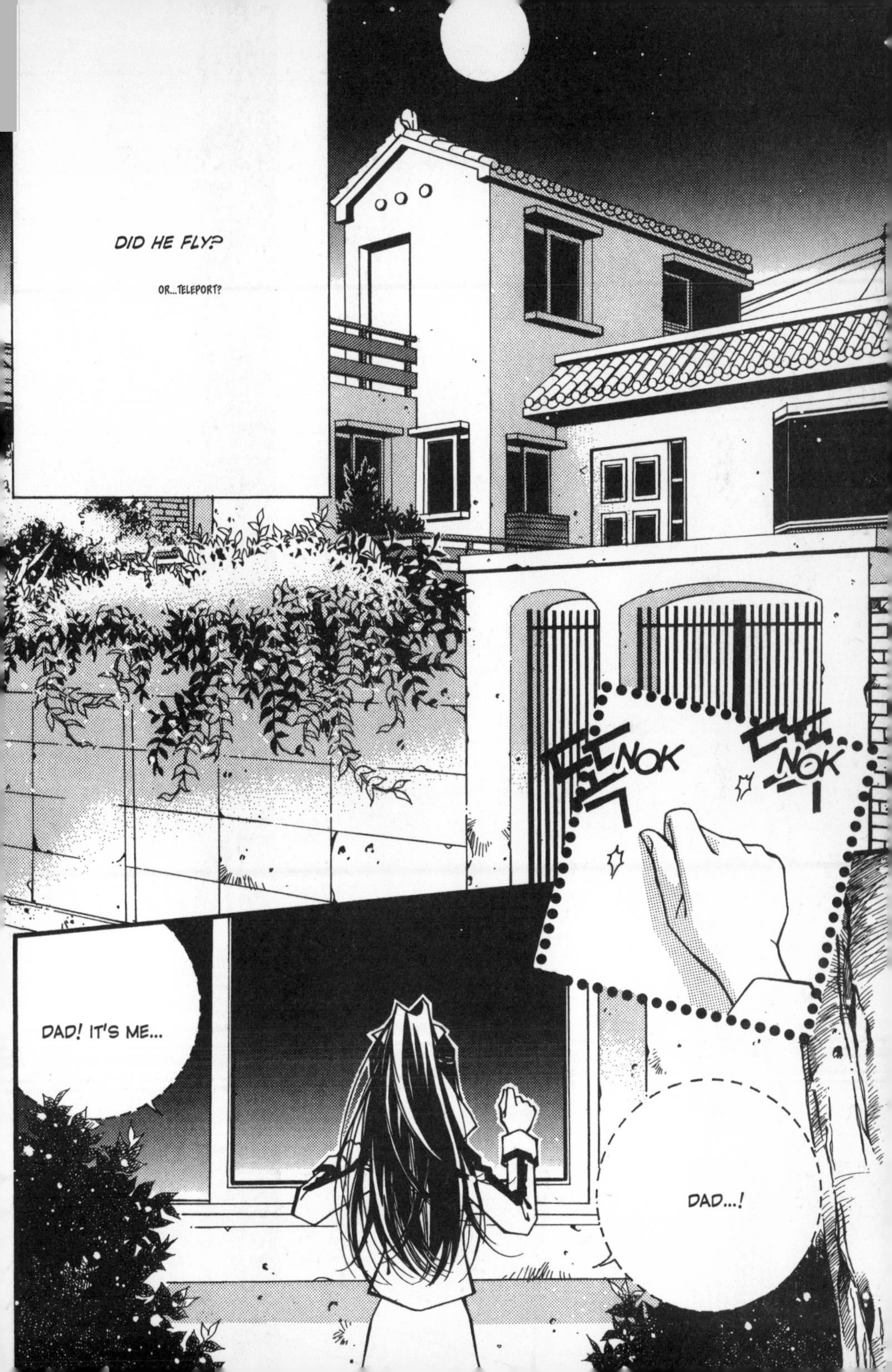
DID HE FLY?
OR...TELEPORT?
NOK
NOK
DAD! IT'S ME...
DAD...!

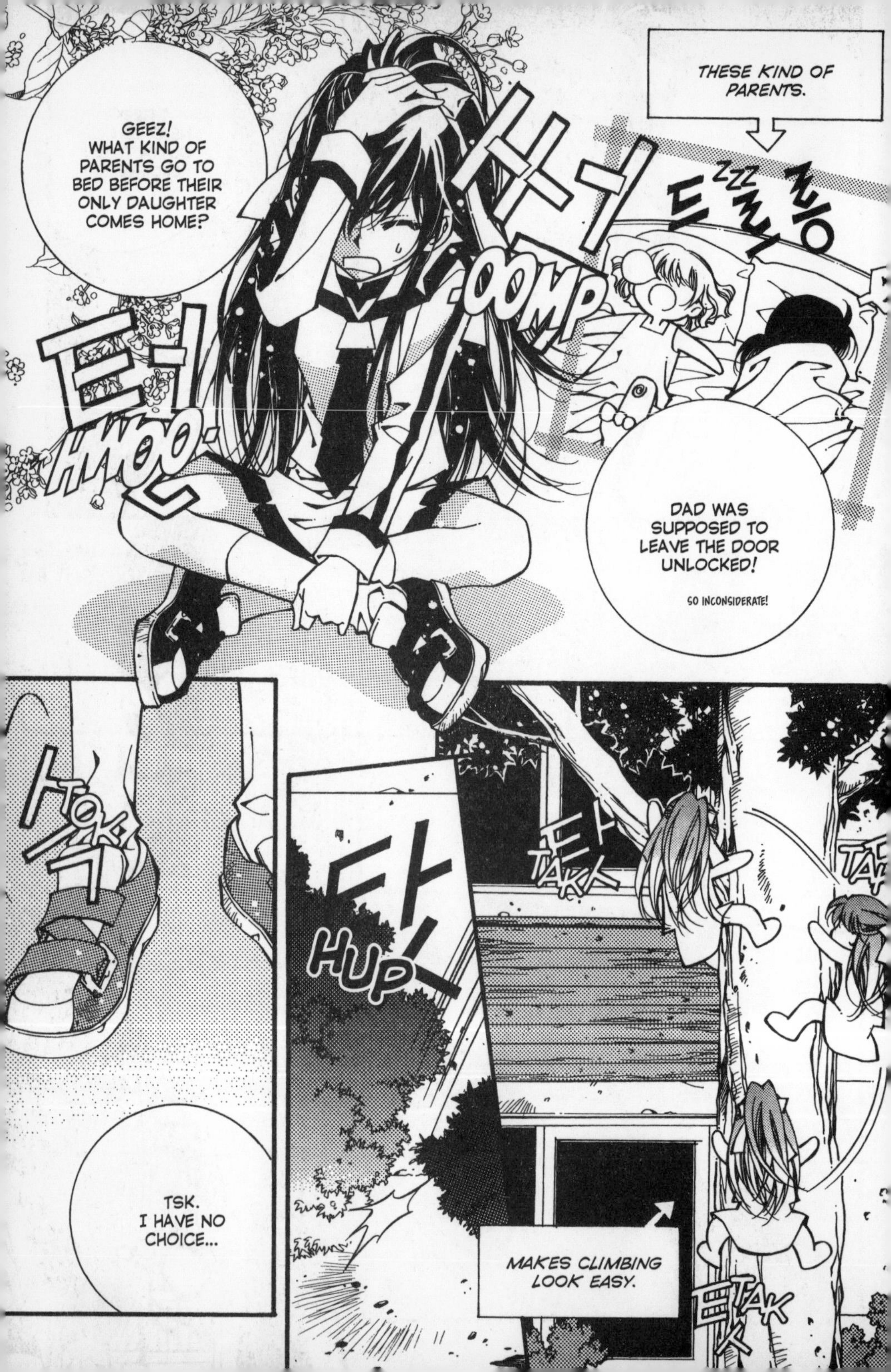
GEEZ! WHAT KIND OF PARENTS GO TO BED BEFORE THEIR ONLY DAUGHTER COMES HOME?
HWOO-
-OOMP
THESE KIND OF PARENTS.
ZZZ
DAD WAS SUPPOSED TO LEAVE THE DOOR UNLOCKED!
SO INCONSIDERATE!
TOK
TSK. I HAVE NO CHOICE...
HUP
TAKK
MAKES CLIMBING LOOK EASY.
TAK

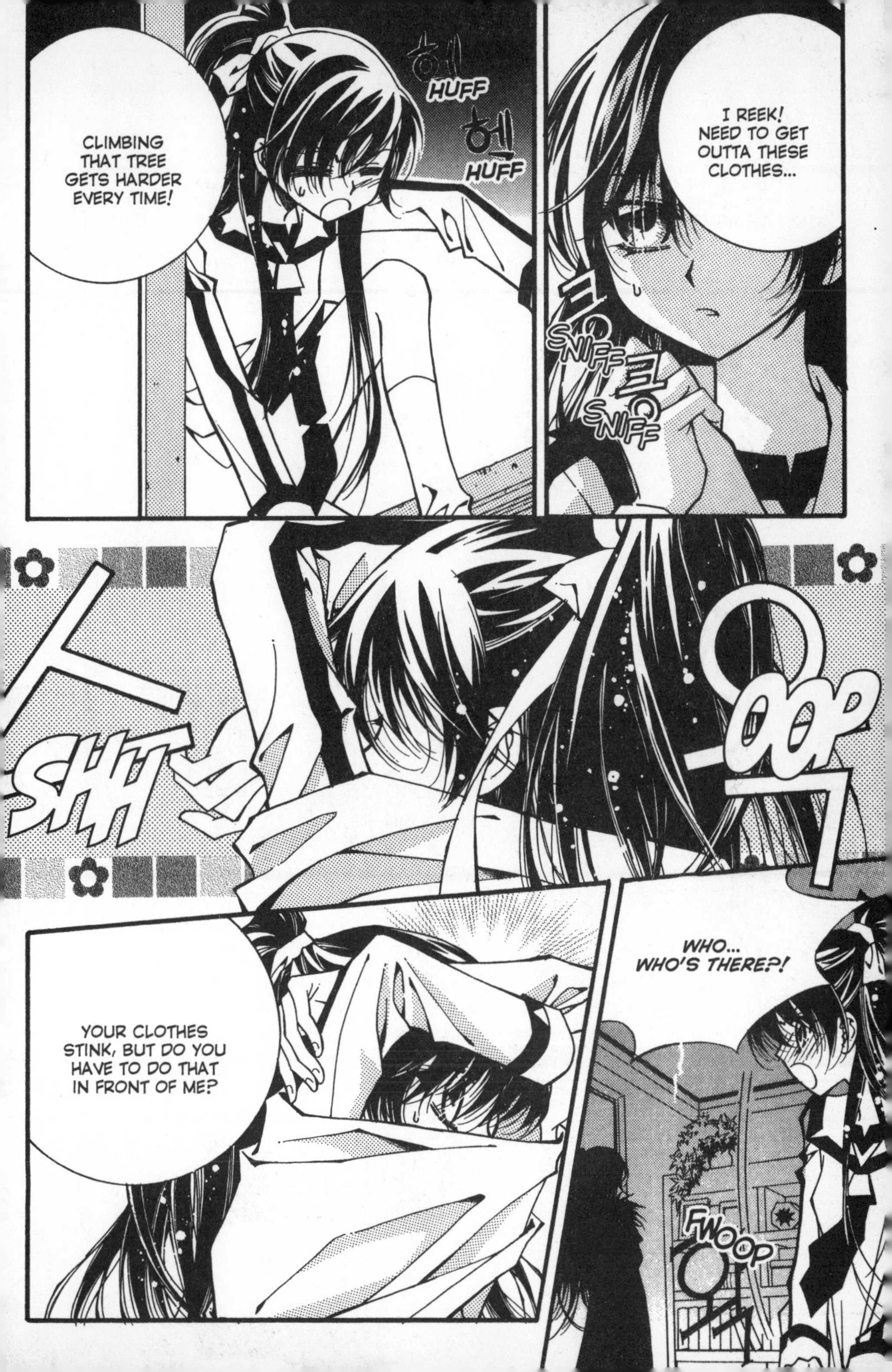
CLIMBING THAT TREE GETS HARDER EVERY TIME!
HUFF
HUFF
I REEK! NEED TO GET OUTTA THESE CLOTHES...
SNIFF
SNIFF
SHH
OOP
YOUR CLOTHES STINK, BUT DO YOU HAVE TO DO THAT IN FRONT OF ME?
WHO... WHO'S THERE?!
FWOOP

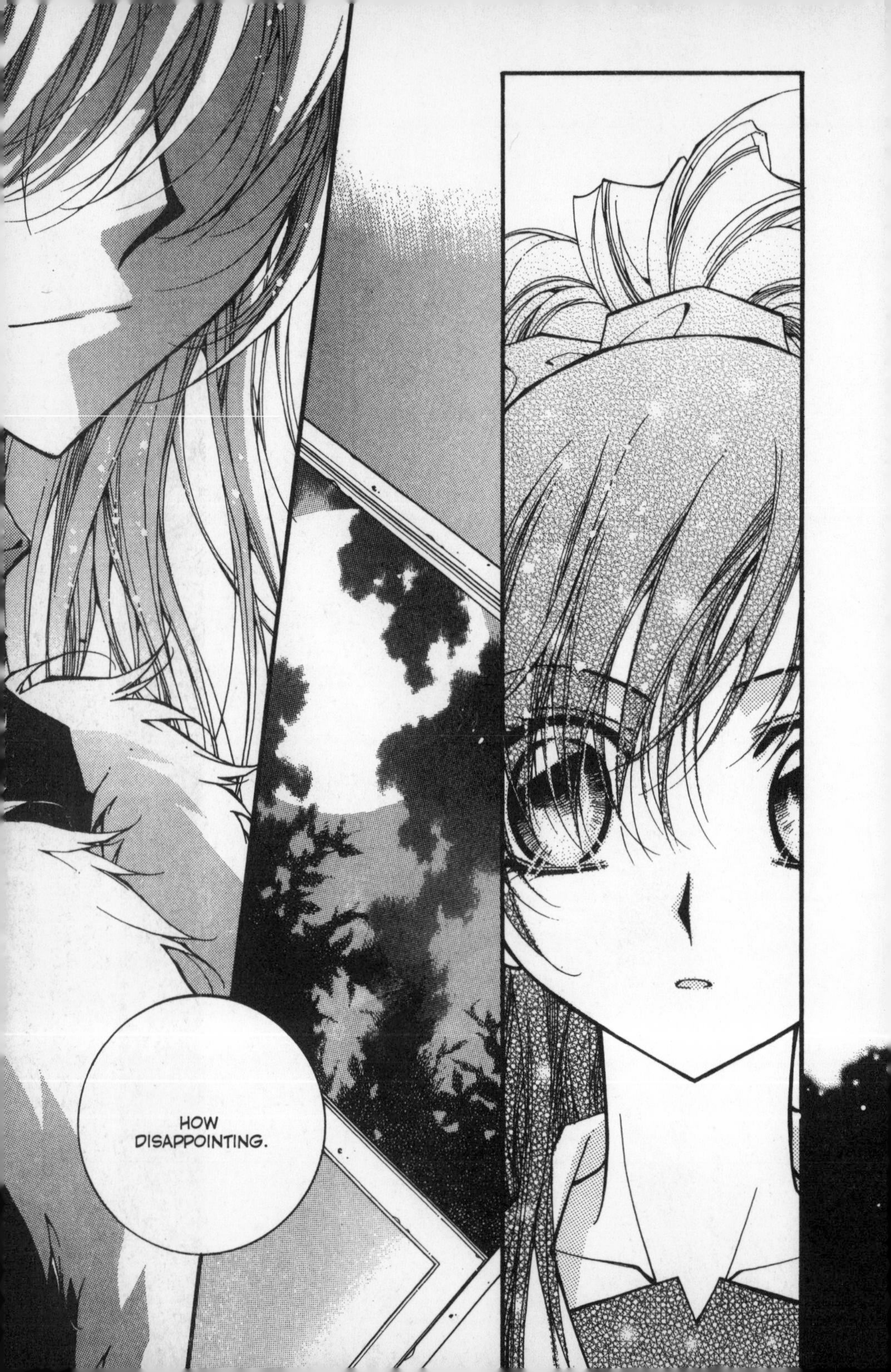
HOW DISAPPOINTING.

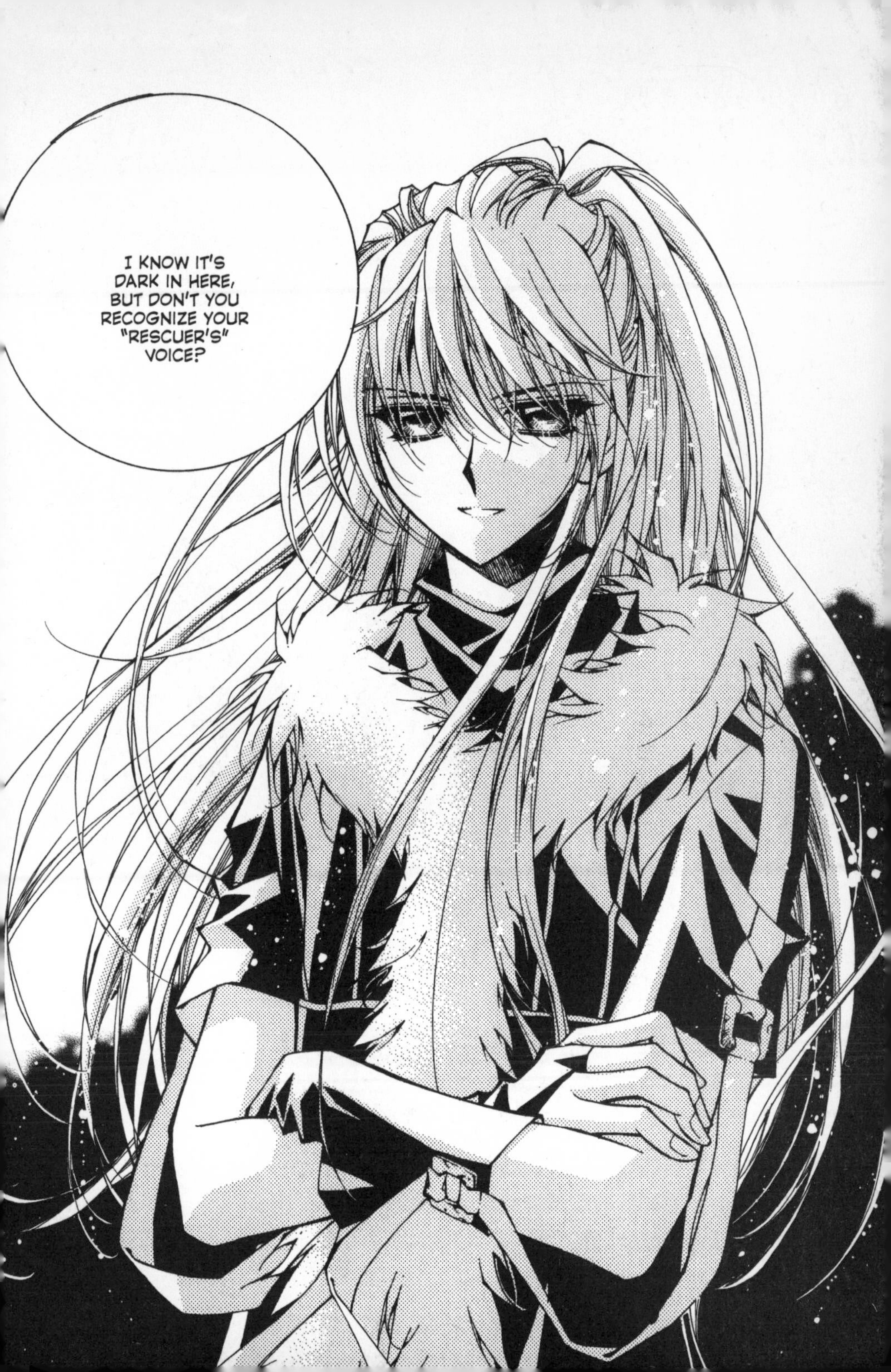
I KNOW IT'S DARK IN HERE, BUT DON'T YOU RECOGNIZE YOUR "RESCUER'S" VOICE?

MINI INTERVIEW

NAME: NO-AH JOO
AGE: 16
BLOOD TYPE: A
HEIGHT: 174 CM
WEIGHT: 61 KG

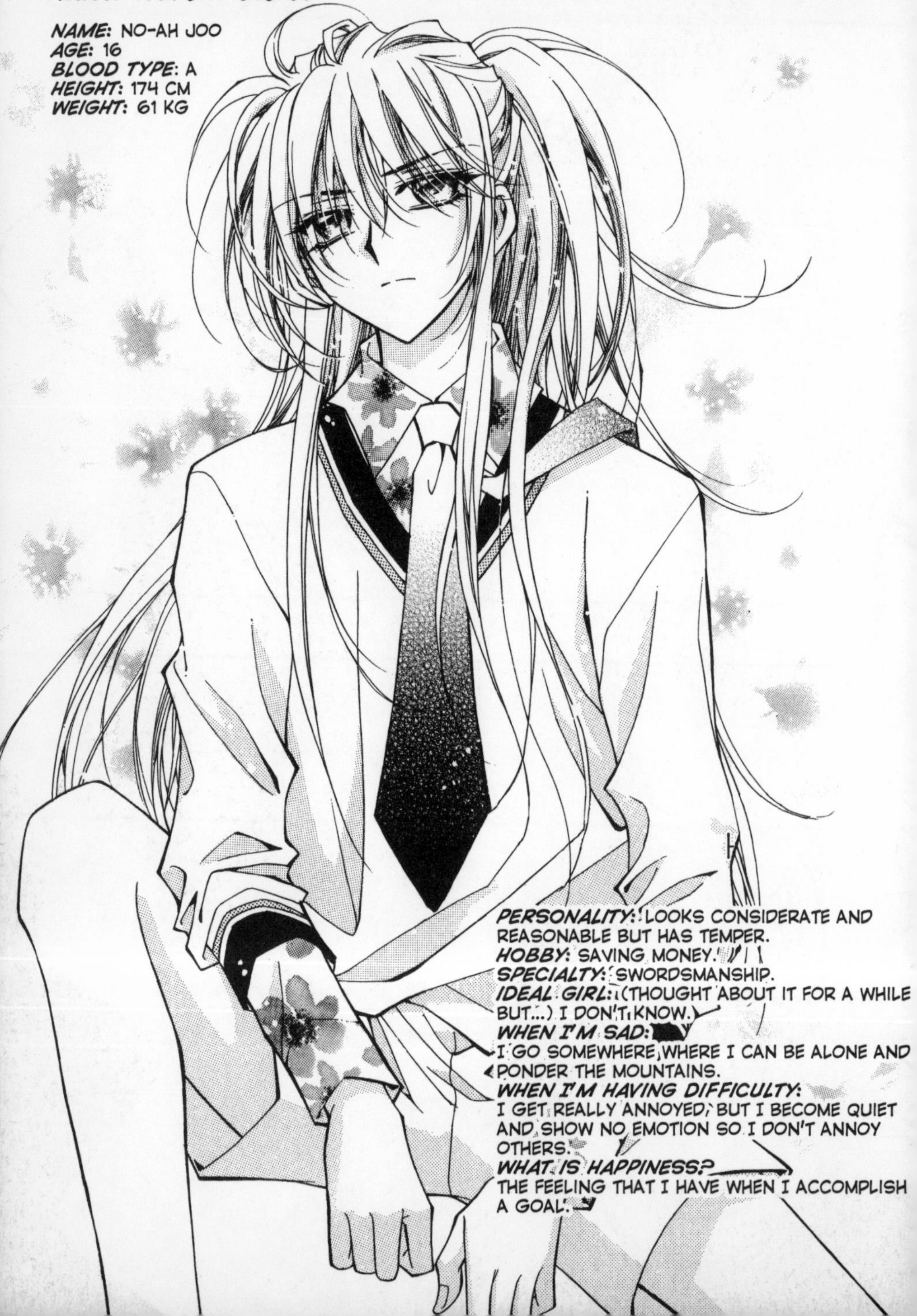

PERSONALITY: LOOKS CONSIDERATE AND REASONABLE BUT HAS TEMPER.
HOBBY: SAVING MONEY.
SPECIALTY: SWORDSMANSHIP.
IDEAL GIRL: (THOUGHT ABOUT IT FOR A WHILE BUT...) I DON'T KNOW.
WHEN I'M SAD:
I GO SOMEWHERE WHERE I CAN BE ALONE AND PONDER THE MOUNTAINS.
WHEN I'M HAVING DIFFICULTY:
I GET REALLY ANNOYED, BUT I BECOME QUIET AND SHOW NO EMOTION SO I DON'T ANNOY OTHERS.
WHAT IS HAPPINESS?
THE FEELING THAT I HAVE WHEN I ACCOMPLISH A GOAL.

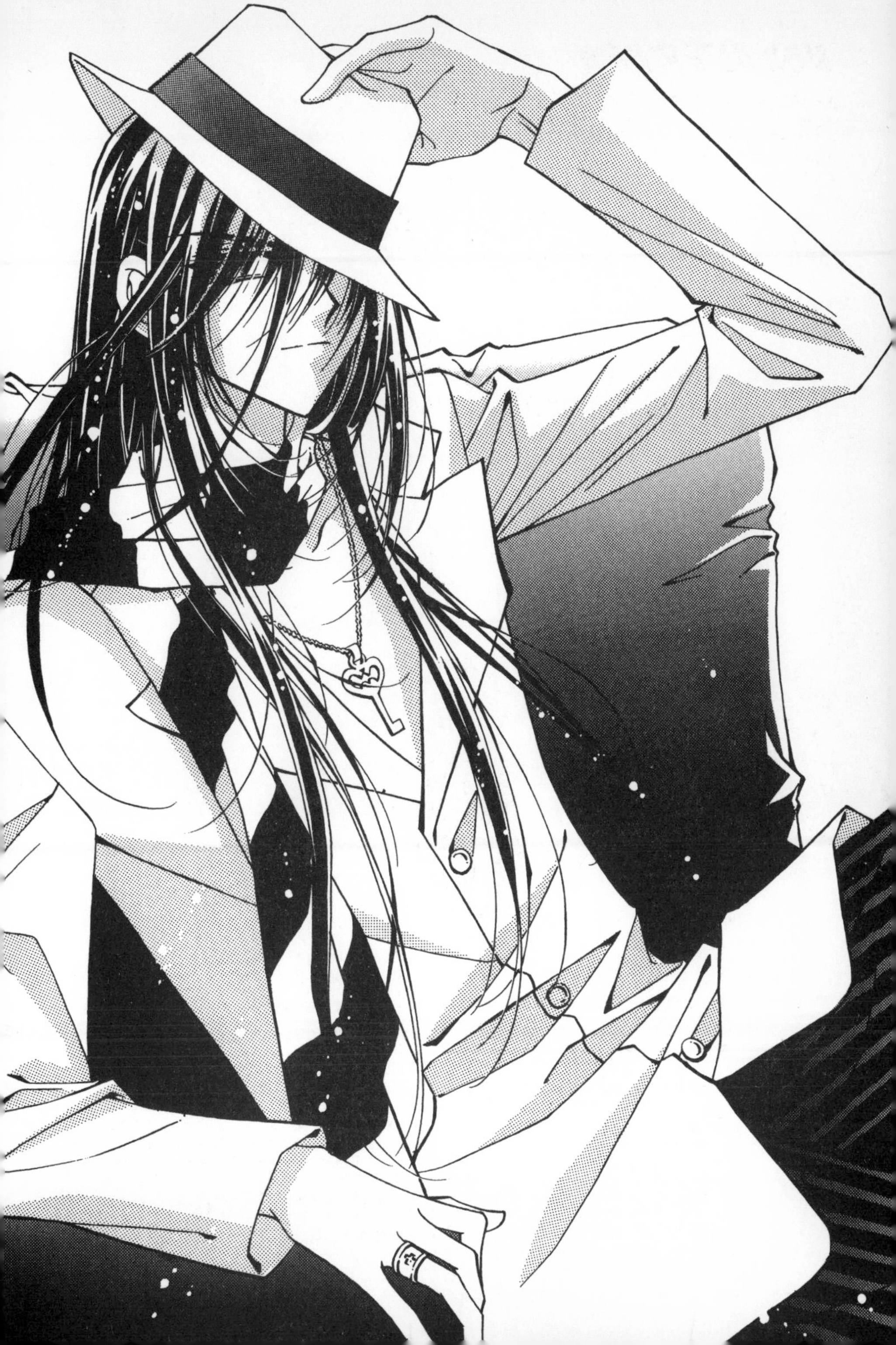

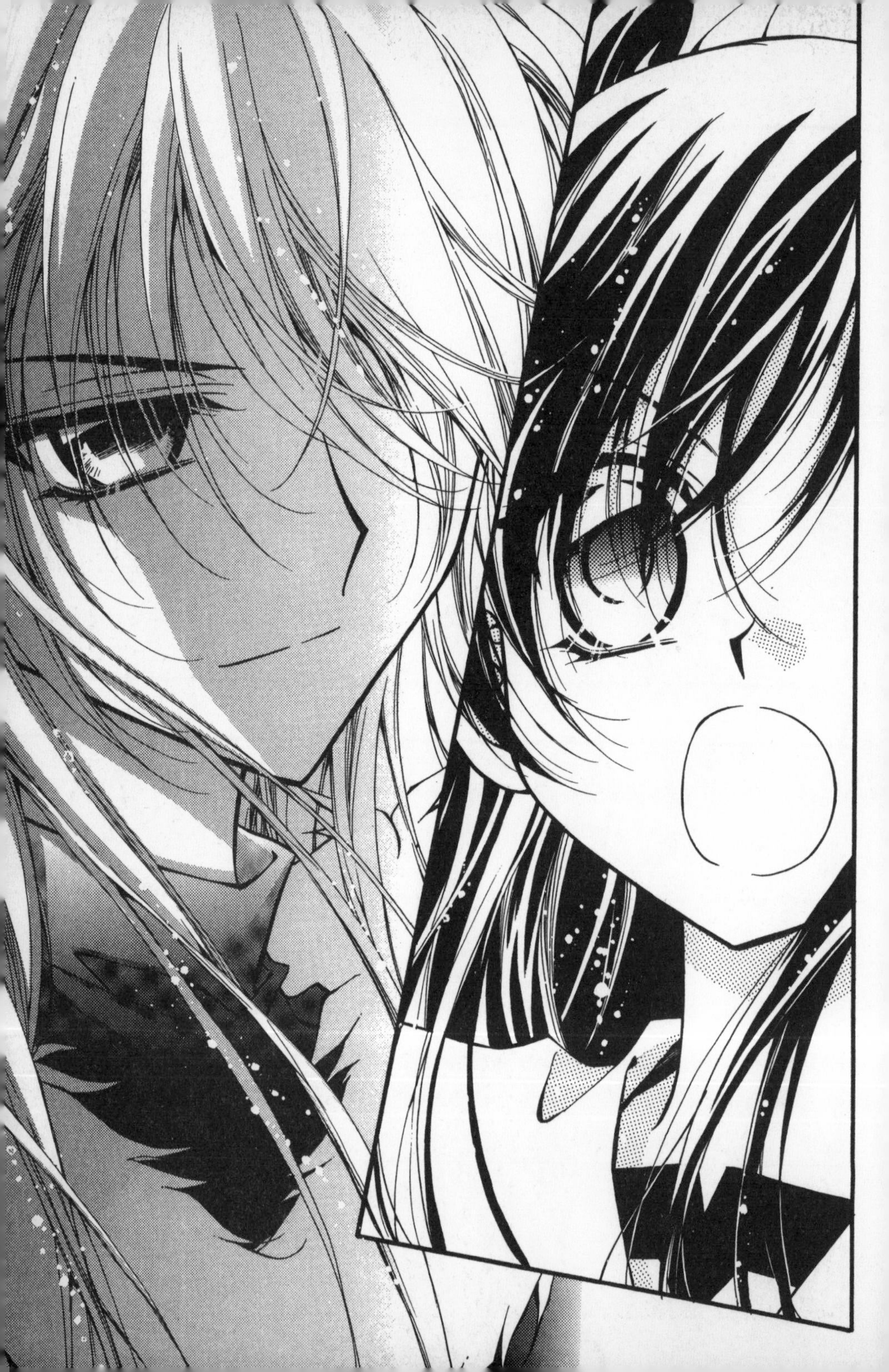

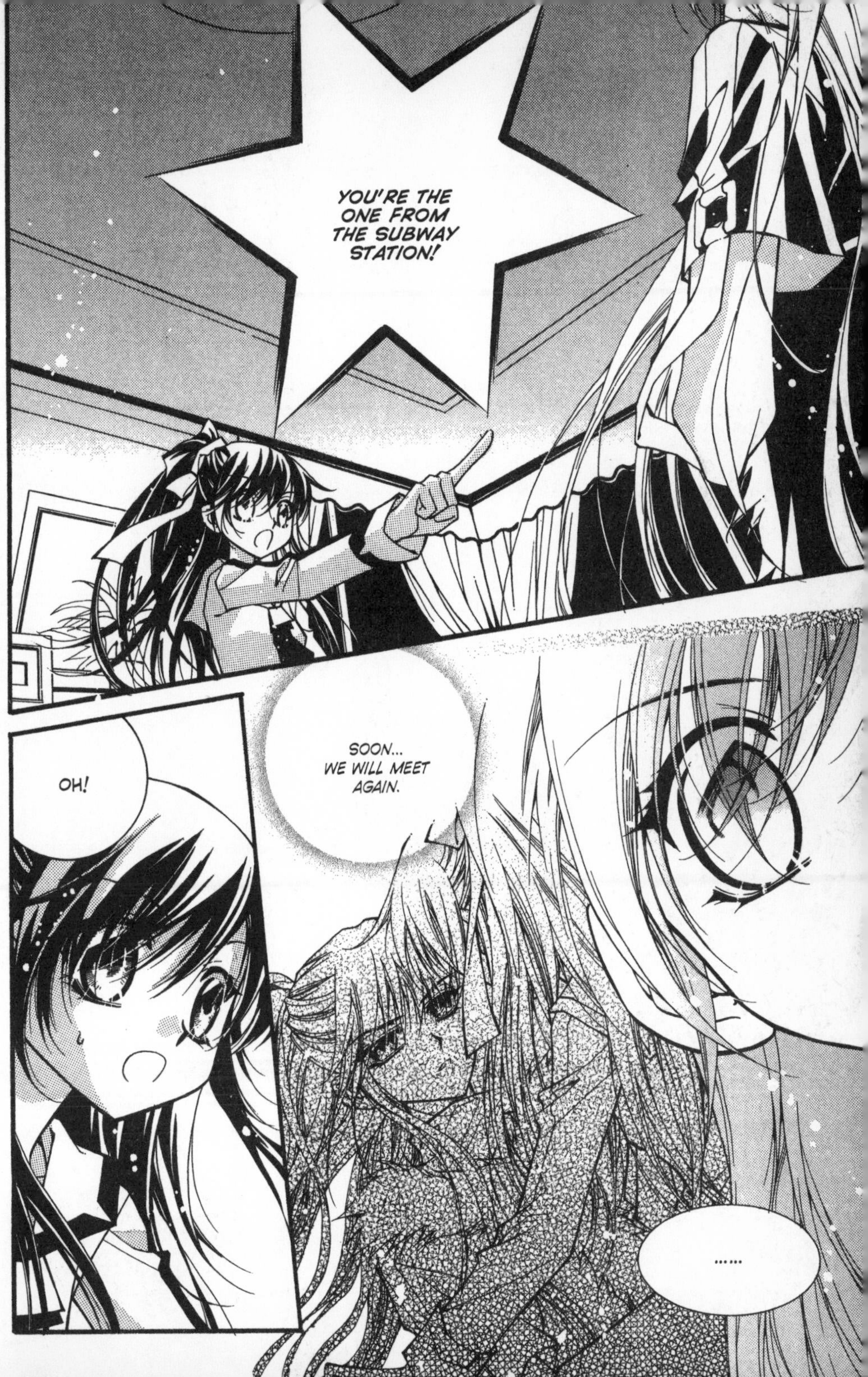
YOU'RE THE ONE FROM THE SUBWAY STATION!
OH!
SOON... WE WILL MEET AGAIN.
......

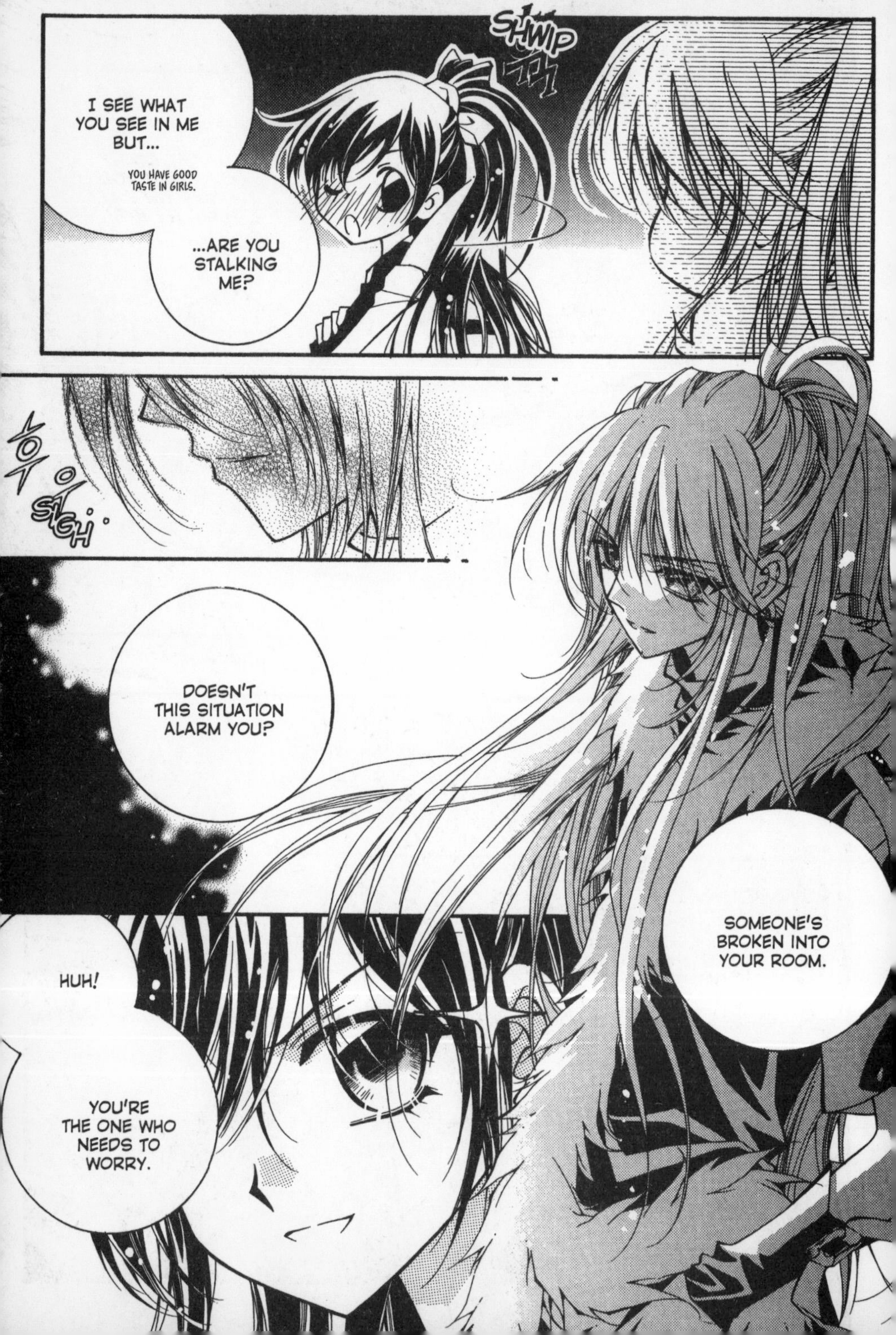

I SEE WHAT YOU SEE IN ME BUT...
YOU HAVE GOOD TASTE IN GIRLS.
...ARE YOU STALKING ME?
SHWIP
SIGH
DOESN'T THIS SITUATION ALARM YOU?
HUH!
YOU'RE THE ONE WHO NEEDS TO WORRY.
SOMEONE'S BROKEN INTO YOUR ROOM.

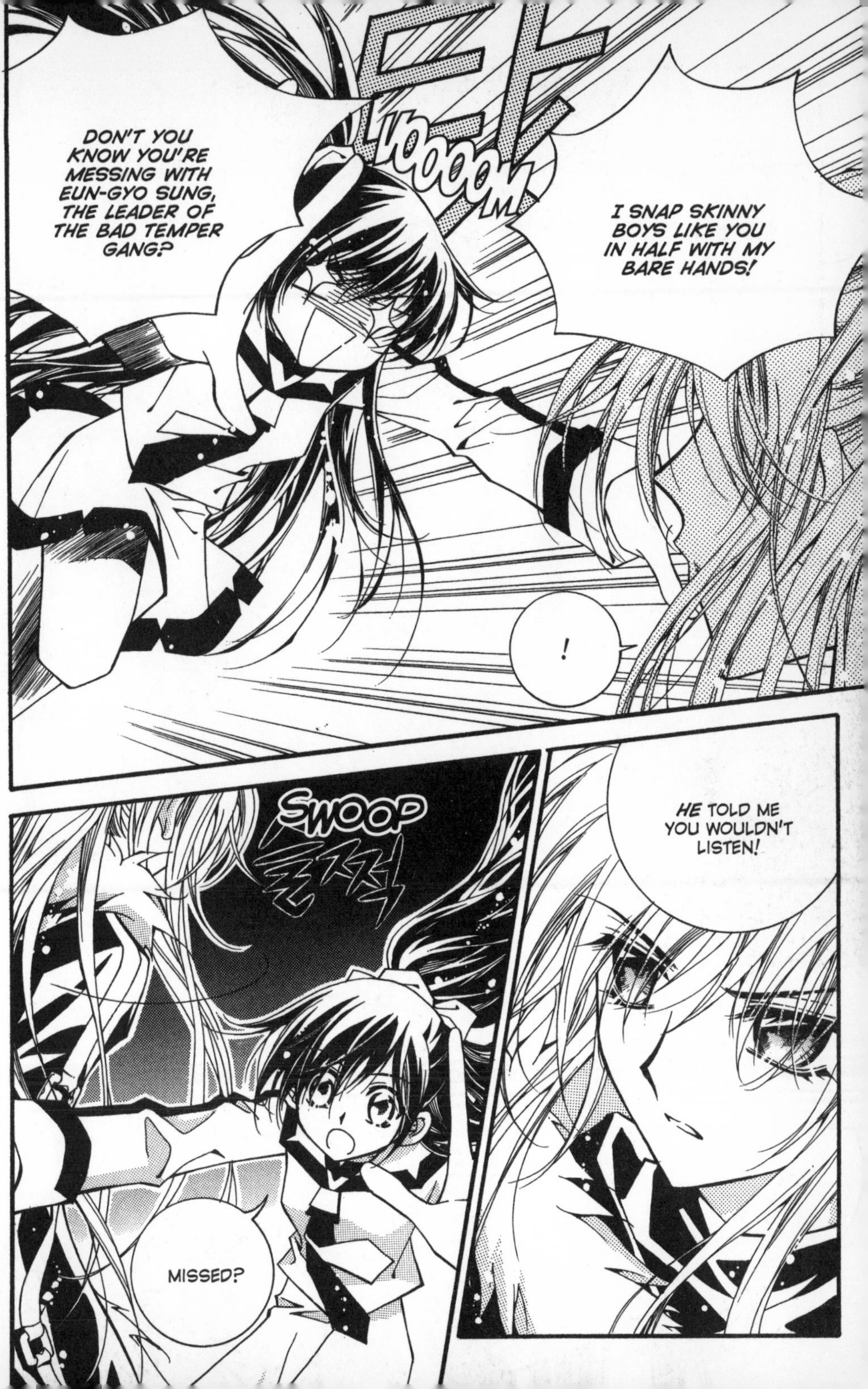
VOOOOM
DON'T YOU KNOW YOU'RE MESSING WITH EUN-GYO SUNG, THE LEADER OF THE BAD TEMPER GANG?
I SNAP SKINNY BOYS LIKE YOU IN HALF WITH MY BARE HANDS!
!
SWOOP
MISSED?
HE TOLD ME YOU WOULDN'T LISTEN!

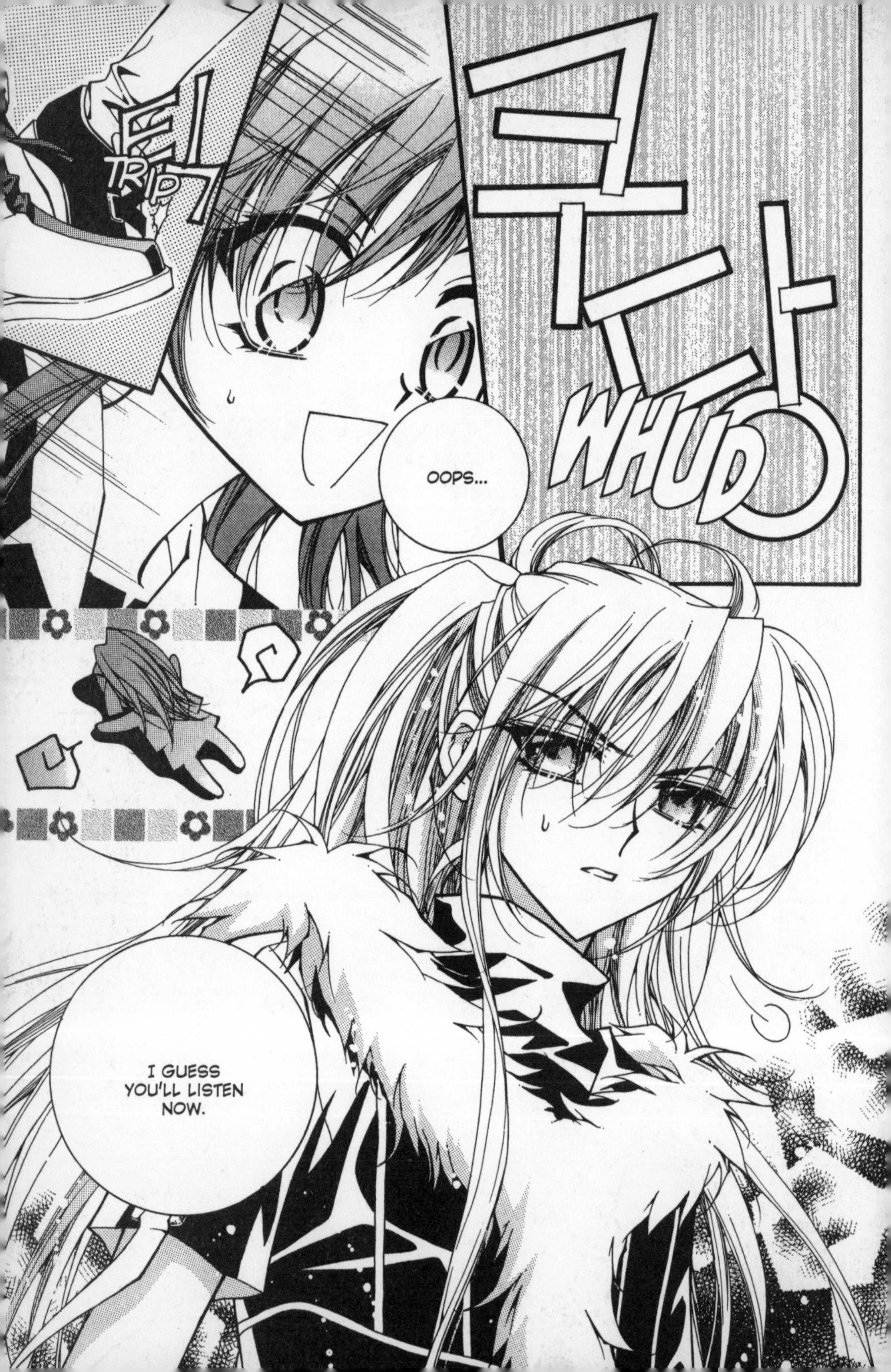

TRIP
OOPS...
WHUD
I GUESS YOU'LL LISTEN NOW.

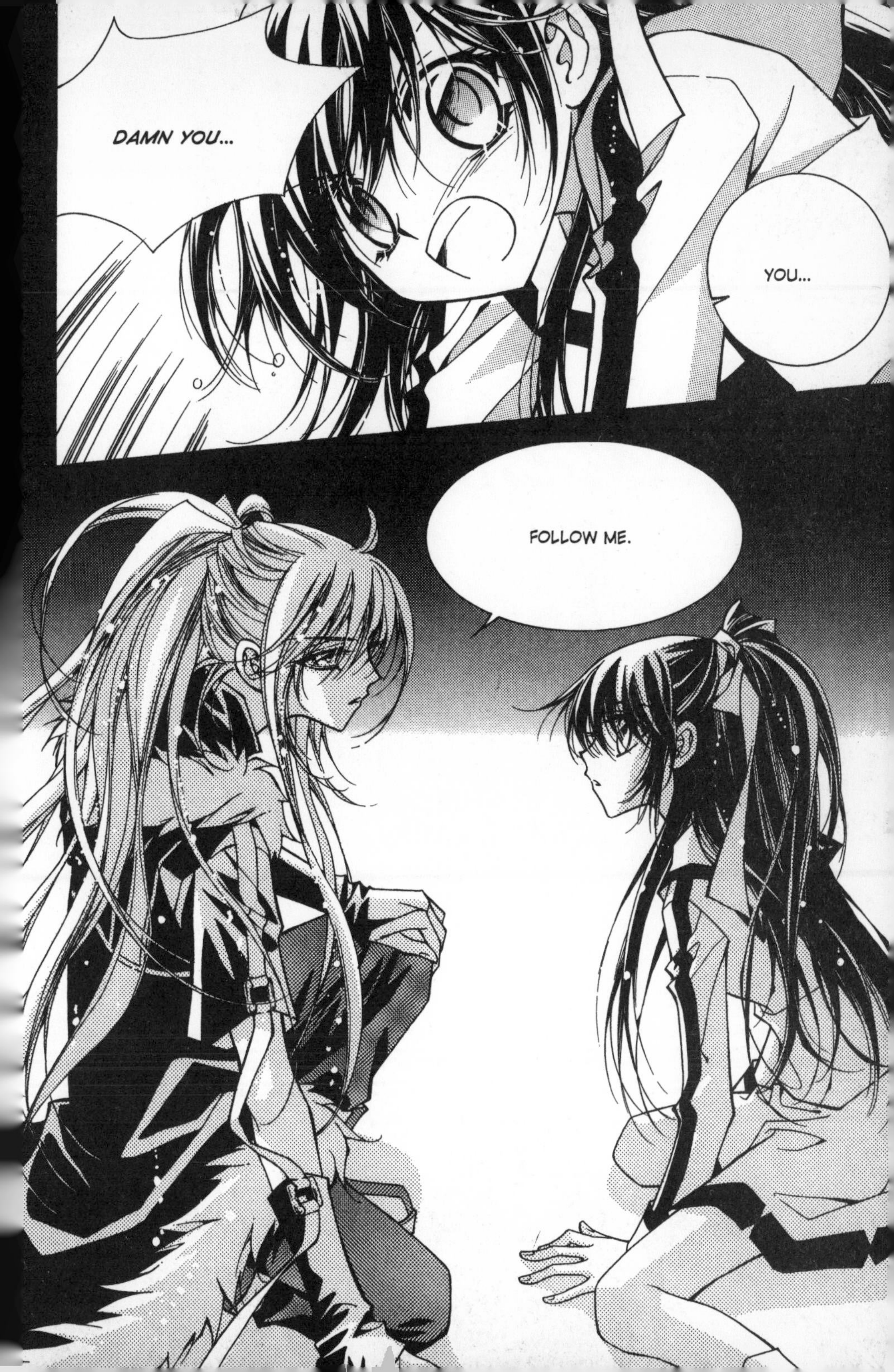
DAMN YOU...
YOU...
FOLLOW ME.

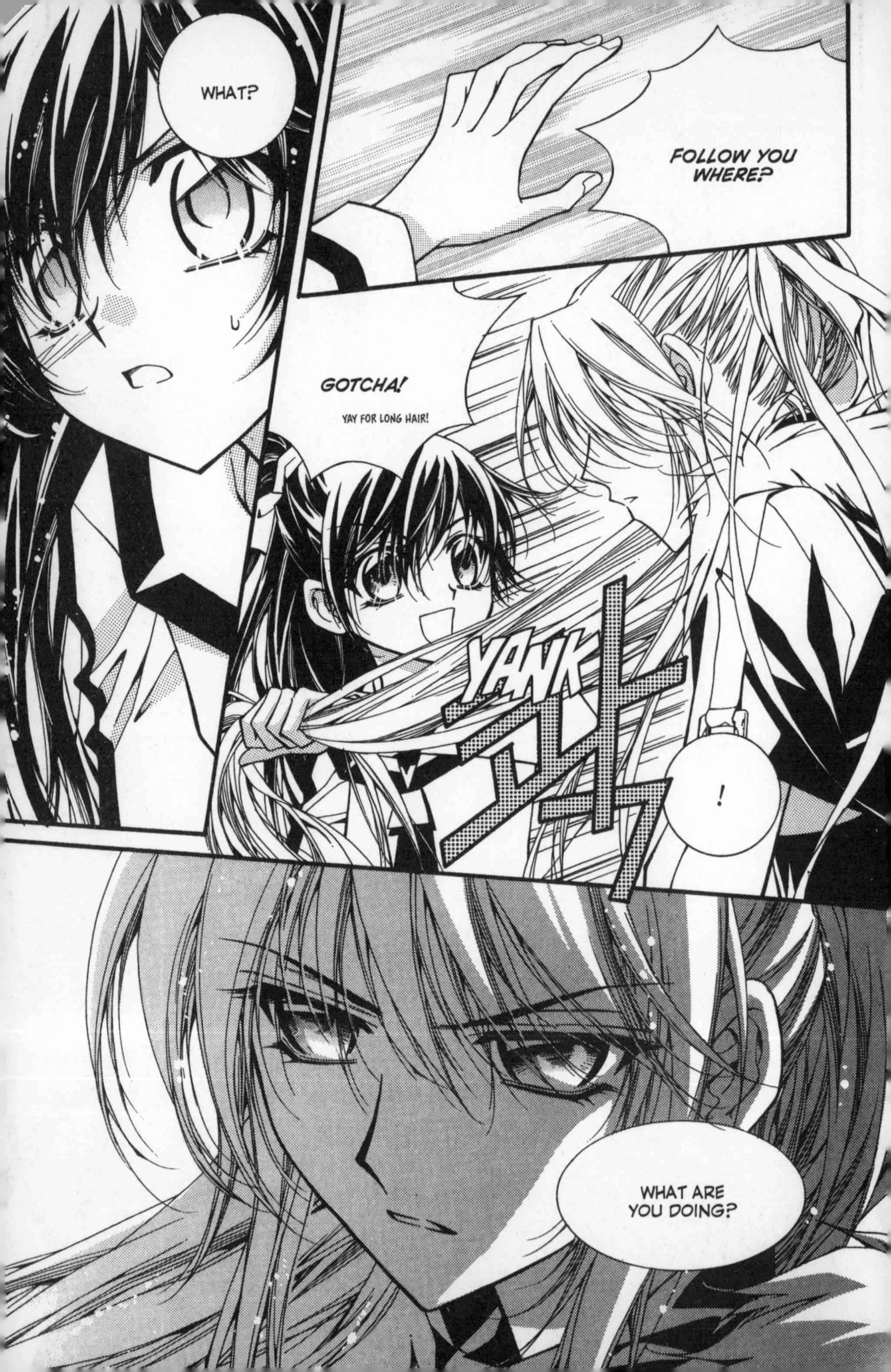
WHAT?
FOLLOW YOU WHERE?
GOTCHA!
YAY FOR LONG HAIR!
YANK
!
WHAT ARE YOU DOING?

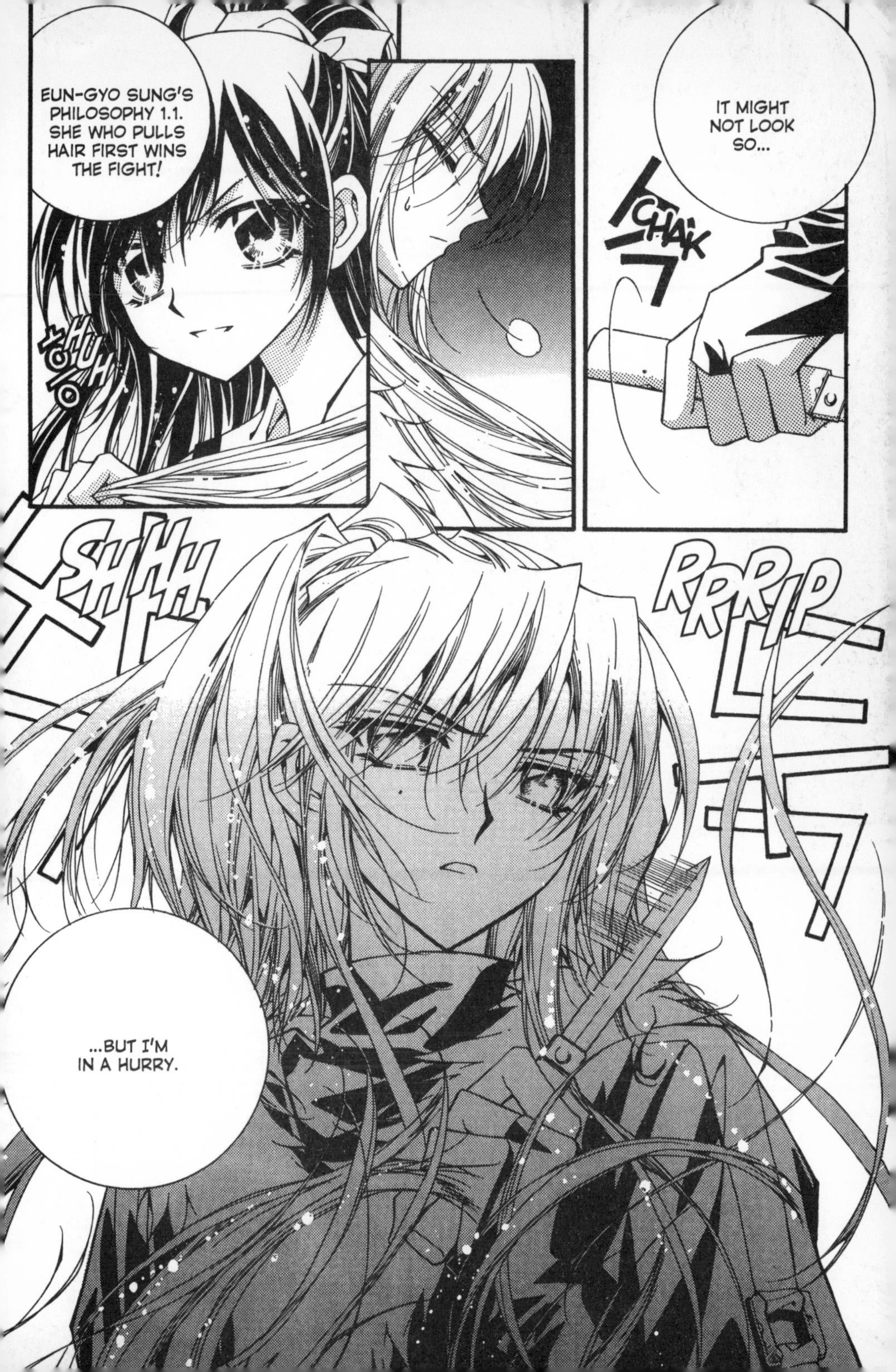
EUN-GYO SUNG'S PHILOSOPHY 1.1. SHE WHO PULLS HAIR FIRST WINS THE FIGHT!
HUH
IT MIGHT NOT LOOK SO...
CHAK
SHHH
RRRIP
...BUT I'M IN A HURRY.

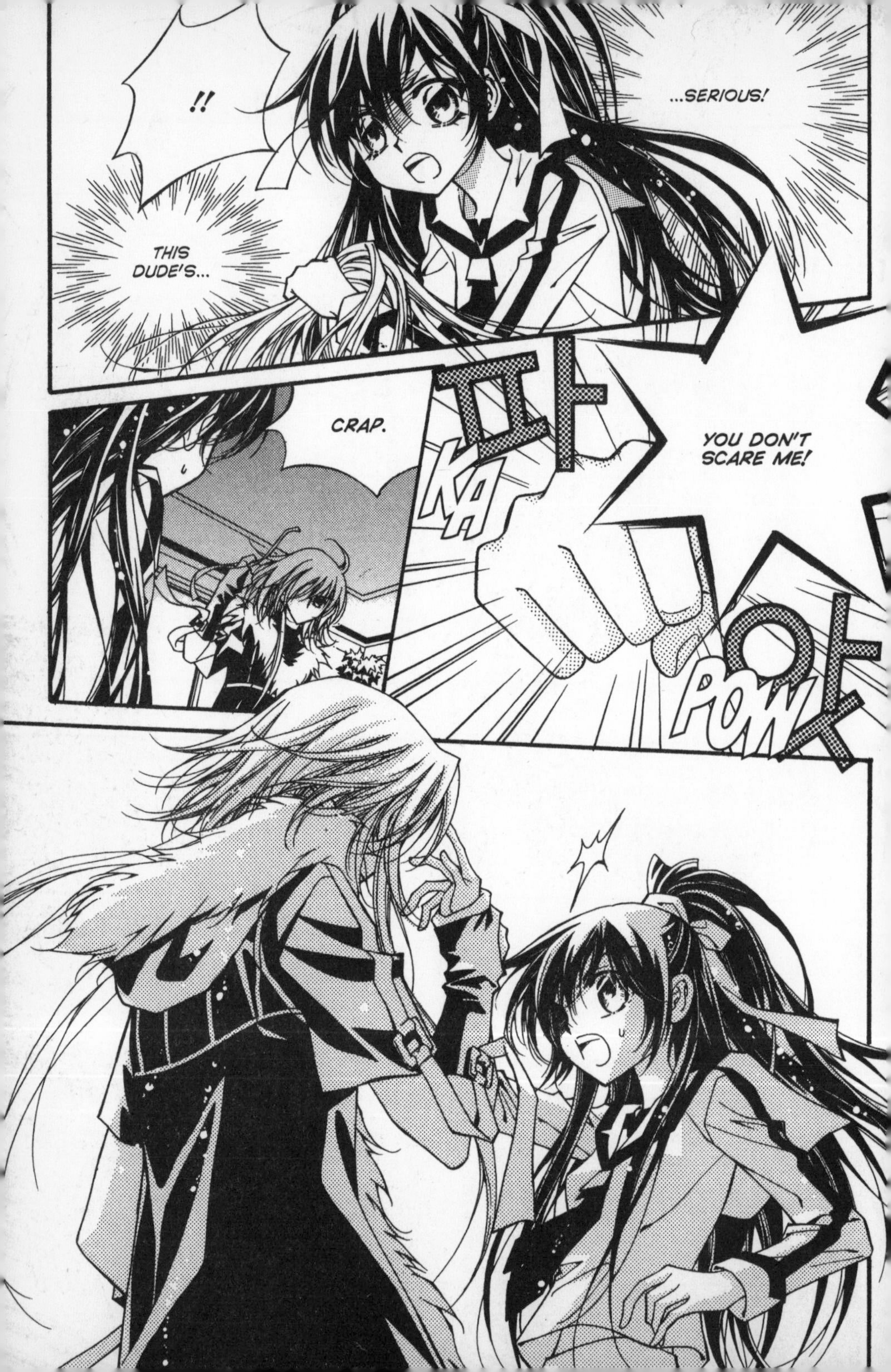
!!
THIS DUDE'S...
...SERIOUS!
CRAP.
KA
YOU DON'T SCARE ME!
POW

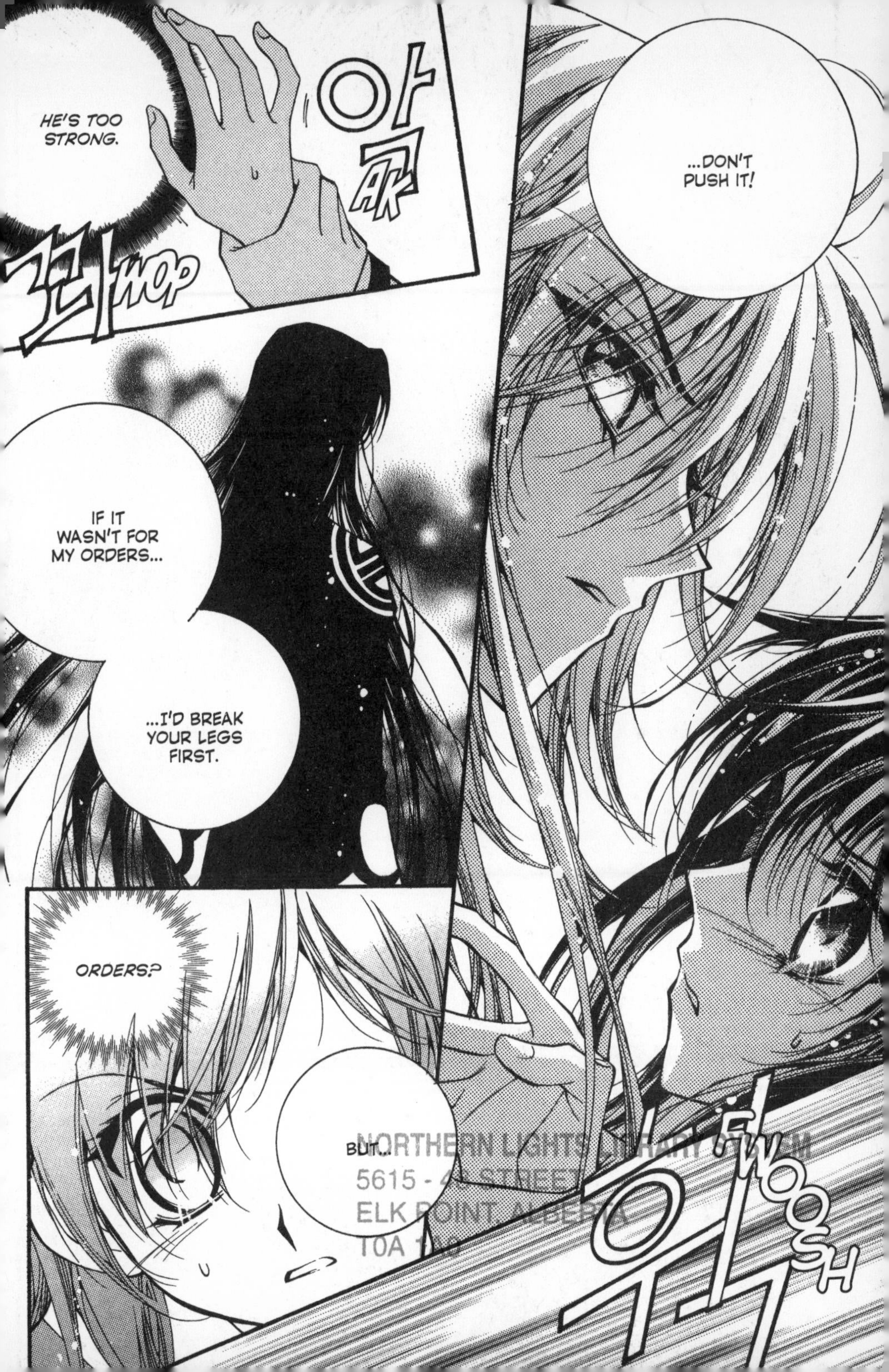
HE'S TOO STRONG.
AK
WOP
IF IT WASN'T FOR MY ORDERS...
...I'D BREAK YOUR LEGS FIRST.
...DON'T PUSH IT!
ORDERS?
BUT...
FWOOSH

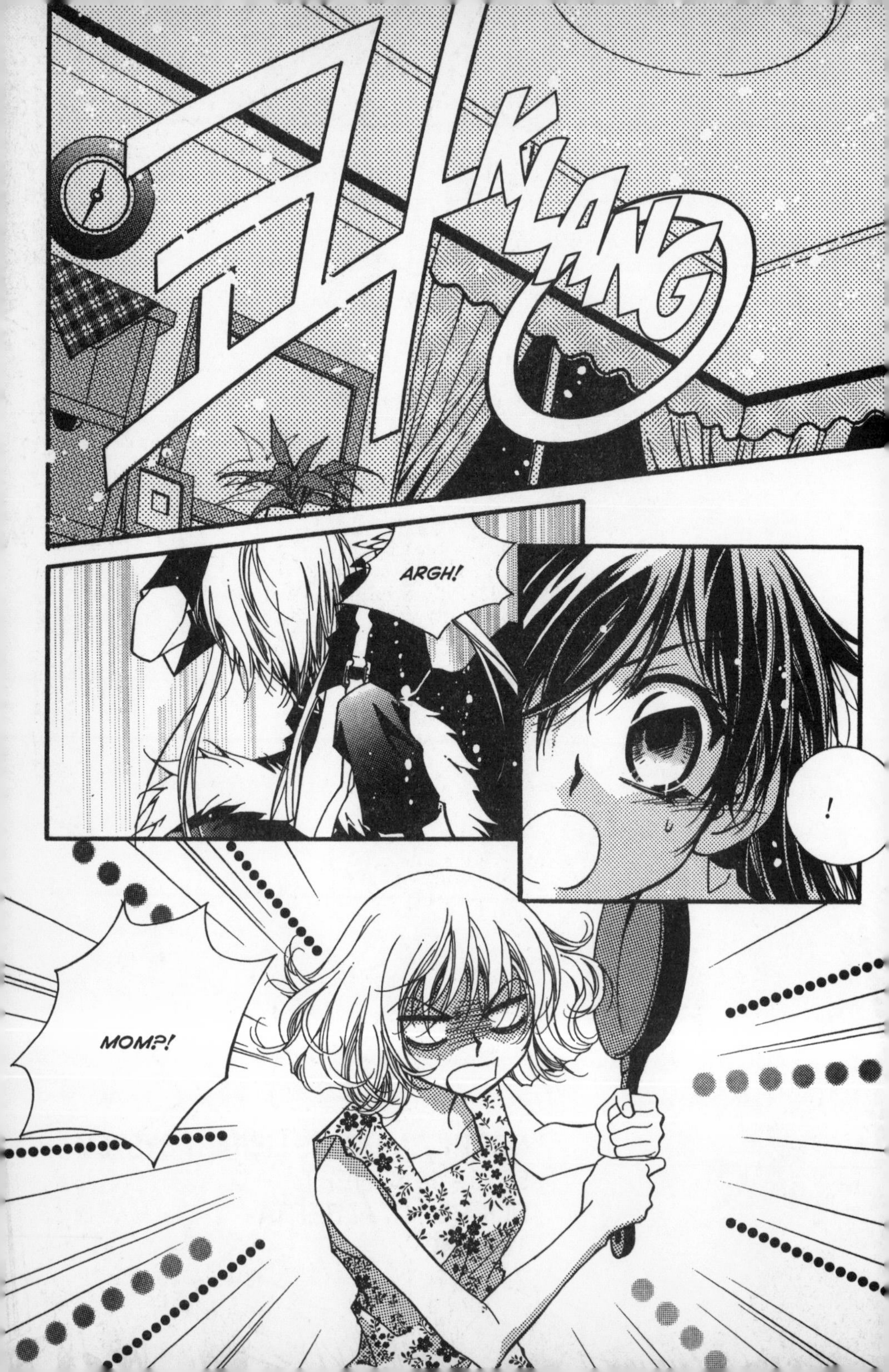

KLANG
ARGH!
!
MOM?!

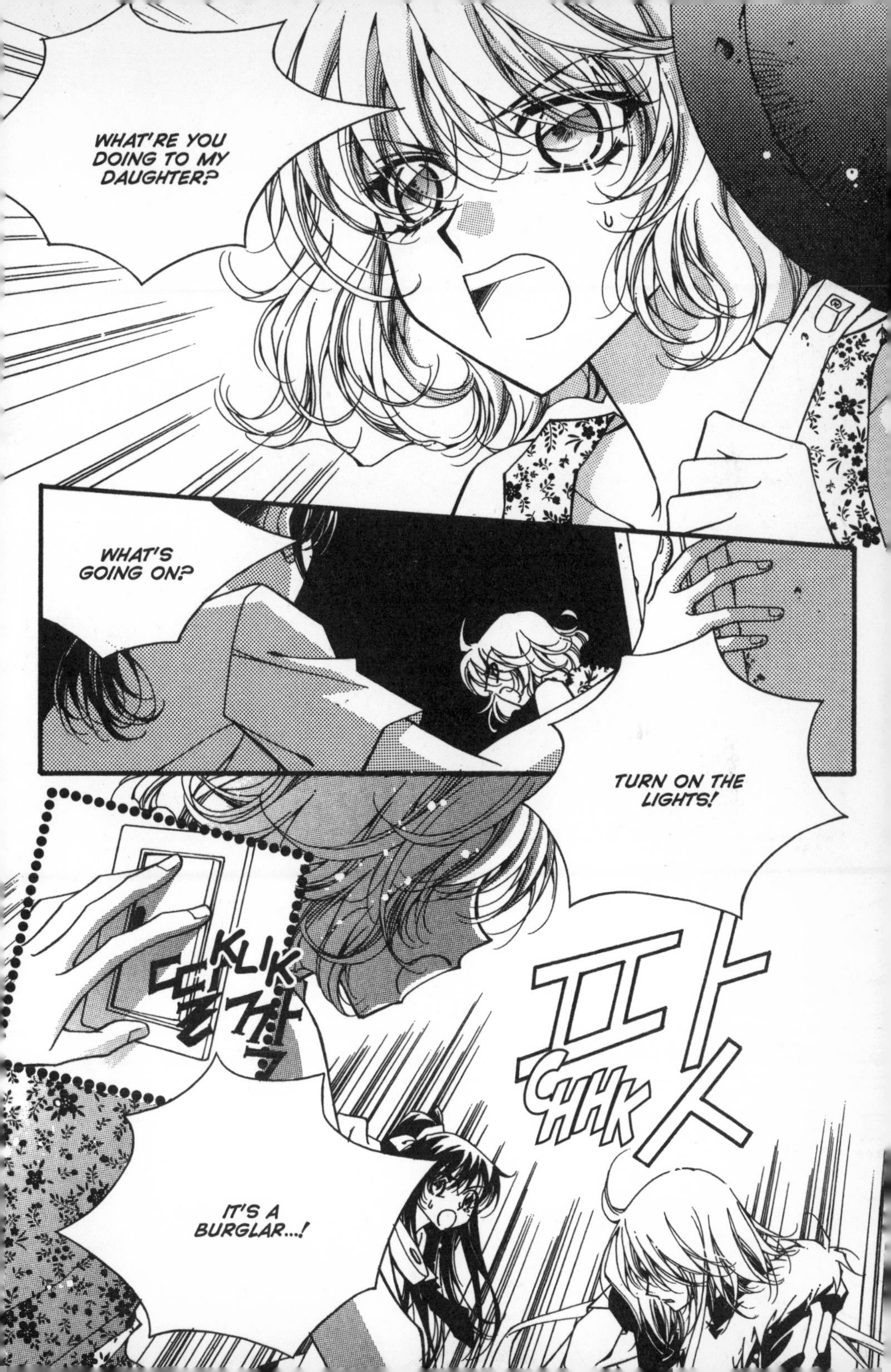
WHAT'RE YOU DOING TO MY DAUGHTER?
WHAT'S GOING ON?
TURN ON THE LIGHTS!
KLIK
CHHK
IT'S A BURGLAR...!

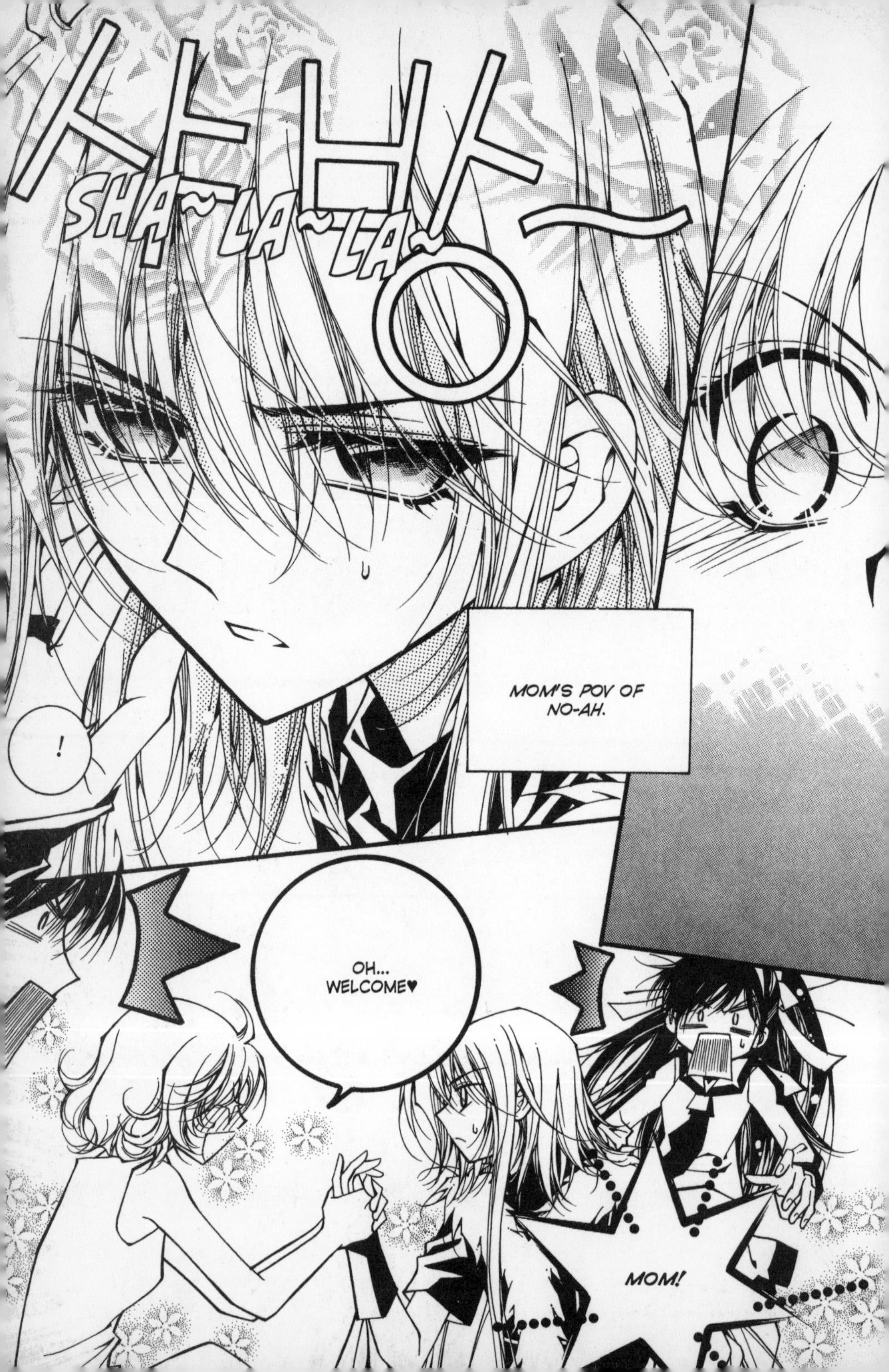
SHA~LA~LA~!
!
MOM'S POV OF NO-AH.
OH... WELCOME♥
MOM!

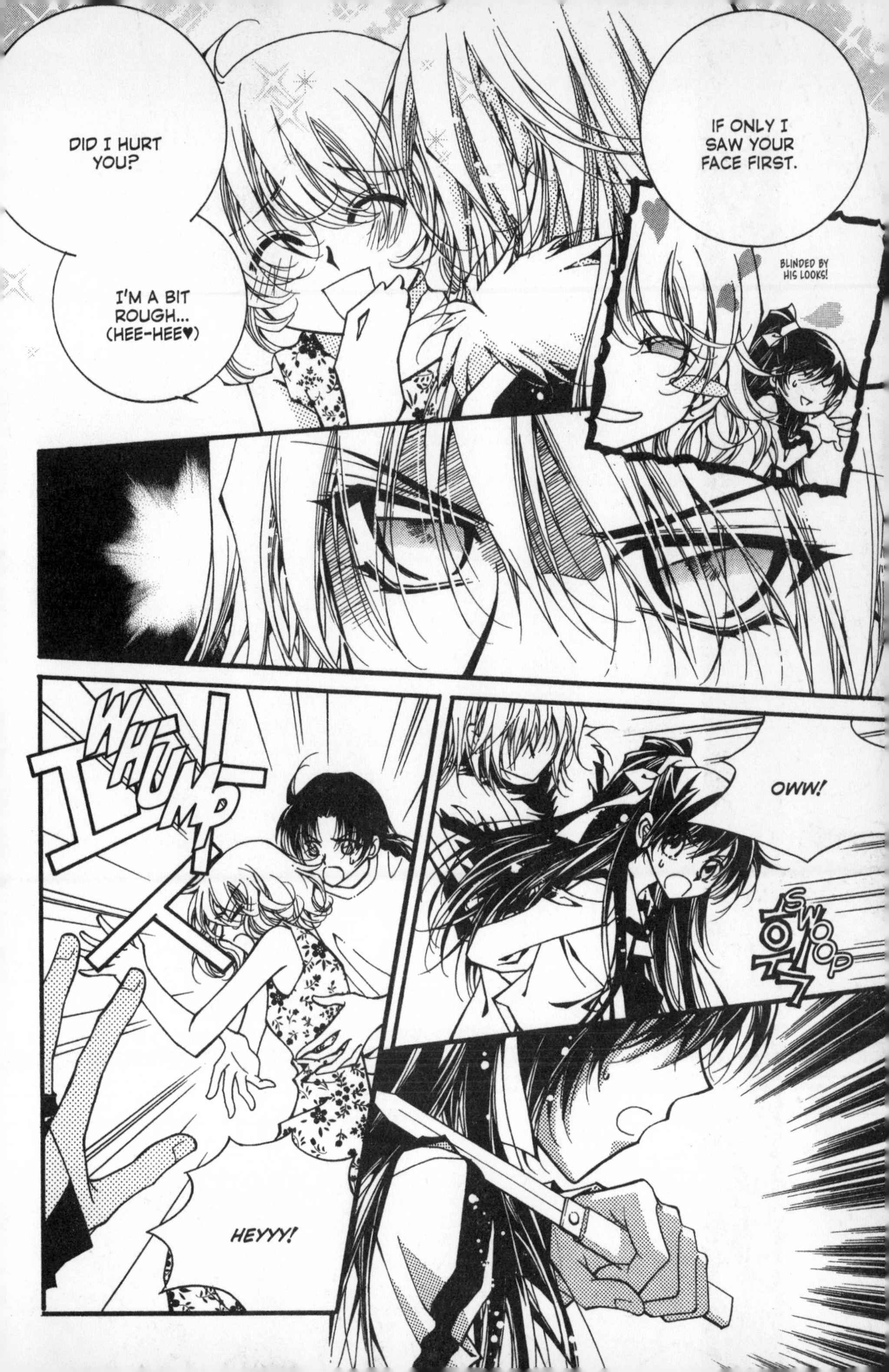
DID I HURT YOU?
I'M A BIT ROUGH... (HEE-HEE♥)
IF ONLY I SAW YOUR FACE FIRST.
BLINDED BY HIS LOOKS!
WHUMP!
OWW!
SWOOP
HEYYY!

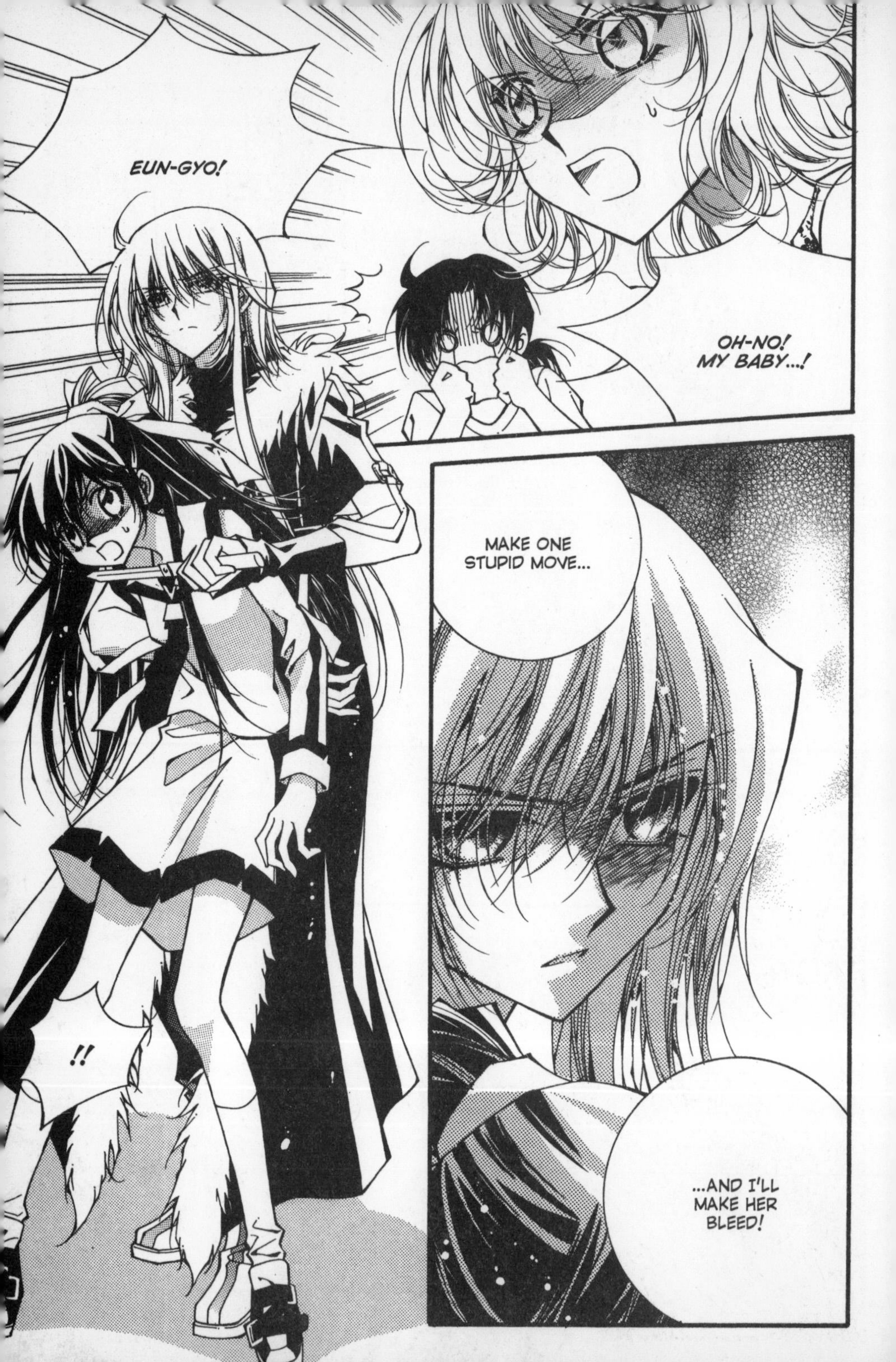
EUN-GYO!
!!
OH-NO! MY BABY...!
MAKE ONE STUPID MOVE...
...AND I'LL MAKE HER BLEED!

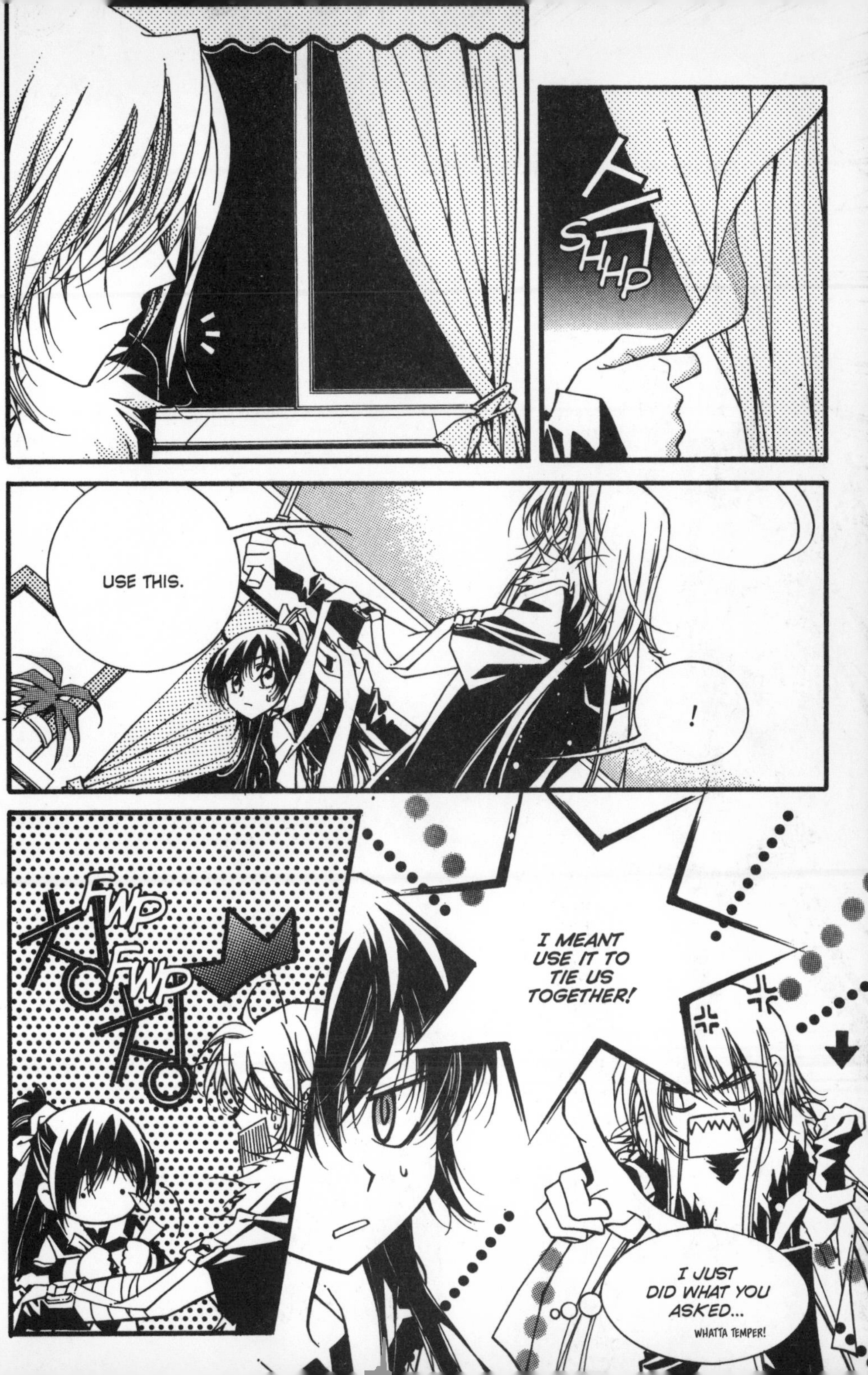
SHHP
USE THIS.
!
FWP
FWP
I MEANT USE IT TO TIE US TOGETHER!
I JUST DID WHAT YOU ASKED...
WHATTA TEMPER!

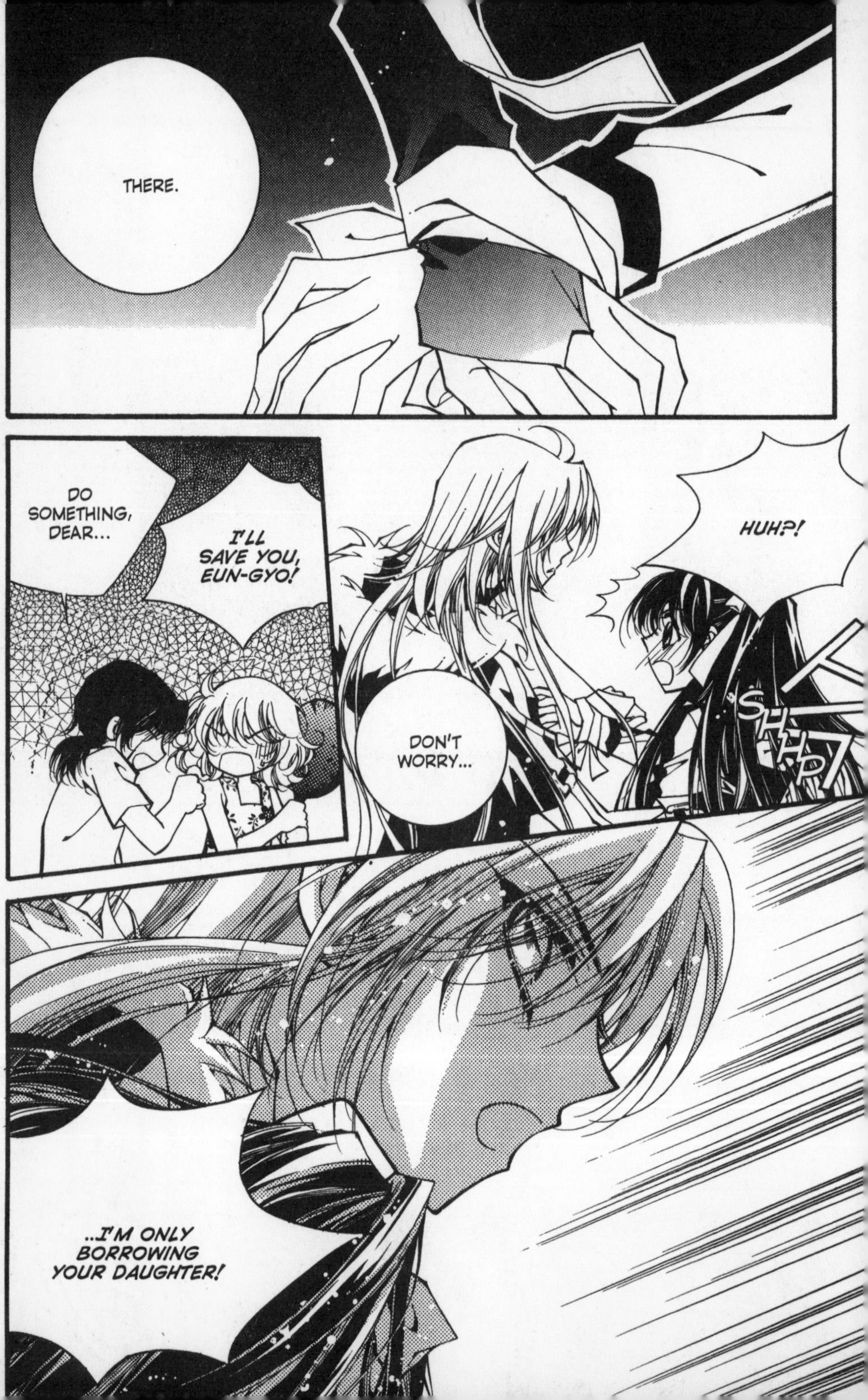

THERE.
DO SOMETHING, DEAR...
I'LL SAVE YOU, EUN-GYO!
HUH?!
DON'T WORRY...
SHHHP
...I'M ONLY BORROWING YOUR DAUGHTER!

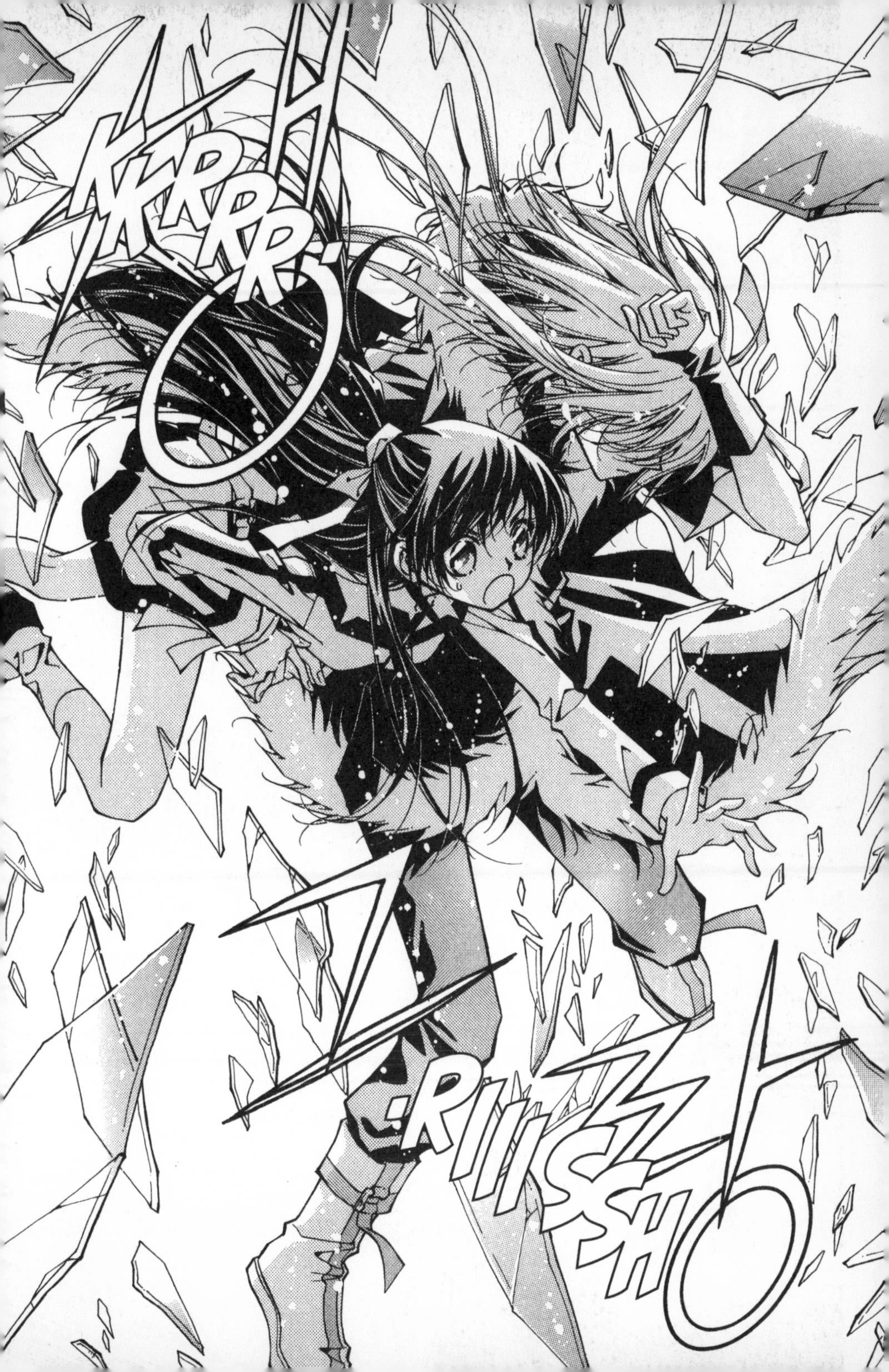
KRRRR
RIIISH

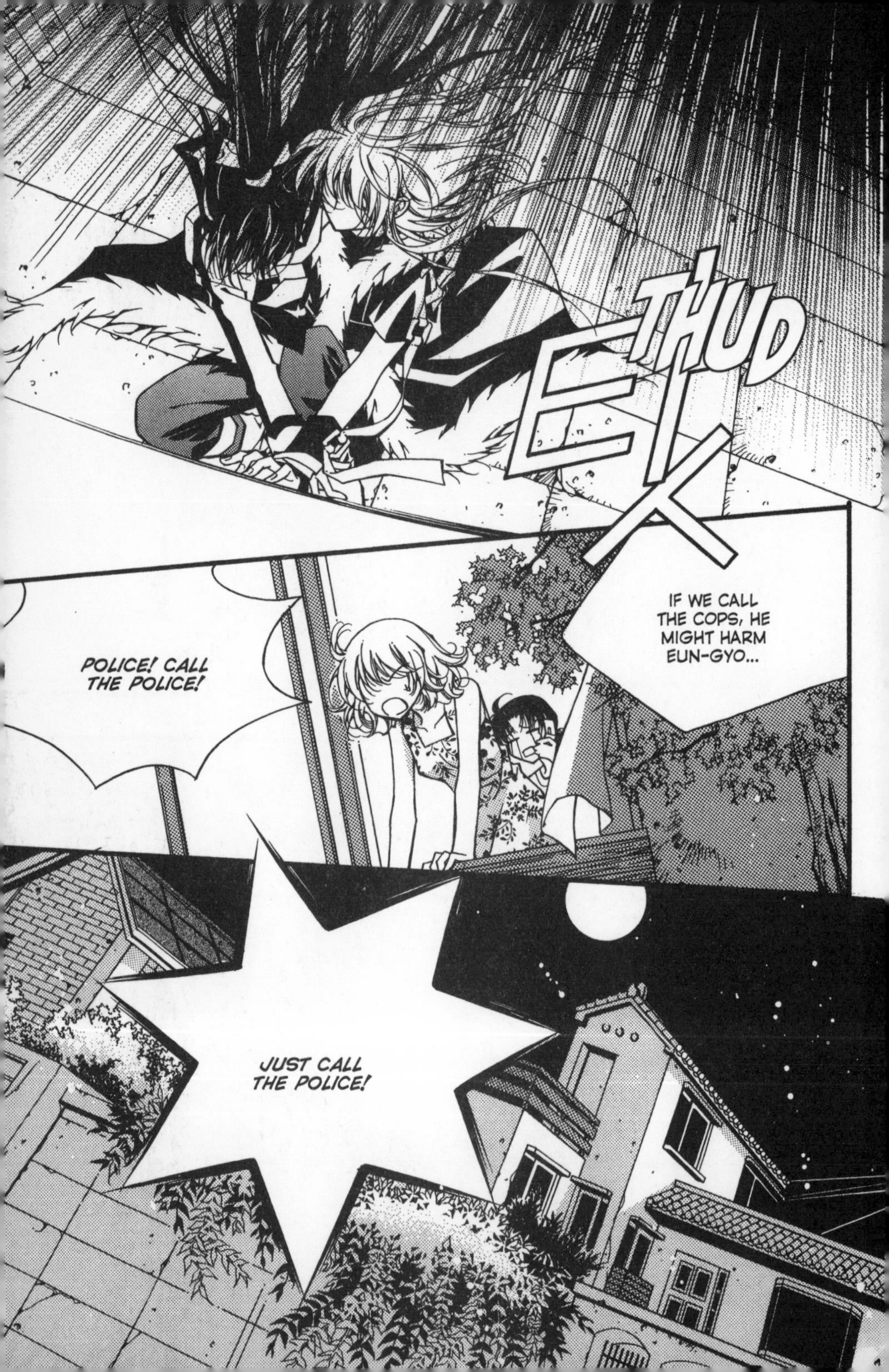
THUD
POLICE! CALL THE POLICE!
IF WE CALL THE COPS, HE MIGHT HARM EUN-GYO...
JUST CALL THE POLICE!

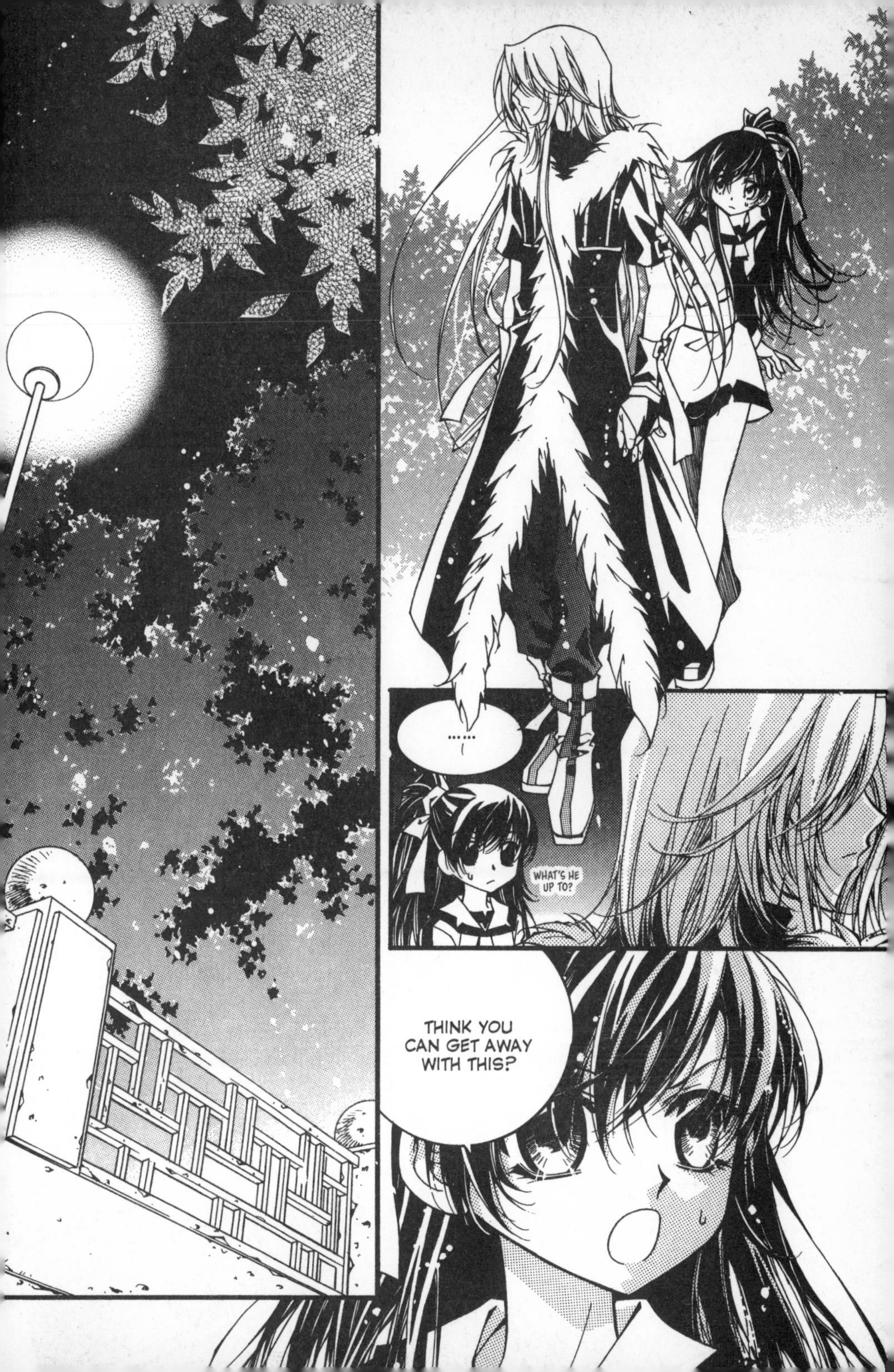
......
WHAT'S HE UP TO?
THINK YOU CAN GET AWAY WITH THIS?

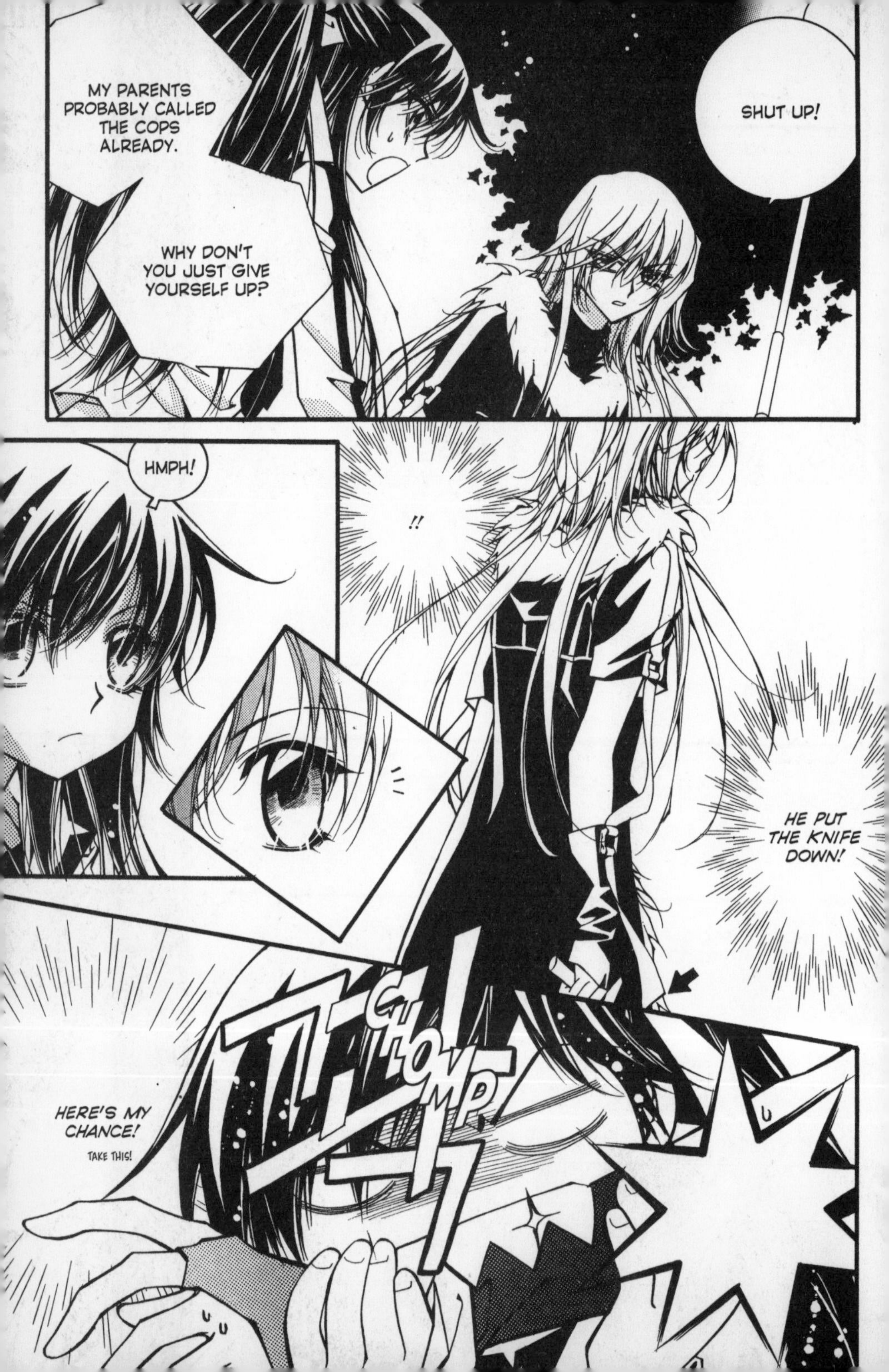
MY PARENTS PROBABLY CALLED THE COPS ALREADY.
WHY DON'T YOU JUST GIVE YOURSELF UP?
SHUT UP!
HMPH!
!!
HE PUT THE KNIFE DOWN!
HERE'S MY CHANCE!
TAKE THIS!
CHOMP

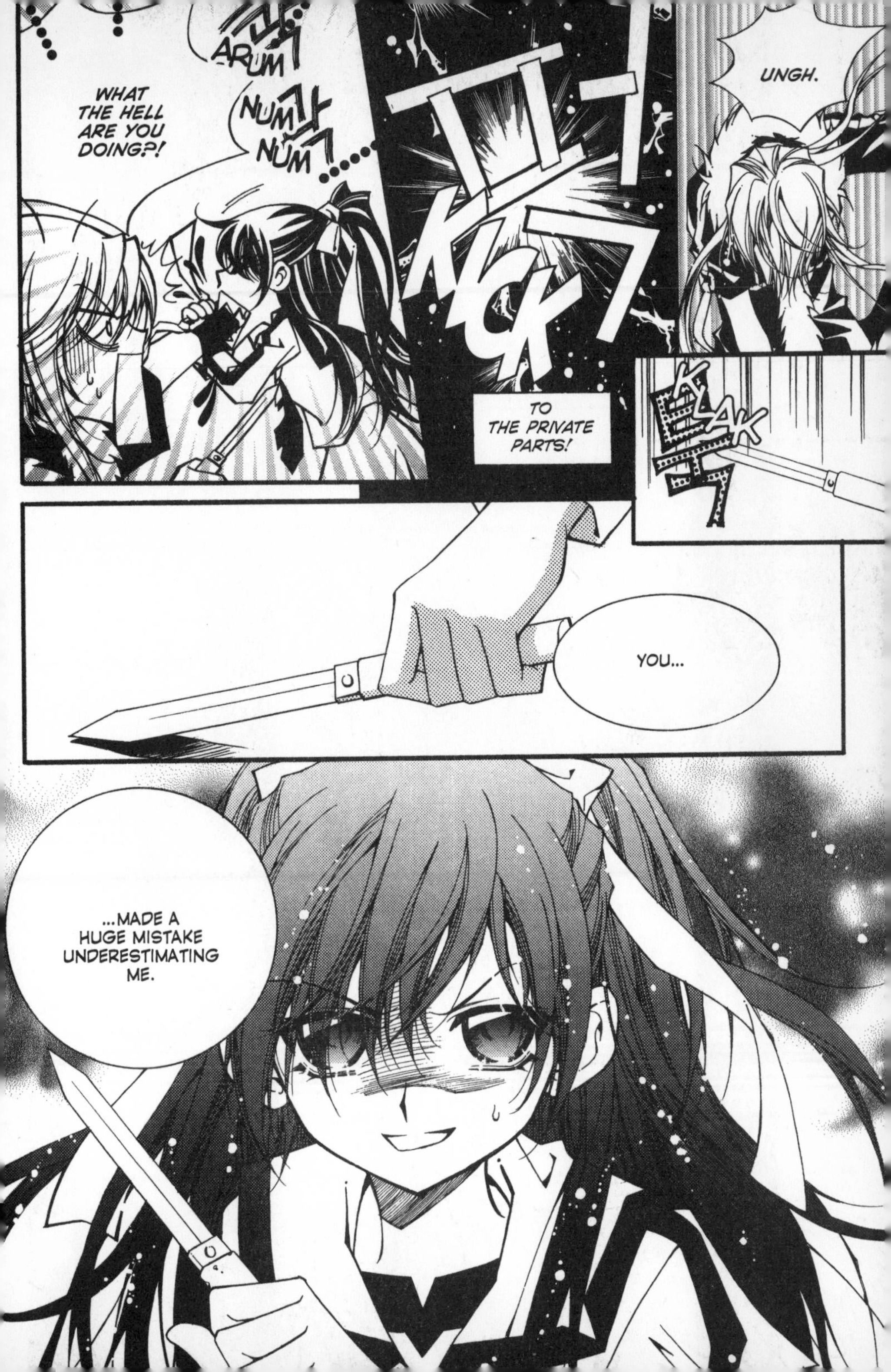
WHAT THE HELL ARE YOU DOING?!
ARUM
NUM NUM......
KICK
TO THE PRIVATE PARTS!
UNGH.
KLAK
YOU...
...MADE A HUGE MISTAKE UNDERESTIMATING ME.

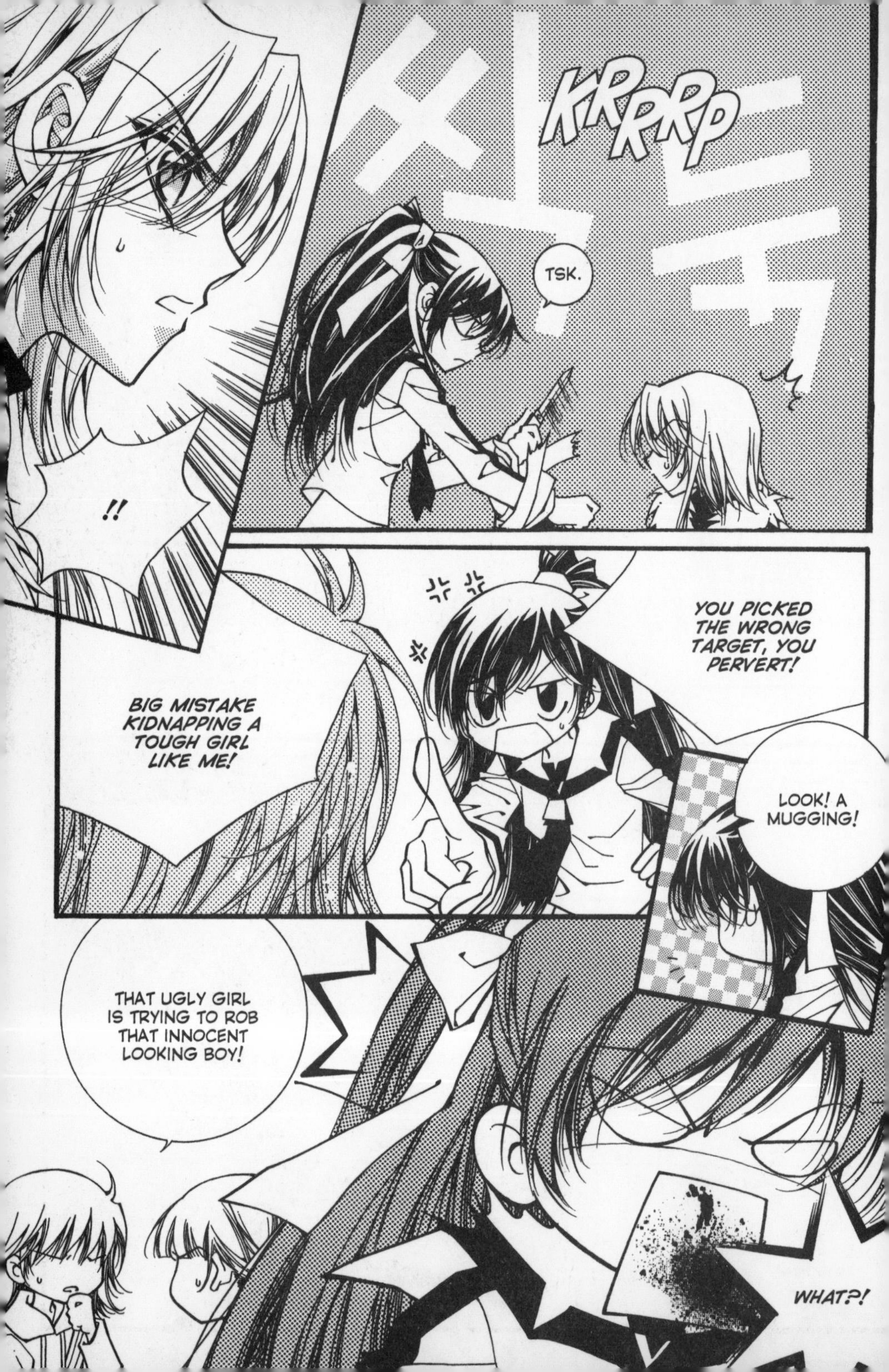
!!
KRRRP
TSK.
BIG MISTAKE KIDNAPPING A TOUGH GIRL LIKE ME!
YOU PICKED THE WRONG TARGET, YOU PERVERT!
LOOK! A MUGGING!
THAT UGLY GIRL IS TRYING TO ROB THAT INNOCENT LOOKING BOY!
WHAT?!

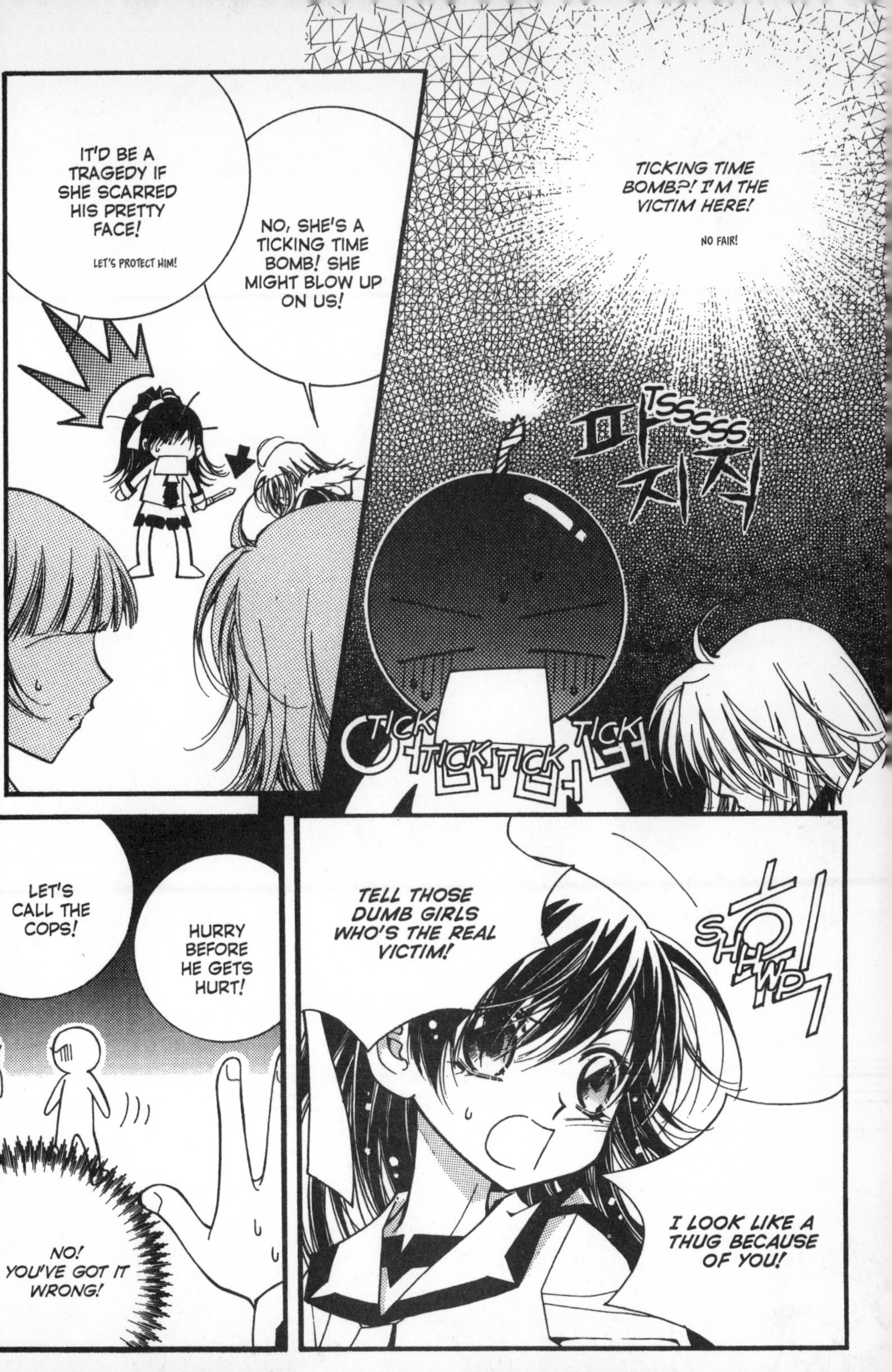
IT'D BE A TRAGEDY IF SHE SCARRED HIS PRETTY FACE!
LET'S PROTECT HIM!
NO, SHE'S A TICKING TIME BOMB! SHE MIGHT BLOW UP ON US!
TICKING TIME BOMB?! I'M THE VICTIM HERE!
NO FAIR!
TSSSSSS
파지직
TICK TICK TICK TICK
LET'S CALL THE COPS!
HURRY BEFORE HE GETS HURT!
NO! YOU'VE GOT IT WRONG!
TELL THOSE DUMB GIRLS WHO'S THE REAL VICTIM!
I LOOK LIKE A THUG BECAUSE OF YOU!

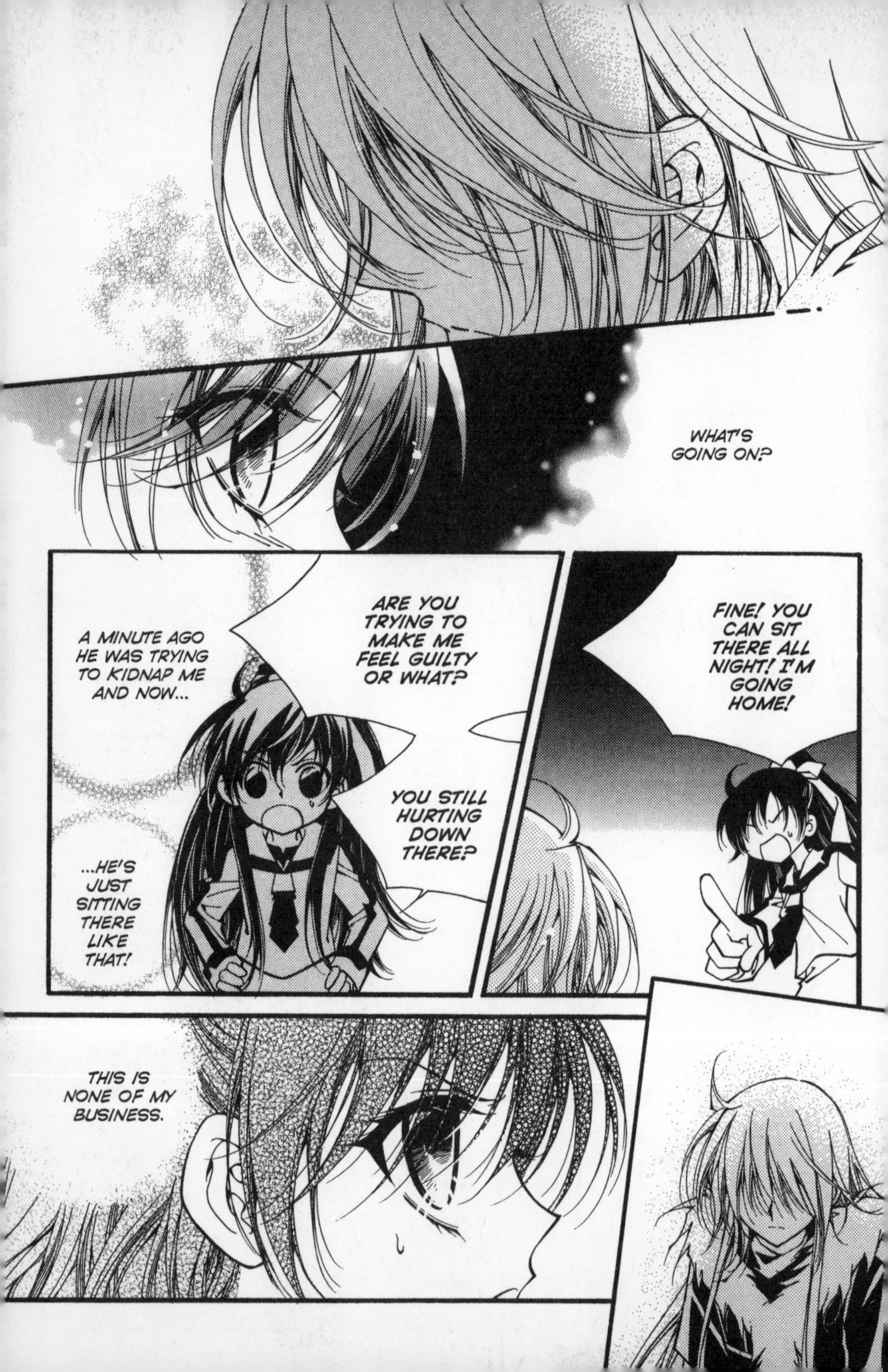
WHAT'S GOING ON?
A MINUTE AGO HE WAS TRYING TO KIDNAP ME AND NOW...
...HE'S JUST SITTING THERE LIKE THAT!
ARE YOU TRYING TO MAKE ME FEEL GUILTY OR WHAT?
YOU STILL HURTING DOWN THERE?
FINE! YOU CAN SIT THERE ALL NIGHT! I'M GOING HOME!
THIS IS NONE OF MY BUSINESS.

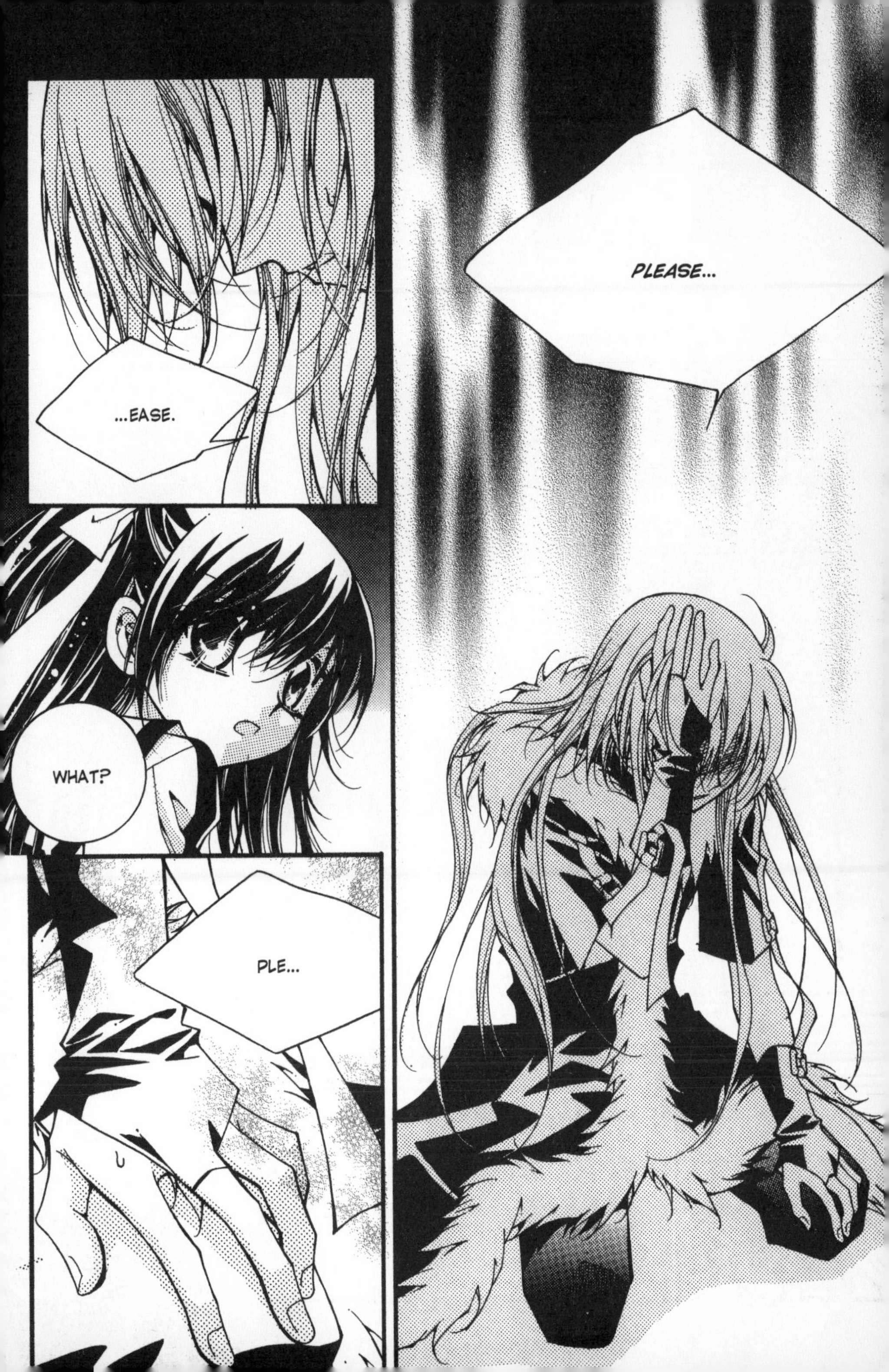
PLEASE...
...EASE.
WHAT?
PLE...

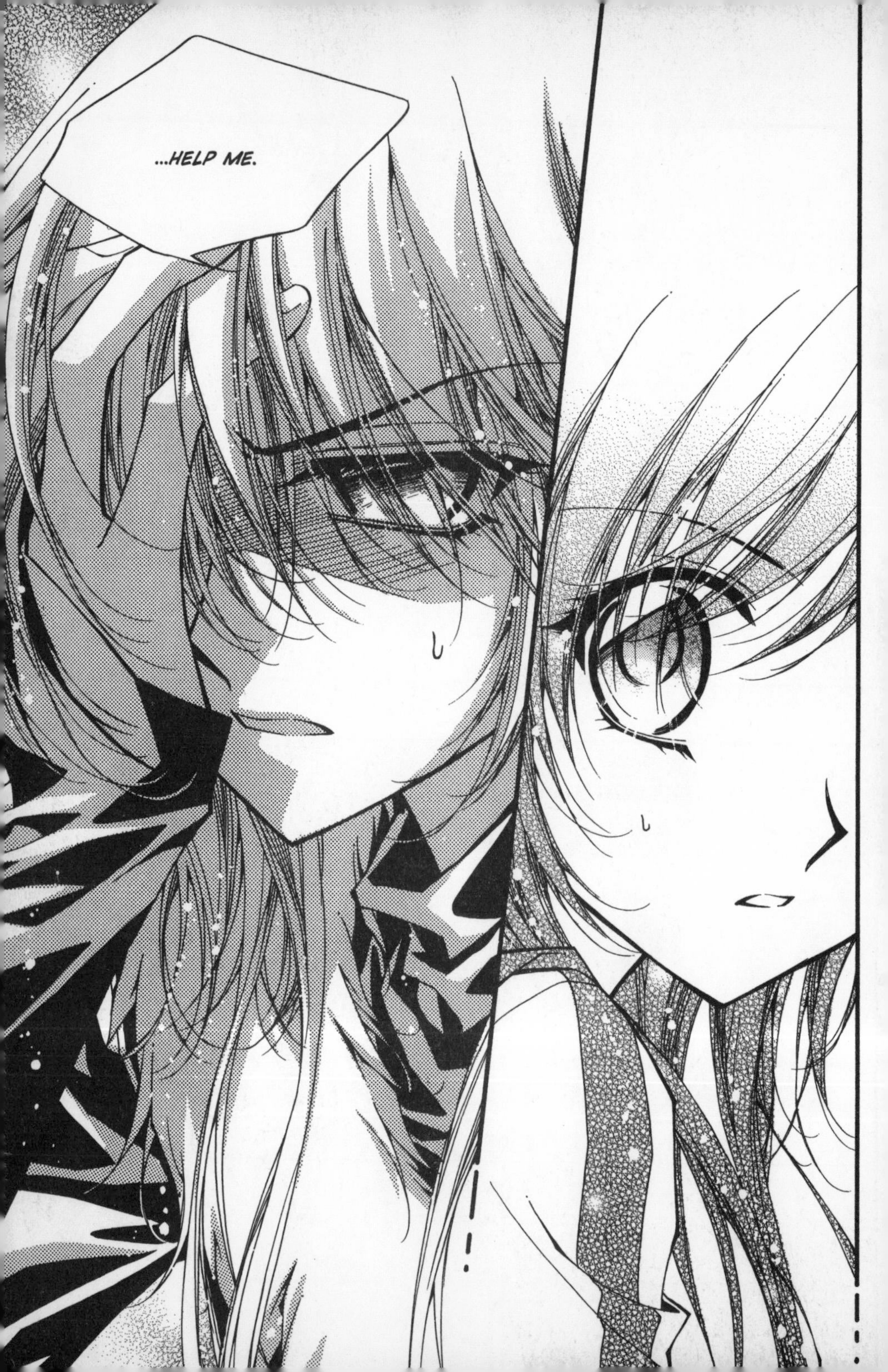
...HELP ME.

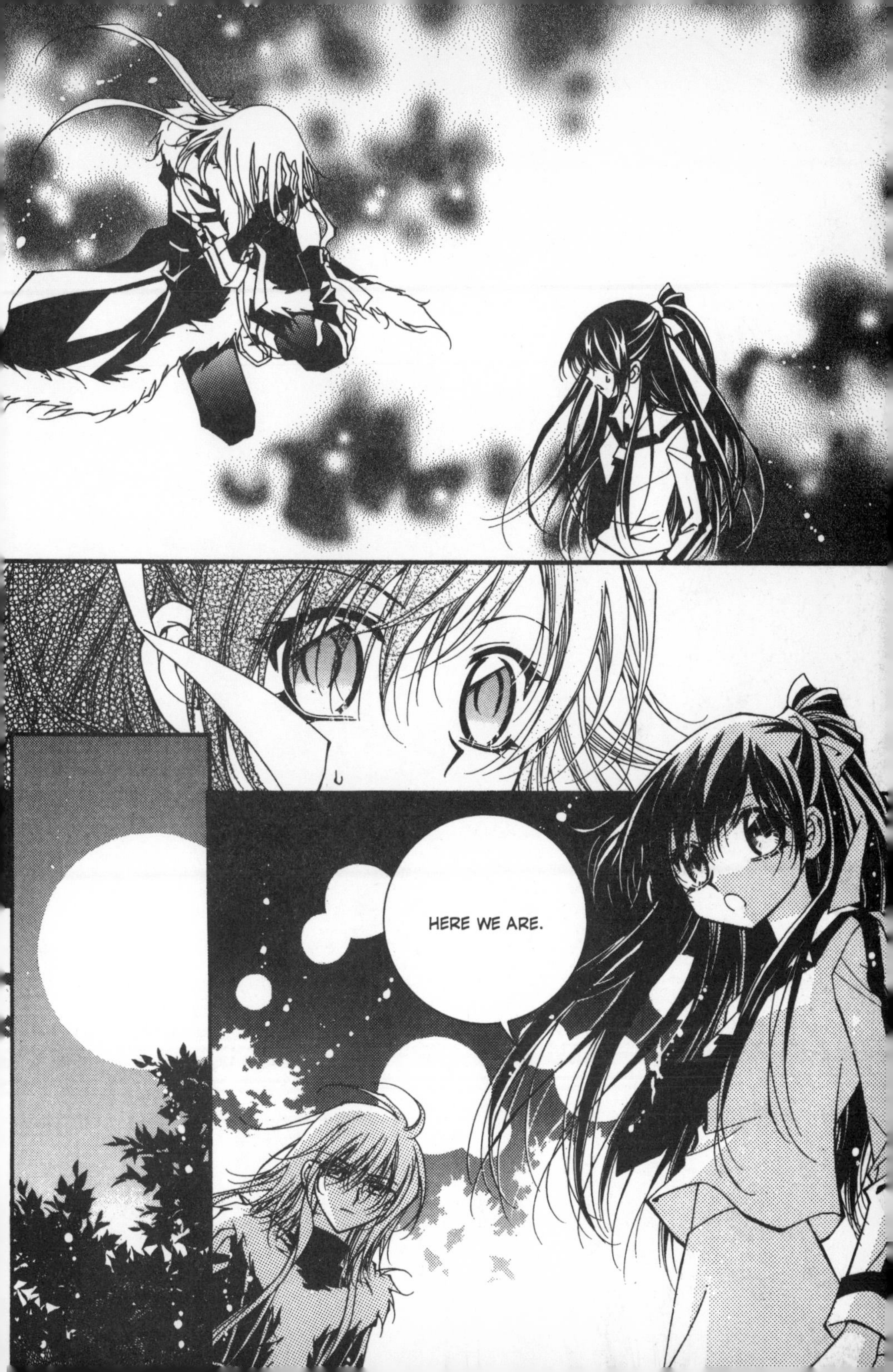
HERE WE ARE.

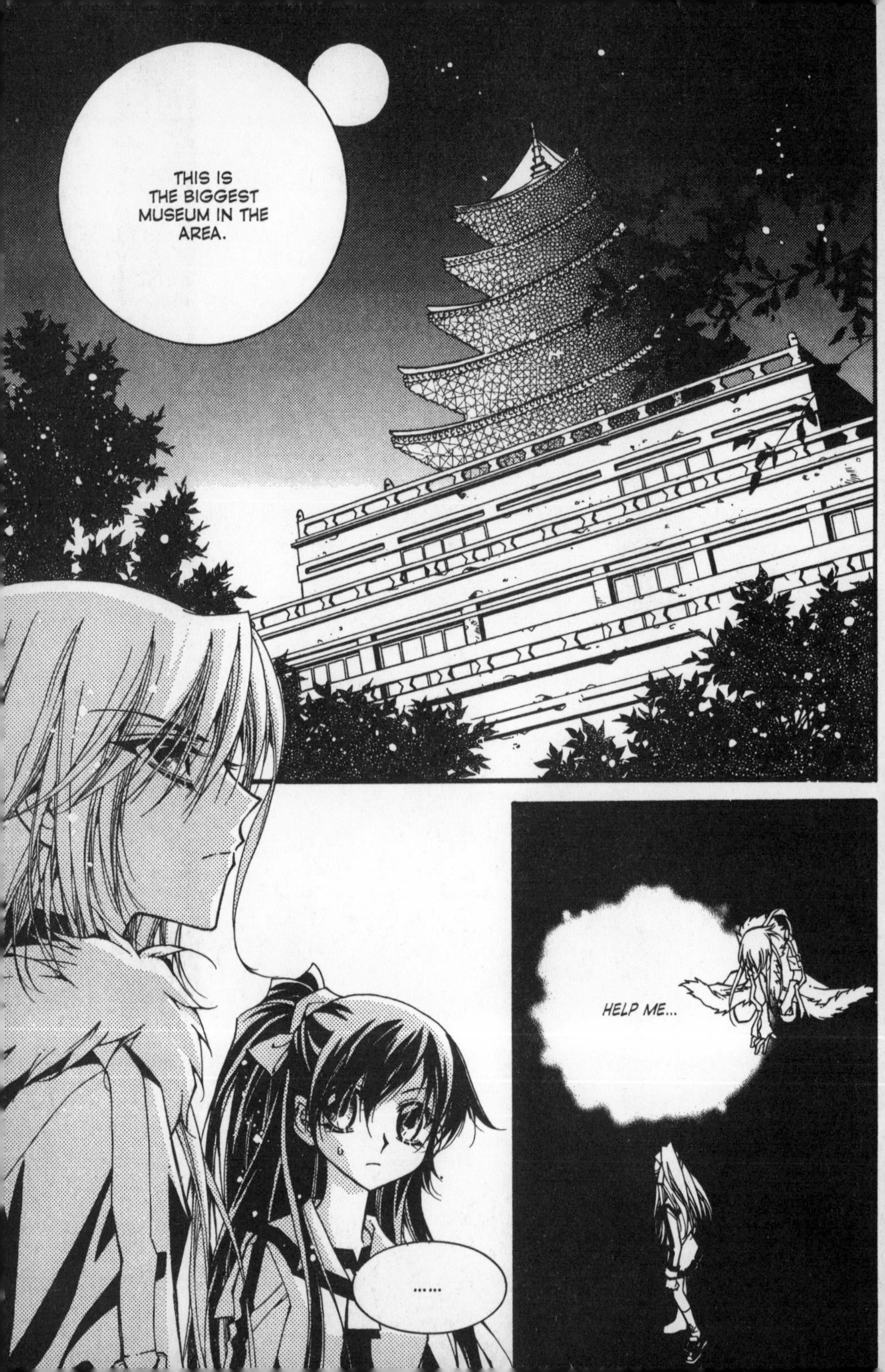
THIS IS THE BIGGEST MUSEUM IN THE AREA.
......
HELP ME...

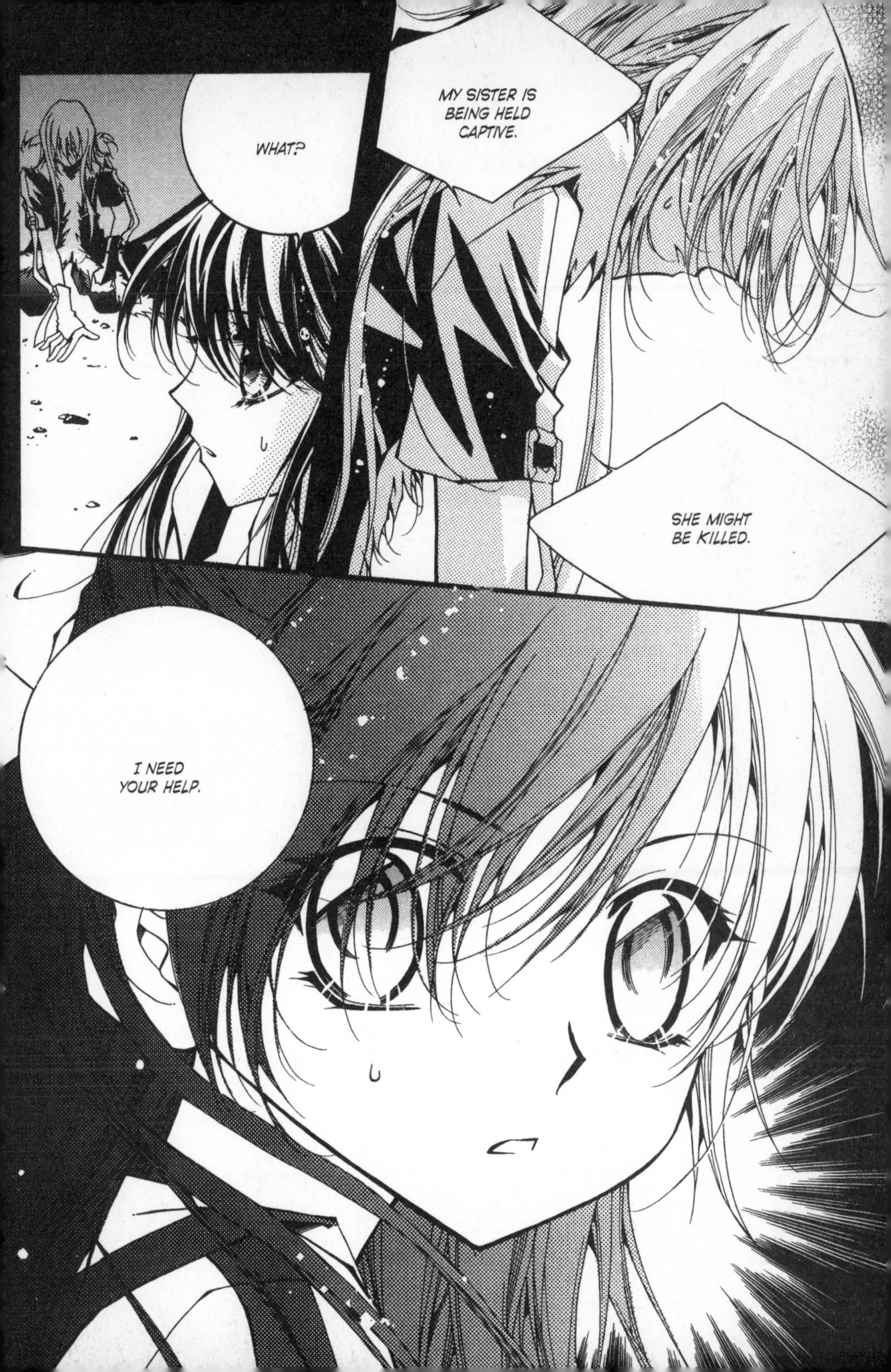
WHAT?
MY SISTER IS BEING HELD CAPTIVE.
SHE MIGHT BE KILLED.
I NEED YOUR HELP.

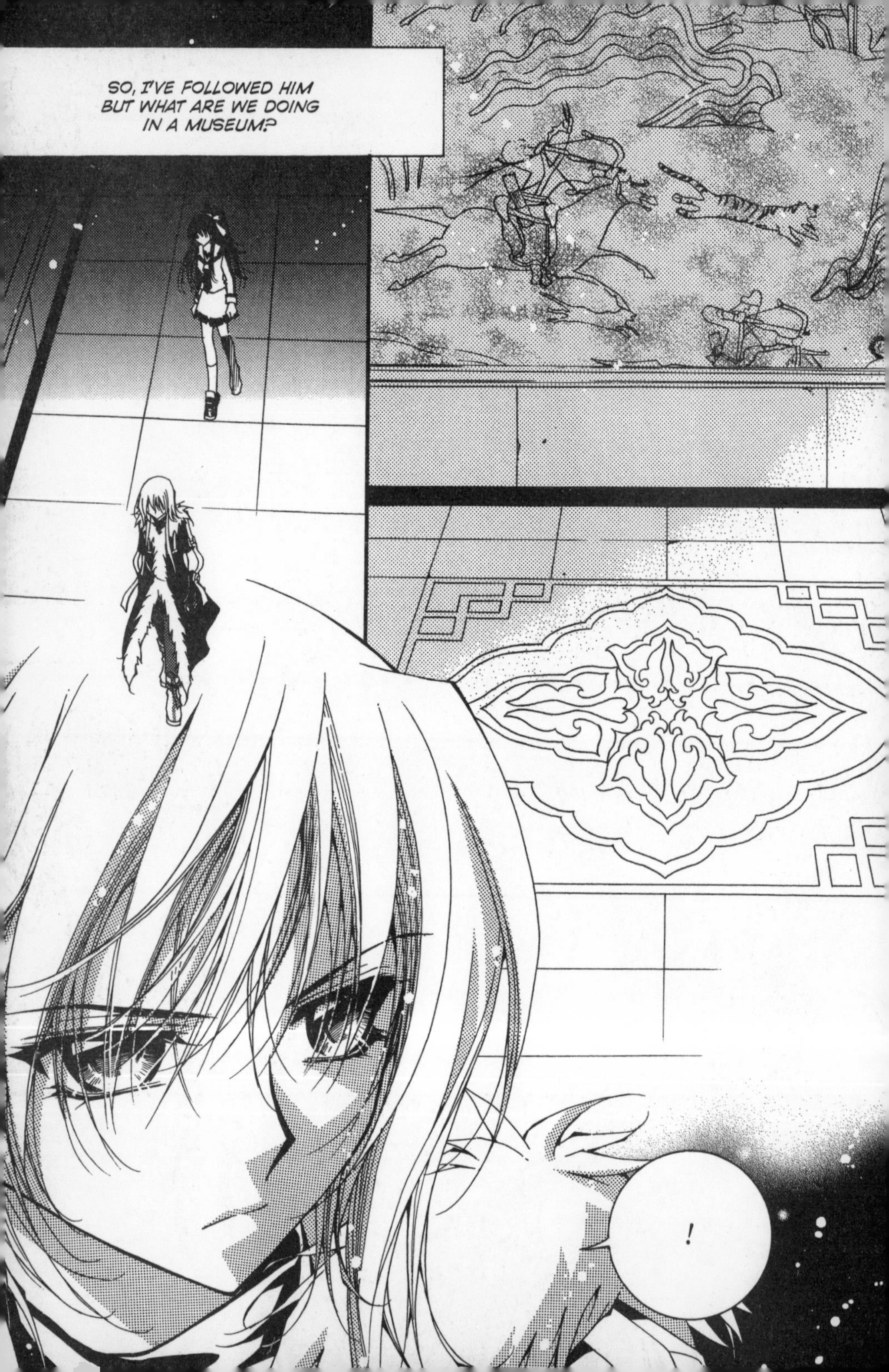
SO, I'VE FOLLOWED HIM BUT WHAT ARE WE DOING IN A MUSEUM?
!

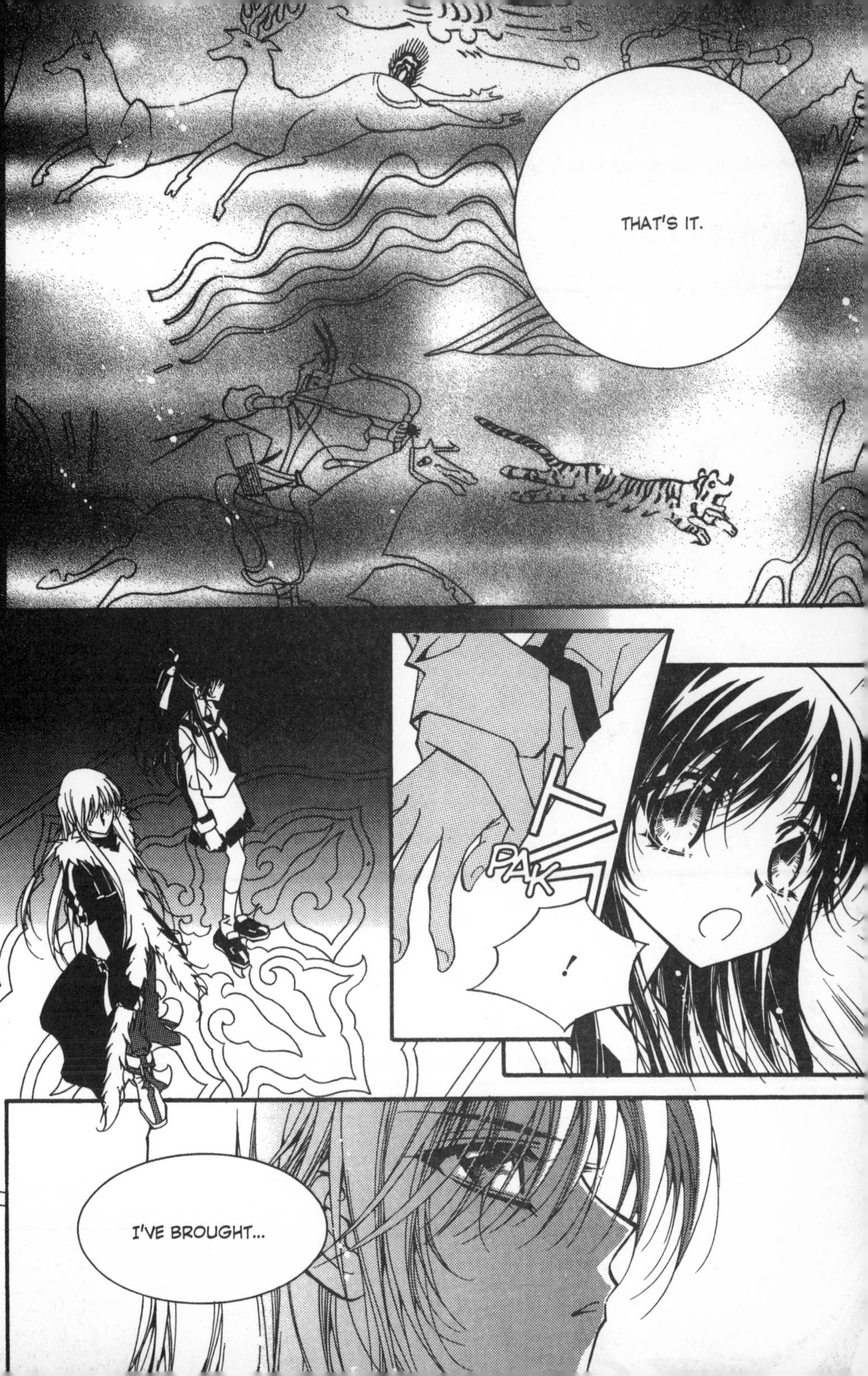
THAT'S IT.
PAK
!
I'VE BROUGHT...

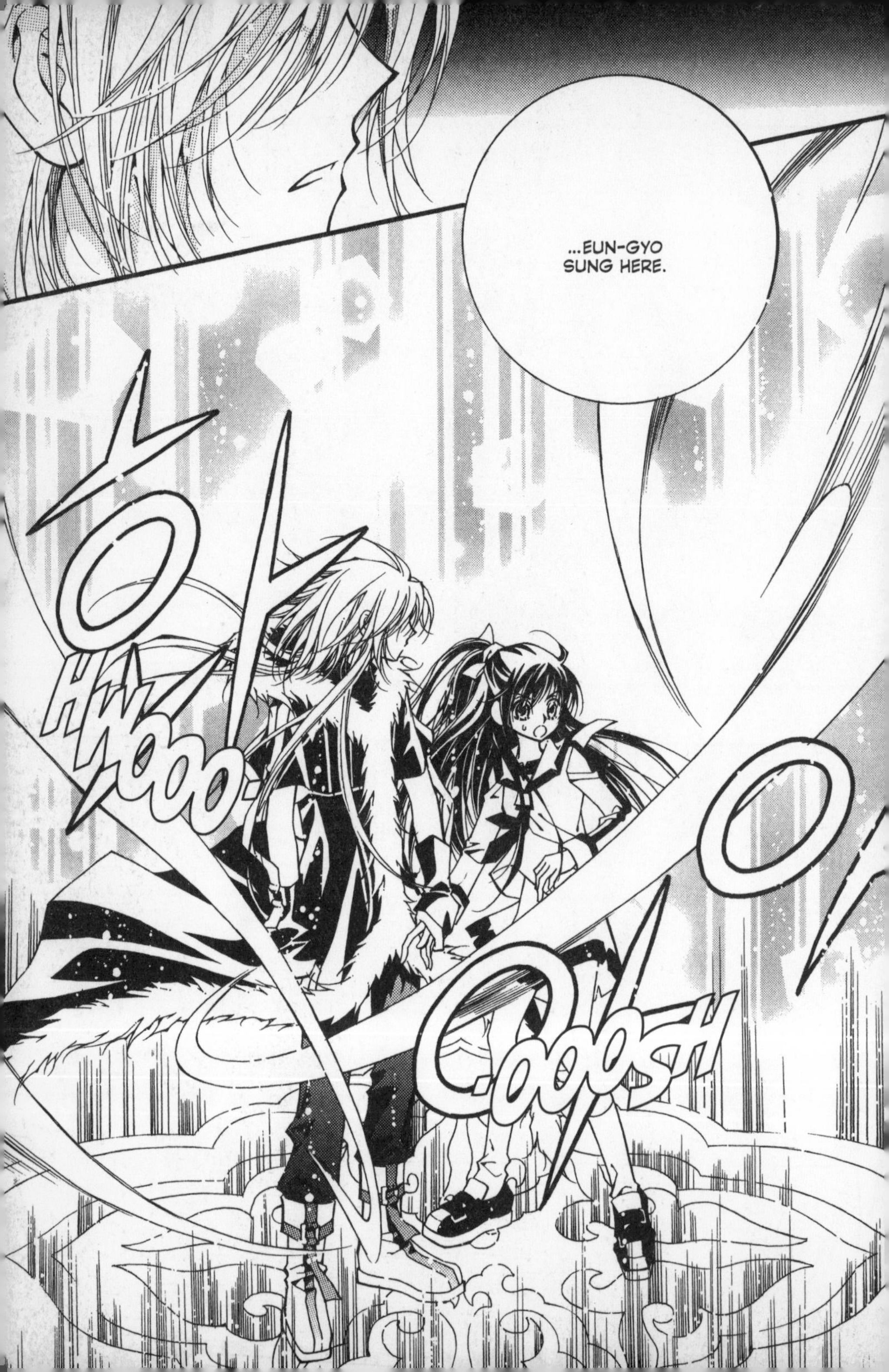
...EUN-GYO SUNG HERE.

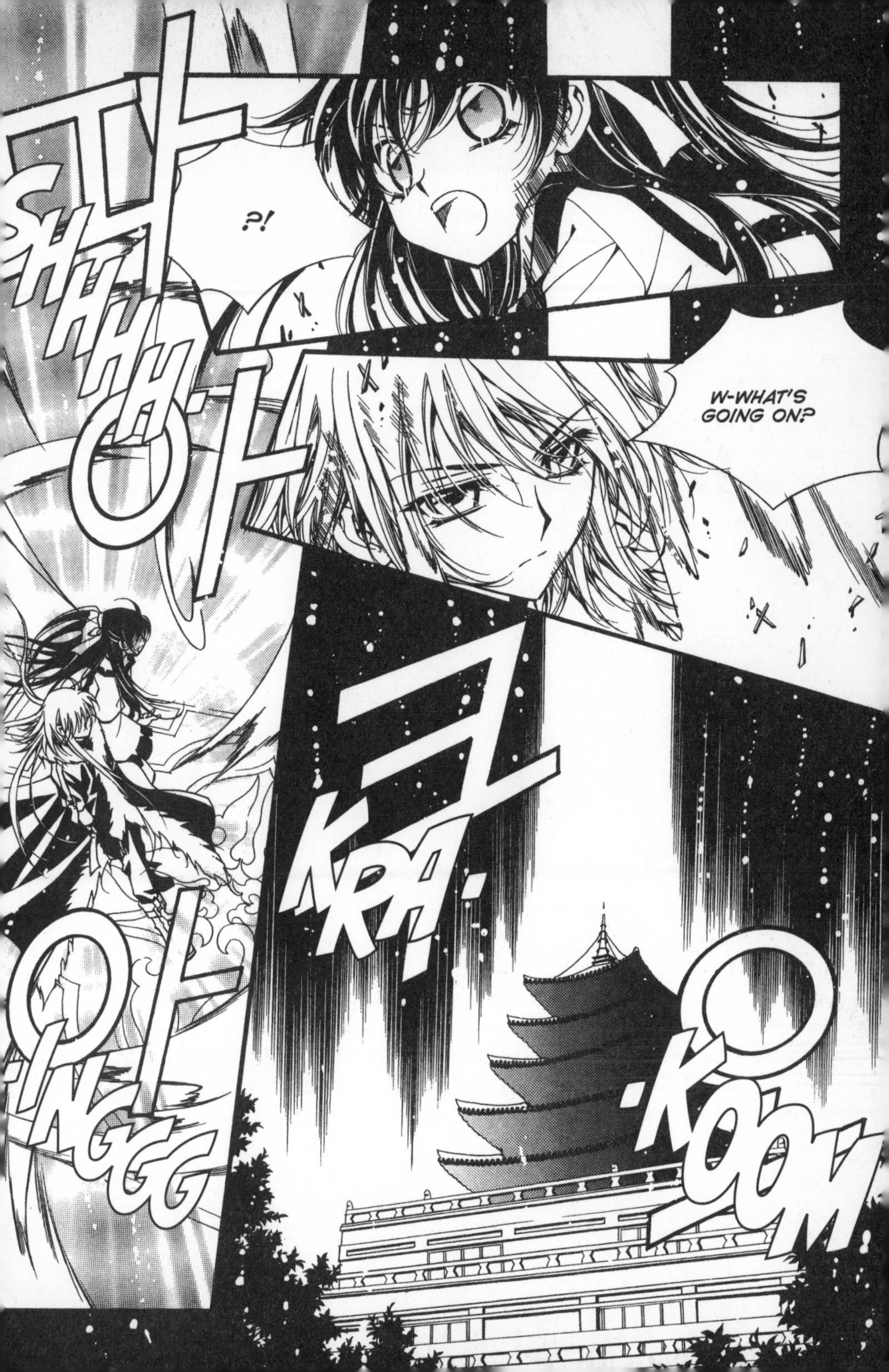
SHHHH
?!
W-WHAT'S GOING ON?
INGGG
KRA
KOOM

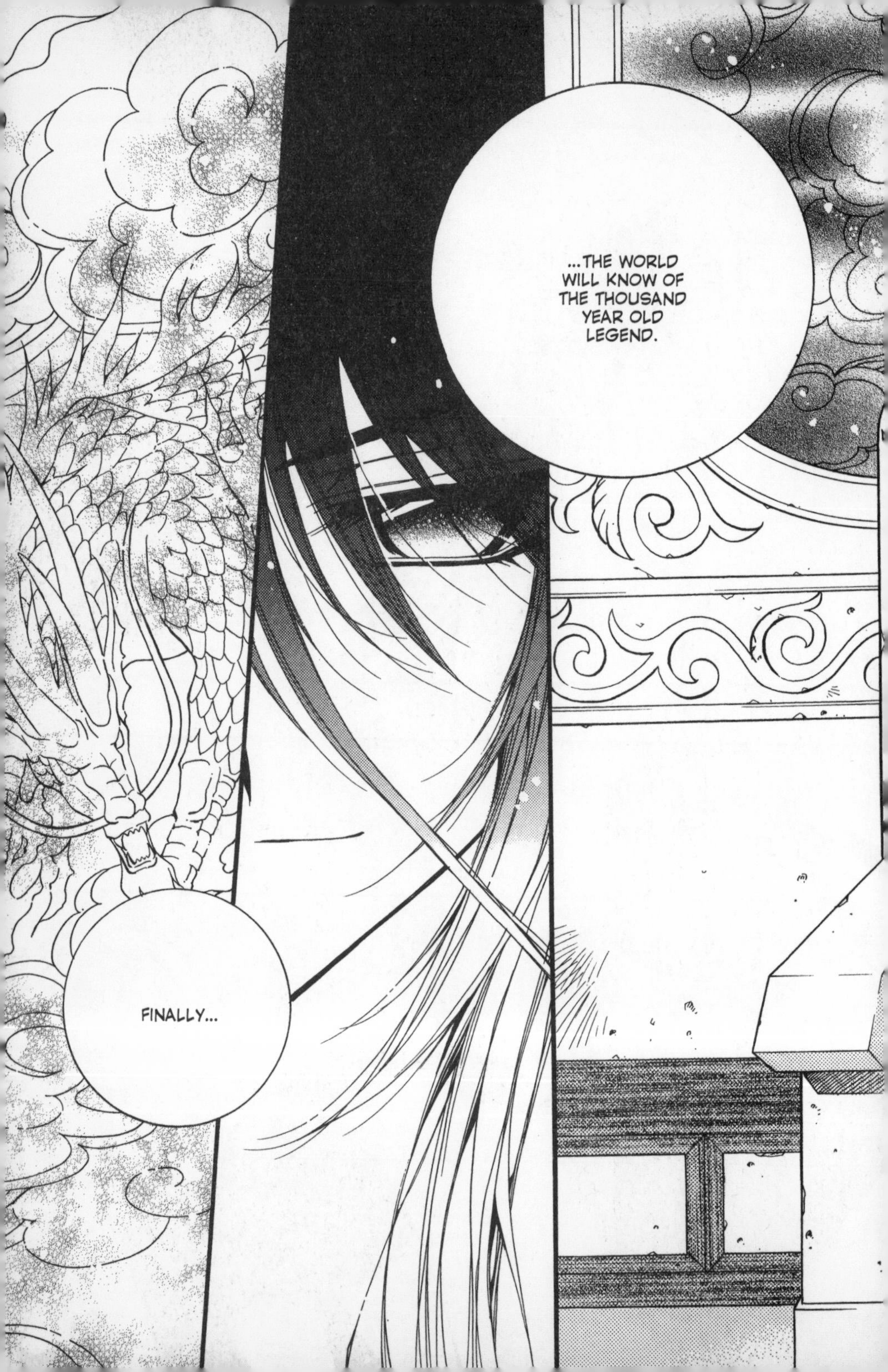
FINALLY...
...THE WORLD WILL KNOW OF THE THOUSAND YEAR OLD LEGEND.

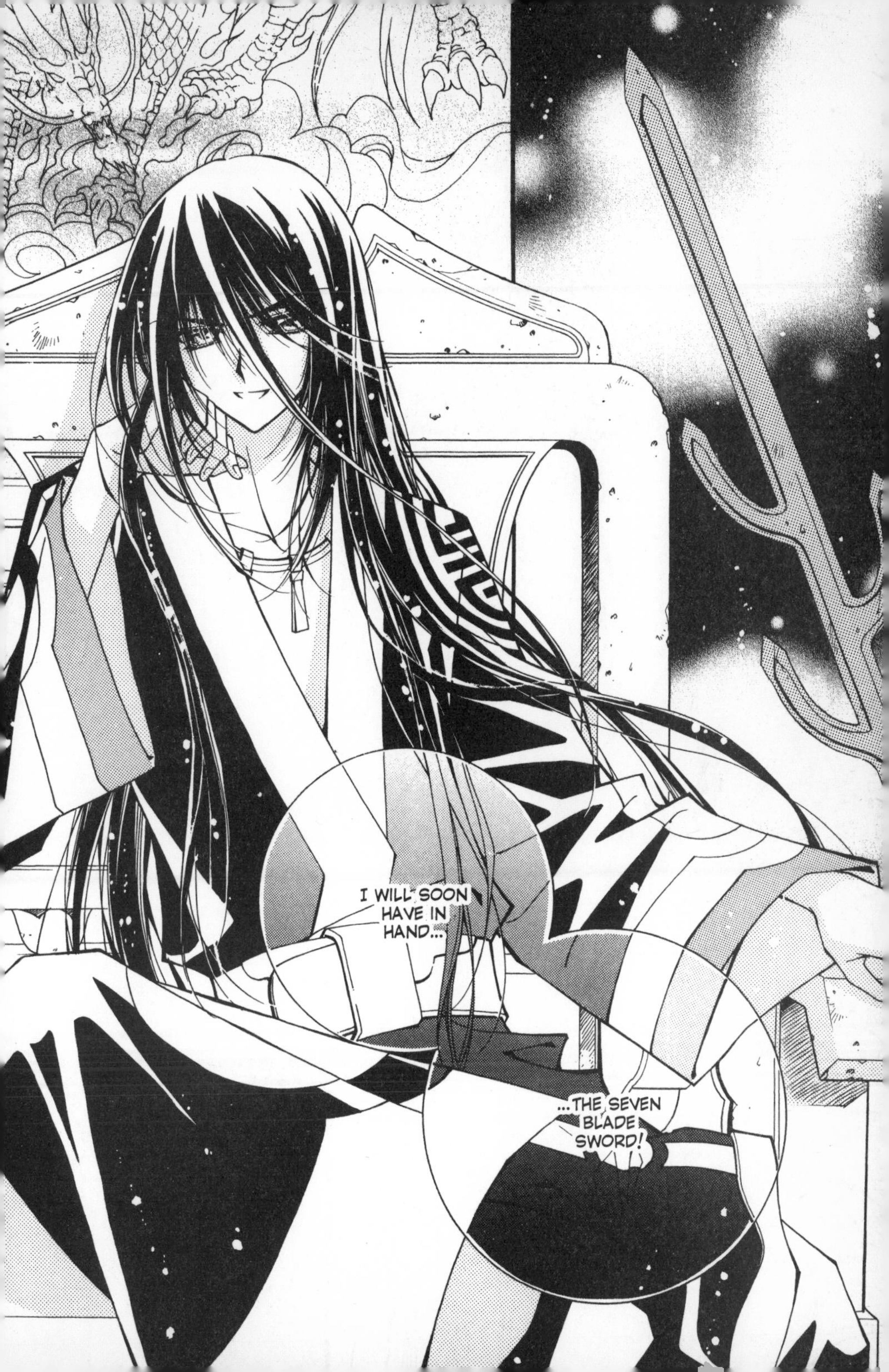
I WILL SOON HAVE IN HAND...
...THE SEVEN BLADE SWORD!

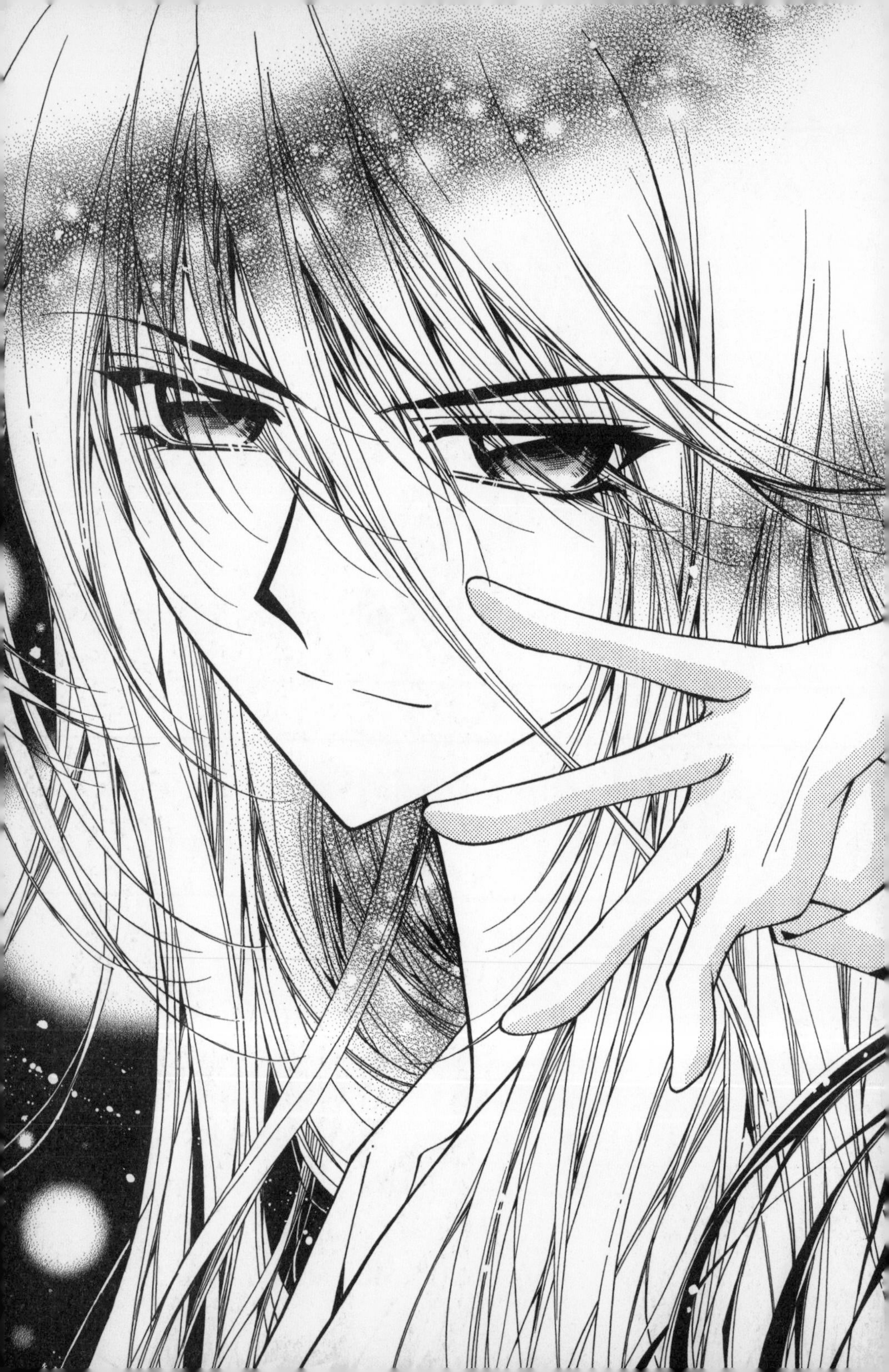

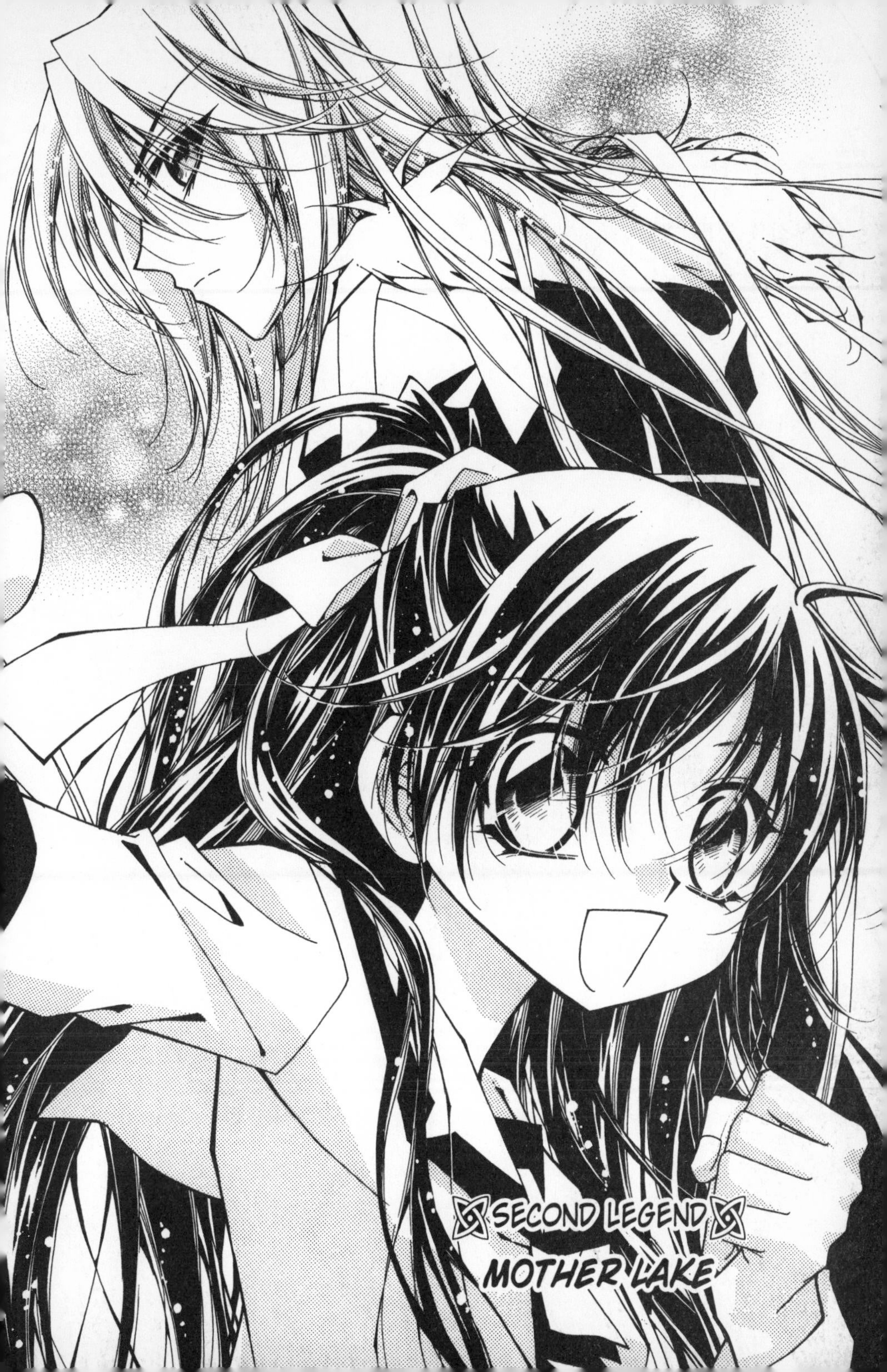
SECOND LEGEND
MOTHER LAKE

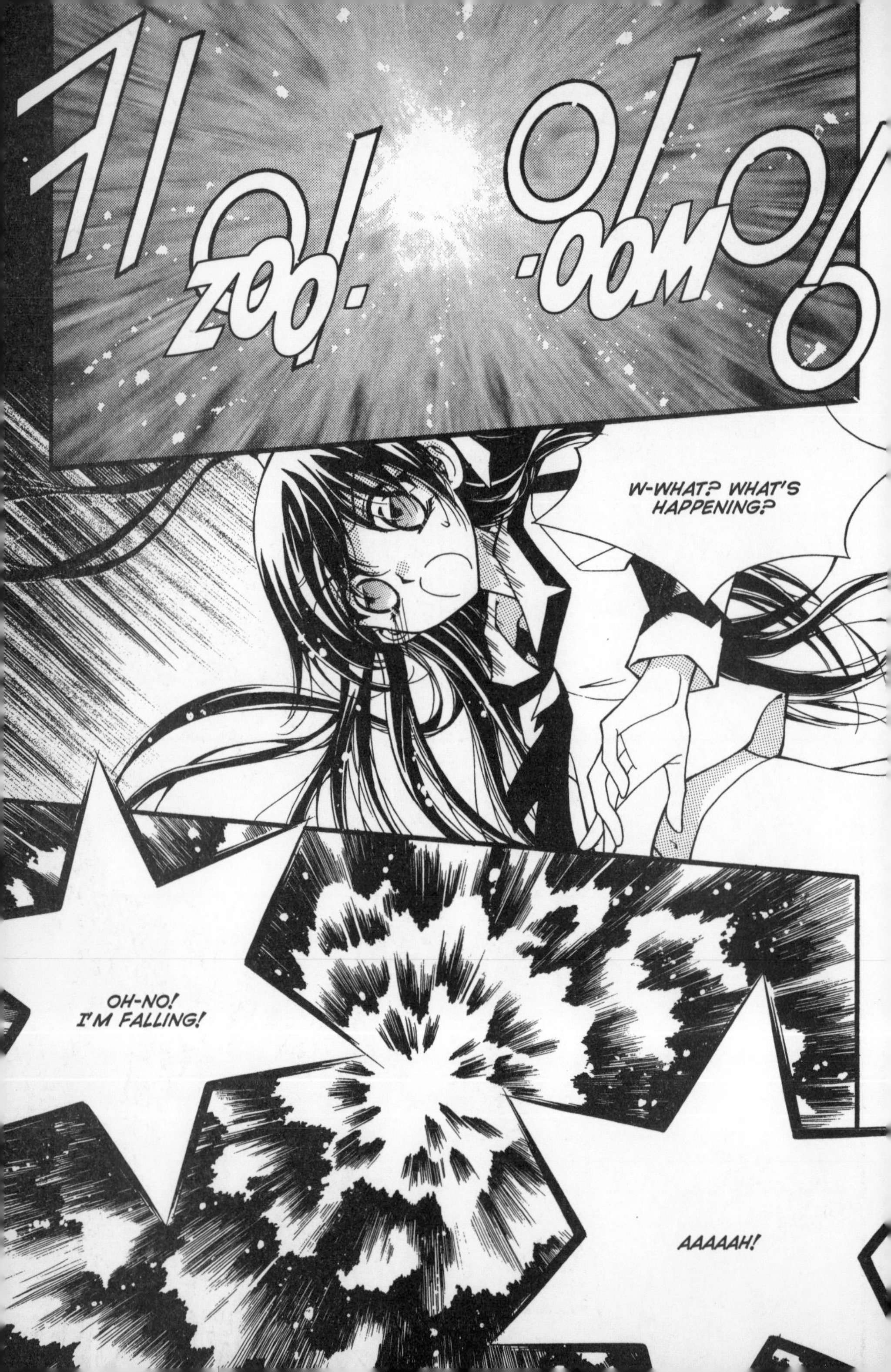
ZOO-
-OOM
W-WHAT? WHAT'S HAPPENING?
OH-NO! I'M FALLING!
AAAAAH!

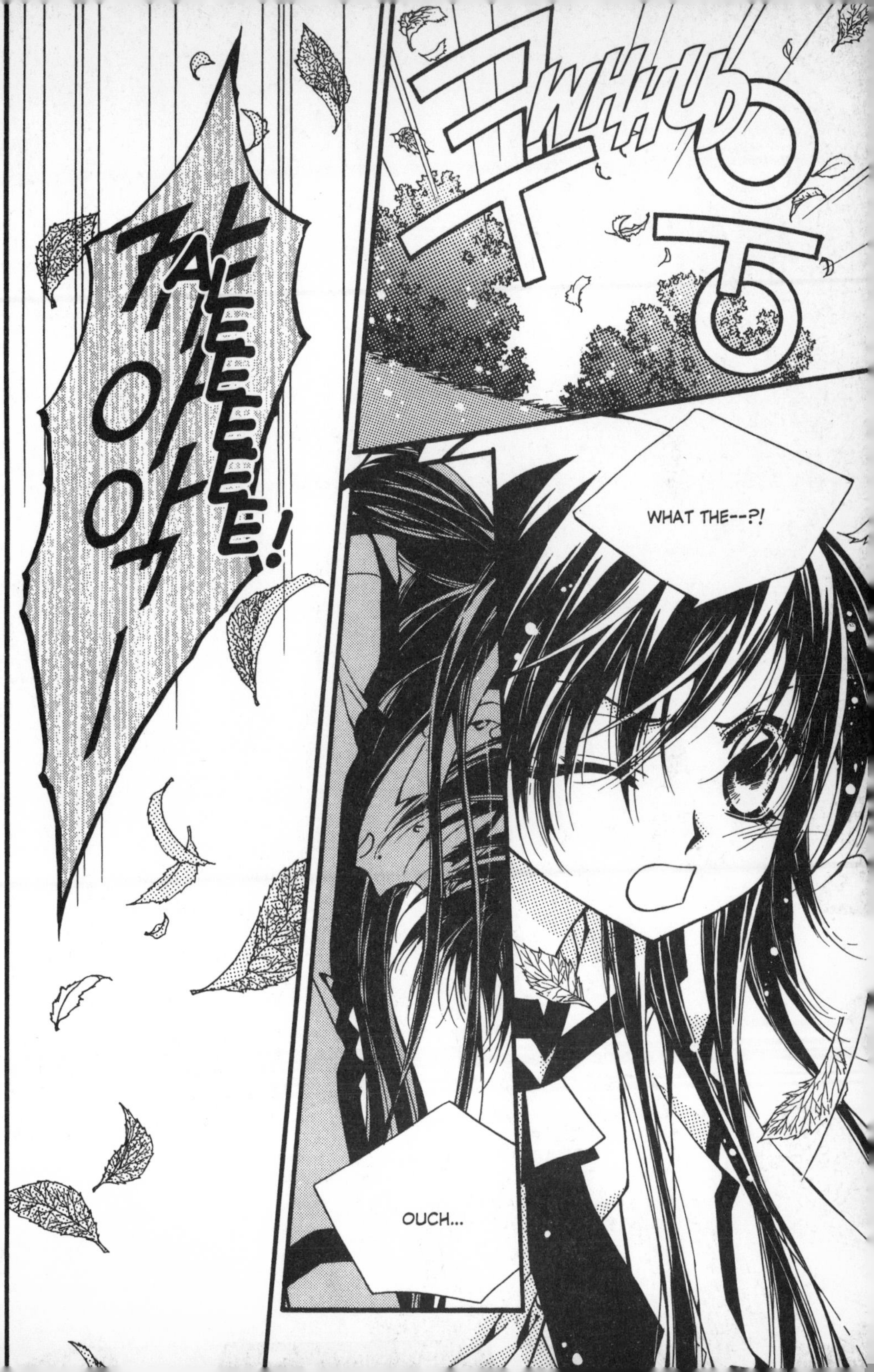
WHUD
WHAT THE--?!
OUCH...

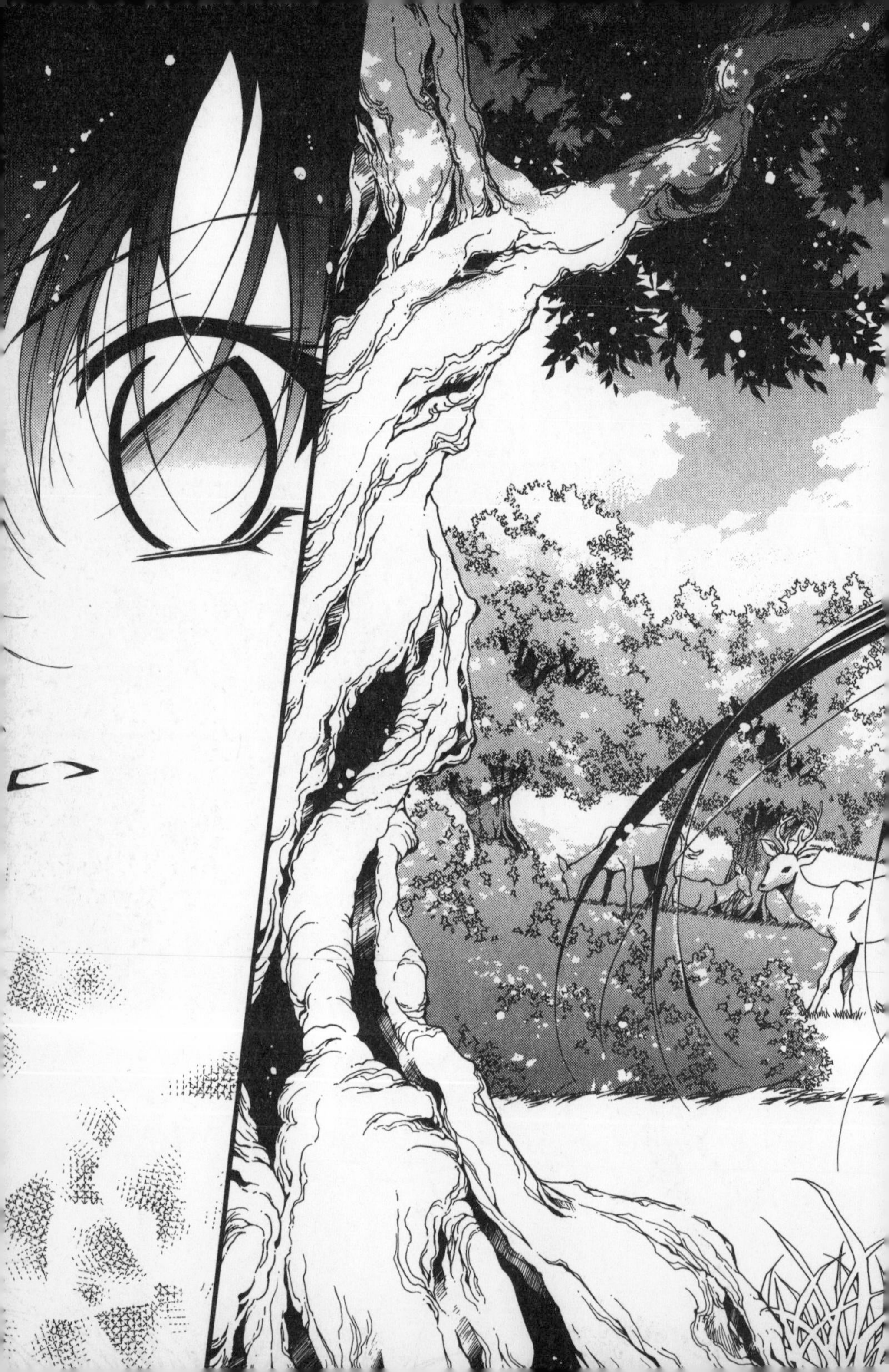

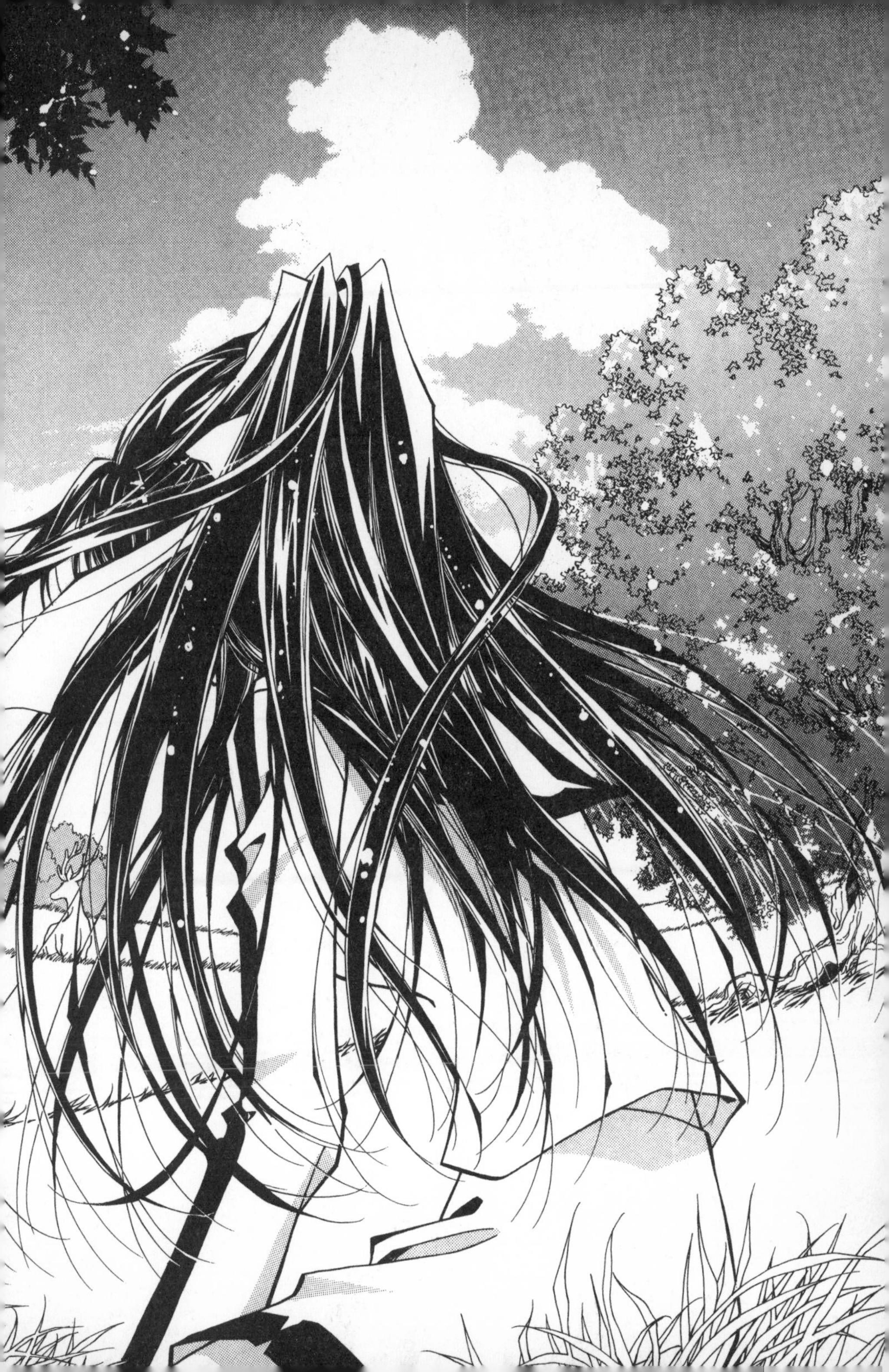

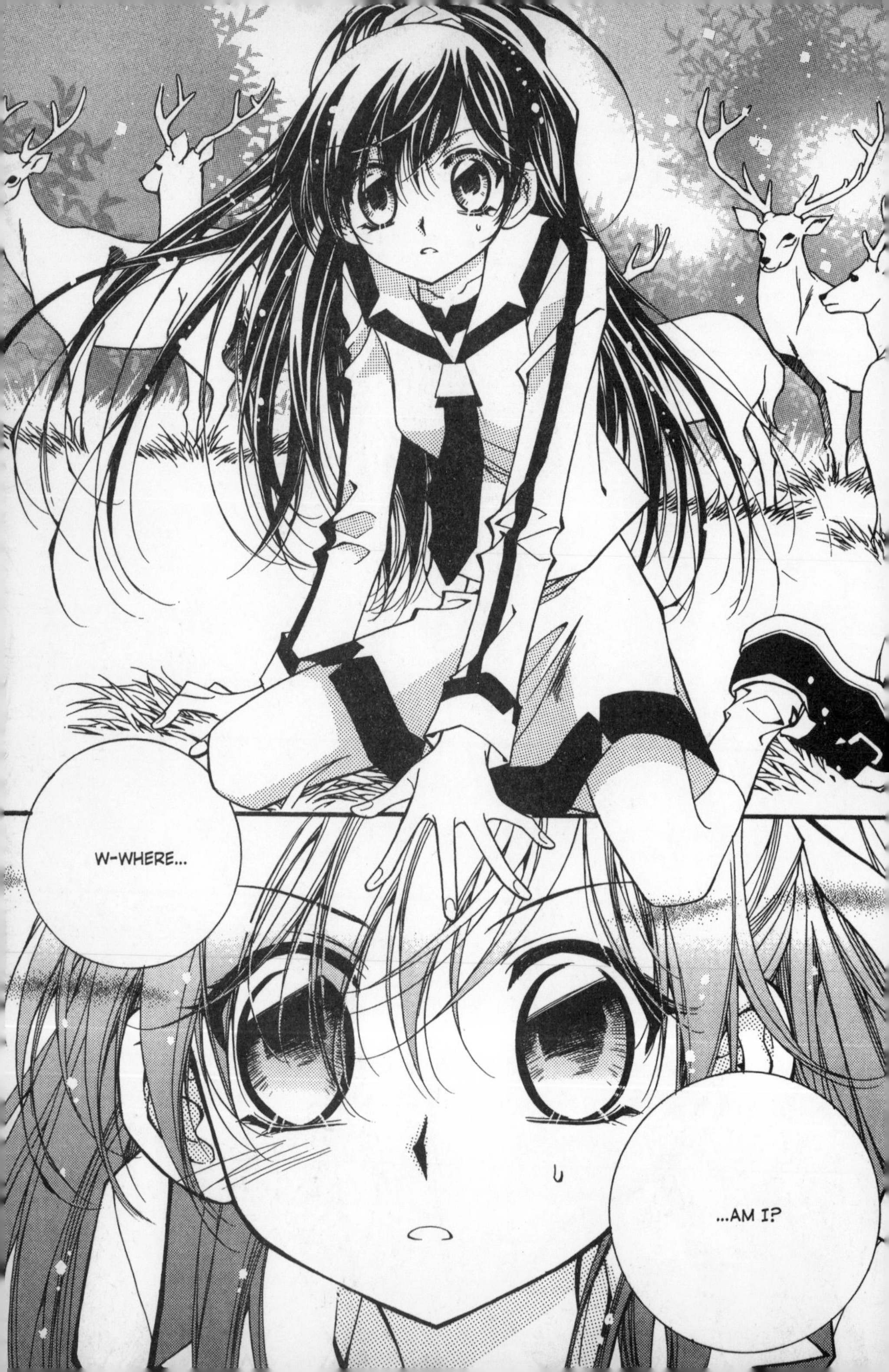
W-WHERE...
...AM I?

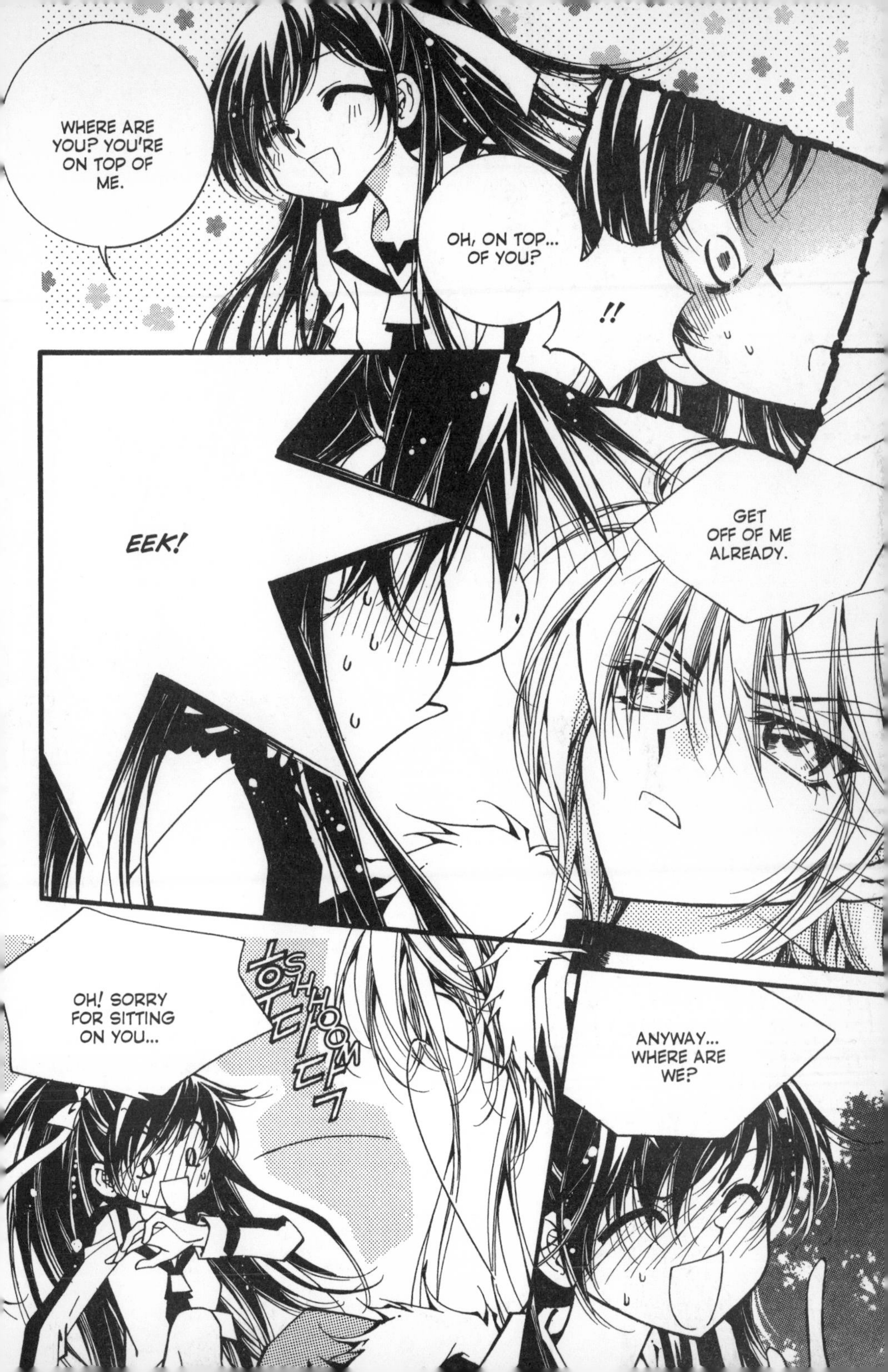
WHERE ARE YOU? YOU'RE ON TOP OF ME.
OH, ON TOP... OF YOU?
!!
EEK!
GET OFF OF ME ALREADY.
OH! SORRY FOR SITTING ON YOU...
SHHOOM
ANYWAY... WHERE ARE WE?

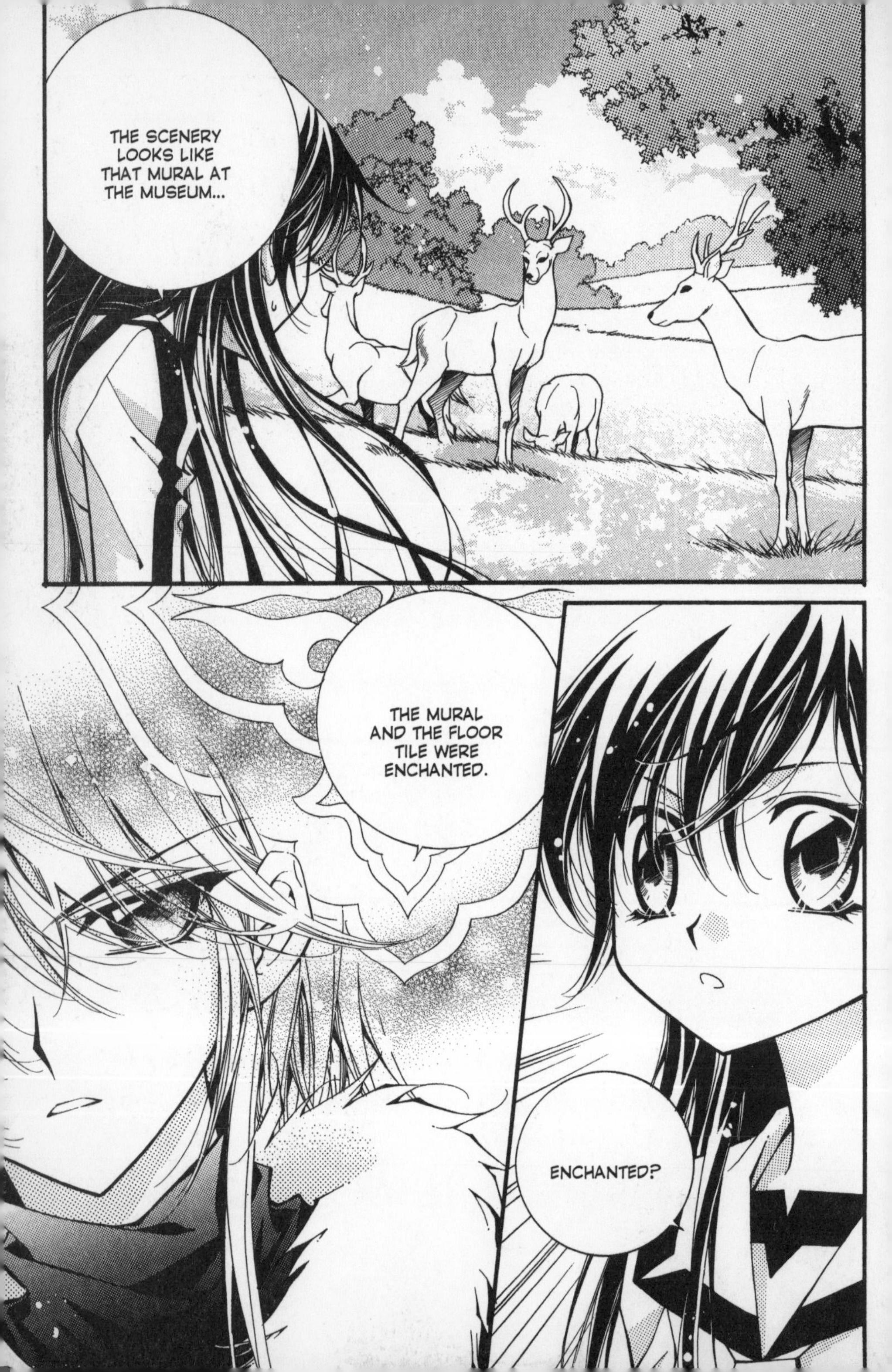
THE SCENERY LOOKS LIKE THAT MURAL AT THE MUSEUM...
THE MURAL AND THE FLOOR TILE WERE ENCHANTED.
ENCHANTED?

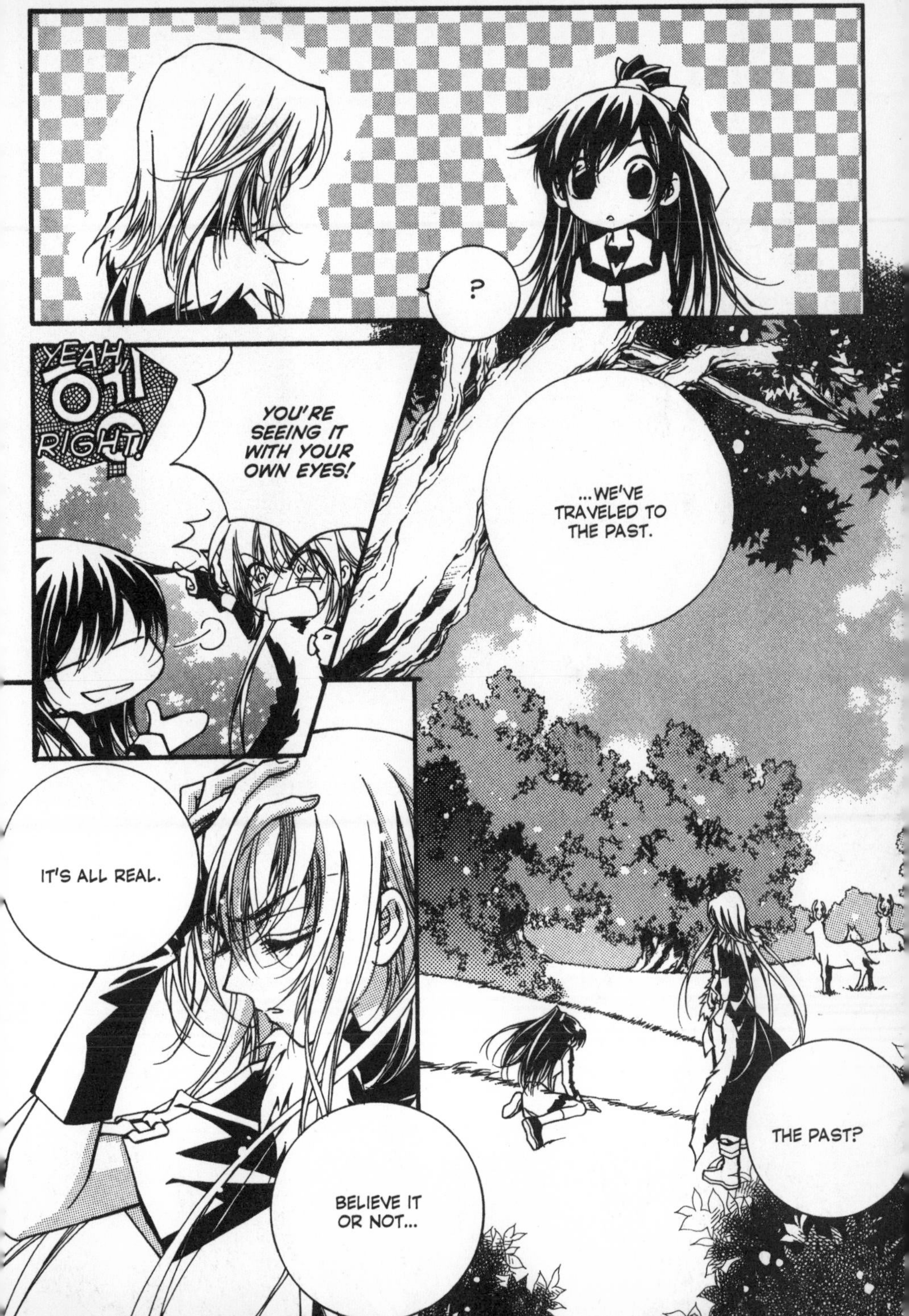

?
YEAH, RIGHT!
YOU'RE SEEING IT WITH YOUR OWN EYES!
IT'S ALL REAL.
BELIEVE IT OR NOT...
...WE'VE TRAVELED TO THE PAST.
THE PAST?

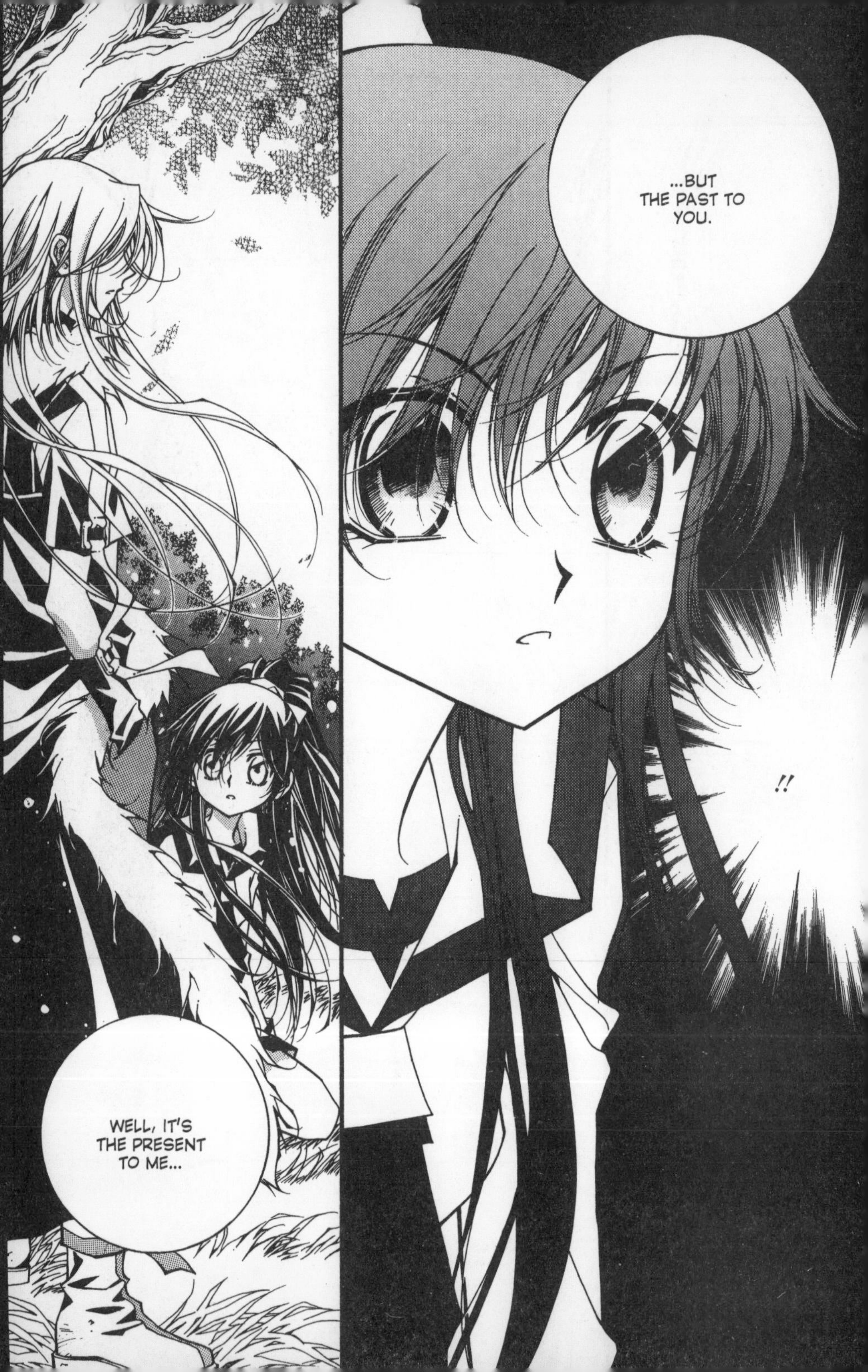
WELL, IT'S THE PRESENT TO ME...
...BUT THE PAST TO YOU.
!!

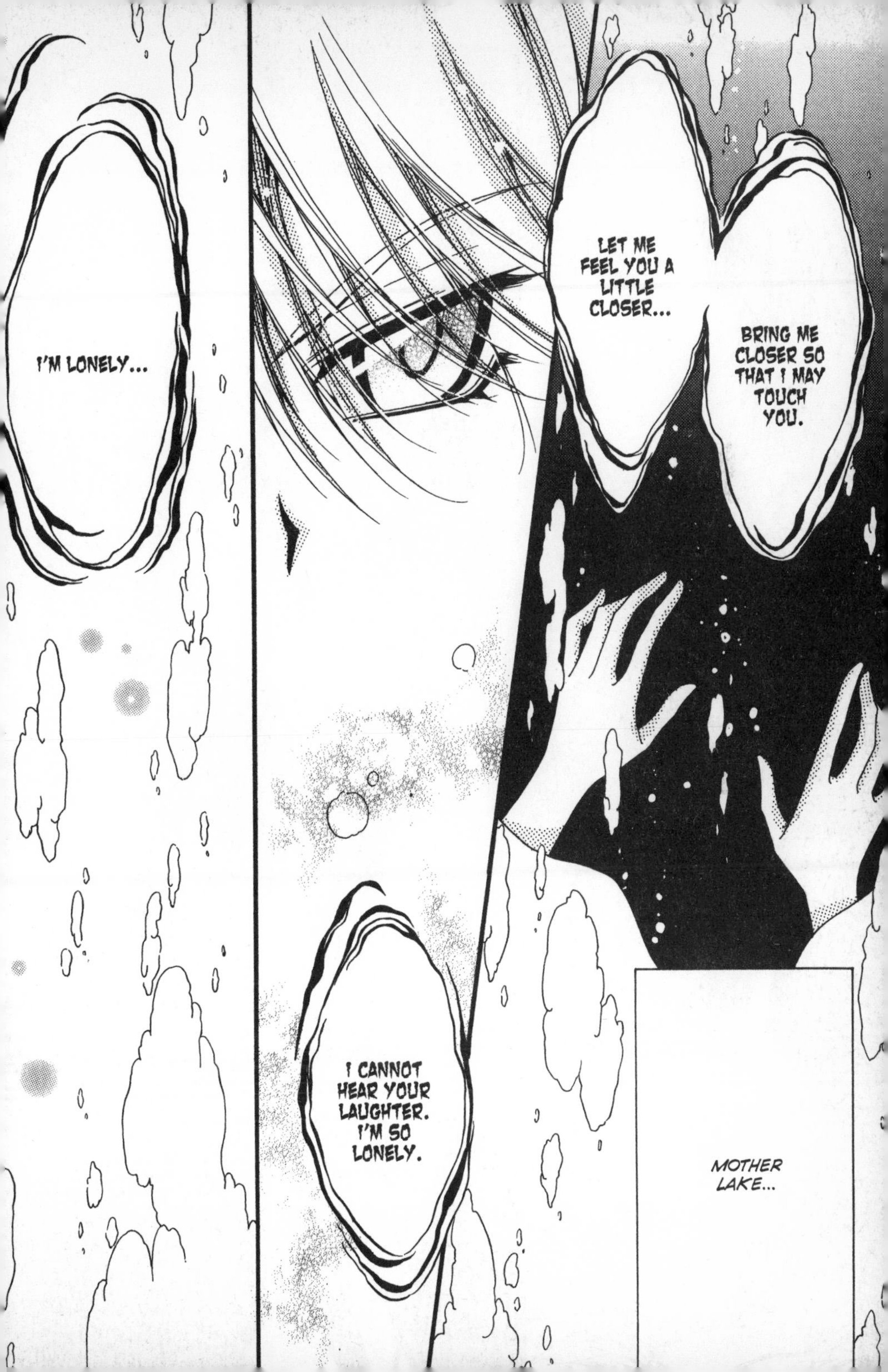
I'M LONELY...
I CANNOT HEAR YOUR LAUGHTER. I'M SO LONELY.
LET ME FEEL YOU A LITTLE CLOSER...
BRING ME CLOSER SO THAT I MAY TOUCH YOU.
MOTHER LAKE...

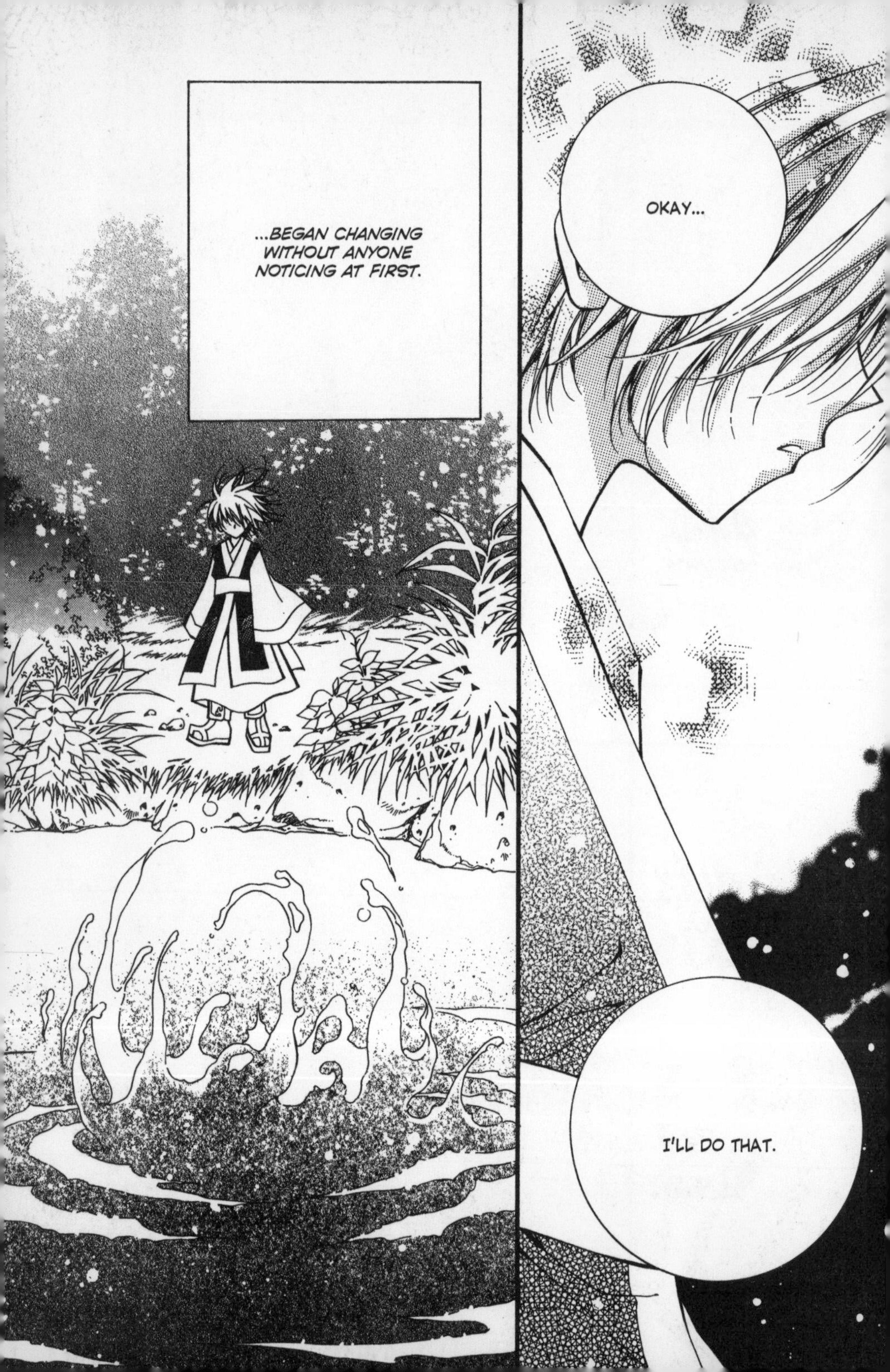
...BEGAN CHANGING WITHOUT ANYONE NOTICING AT FIRST.
OKAY...
I'LL DO THAT.

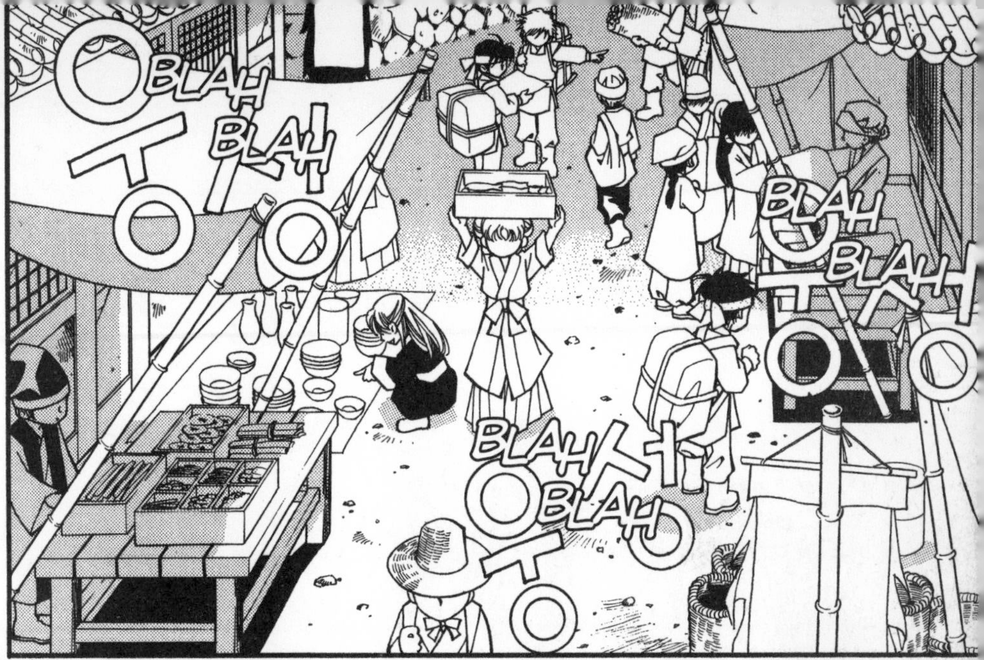
BLAH BLAH
BLAH BLAH
BLAH BLAH

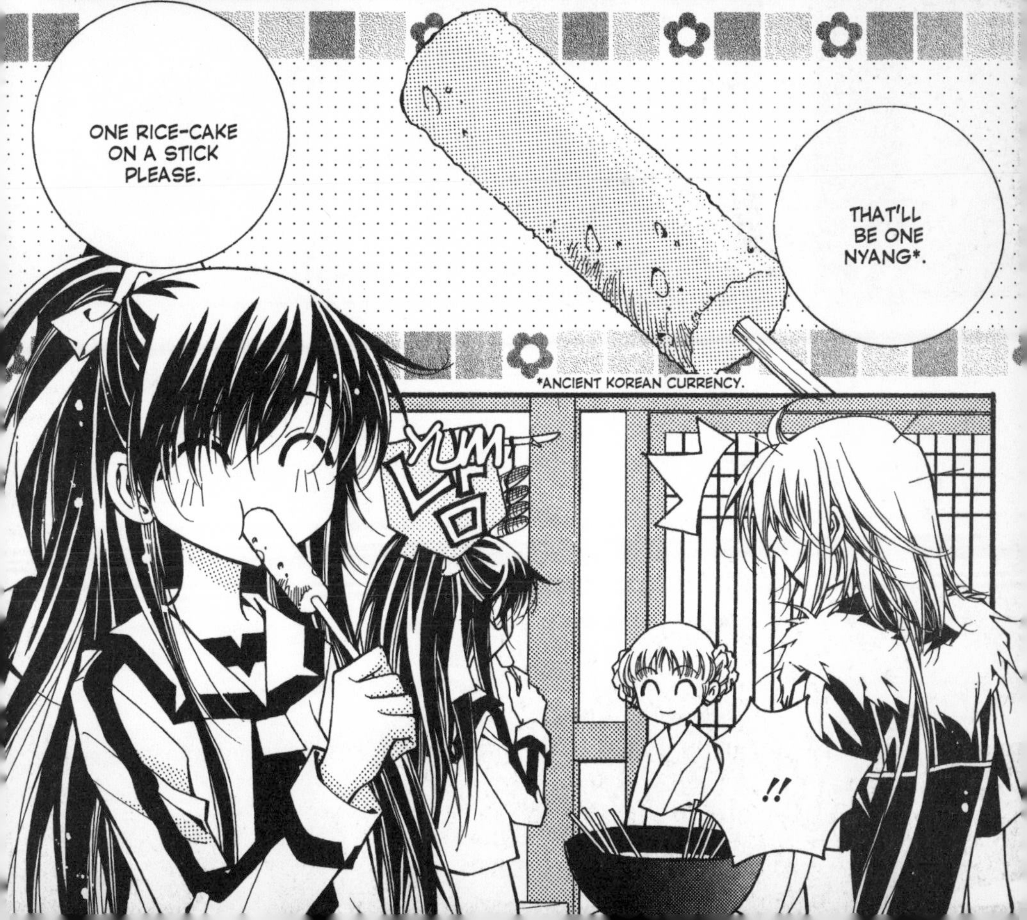
ONE RICE-CAKE ON A STICK PLEASE.
THAT'LL BE ONE NYANG*.
*ANCIENT KOREAN CURRENCY.
YUM
!!

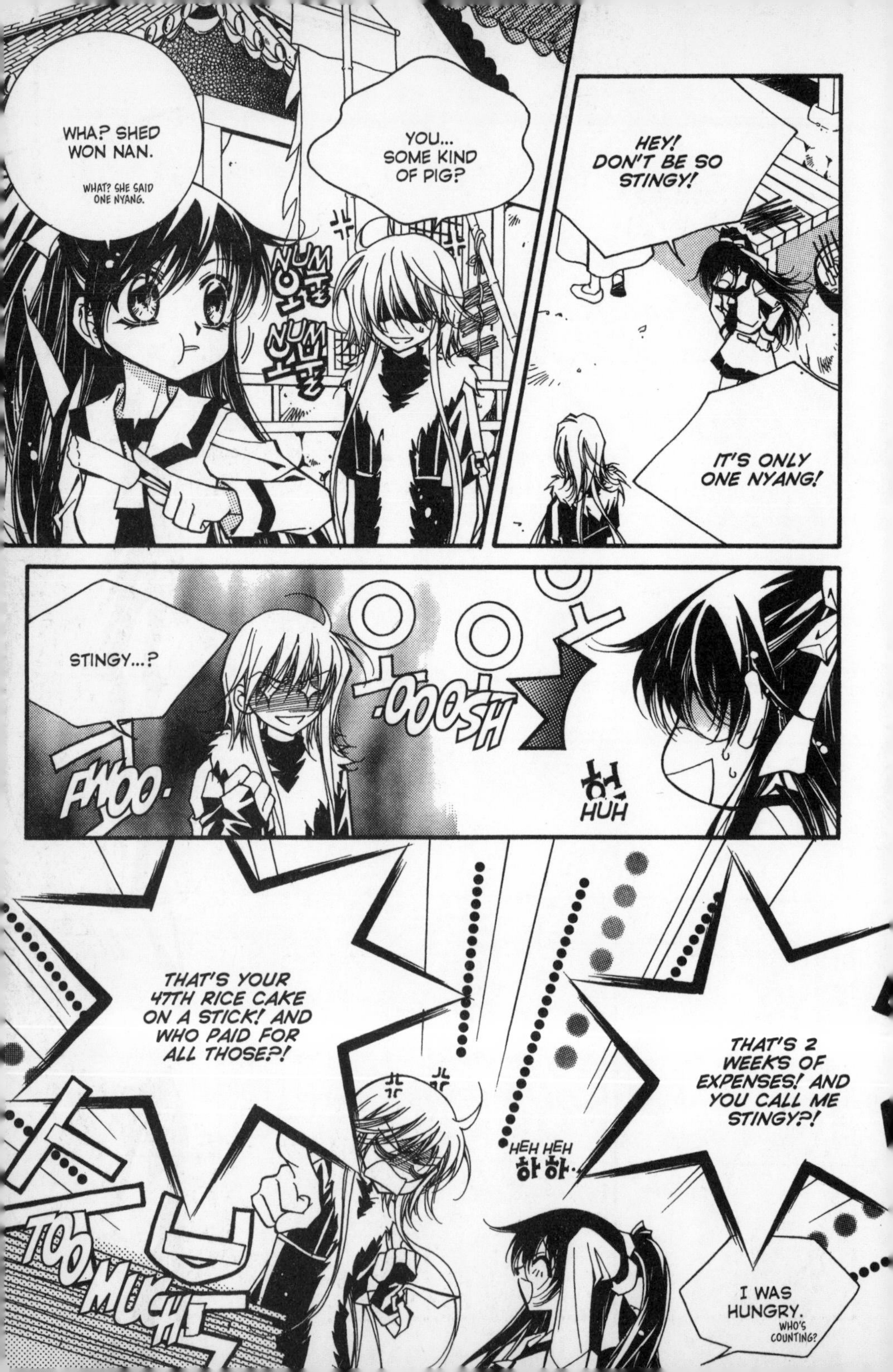
WHA? SHED WON NAN.
WHAT? SHE SAID ONE NYANG.
YOU... SOME KIND OF PIG?
NUM NUM
HEY! DON'T BE SO STINGY!
IT'S ONLY ONE NYANG!
STINGY...?
PHOO-
WOOOSH
HUH
THAT'S YOUR 47TH RICE CAKE ON A STICK! AND WHO PAID FOR ALL THOSE?!
THAT'S 2 WEEKS OF EXPENSES! AND YOU CALL ME STINGY?!
HEH HEH
하하..
TOO MUCH
I WAS HUNGRY.
WHO'S COUNTING?

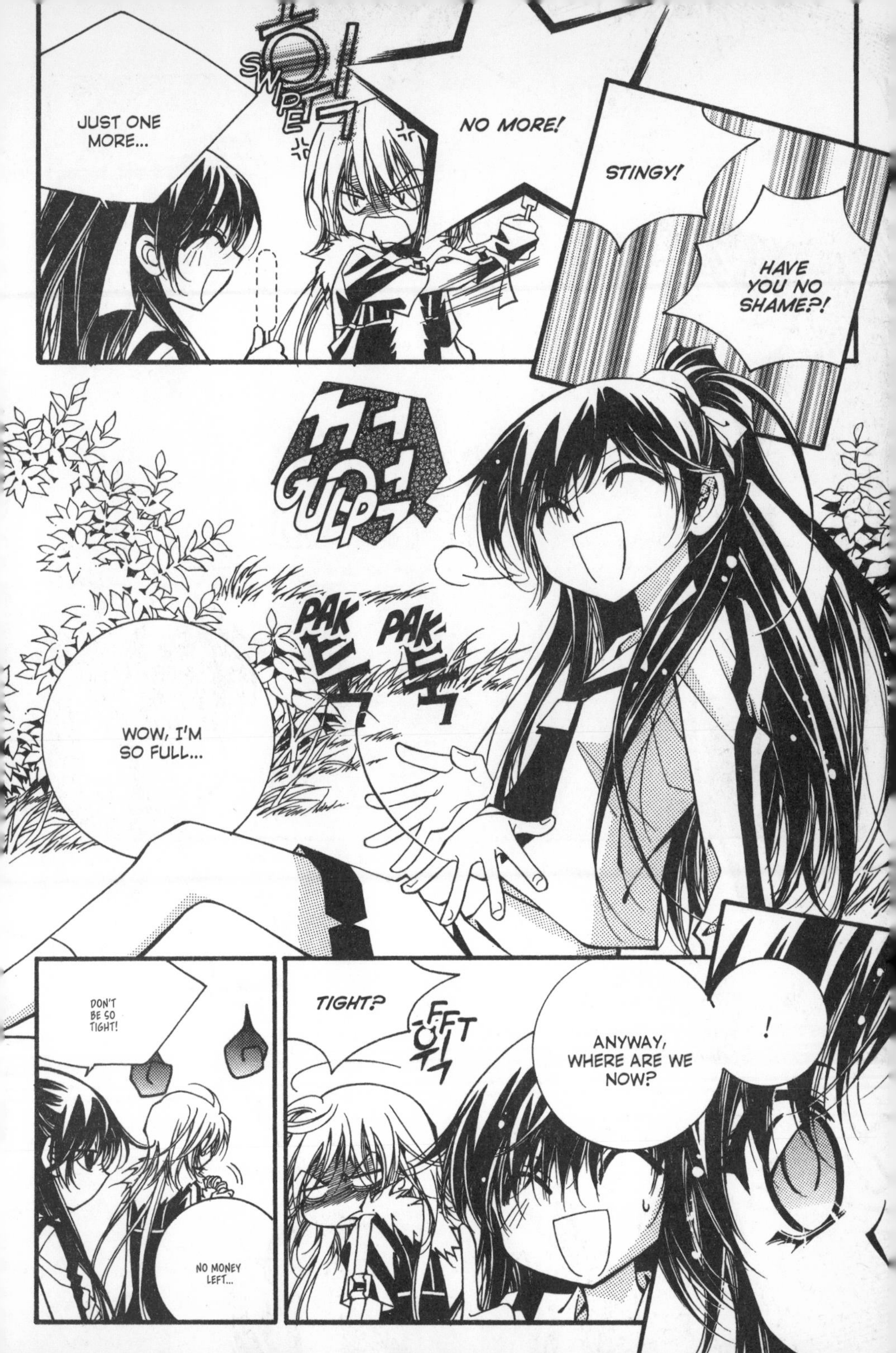
JUST ONE MORE...
SWIPE
NO MORE!
STINGY!
HAVE YOU NO SHAME?!
GULP
PAK PAK
WOW, I'M SO FULL...
DON'T BE SO TIGHT!
NO MONEY LEFT...
TIGHT?
FFFT
!
ANYWAY, WHERE ARE WE NOW?

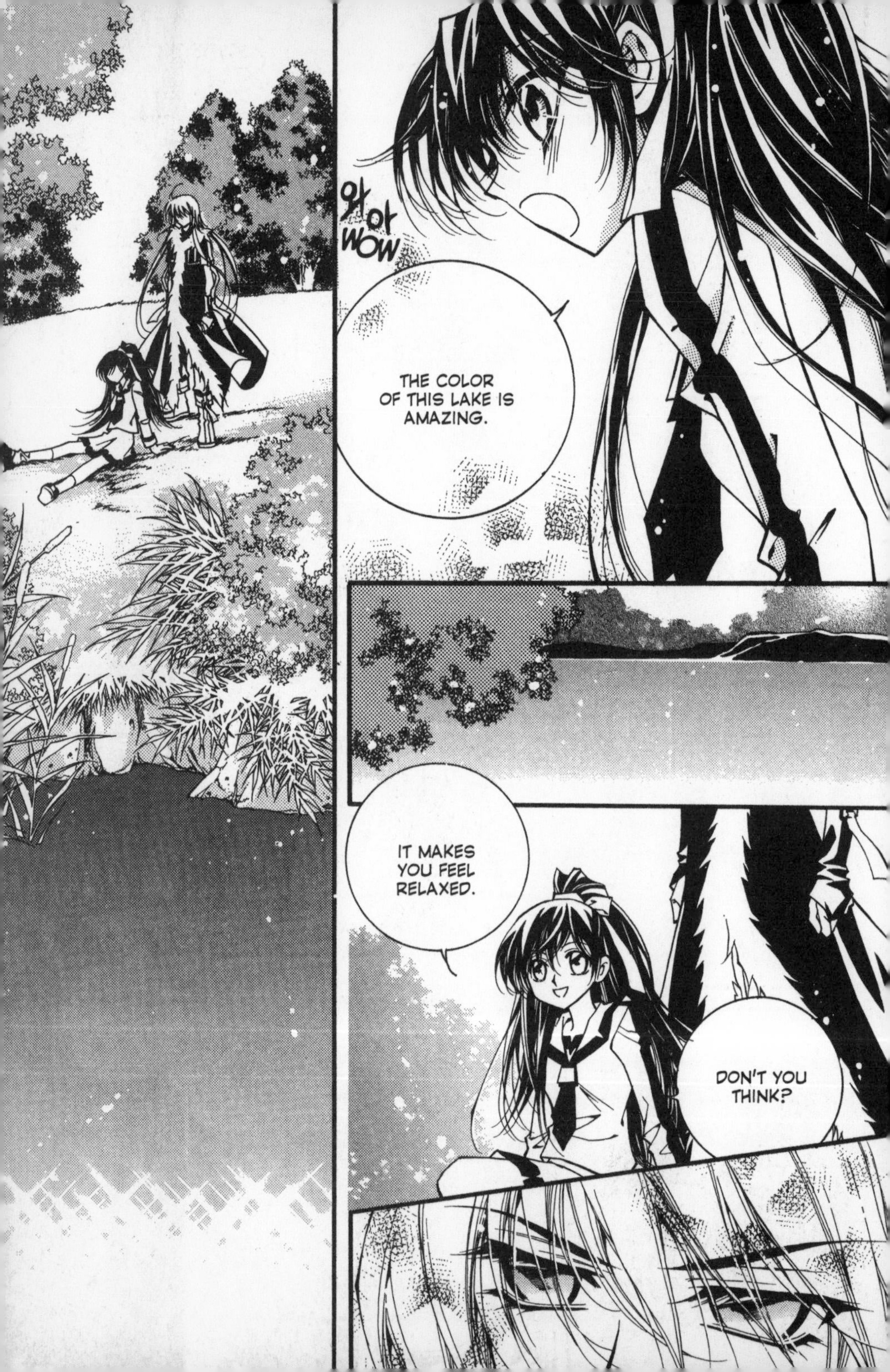
와아
WOW
THE COLOR OF THIS LAKE IS AMAZING.
IT MAKES YOU FEEL RELAXED.
DON'T YOU THINK?

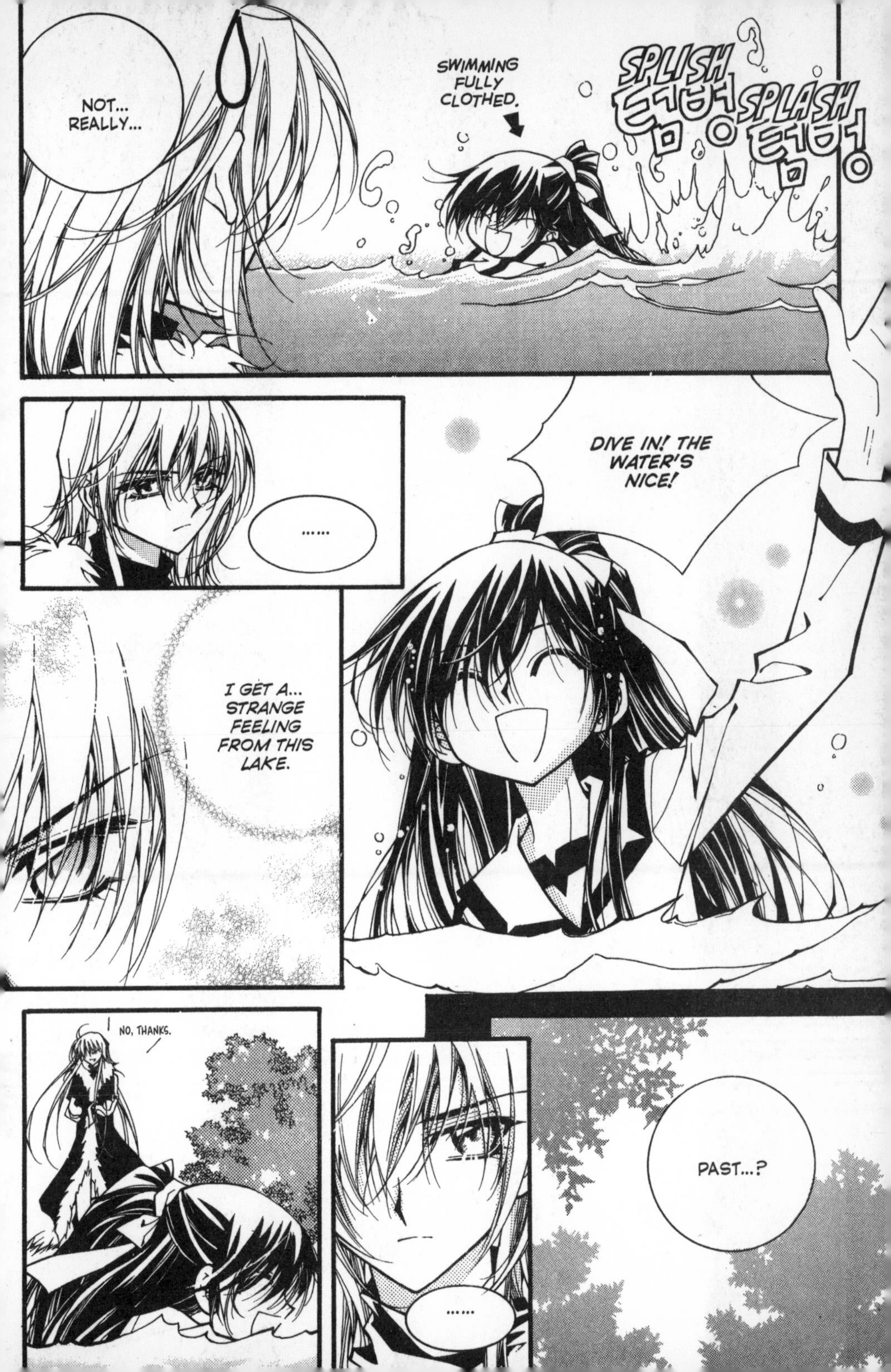
NOT... REALLY...
SWIMMING FULLY CLOTHED.
SPLISH
텀벙
SPLASH
텀벙
......
I GET A... STRANGE FEELING FROM THIS LAKE.
DIVE IN! THE WATER'S NICE!
NO, THANKS.
PAST...?
......

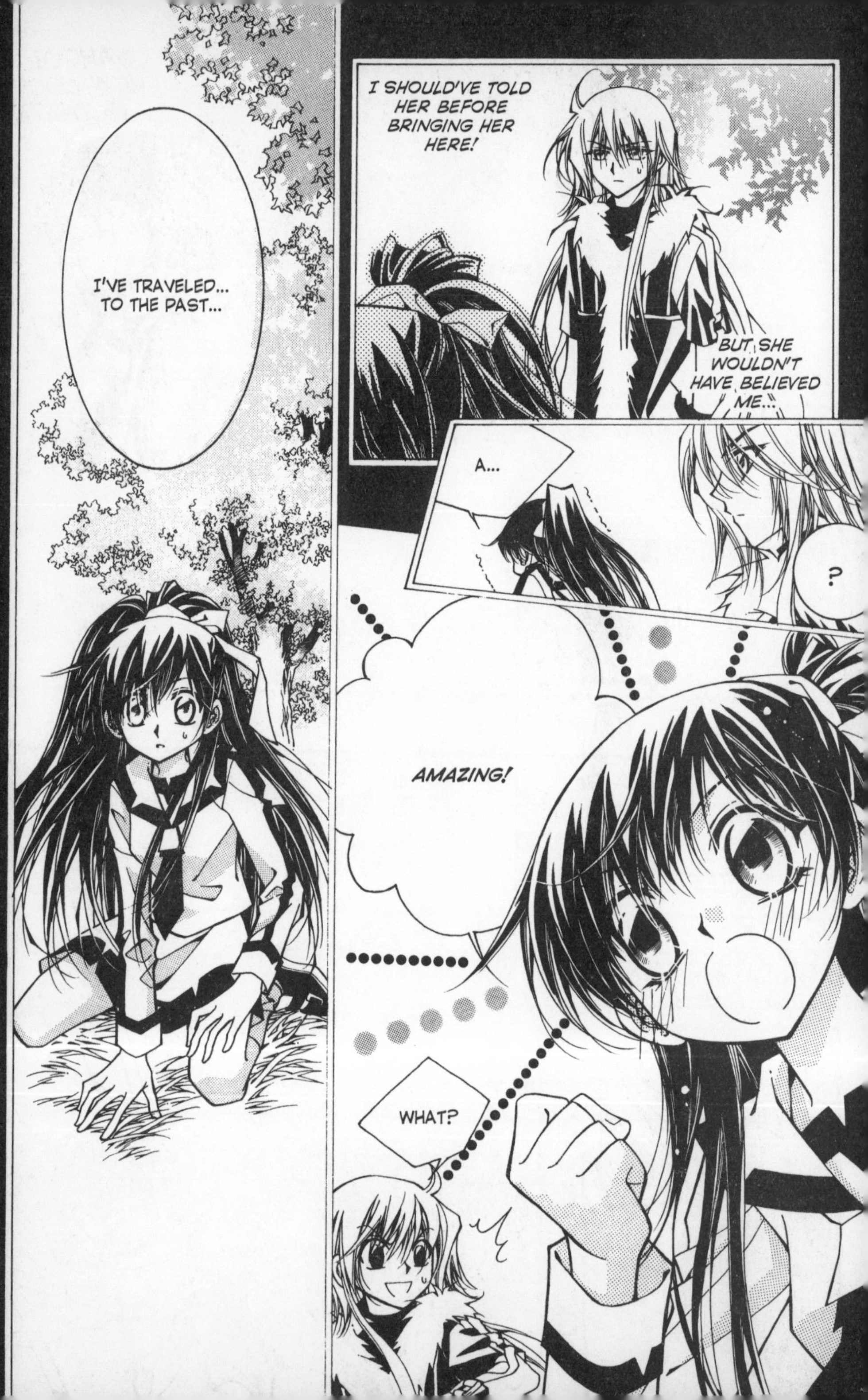
I'VE TRAVELED... TO THE PAST...
I SHOULD'VE TOLD HER BEFORE BRINGING HER HERE!
BUT SHE WOULDN'T HAVE BELIEVED ME...
A...
?
AMAZING!
WHAT?

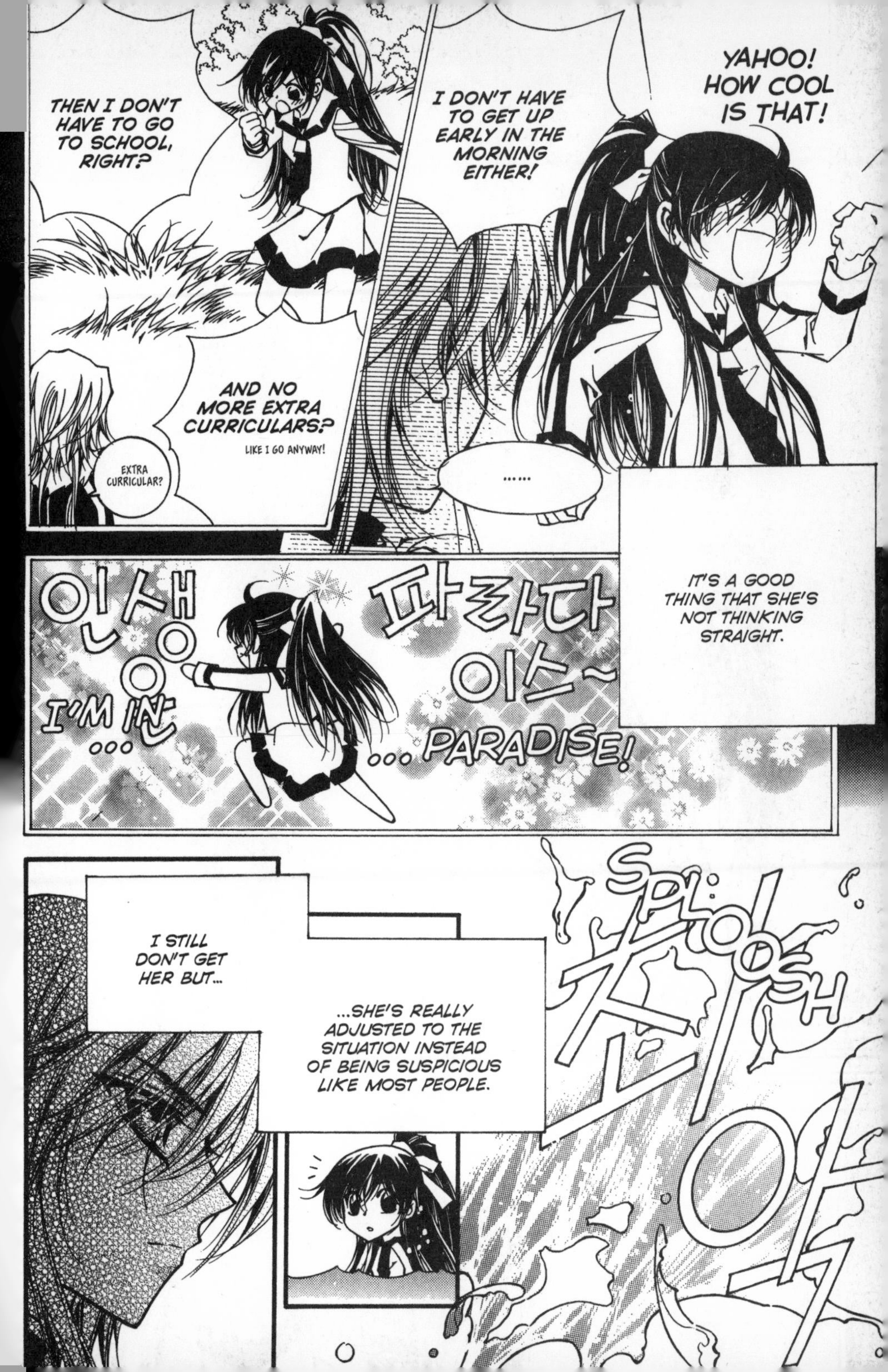
THEN I DON'T HAVE TO GO TO SCHOOL, RIGHT?
AND NO MORE EXTRA CURRICULARS?
LIKE I GO ANYWAY!
EXTRA CURRICULAR?
I DON'T HAVE TO GET UP EARLY IN THE MORNING EITHER!
YAHOO! HOW COOL IS THAT!
......
IT'S A GOOD THING THAT SHE'S NOT THINKING STRAIGHT.
인생은
I'M IN ...
파라다이스~
... PARADISE!
I STILL DON'T GET HER BUT...
...SHE'S REALLY ADJUSTED TO THE SITUATION INSTEAD OF BEING SUSPICIOUS LIKE MOST PEOPLE.
SPLOOSH
촤아악

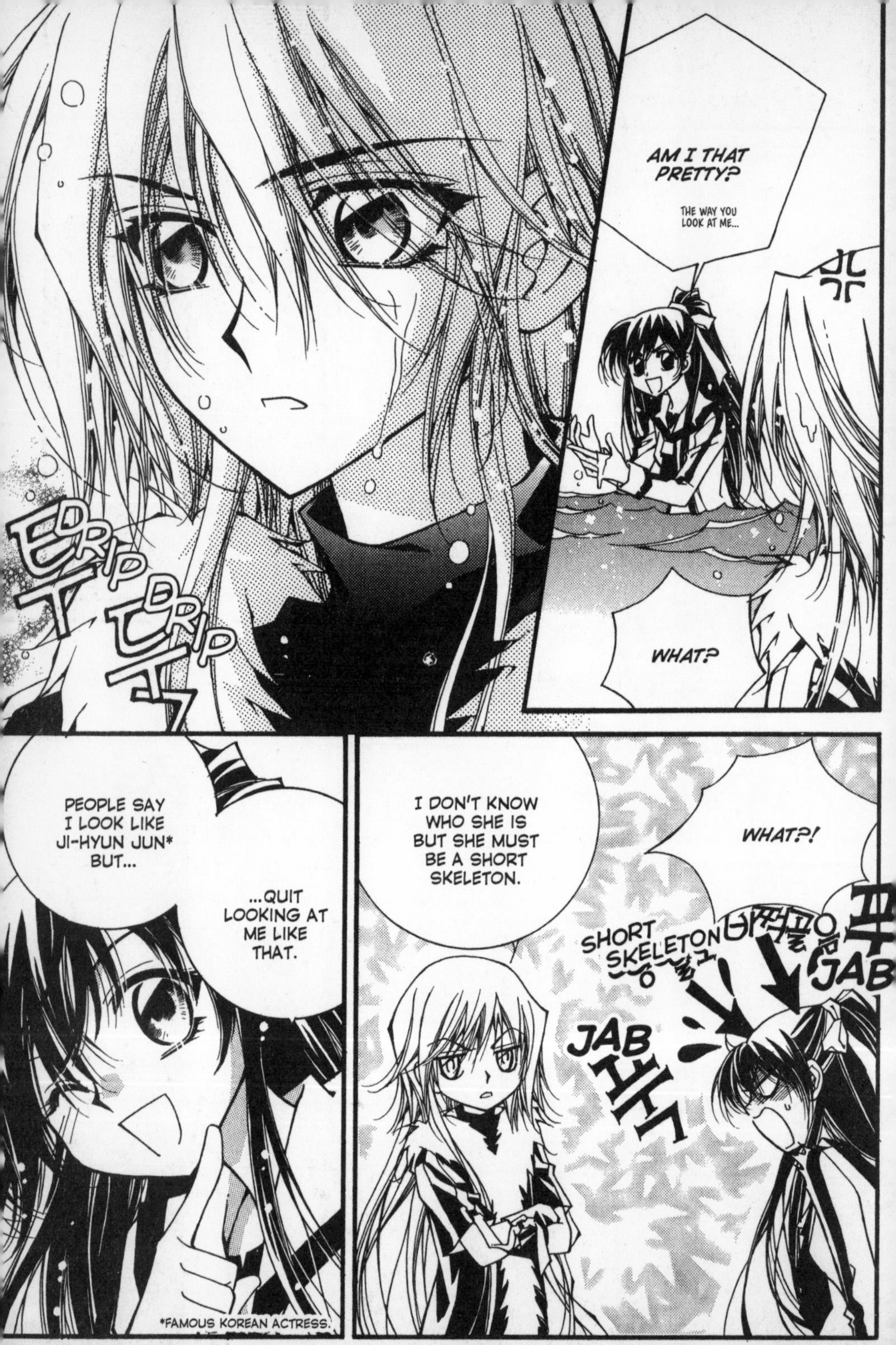

DRIP DRIP
AM I THAT PRETTY?
THE WAY YOU LOOK AT ME...
WHAT?
PEOPLE SAY I LOOK LIKE JI-HYUN JUN* BUT...
...QUIT LOOKING AT ME LIKE THAT.
*FAMOUS KOREAN ACTRESS.
I DON'T KNOW WHO SHE IS BUT SHE MUST BE A SHORT SKELETON.
WHAT?!
SHORT SKELETON
JAB
JAB

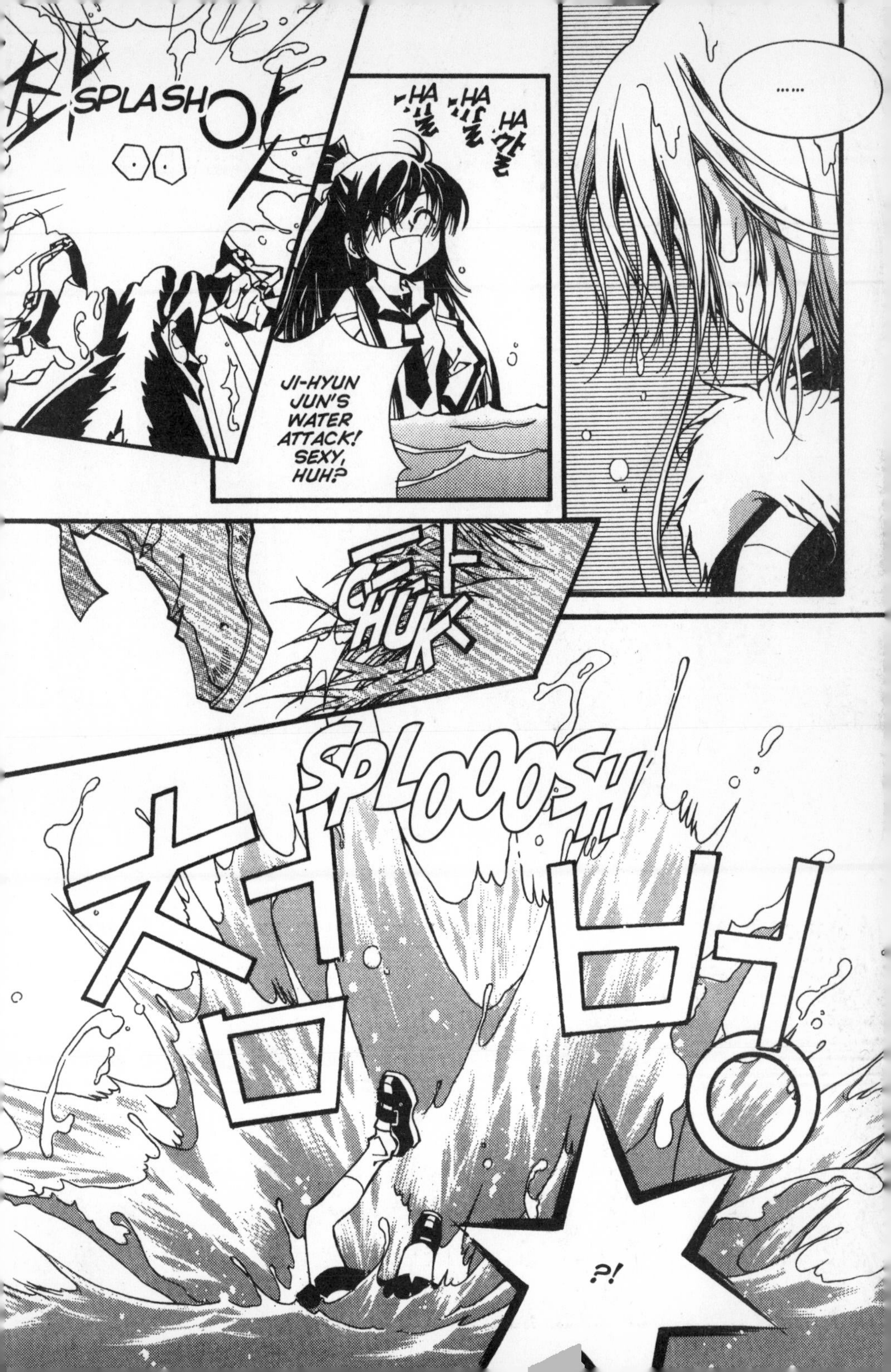
SPLASH
HA HA HA
JI-HYUN JUN'S WATER ATTACK! SEXY, HUH?
......
CHUK
SPLOOOSH
첨벙
?!

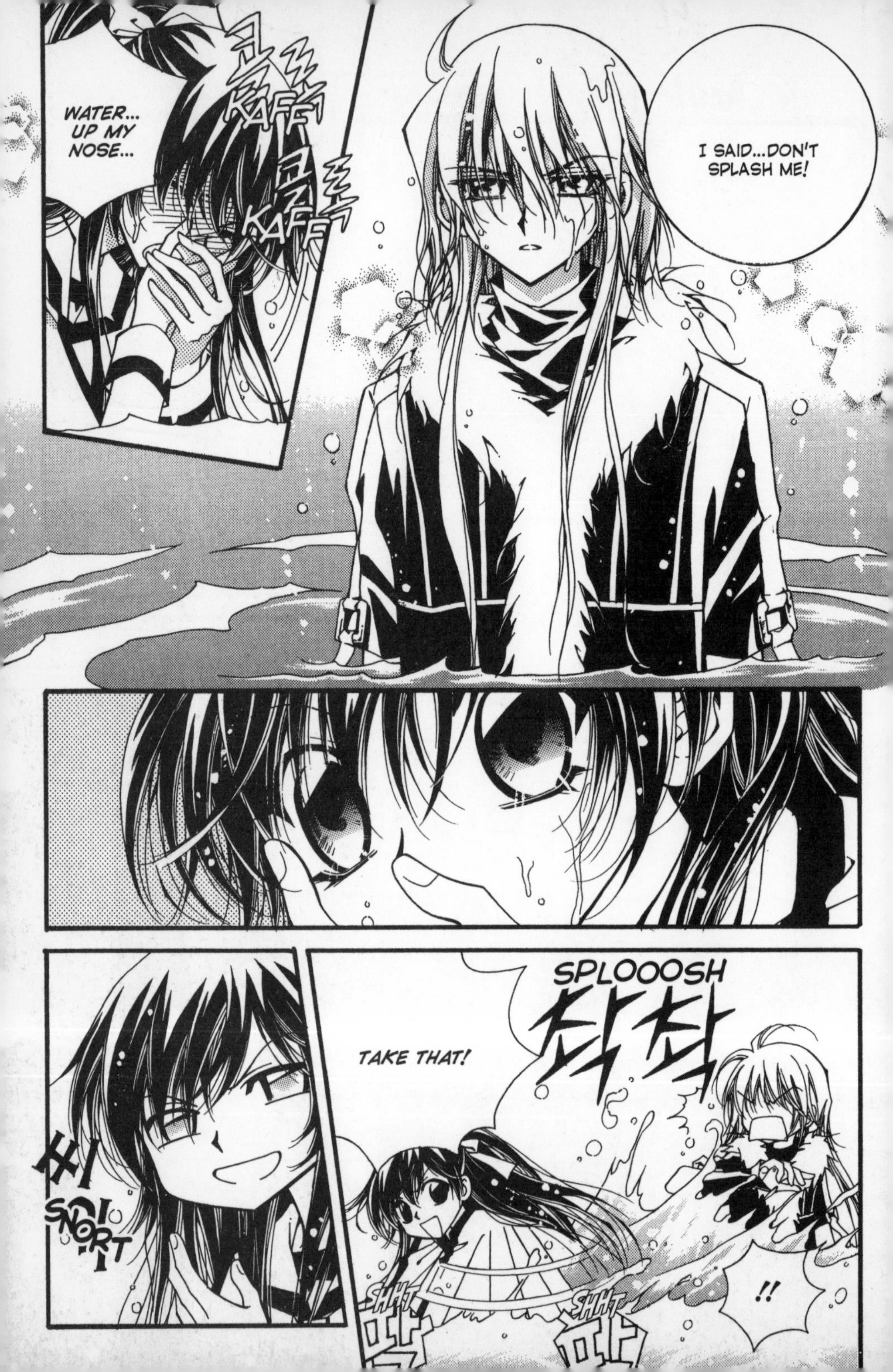
WATER... UP MY NOSE...
KAFF
KAFF
I SAID...DON'T SPLASH ME!
SNORT
TAKE THAT!
SPLOOOSH
SHHT
SHHT
!!

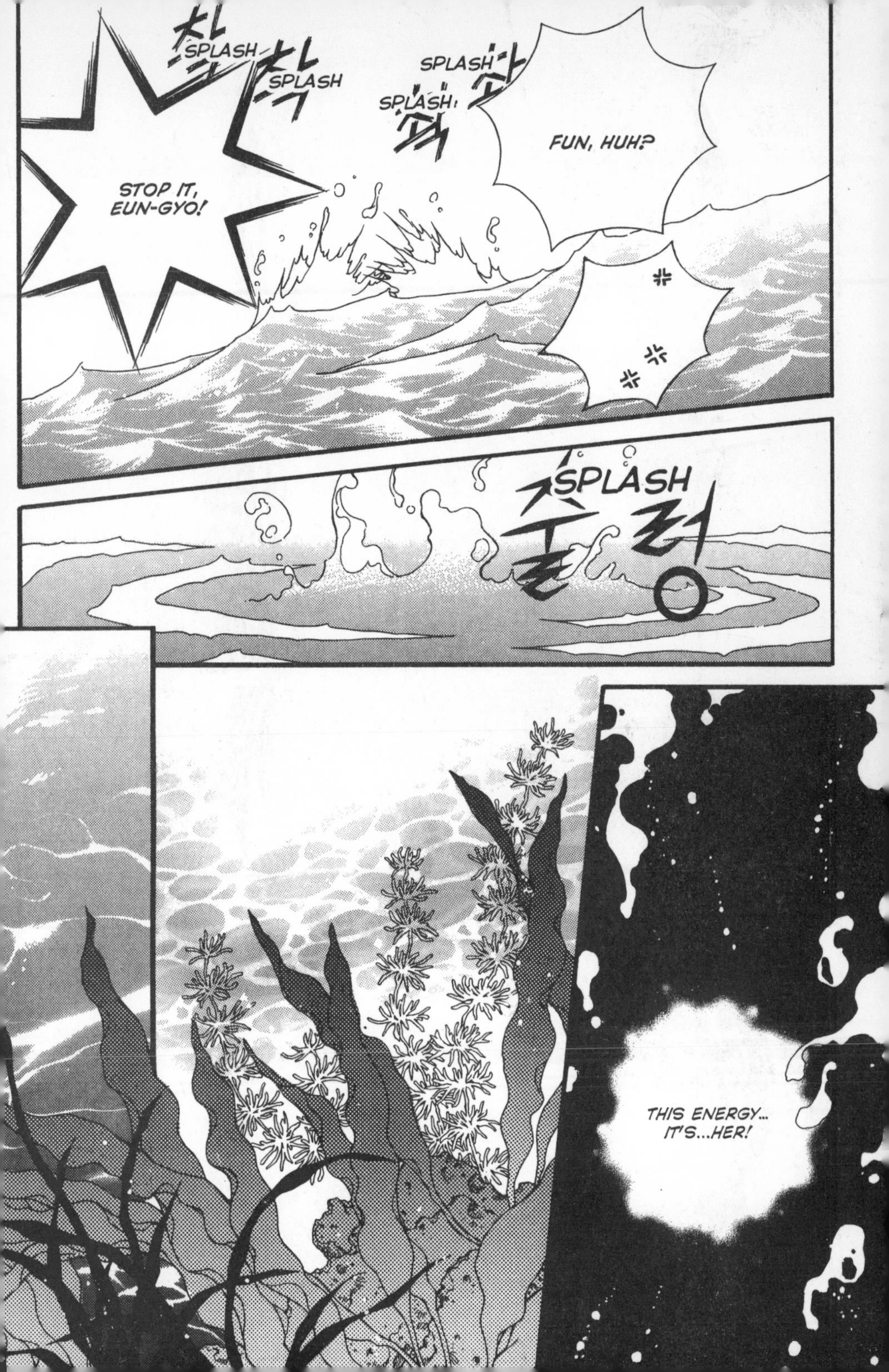
SPLASH
SPLASH
STOP IT, EUN-GYO!
SPLASH
SPLASH
FUN, HUH?
SPLASH
THIS ENERGY... IT'S...HER!

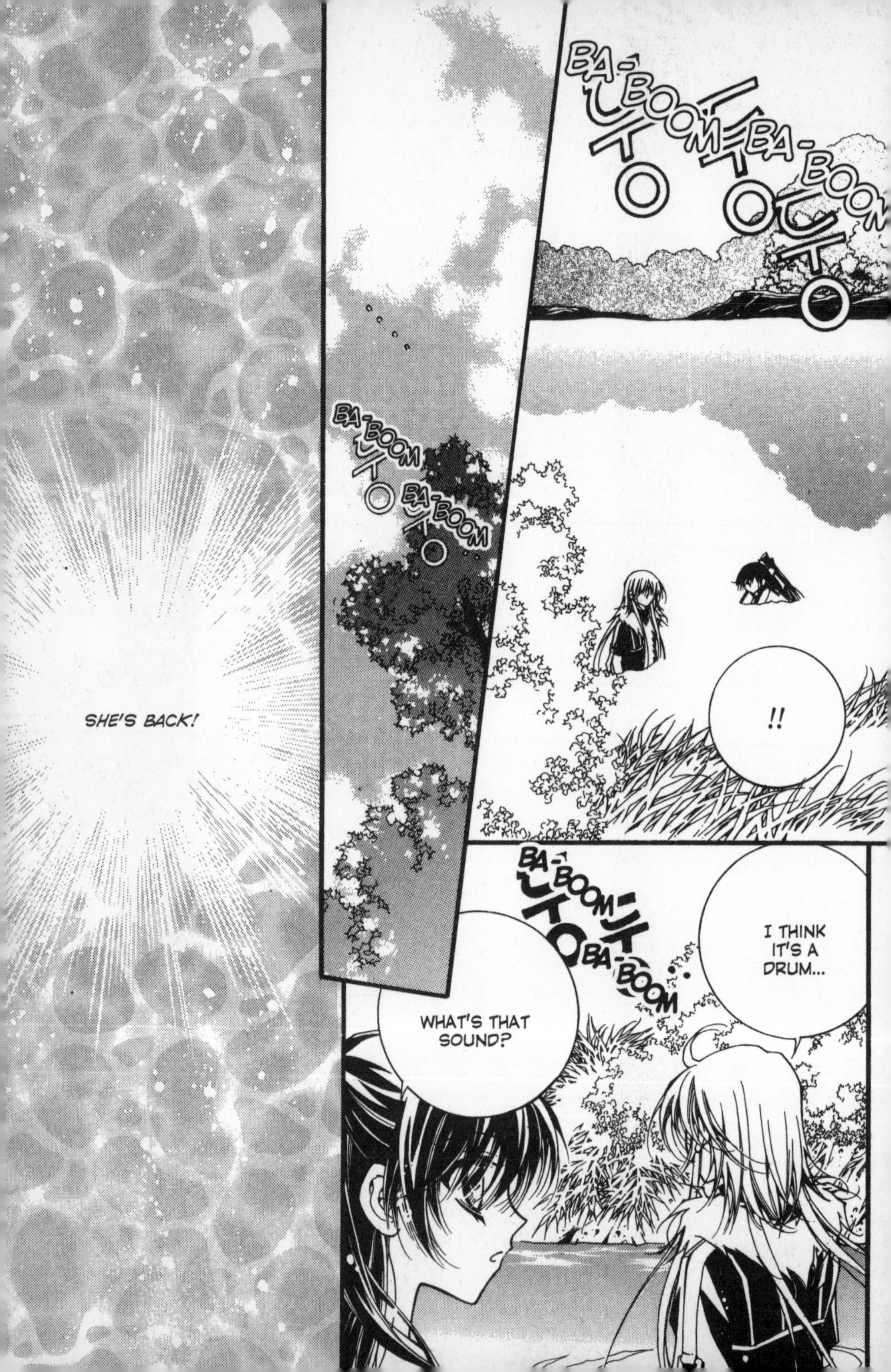
SHE'S BACK!
BA-BOOM BA-BOOM
BA-BOOM BA-BOOM
!!
BA-BOOM BA-BOOM
WHAT'S THAT SOUND?
I THINK IT'S A DRUM...

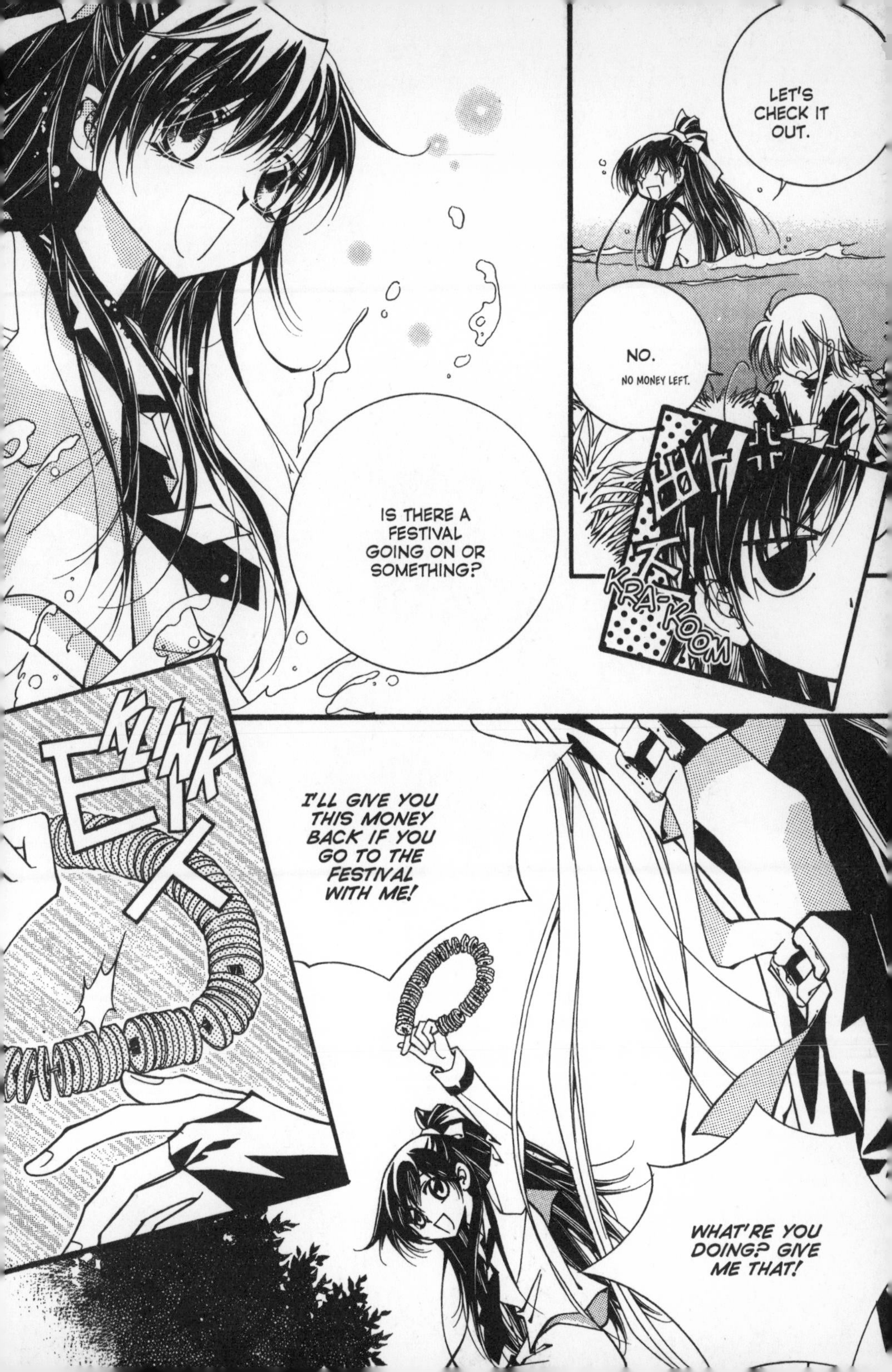
IS THERE A FESTIVAL GOING ON OR SOMETHING?
LET'S CHECK IT OUT.
NO.
NO MONEY LEFT.
KRA-KOOM
KLINK
I'LL GIVE YOU THIS MONEY BACK IF YOU GO TO THE FESTIVAL WITH ME!
WHAT'RE YOU DOING? GIVE ME THAT!

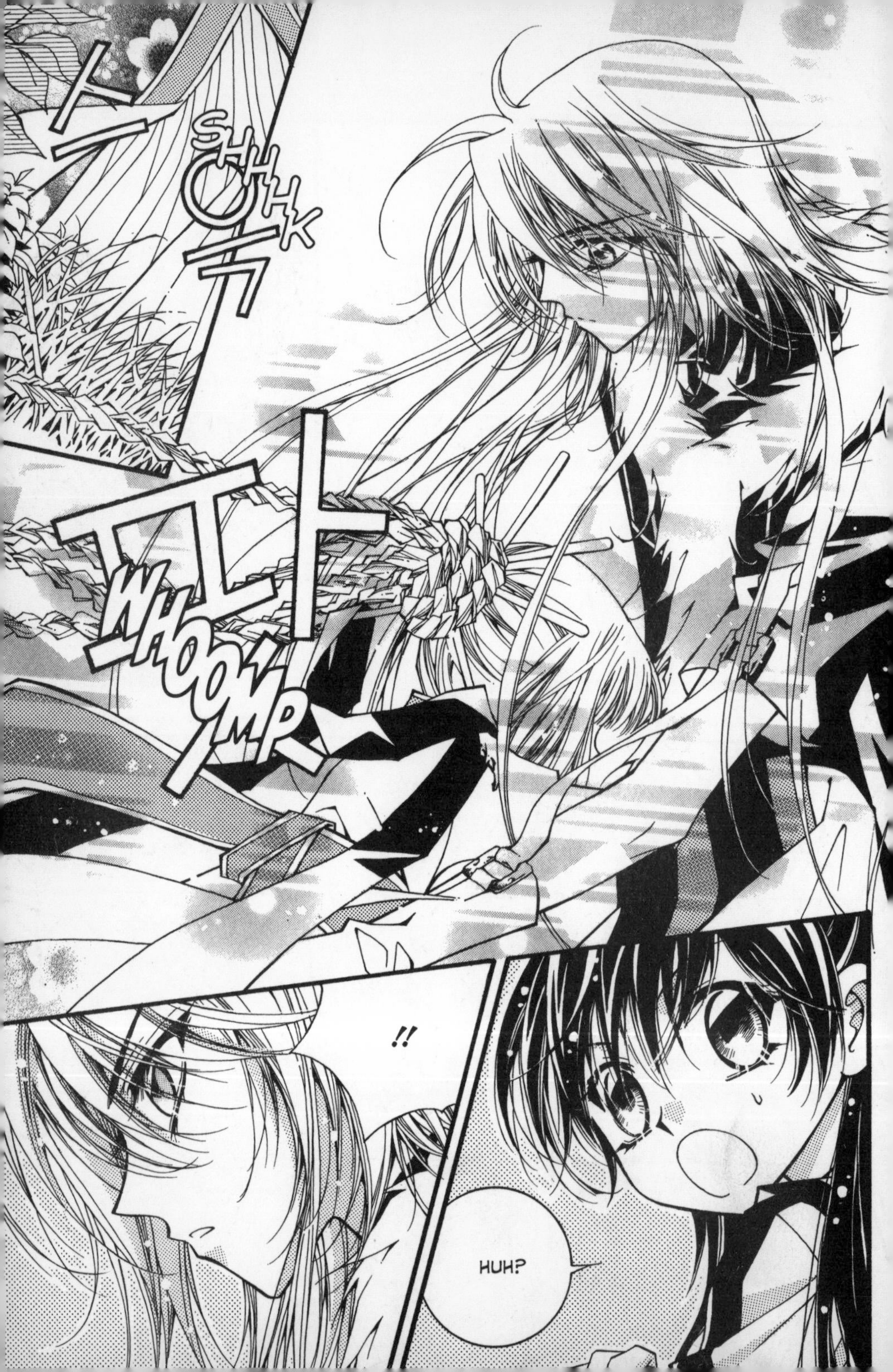
SHHHK
WHOOMP
!!
HUH?

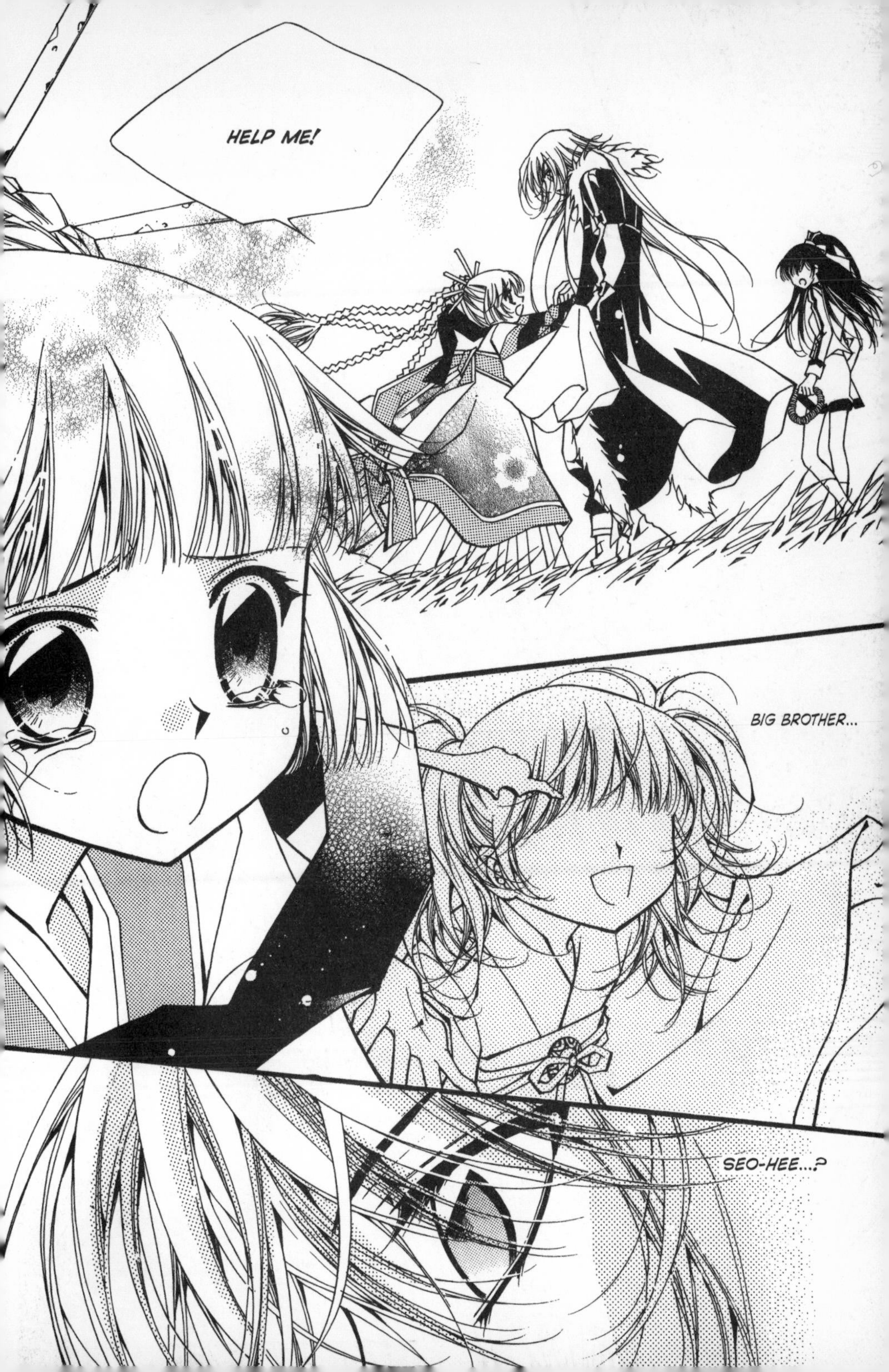
HELP ME!
BIG BROTHER...
SEO-HEE...?

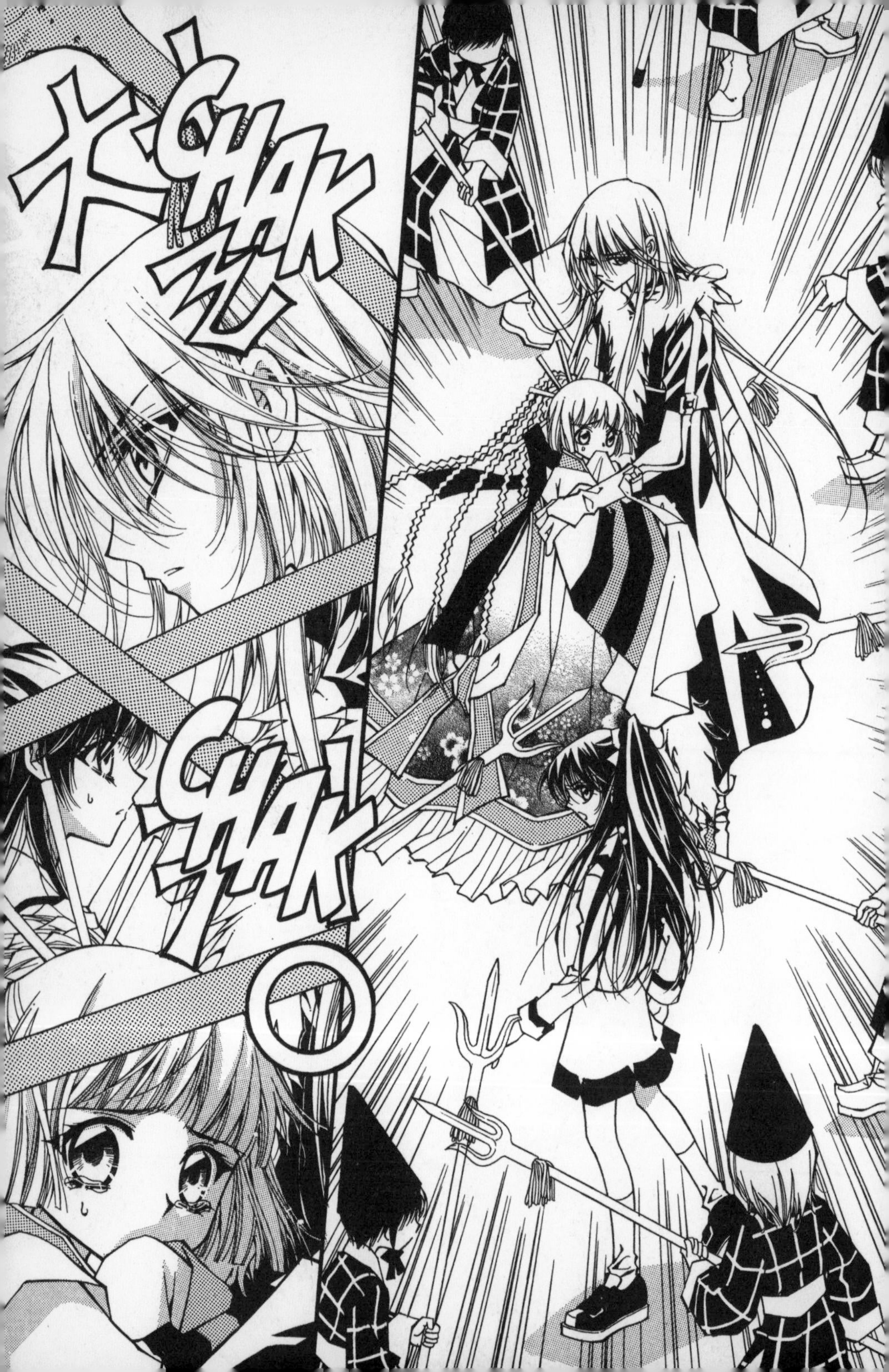
CHAK
CHAK

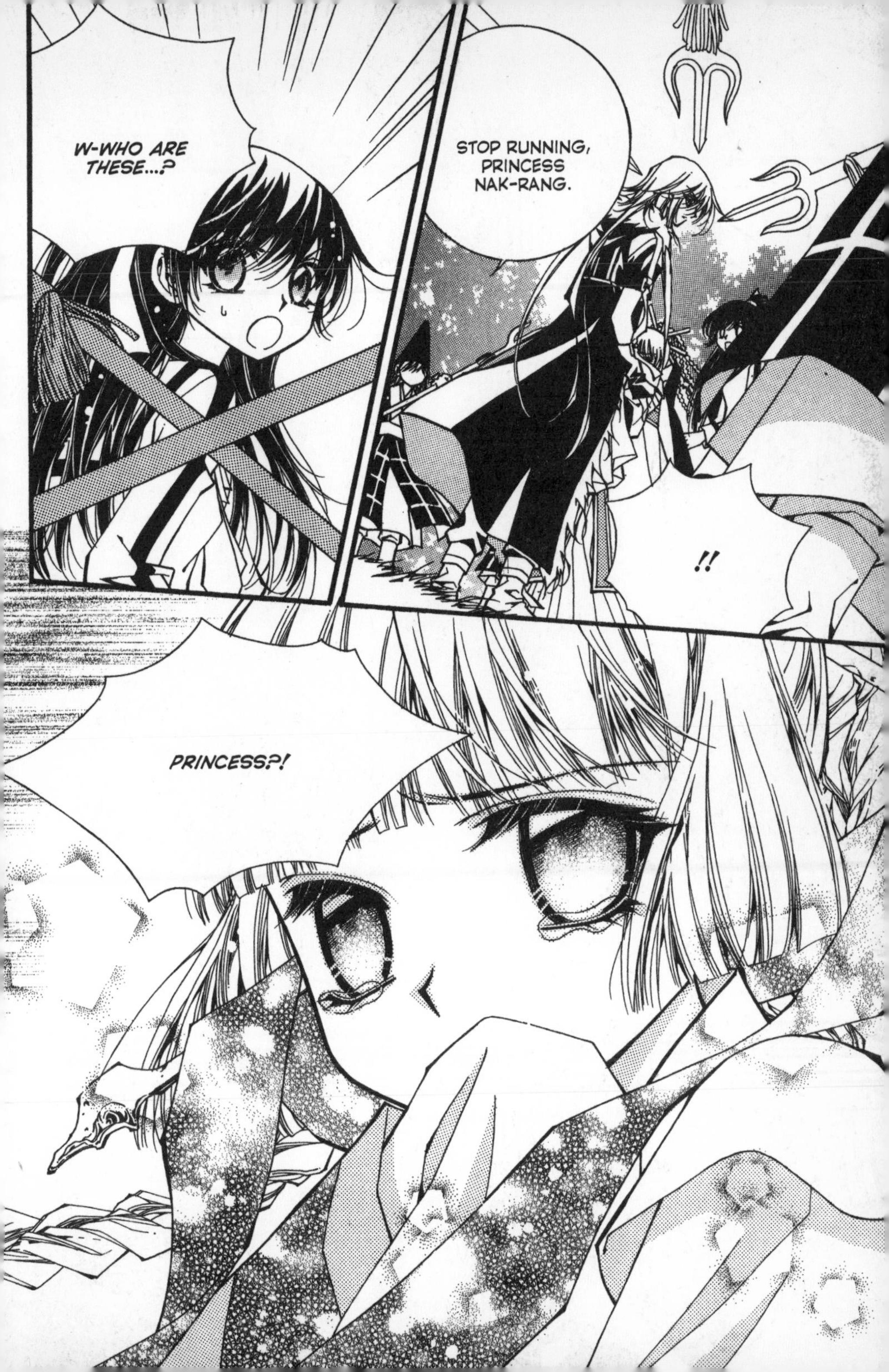
W-WHO ARE THESE...?
STOP RUNNING, PRINCESS NAK-RANG.
!!
PRINCESS?!

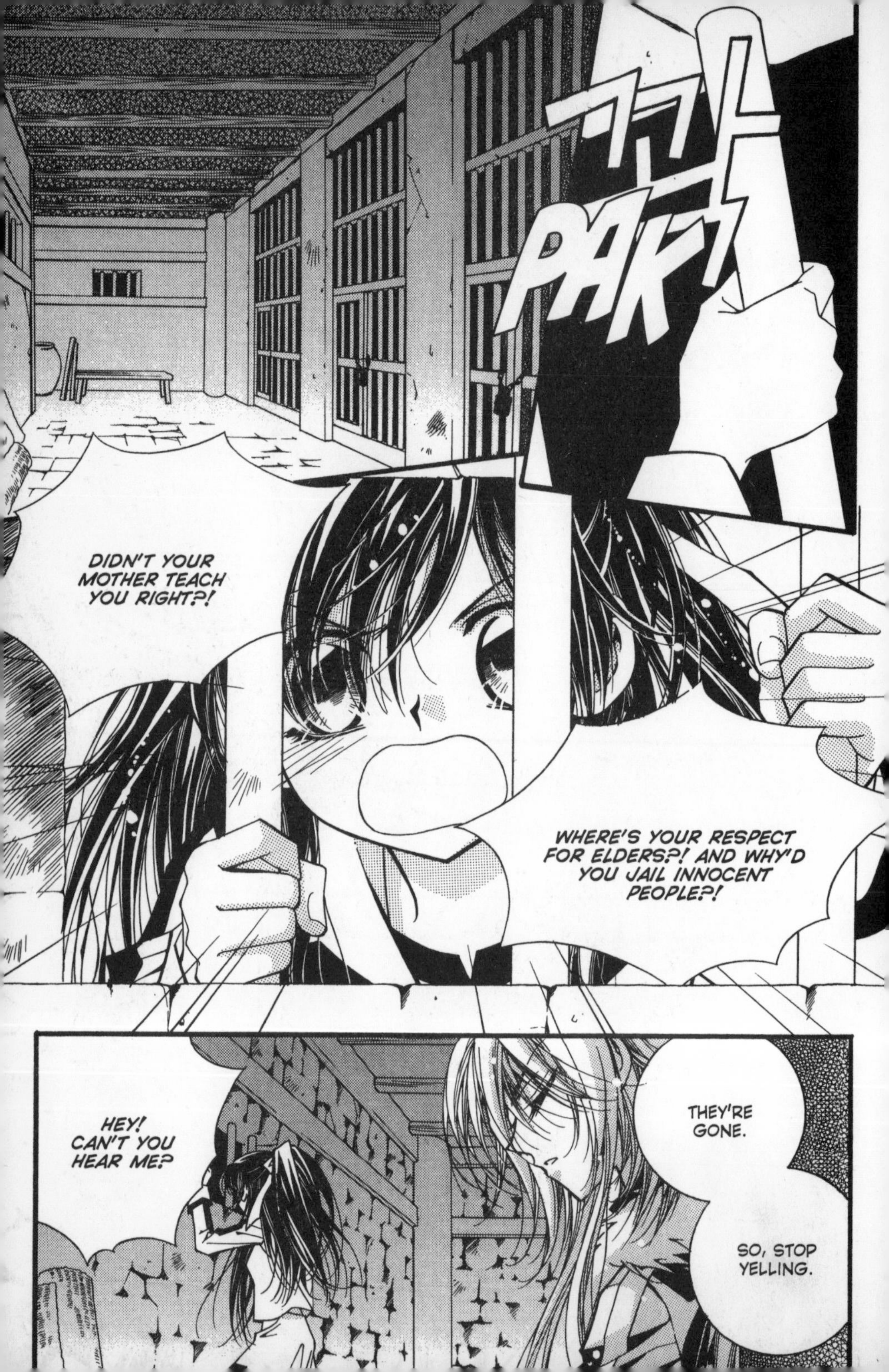
PAK!
DIDN'T YOUR MOTHER TEACH YOU RIGHT?!
WHERE'S YOUR RESPECT FOR ELDERS?! AND WHY'D YOU JAIL INNOCENT PEOPLE?!
HEY! CAN'T YOU HEAR ME?
THEY'RE GONE.
SO, STOP YELLING.

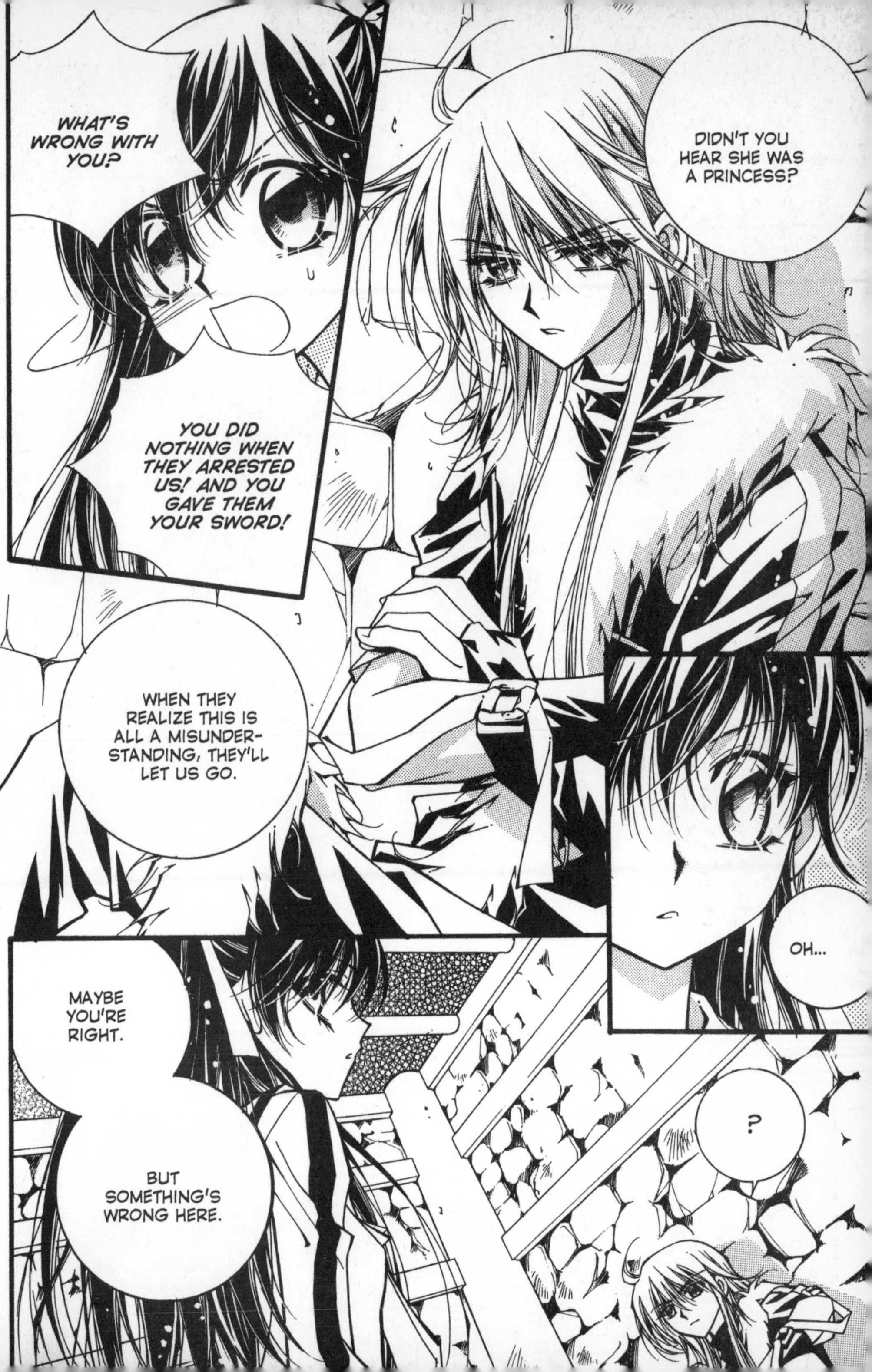
WHAT'S WRONG WITH YOU?
YOU DID NOTHING WHEN THEY ARRESTED US! AND YOU GAVE THEM YOUR SWORD!
DIDN'T YOU HEAR SHE WAS A PRINCESS?
WHEN THEY REALIZE THIS IS ALL A MISUNDER-STANDING, THEY'LL LET US GO.
OH...
MAYBE YOU'RE RIGHT.
BUT SOMETHING'S WRONG HERE.
?

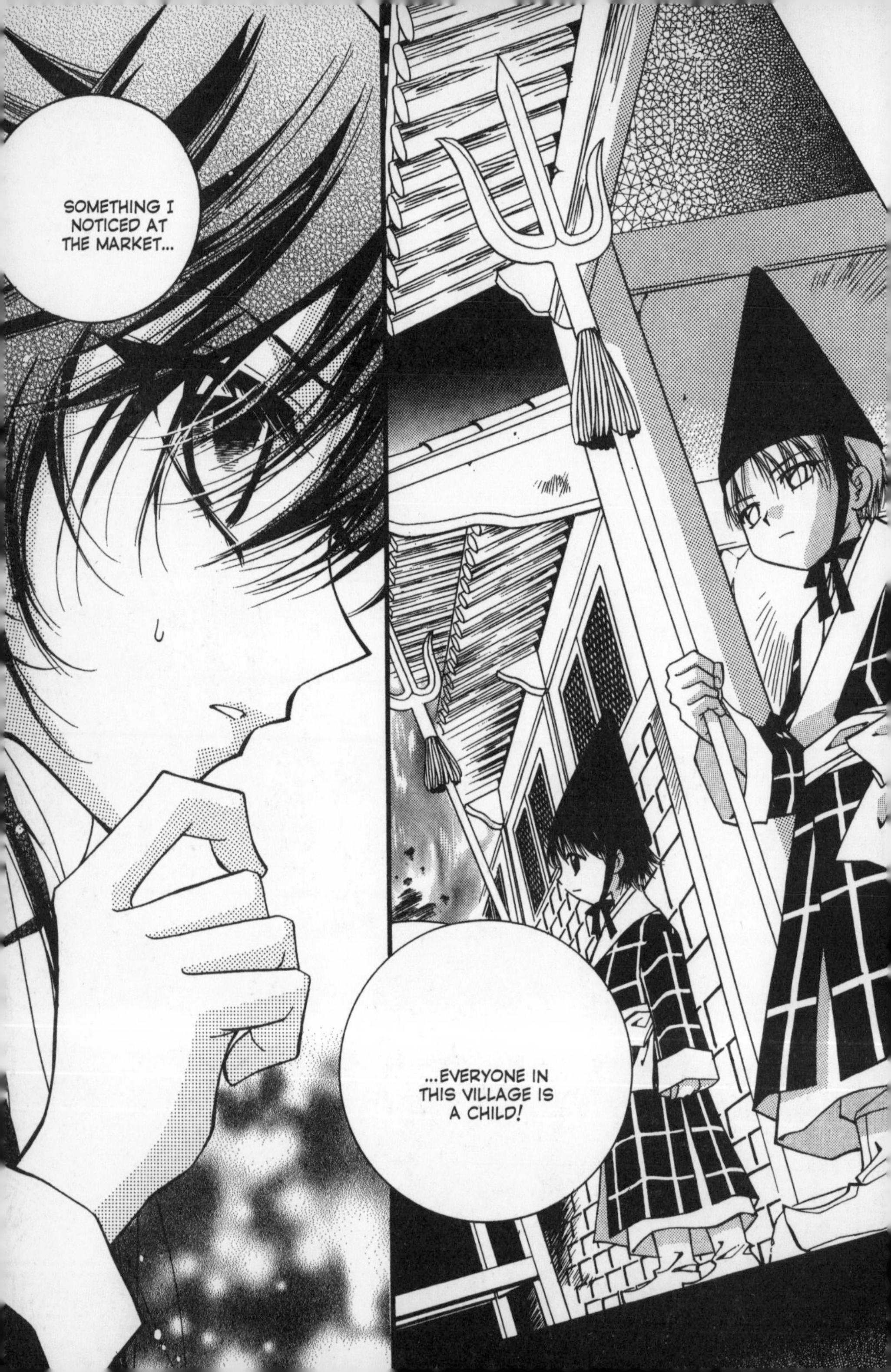
SOMETHING I NOTICED AT THE MARKET...
...EVERYONE IN THIS VILLAGE IS A CHILD!

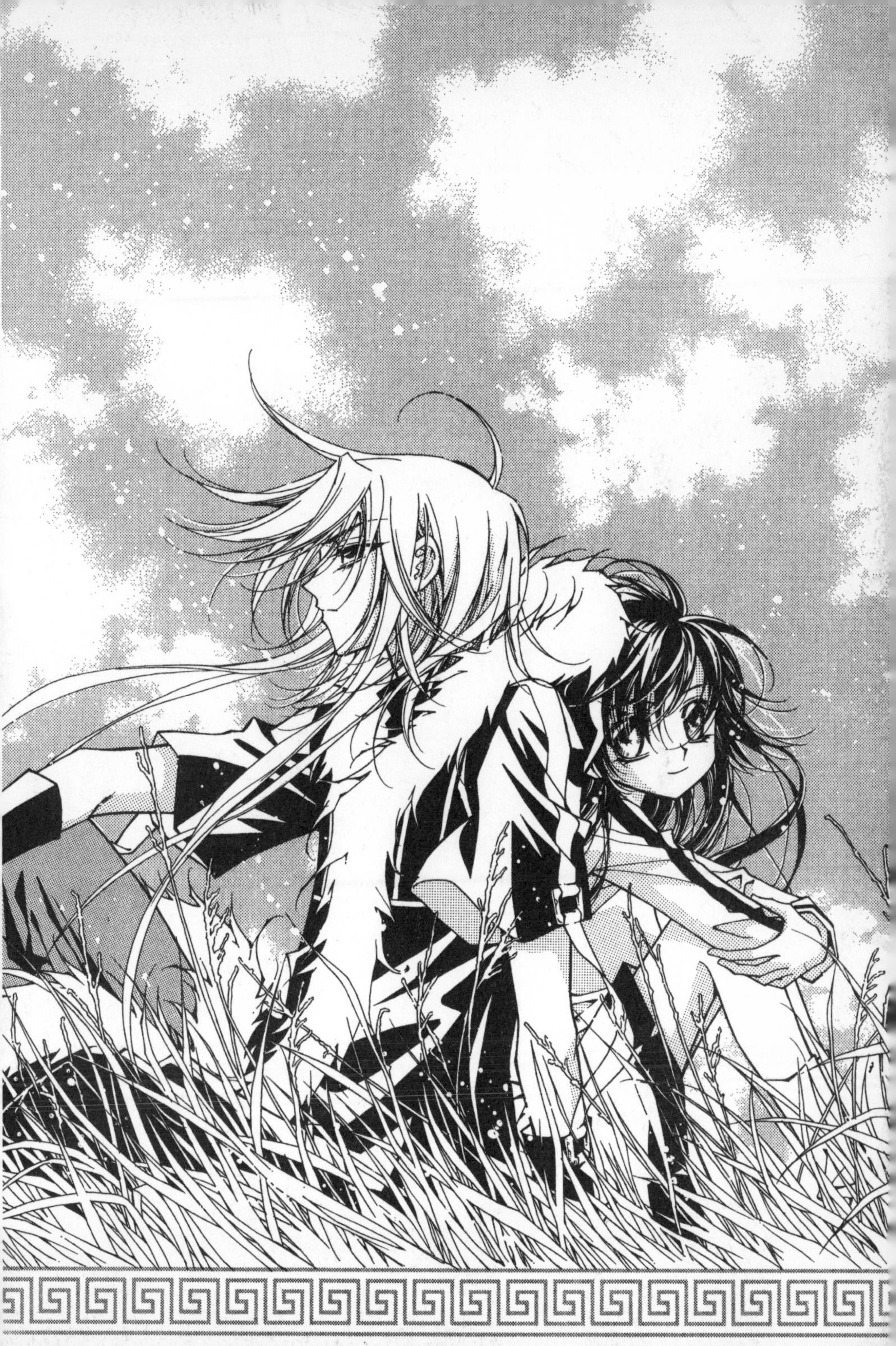

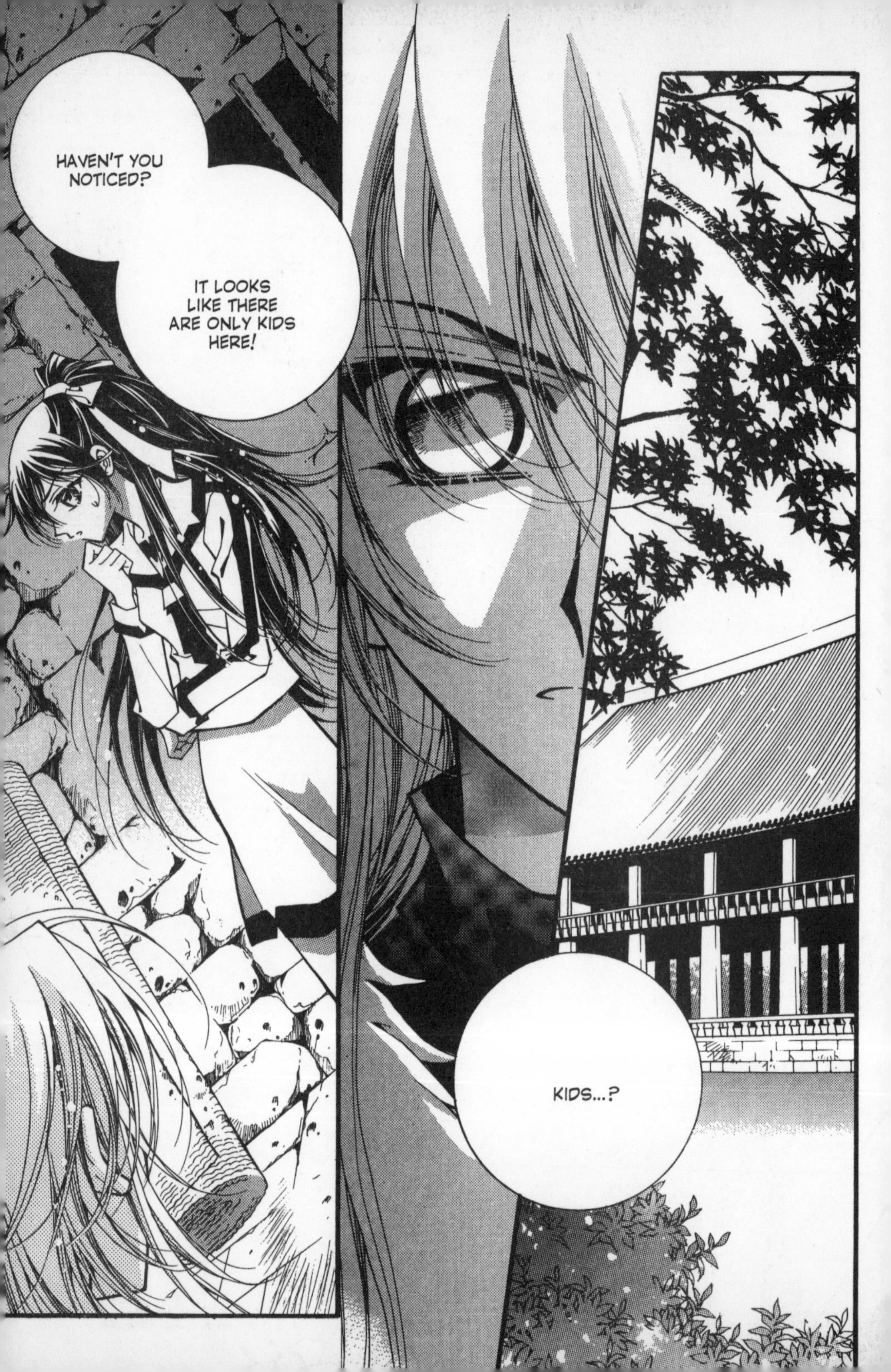
HAVEN'T YOU NOTICED?
IT LOOKS LIKE THERE ARE ONLY KIDS HERE!
KIDS...?

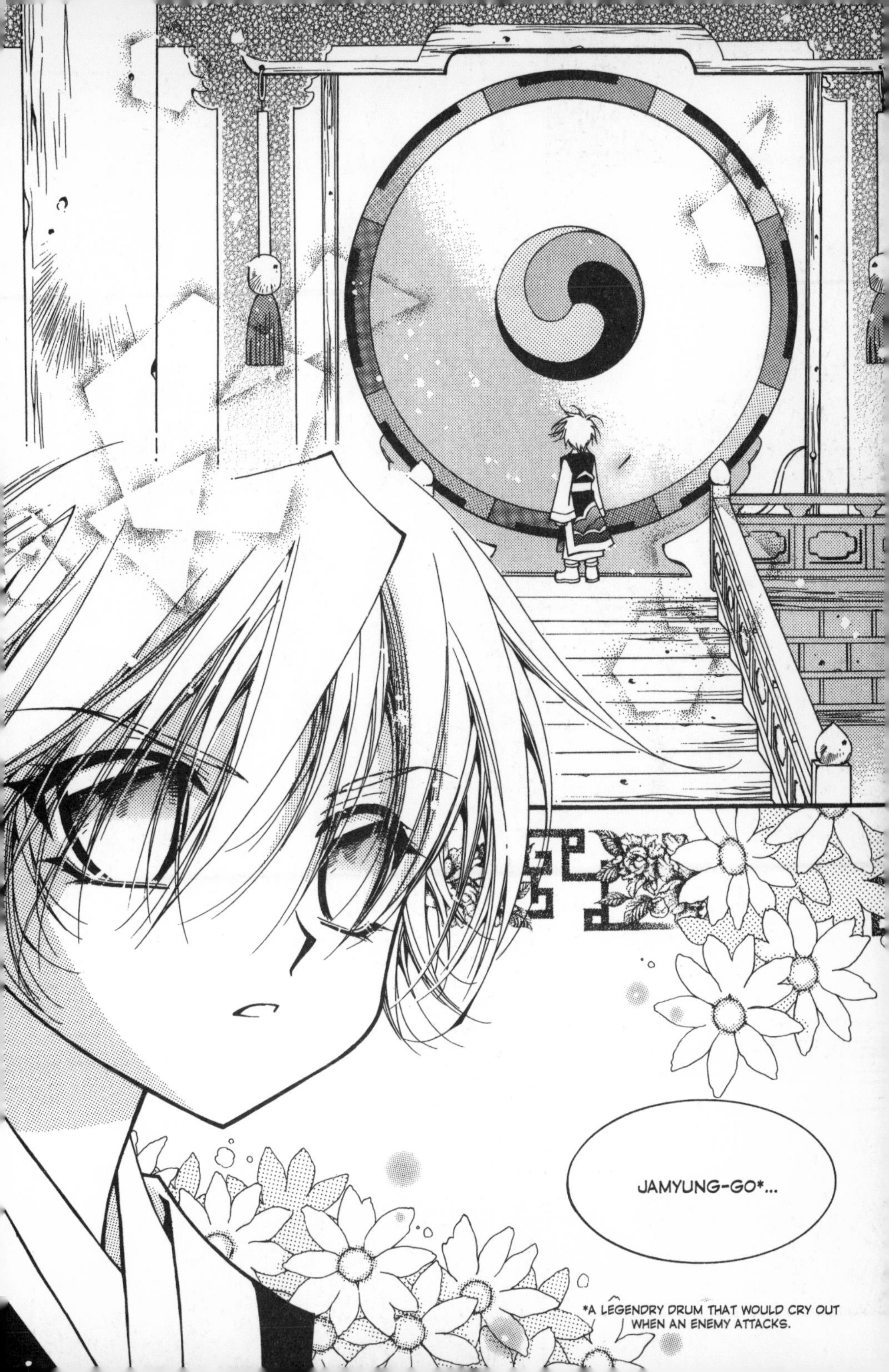
JAMYUNG-GO*...
*A LEGENDRY DRUM THAT WOULD CRY OUT WHEN AN ENEMY ATTACKS.

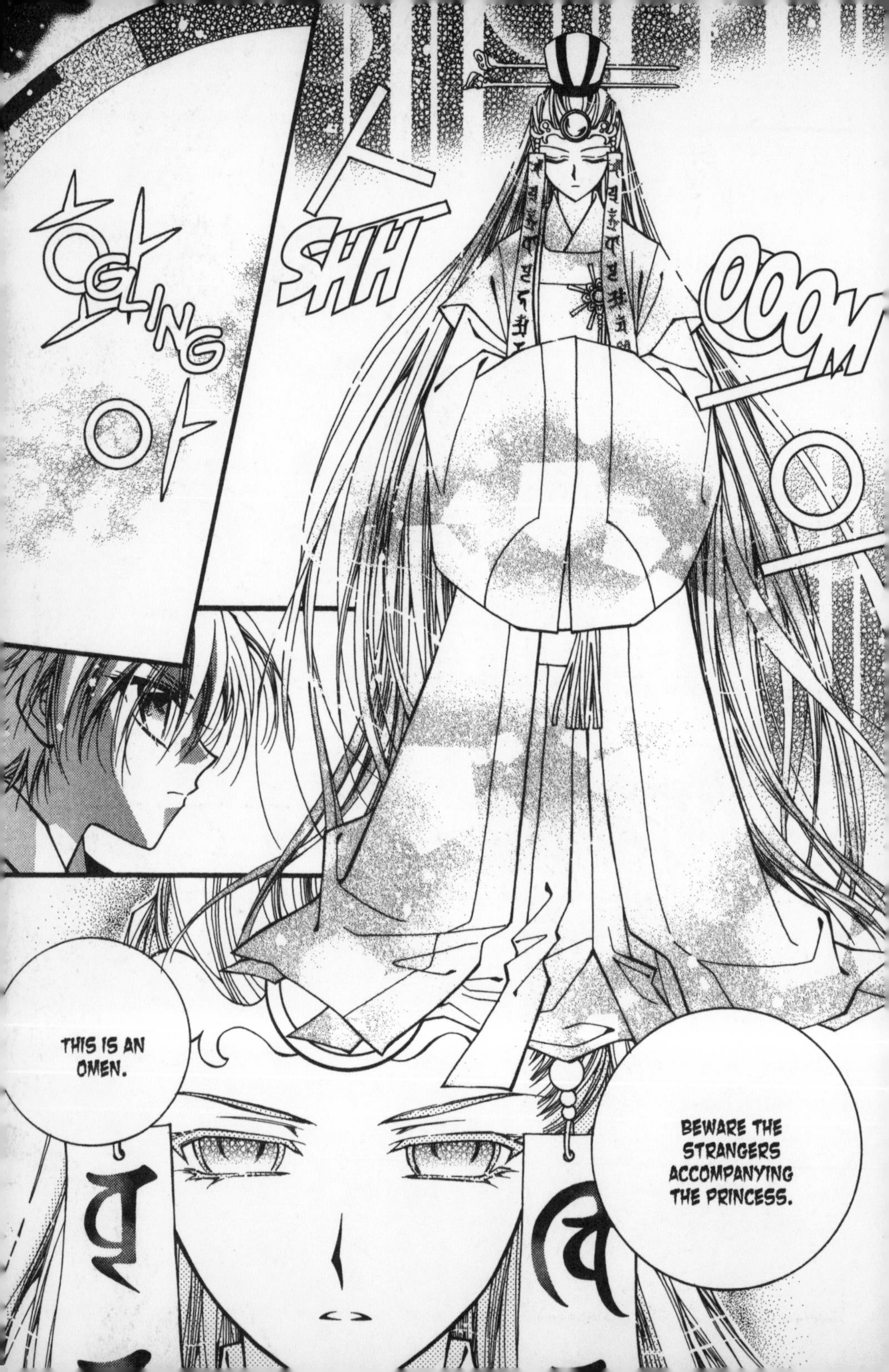
GLING
SHH
OOOM
THIS IS AN OMEN.
BEWARE THE STRANGERS ACCOMPANYING THE PRINCESS.

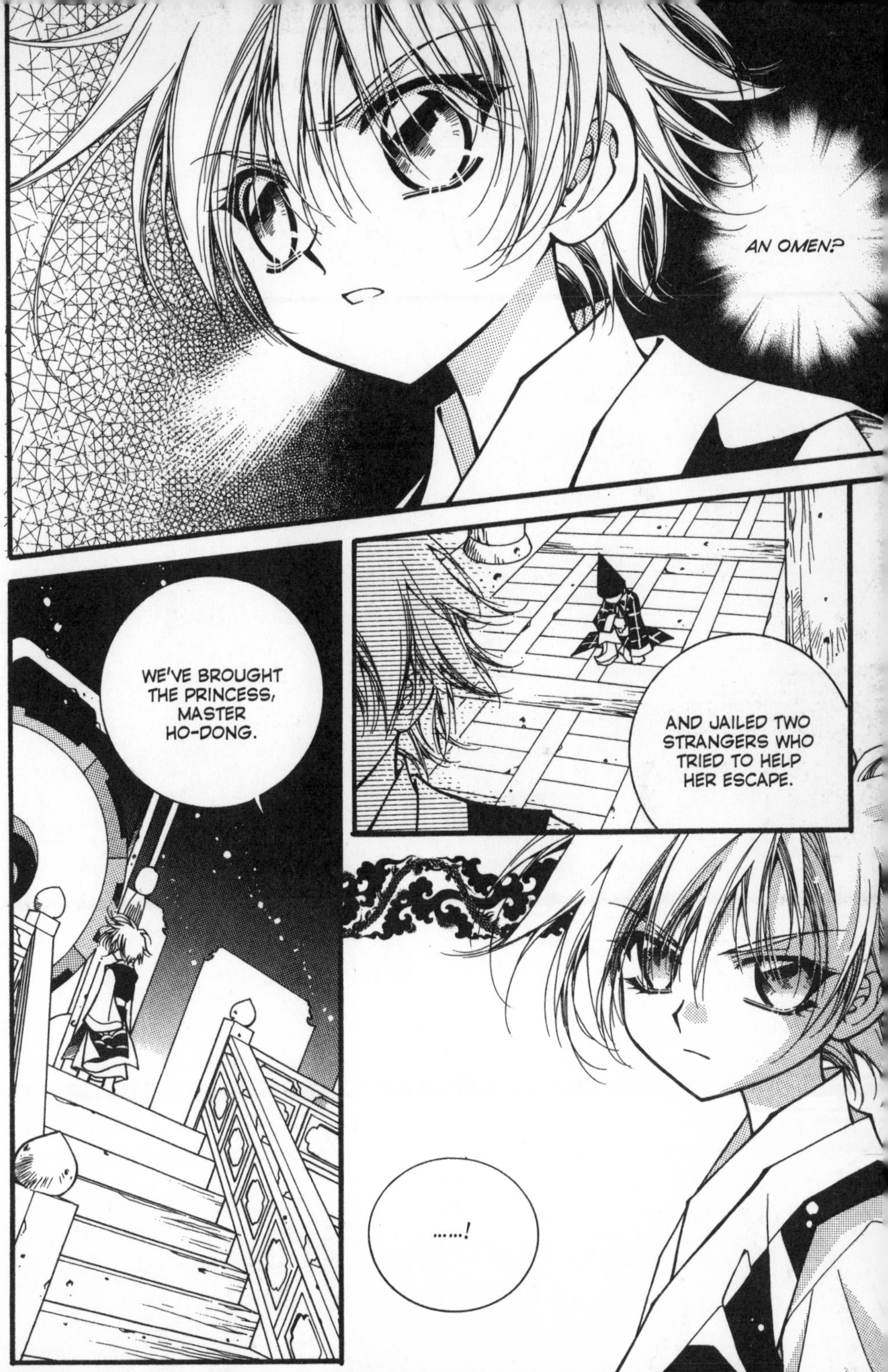
AN OMEN?
WE'VE BROUGHT THE PRINCESS, MASTER HO-DONG.
AND JAILED TWO STRANGERS WHO TRIED TO HELP HER ESCAPE.
......!

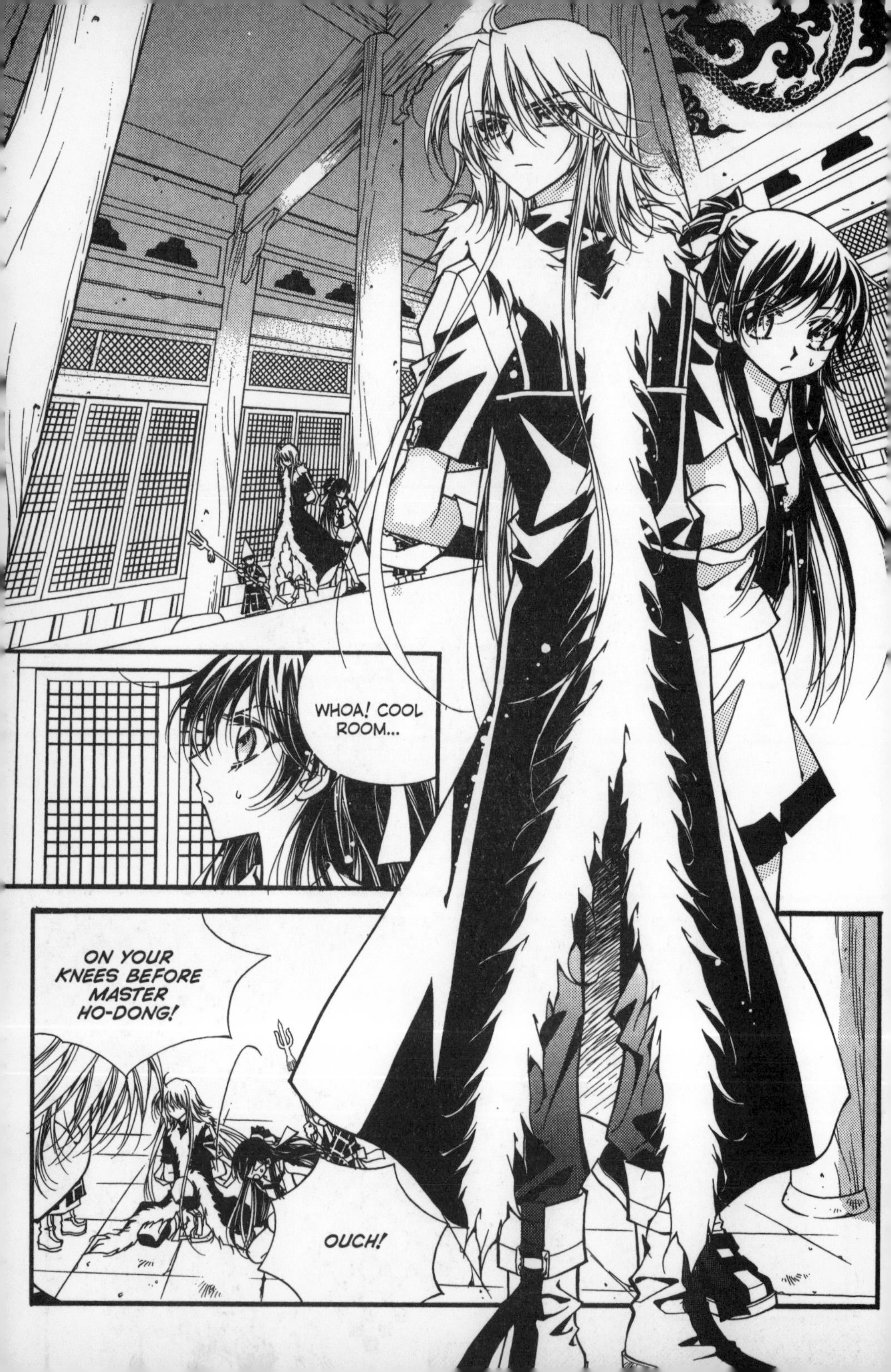
WHOA! COOL ROOM...
ON YOUR KNEES BEFORE MASTER HO-DONG!
OUCH!

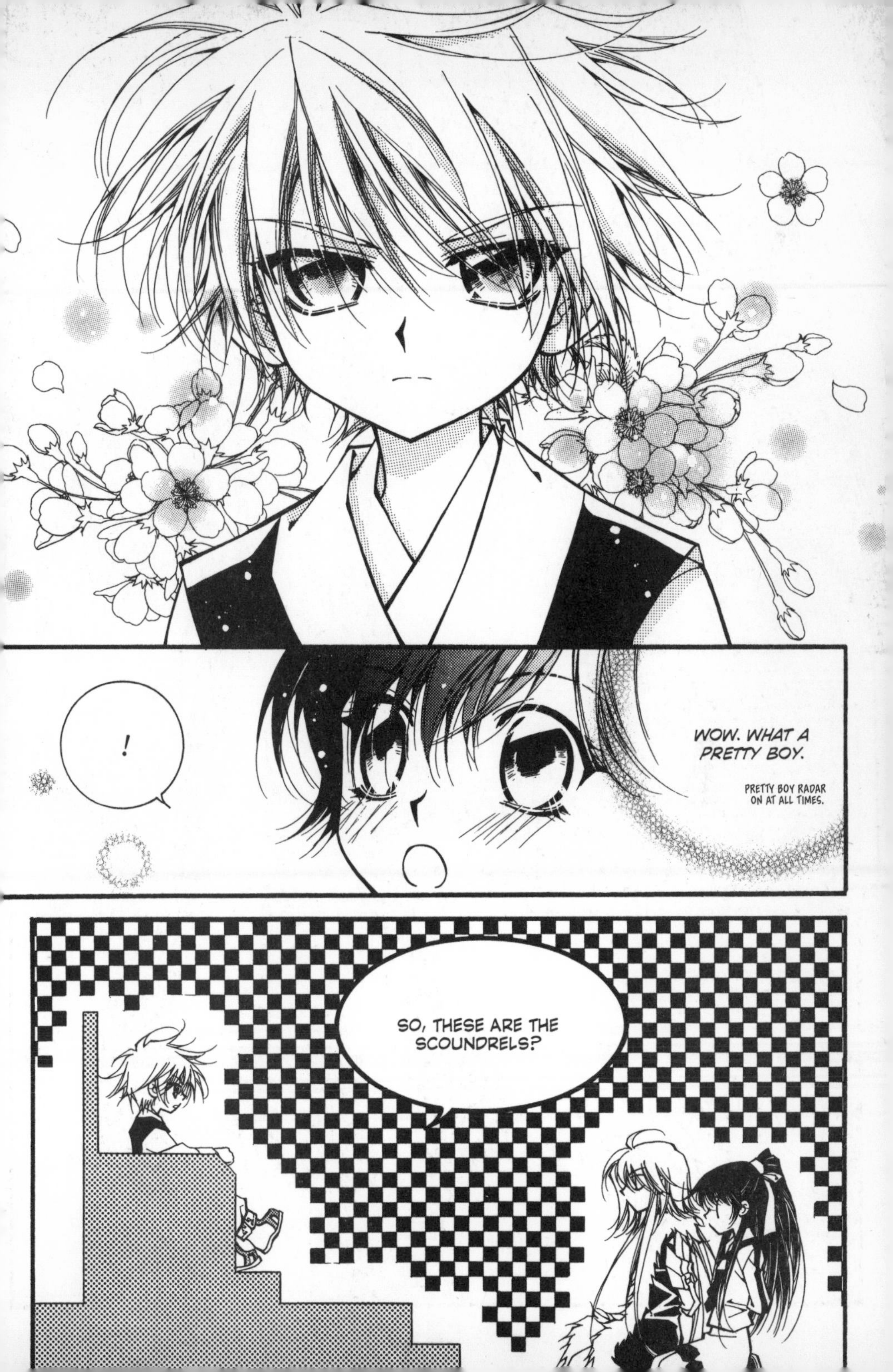
!
WOW. WHAT A PRETTY BOY.
PRETTY BOY RADAR ON AT ALL TIMES.
SO, THESE ARE THE SCOUNDRELS?

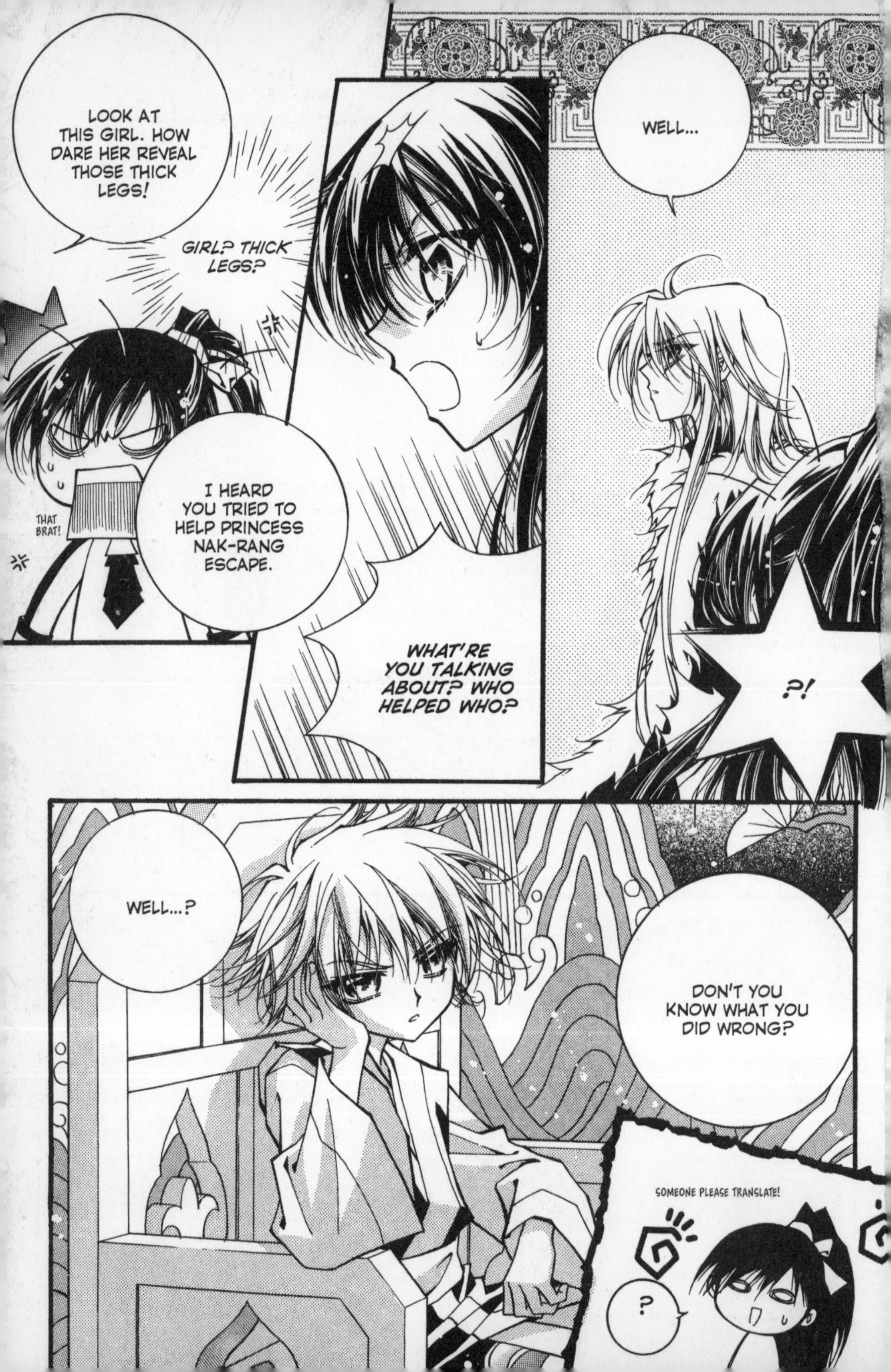
LOOK AT THIS GIRL. HOW DARE HER REVEAL THOSE THICK LEGS!
GIRL? THICK LEGS?
THAT BRAT!
I HEARD YOU TRIED TO HELP PRINCESS NAK-RANG ESCAPE.
WHAT'RE YOU TALKING ABOUT? WHO HELPED WHO?
WELL...
?!
WELL...?
DON'T YOU KNOW WHAT YOU DID WRONG?
SOMEONE PLEASE TRANSLATE!
?

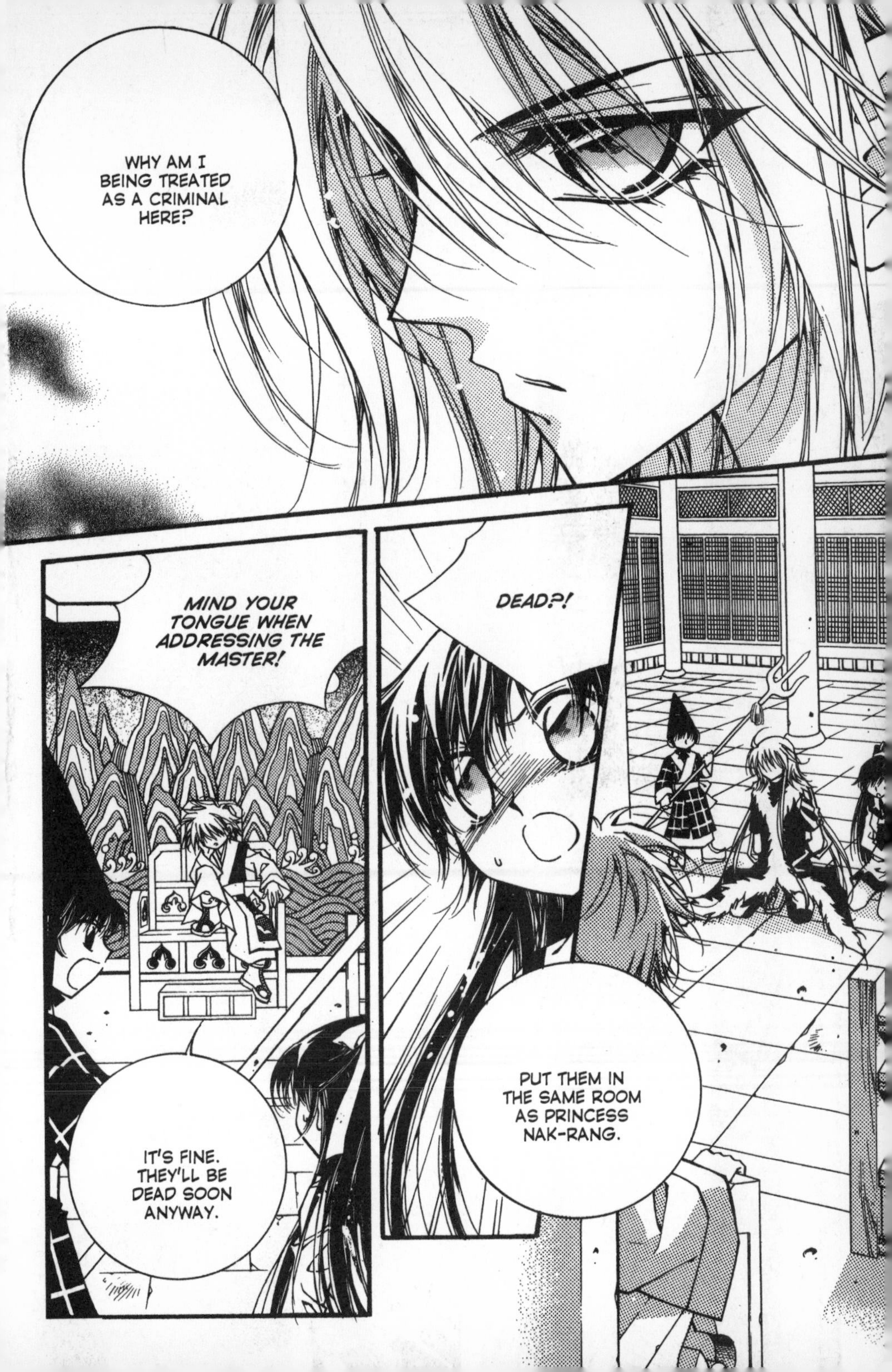
WHY AM I BEING TREATED AS A CRIMINAL HERE?
MIND YOUR TONGUE WHEN ADDRESSING THE MASTER!
IT'S FINE. THEY'LL BE DEAD SOON ANYWAY.
DEAD?!
PUT THEM IN THE SAME ROOM AS PRINCESS NAK-RANG.

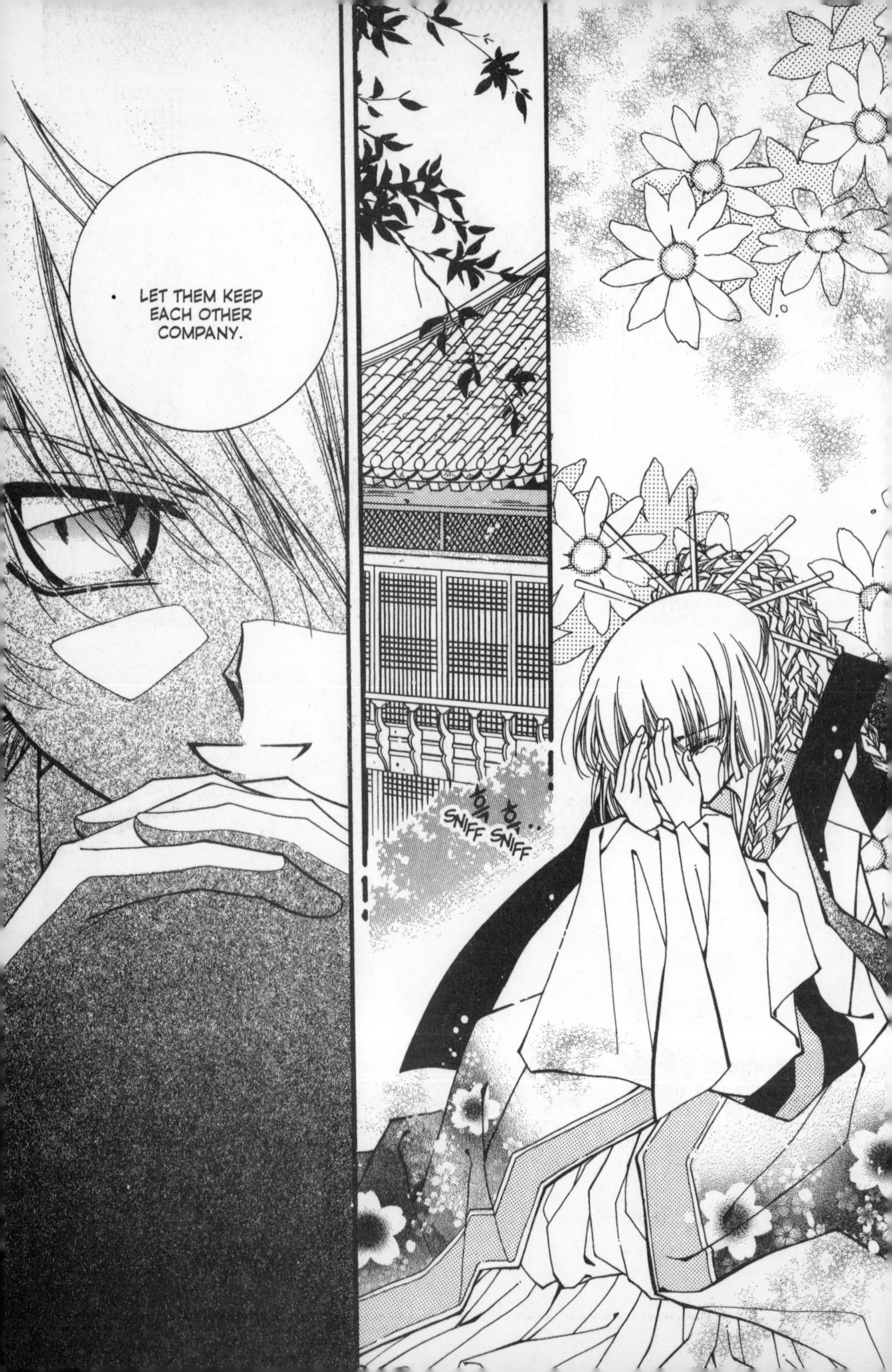
LET THEM KEEP EACH OTHER COMPANY.
SNIFF SNIFF

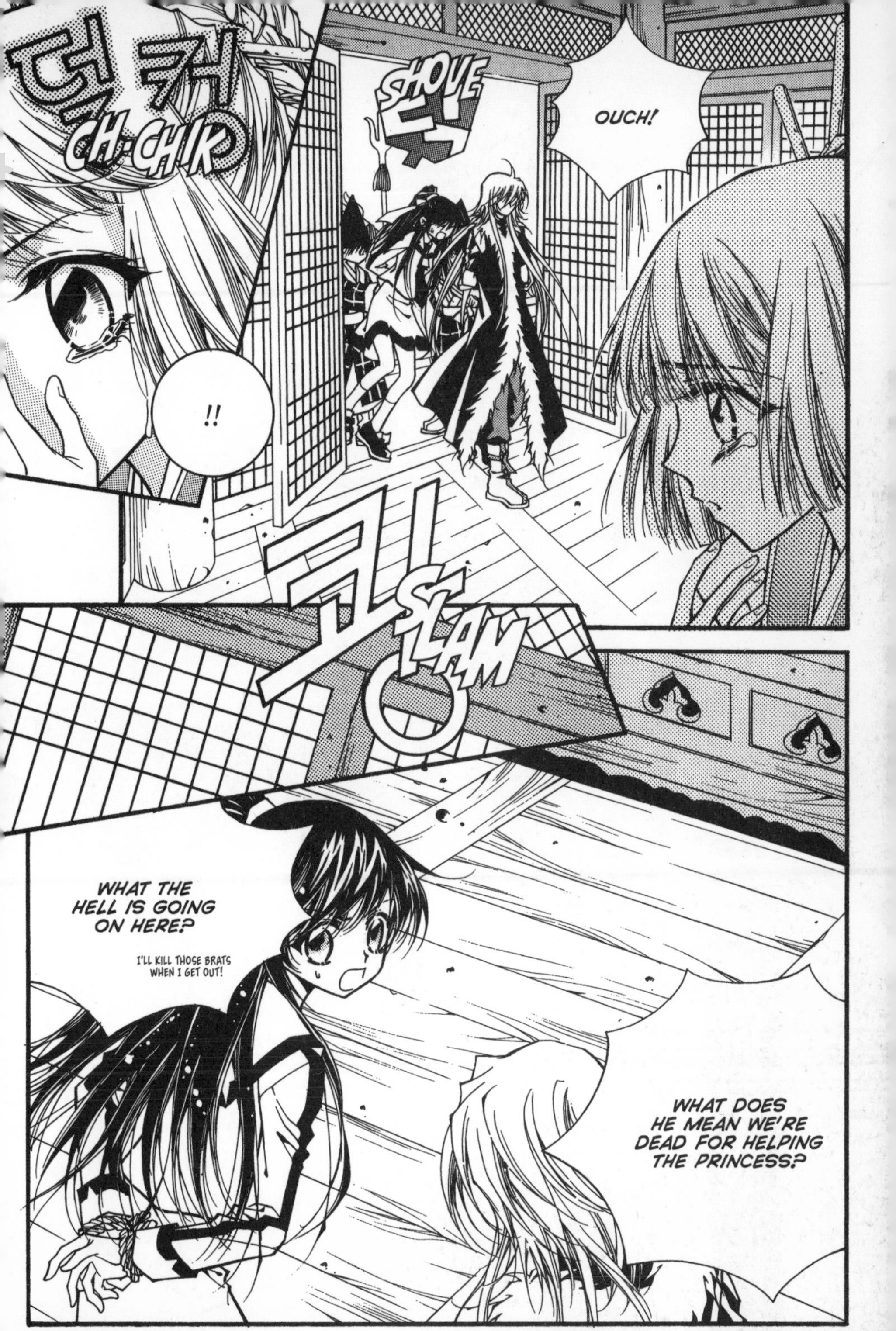
CH-CHIK
!!
SHOVE
OUCH!
쾅
SLAM
WHAT THE HELL IS GOING ON HERE?
I'LL KILL THOSE BRATS WHEN I GET OUT!
WHAT DOES HE MEAN WE'RE DEAD FOR HELPING THE PRINCESS?

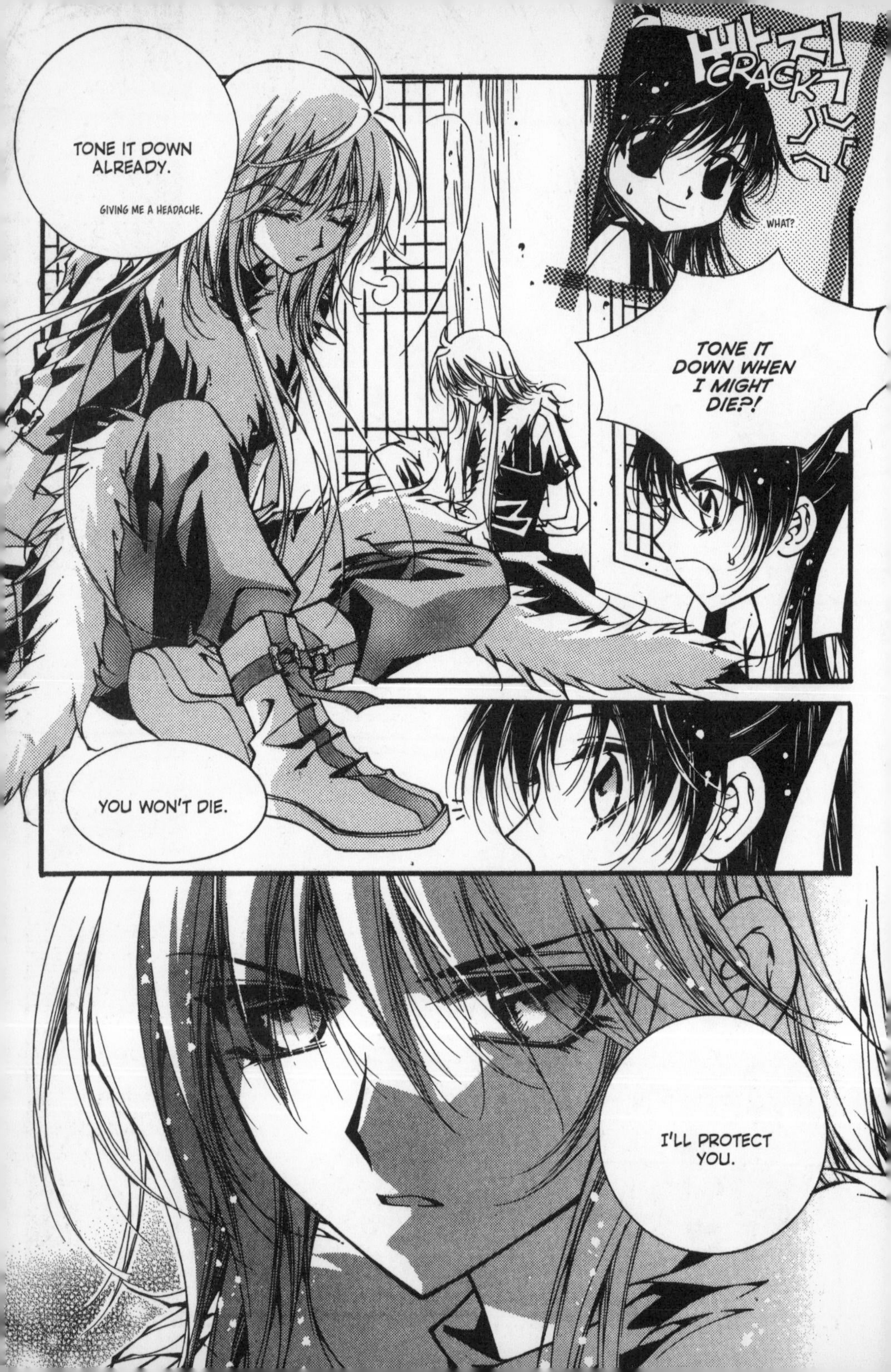
TONE IT DOWN ALREADY.
GIVING ME A HEADACHE.
CRACK
WHAT?
TONE IT DOWN WHEN I MIGHT DIE?!
YOU WON'T DIE.
I'LL PROTECT YOU.

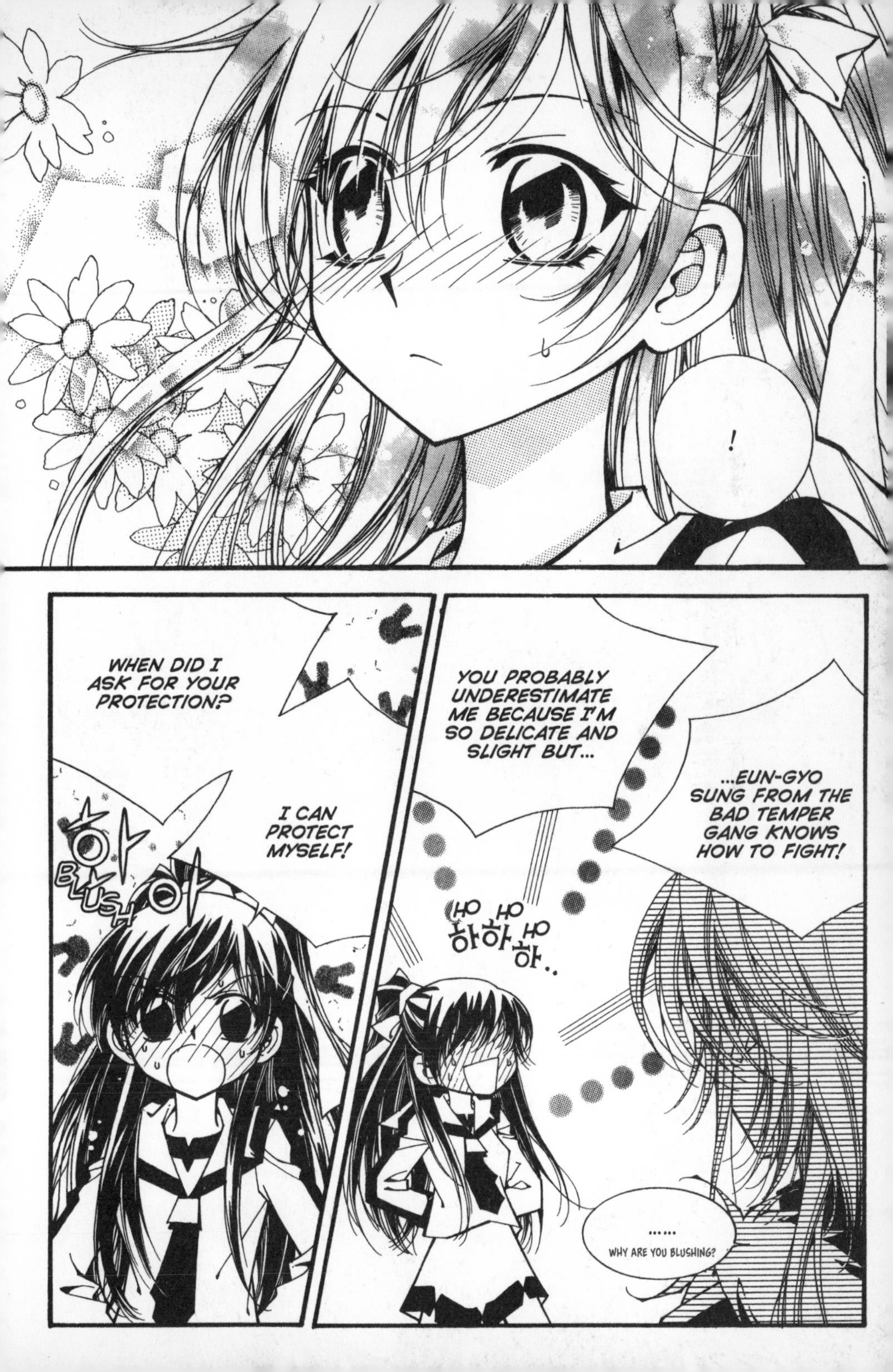
!
WHEN DID I ASK FOR YOUR PROTECTION?
I CAN PROTECT MYSELF!
BLUSH
YOU PROBABLY UNDERESTIMATE ME BECAUSE I'M SO DELICATE AND SLIGHT BUT...
...EUN-GYO SUNG FROM THE BAD TEMPER GANG KNOWS HOW TO FIGHT!
HO HO HO
하하하..
......
WHY ARE YOU BLUSHING?

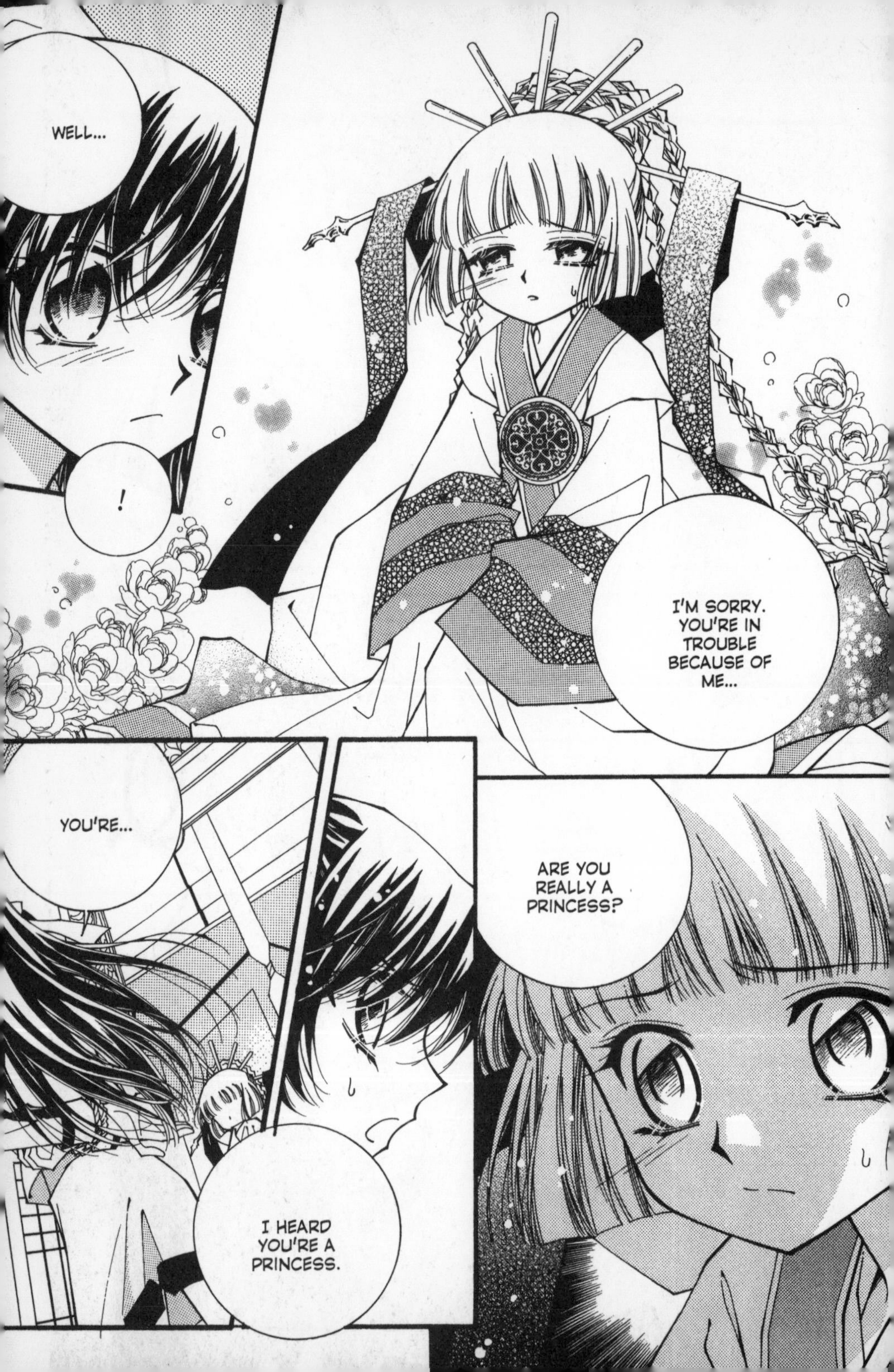
WELL...
!
I'M SORRY. YOU'RE IN TROUBLE BECAUSE OF ME...
YOU'RE...
I HEARD YOU'RE A PRINCESS.
ARE YOU REALLY A PRINCESS?

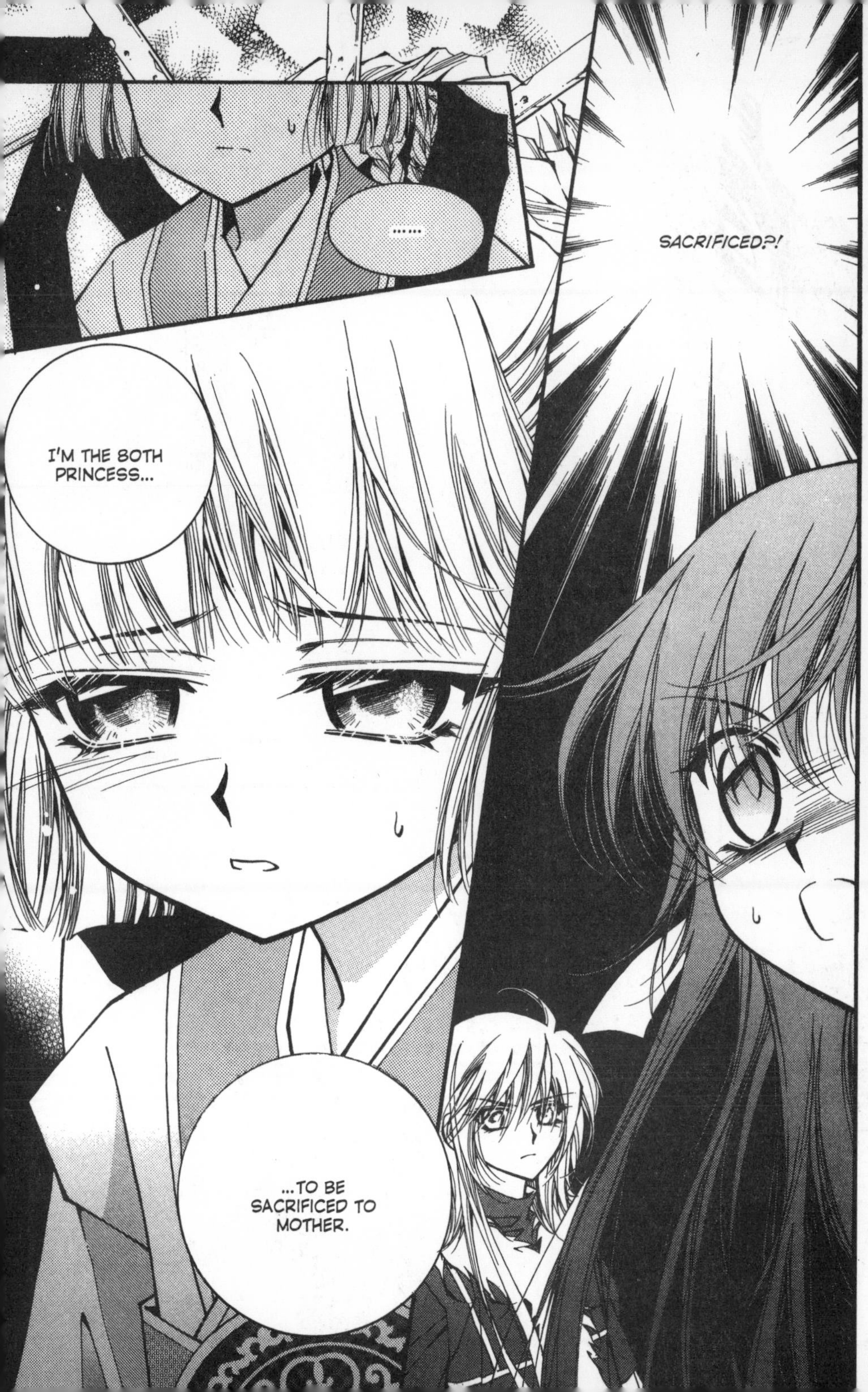
……
I'M THE 80TH PRINCESS...
...TO BE SACRIFICED TO MOTHER.
SACRIFICED?!

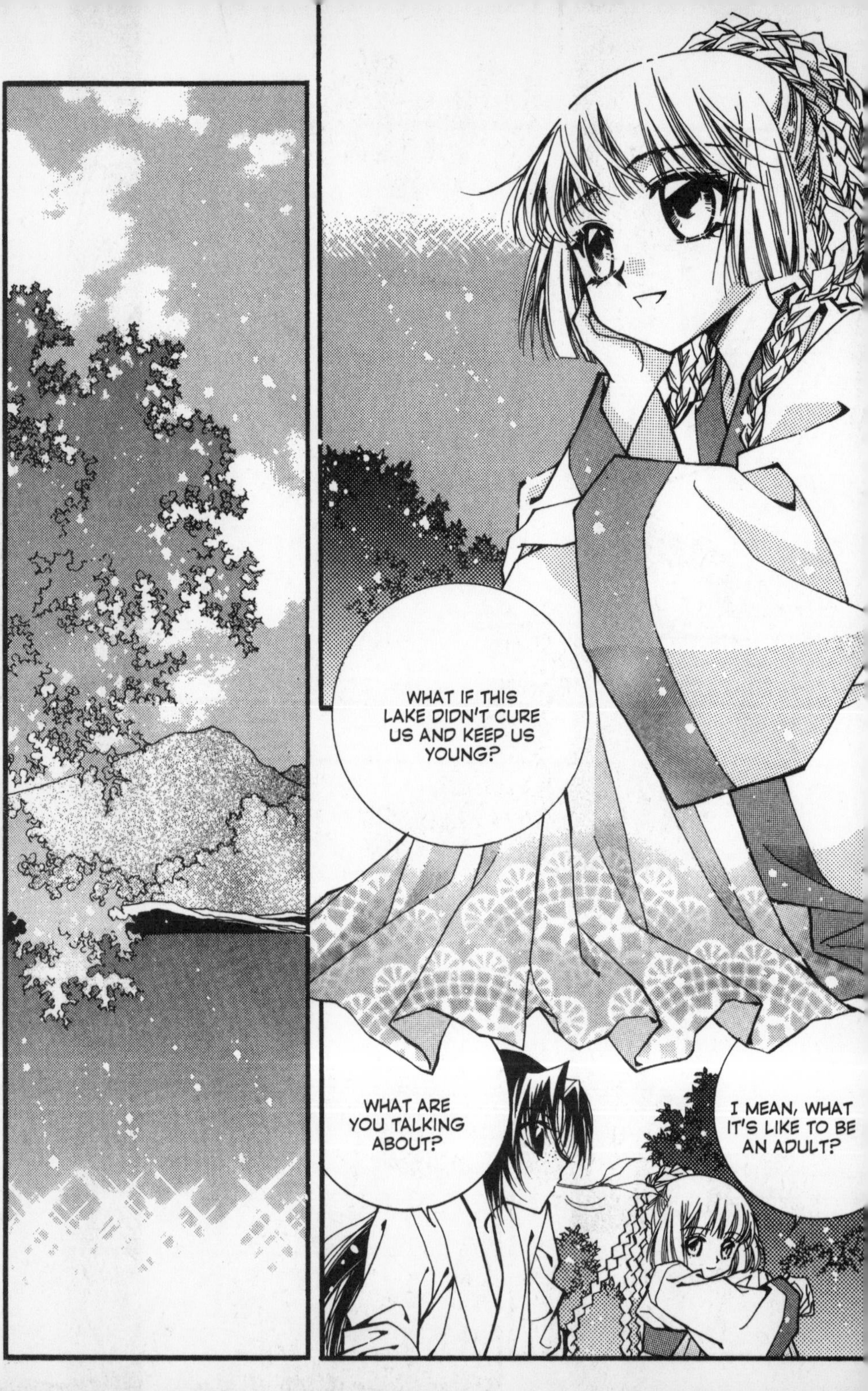
WHAT IF THIS LAKE DIDN'T CURE US AND KEEP US YOUNG?
WHAT ARE YOU TALKING ABOUT?
I MEAN, WHAT IT'S LIKE TO BE AN ADULT?

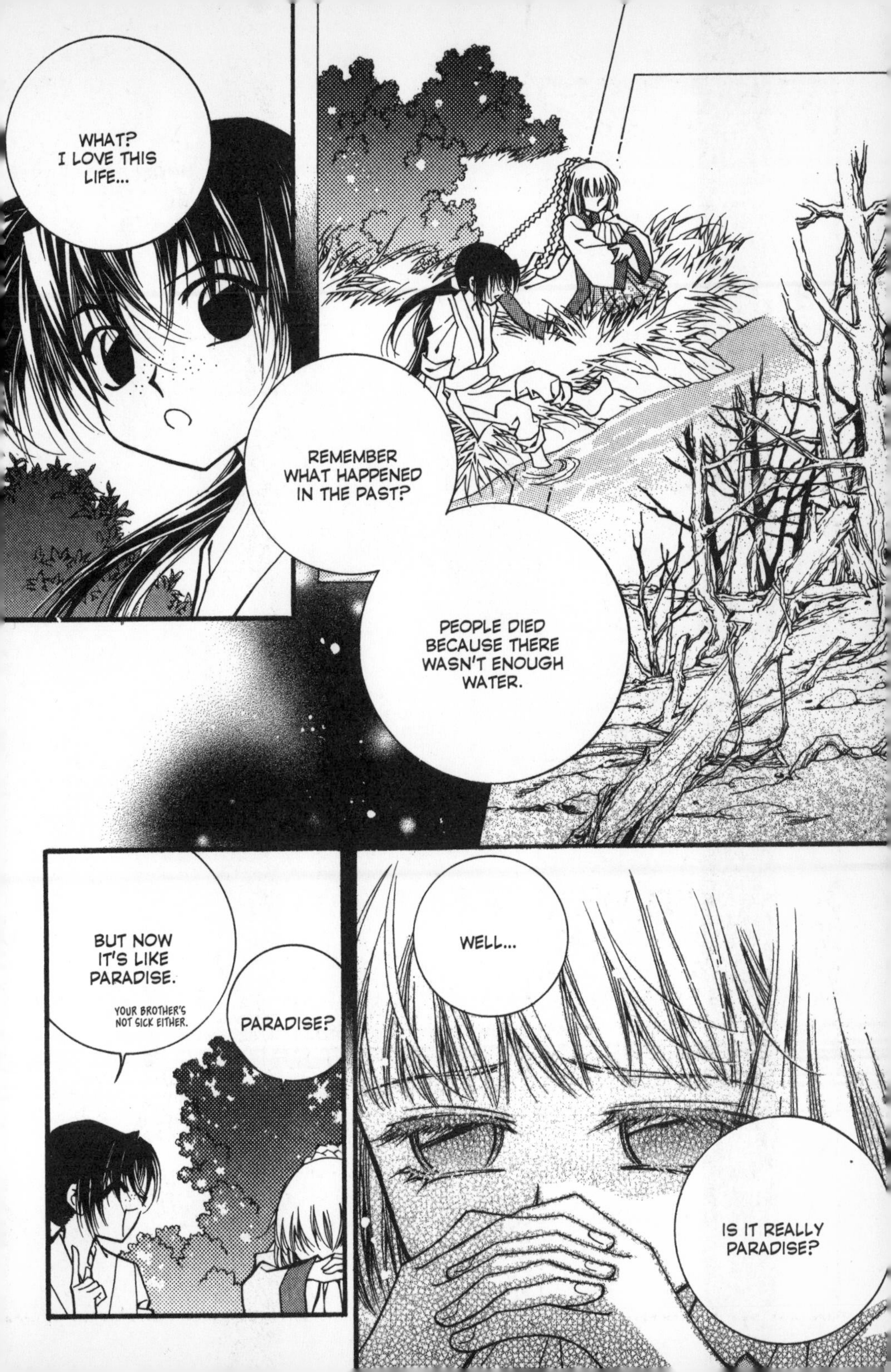
WHAT? I LOVE THIS LIFE...
REMEMBER WHAT HAPPENED IN THE PAST?
PEOPLE DIED BECAUSE THERE WASN'T ENOUGH WATER.
BUT NOW IT'S LIKE PARADISE.
YOUR BROTHER'S NOT SICK EITHER.
PARADISE?
WELL...
IS IT REALLY PARADISE?

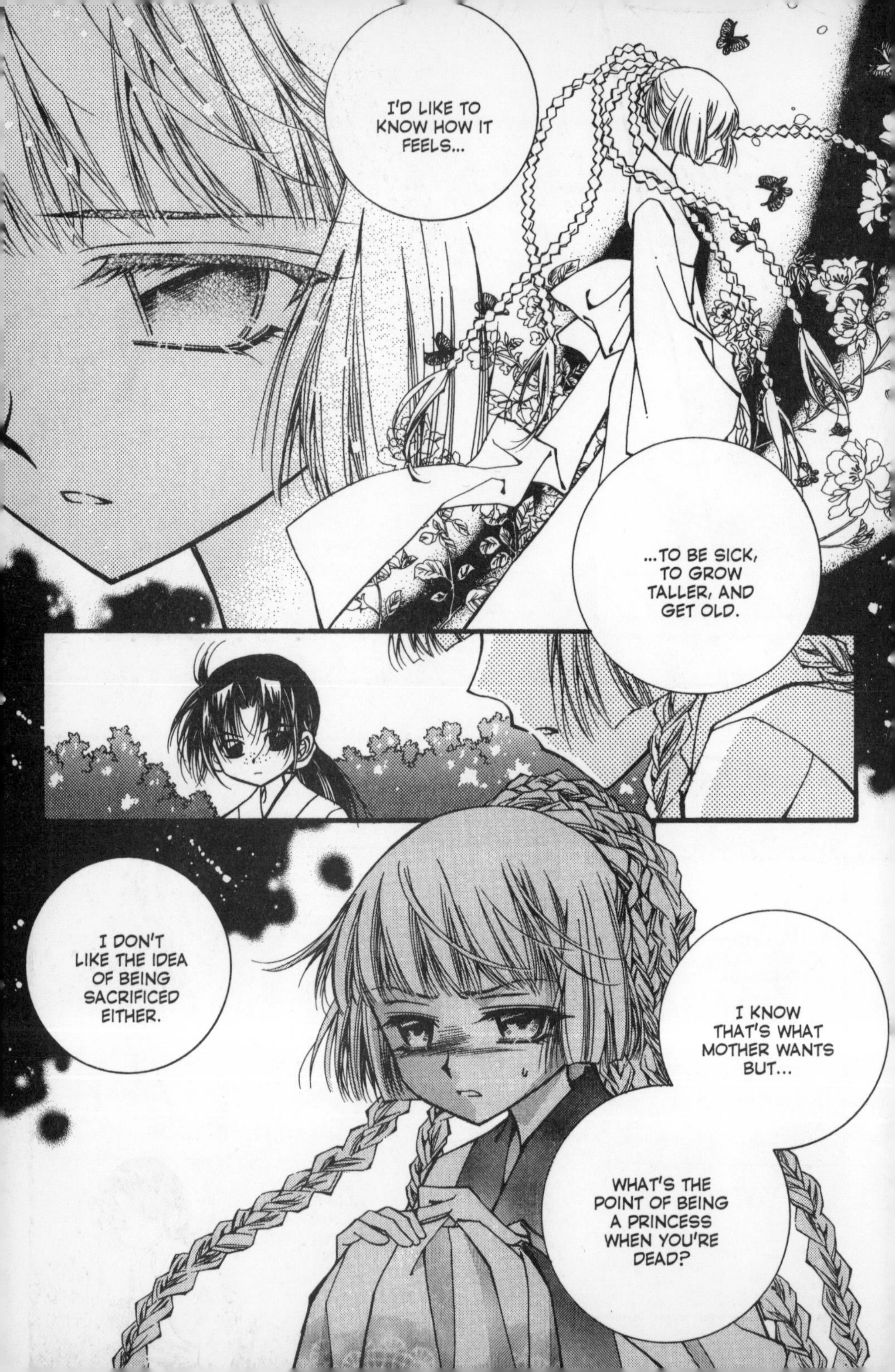
I'D LIKE TO KNOW HOW IT FEELS...
...TO BE SICK, TO GROW TALLER, AND GET OLD.
I DON'T LIKE THE IDEA OF BEING SACRIFICED EITHER.
I KNOW THAT'S WHAT MOTHER WANTS BUT...
WHAT'S THE POINT OF BEING A PRINCESS WHEN YOU'RE DEAD?

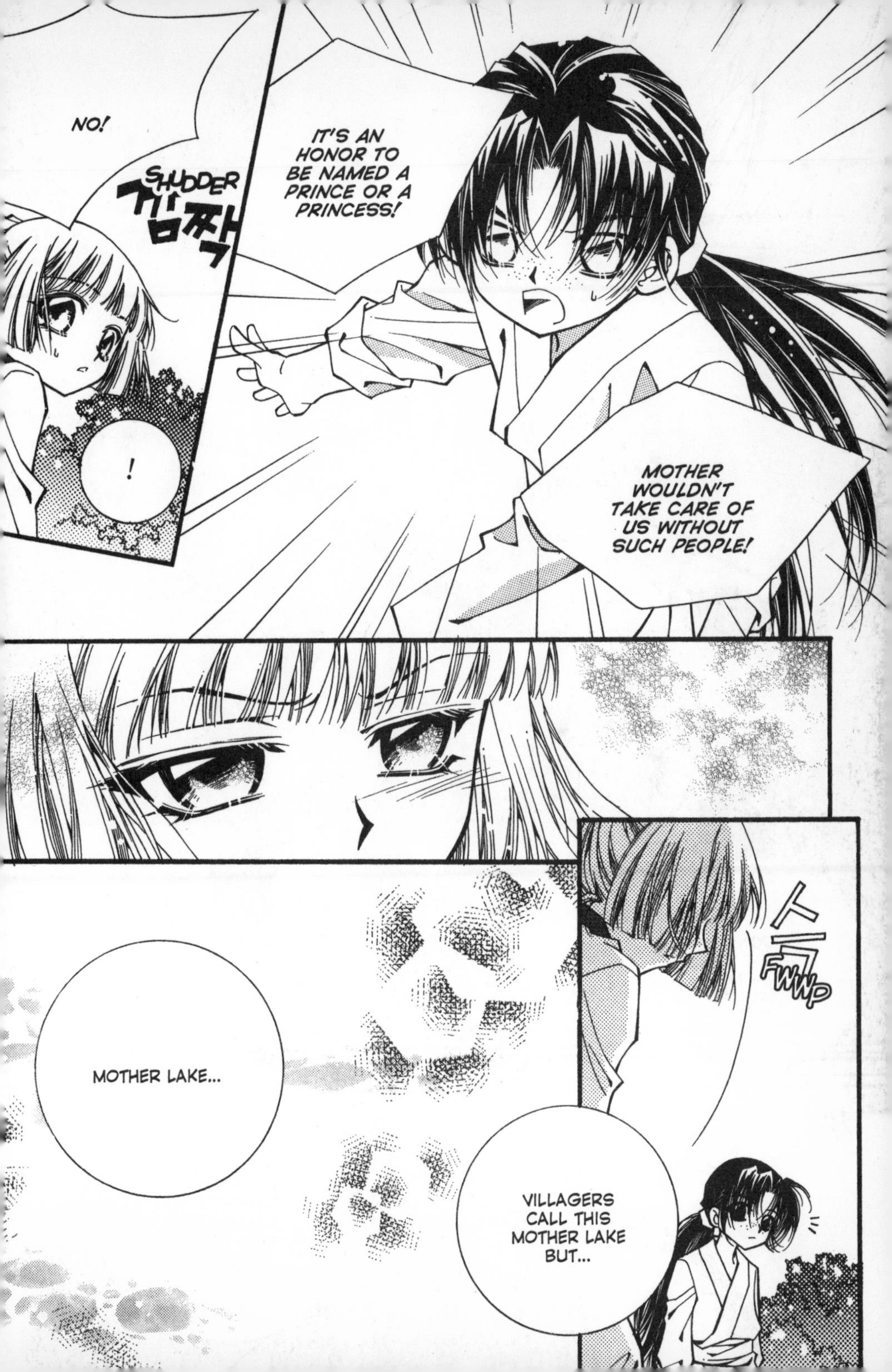

NO!
SHUDDER
깜짝
!
IT'S AN HONOR TO BE NAMED A PRINCE OR A PRINCESS!
MOTHER WOULDN'T TAKE CARE OF US WITHOUT SUCH PEOPLE!
MOTHER LAKE...
FWWP
VILLAGERS CALL THIS MOTHER LAKE BUT...

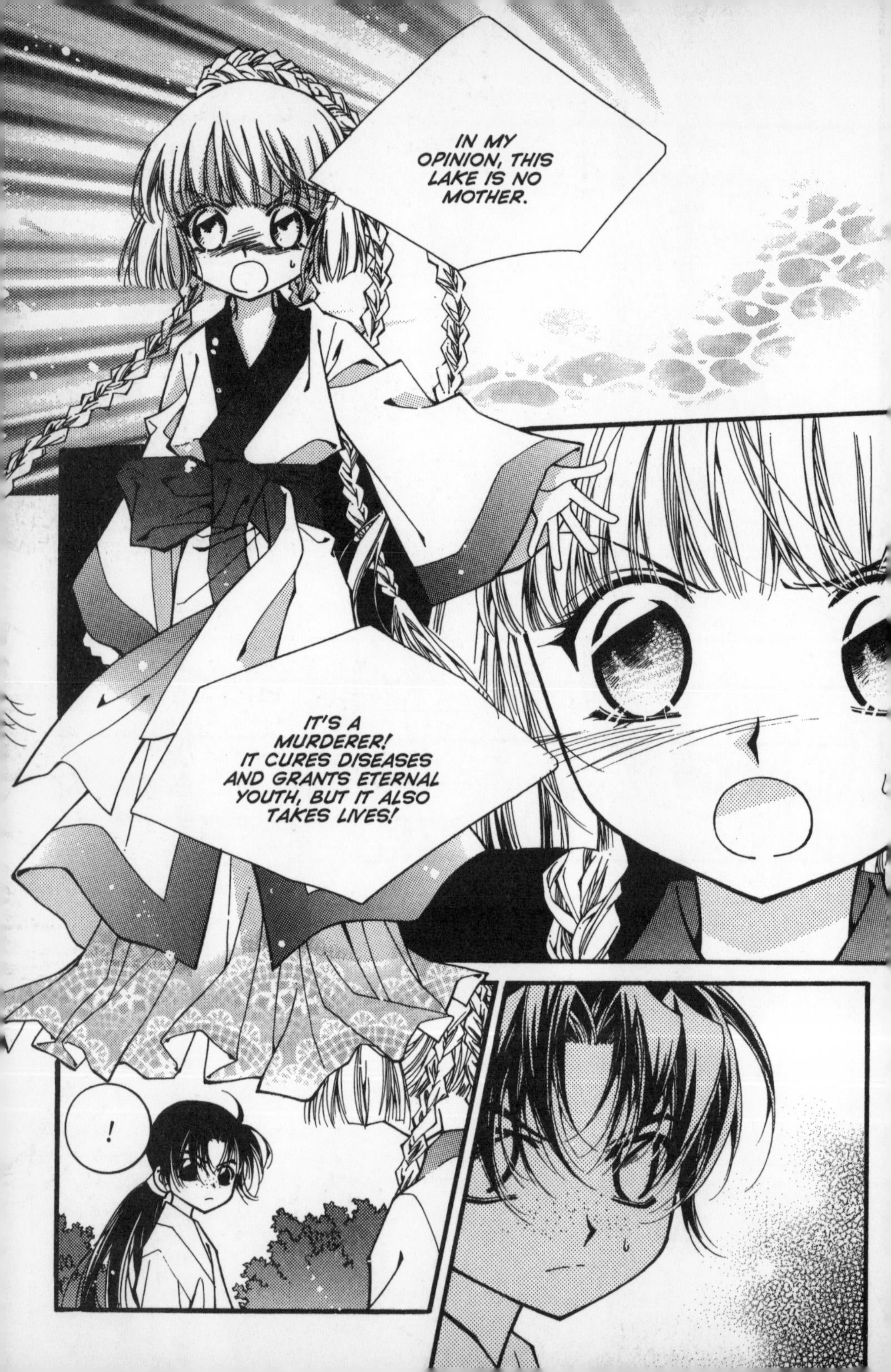
IN MY OPINION, THIS LAKE IS NO MOTHER.
IT'S A MURDERER! IT CURES DISEASES AND GRANTS ETERNAL YOUTH, BUT IT ALSO TAKES LIVES!
!

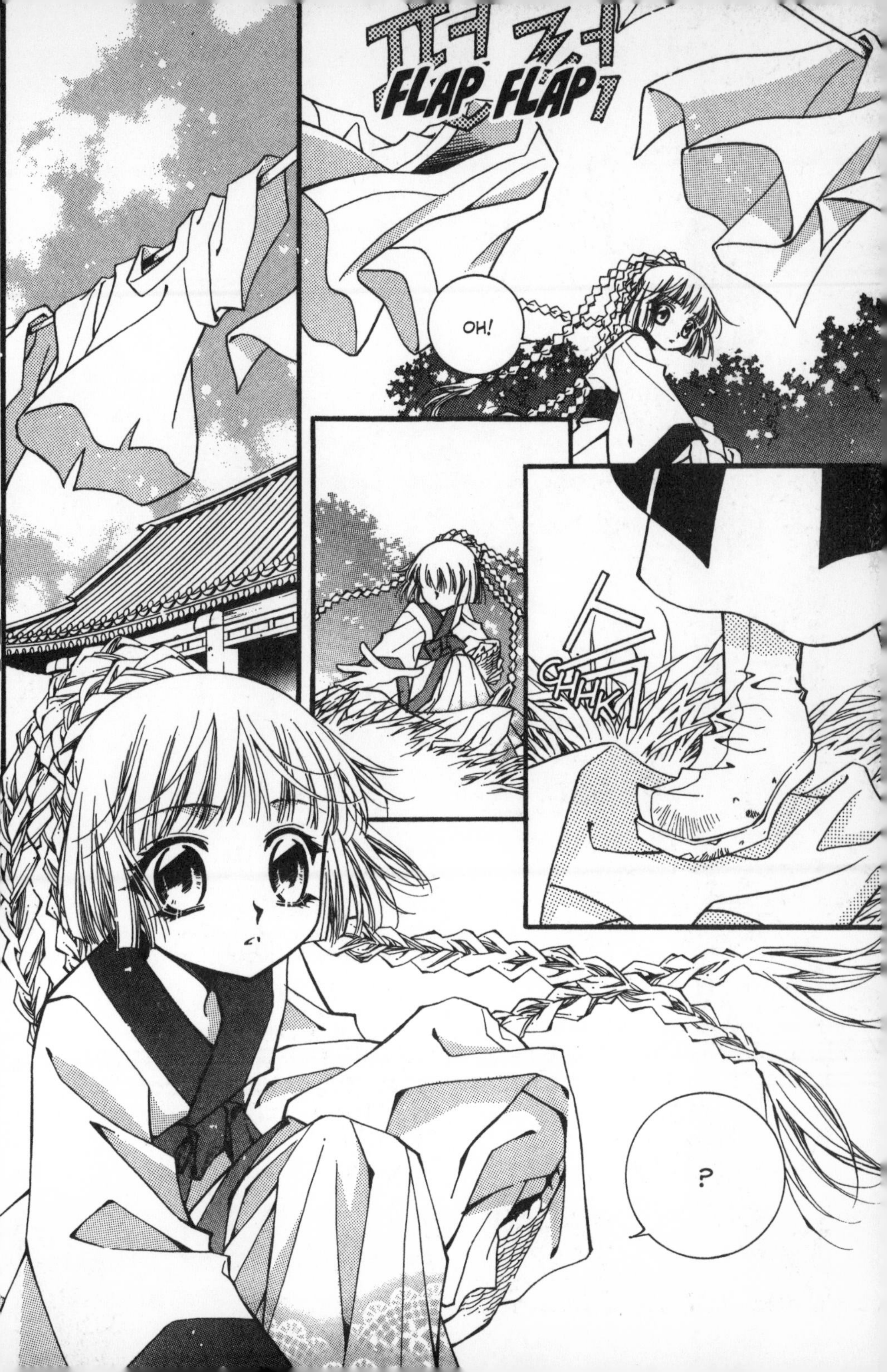
FLAP FLAP
OH!
CHHK
?

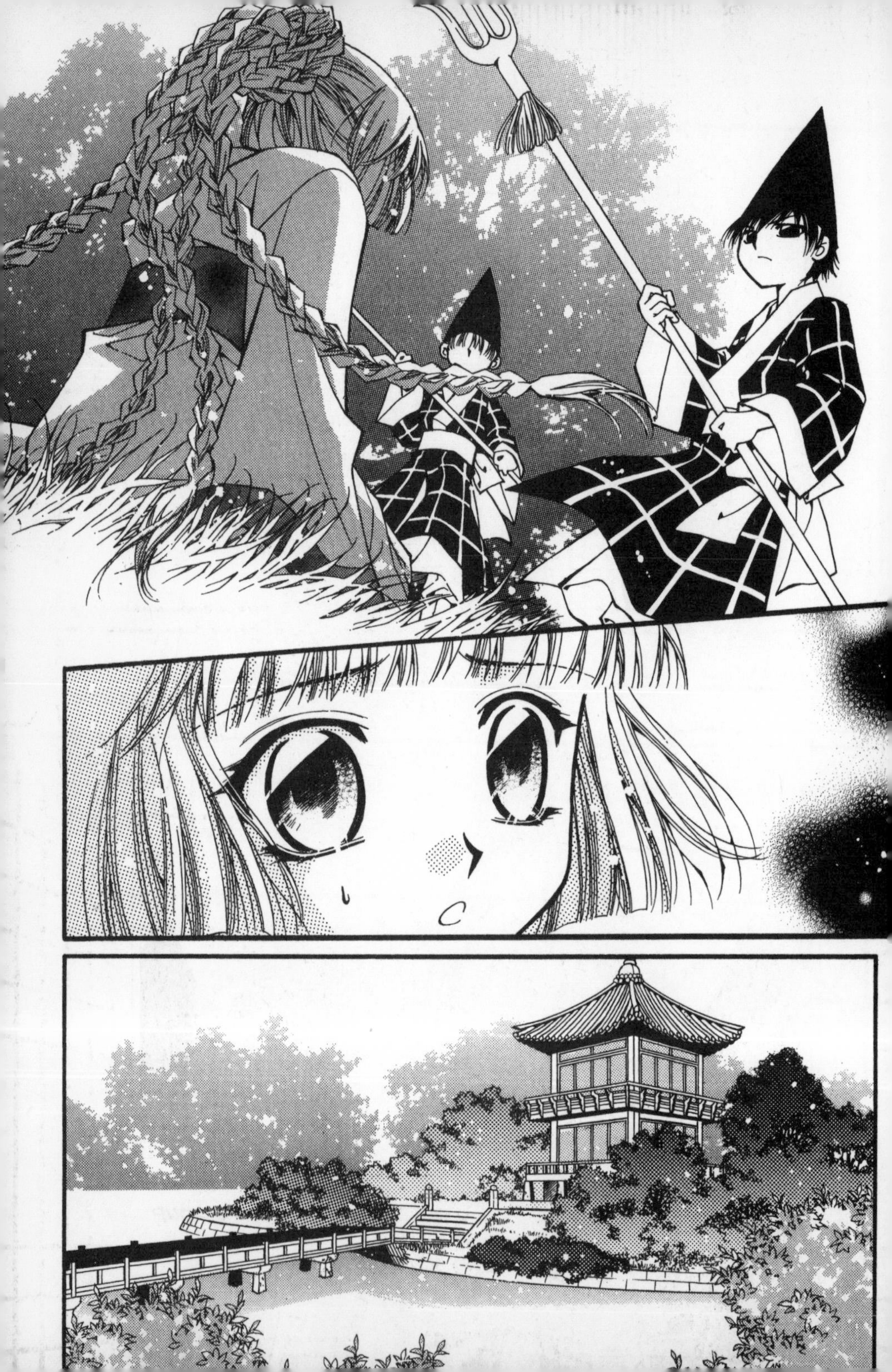

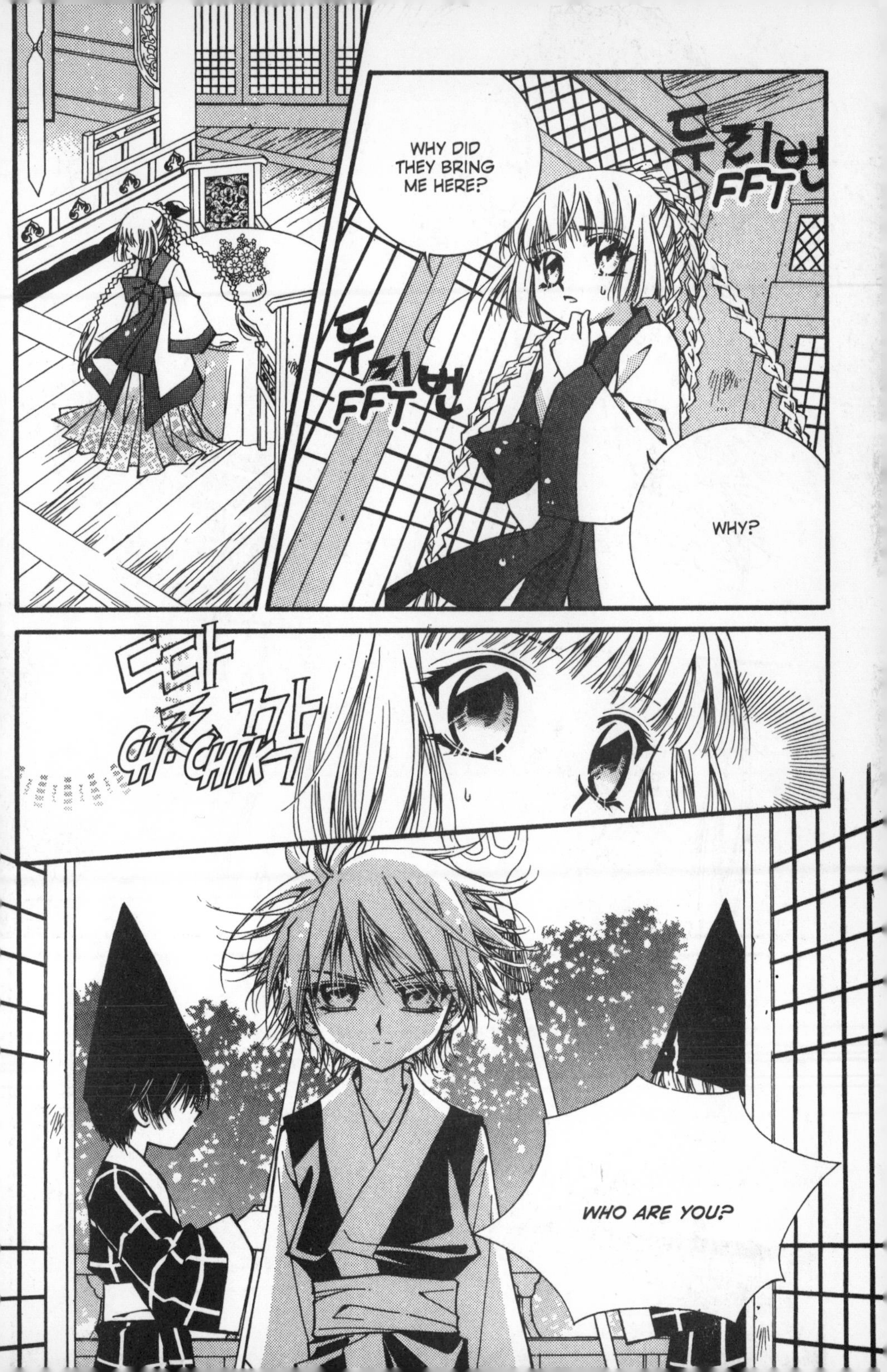
WHY DID THEY BRING ME HERE?
FFT
FFT
WHY?
CH- CHIK
WHO ARE YOU?

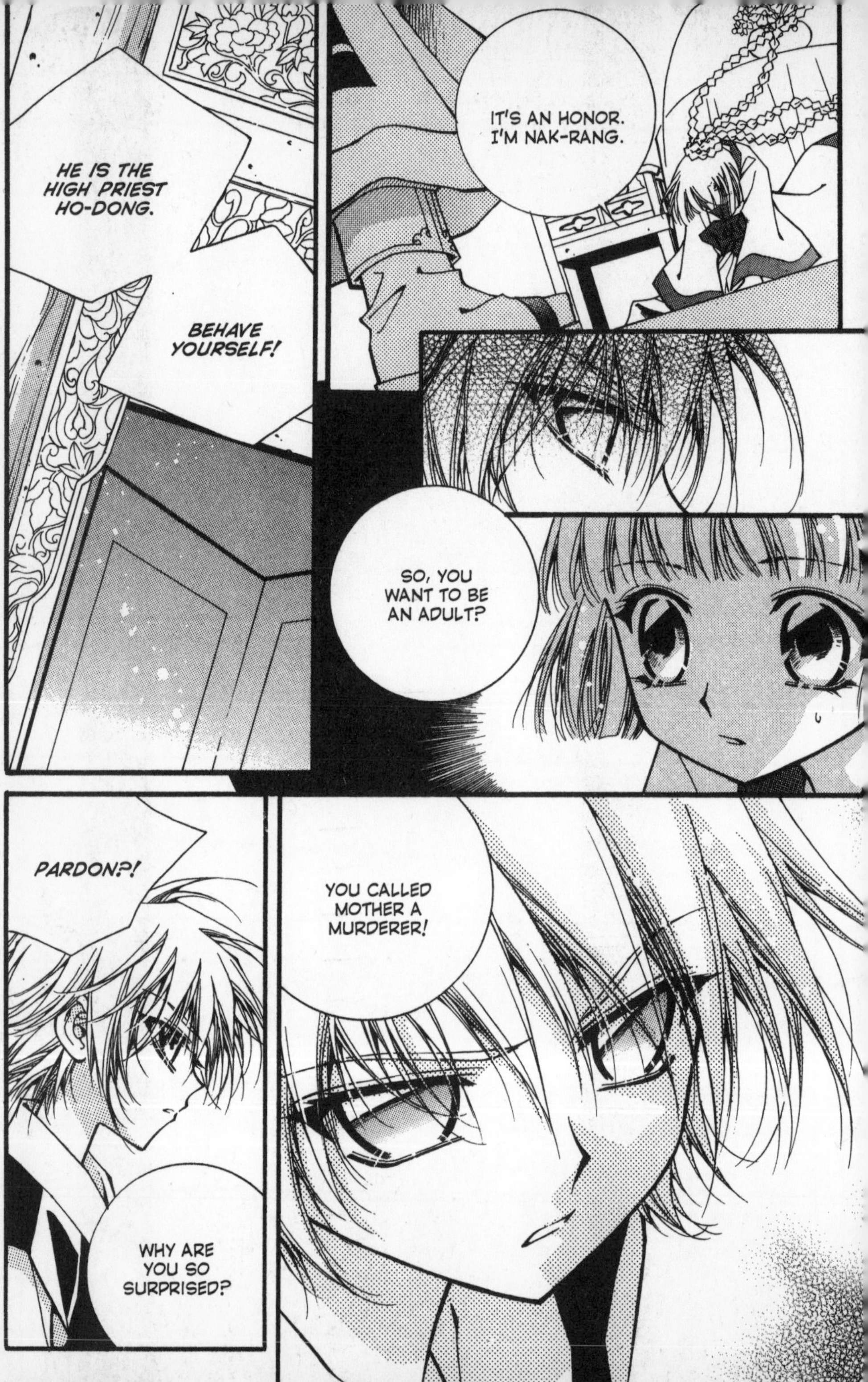
HE IS THE HIGH PRIEST HO-DONG.
BEHAVE YOURSELF!
IT'S AN HONOR. I'M NAK-RANG.
SO, YOU WANT TO BE AN ADULT?
PARDON?!
WHY ARE YOU SO SURPRISED?
YOU CALLED MOTHER A MURDERER!

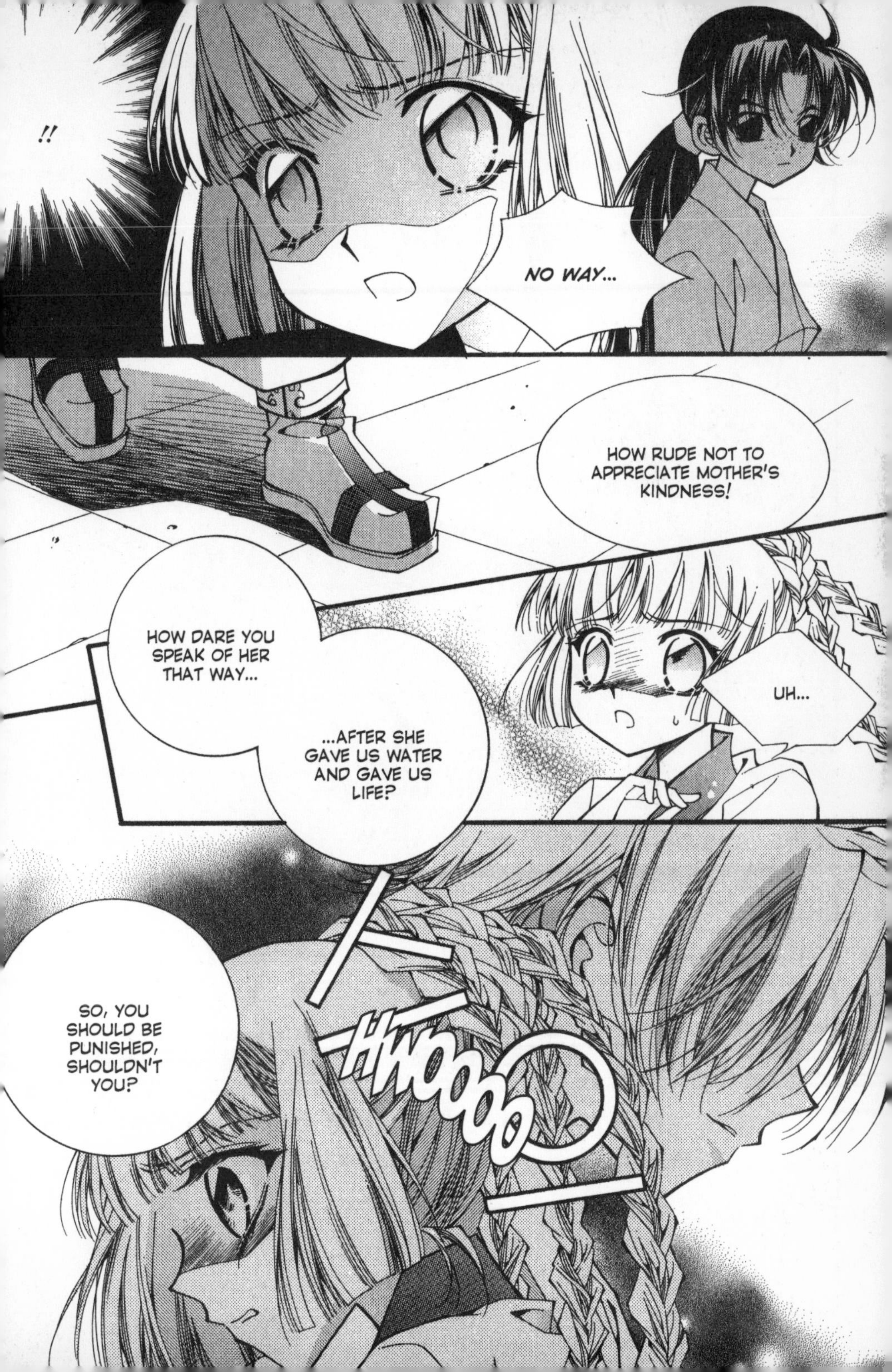

!!
NO WAY...
HOW RUDE NOT TO APPRECIATE MOTHER'S KINDNESS!
HOW DARE YOU SPEAK OF HER THAT WAY...
...AFTER SHE GAVE US WATER AND GAVE US LIFE?
UH...
SO, YOU SHOULD BE PUNISHED, SHOULDN'T YOU?
HWOOOOO

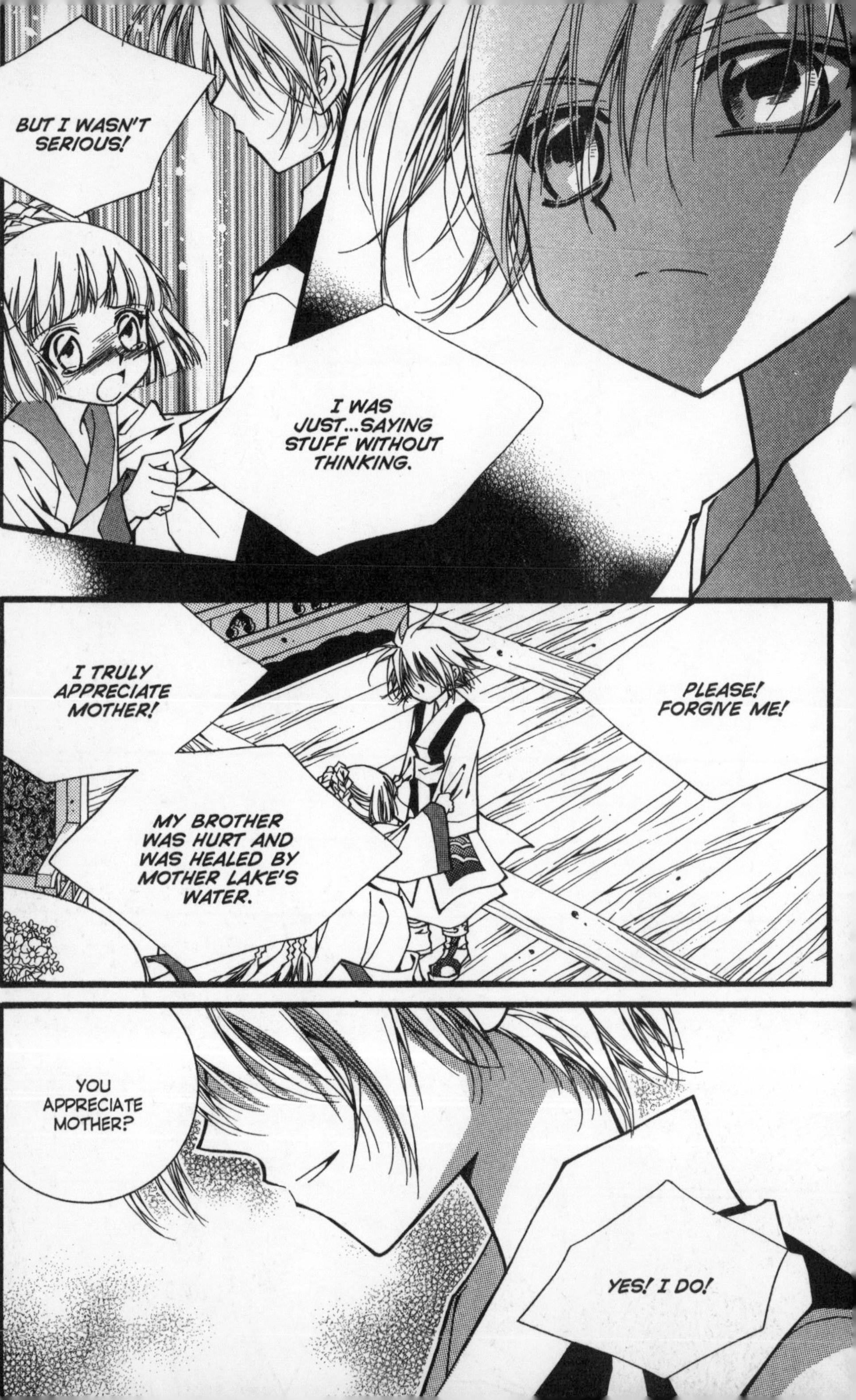
BUT I WASN'T SERIOUS!
I WAS JUST...SAYING STUFF WITHOUT THINKING.
I TRULY APPRECIATE MOTHER!
MY BROTHER WAS HURT AND WAS HEALED BY MOTHER LAKE'S WATER.
PLEASE! FORGIVE ME!
YOU APPRECIATE MOTHER?
YES! I DO!

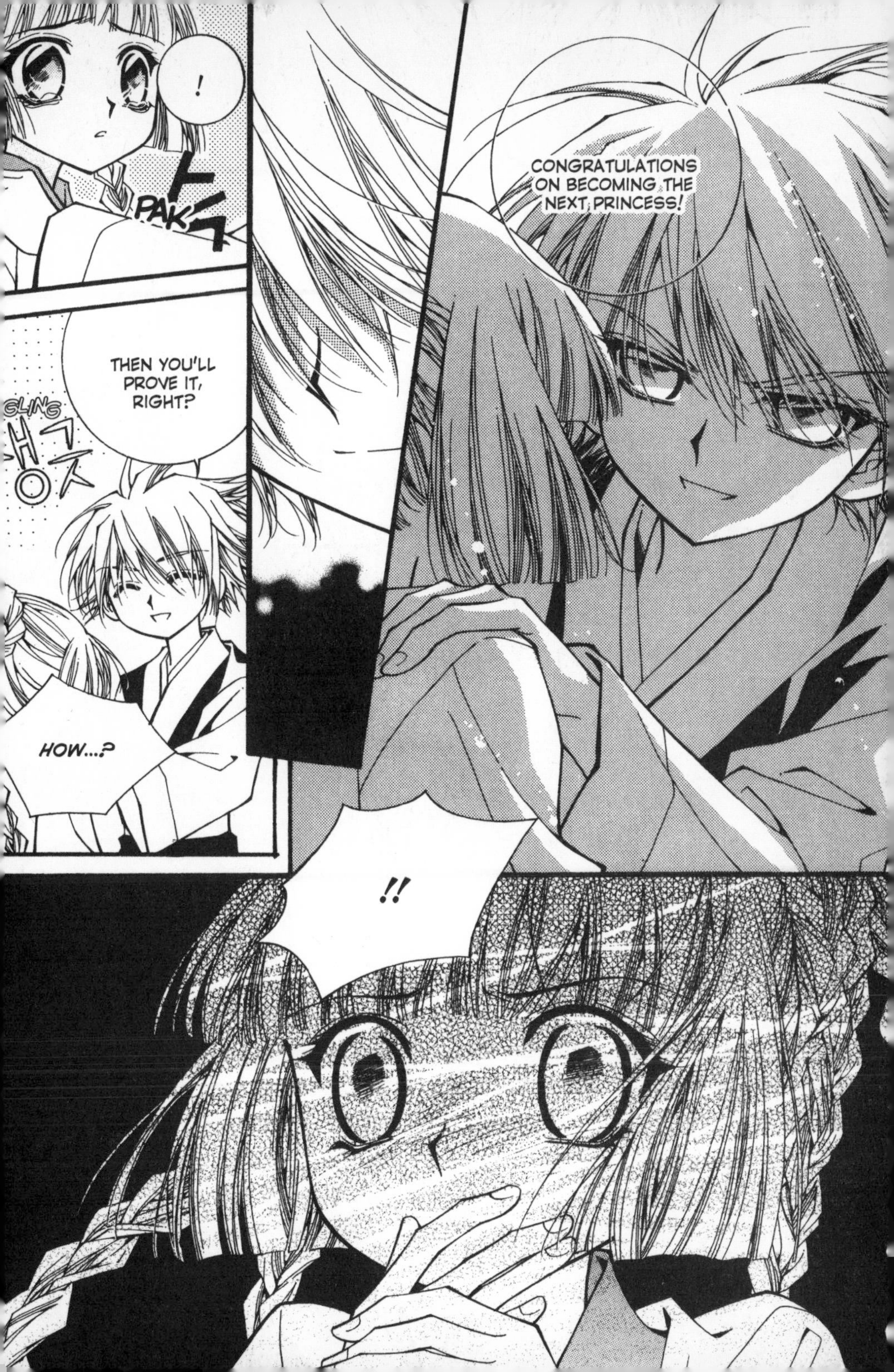
!
PAK
THEN YOU'LL PROVE IT, RIGHT?
GLING
HOW...?
CONGRATULATIONS ON BECOMING THE NEXT PRINCESS!
!!

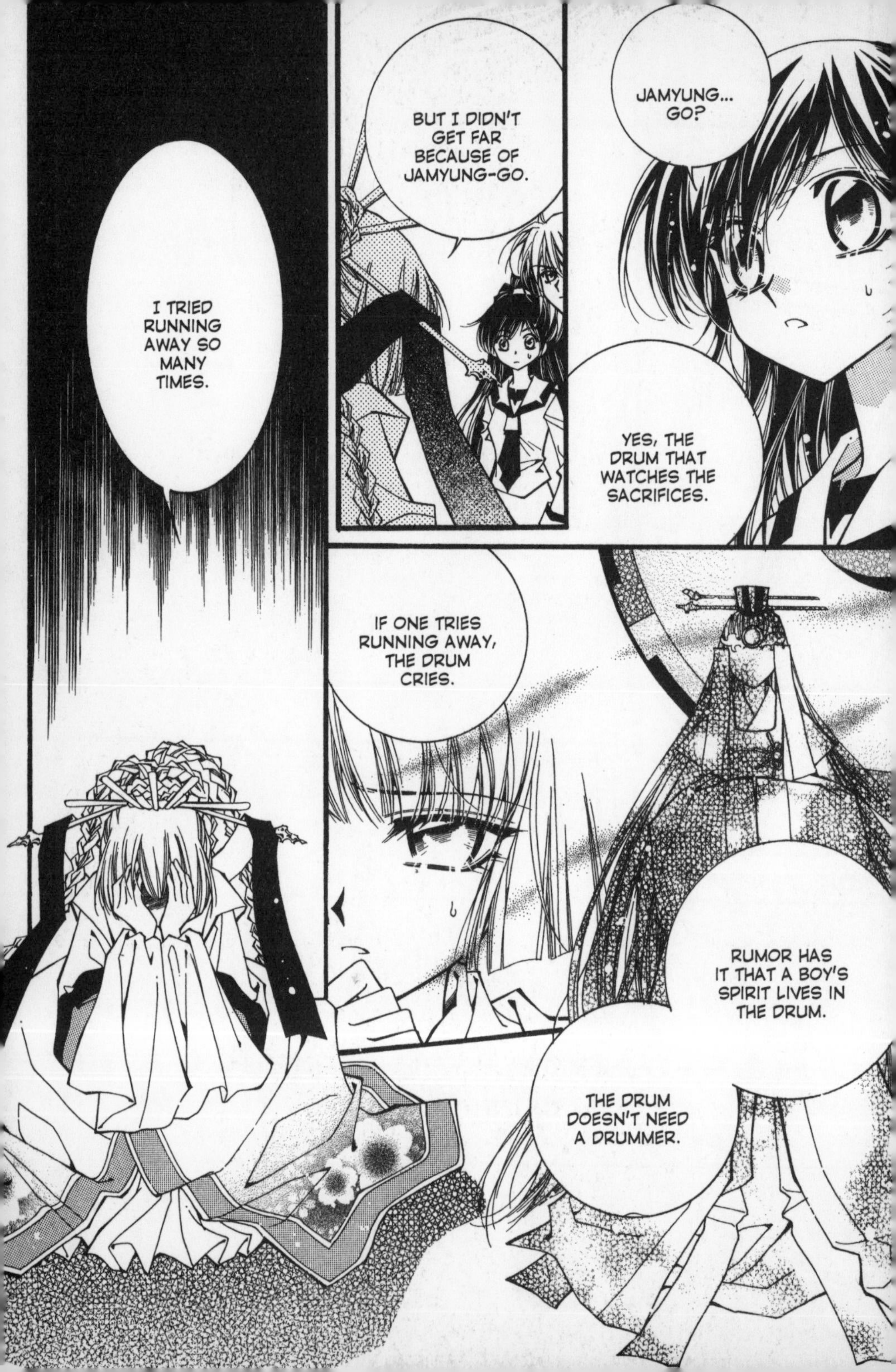
I TRIED RUNNING AWAY SO MANY TIMES.
BUT I DIDN'T GET FAR BECAUSE OF JAMYUNG-GO.
JAMYUNG... GO?
YES, THE DRUM THAT WATCHES THE SACRIFICES.
IF ONE TRIES RUNNING AWAY, THE DRUM CRIES.
RUMOR HAS IT THAT A BOY'S SPIRIT LIVES IN THE DRUM.
THE DRUM DOESN'T NEED A DRUMMER.

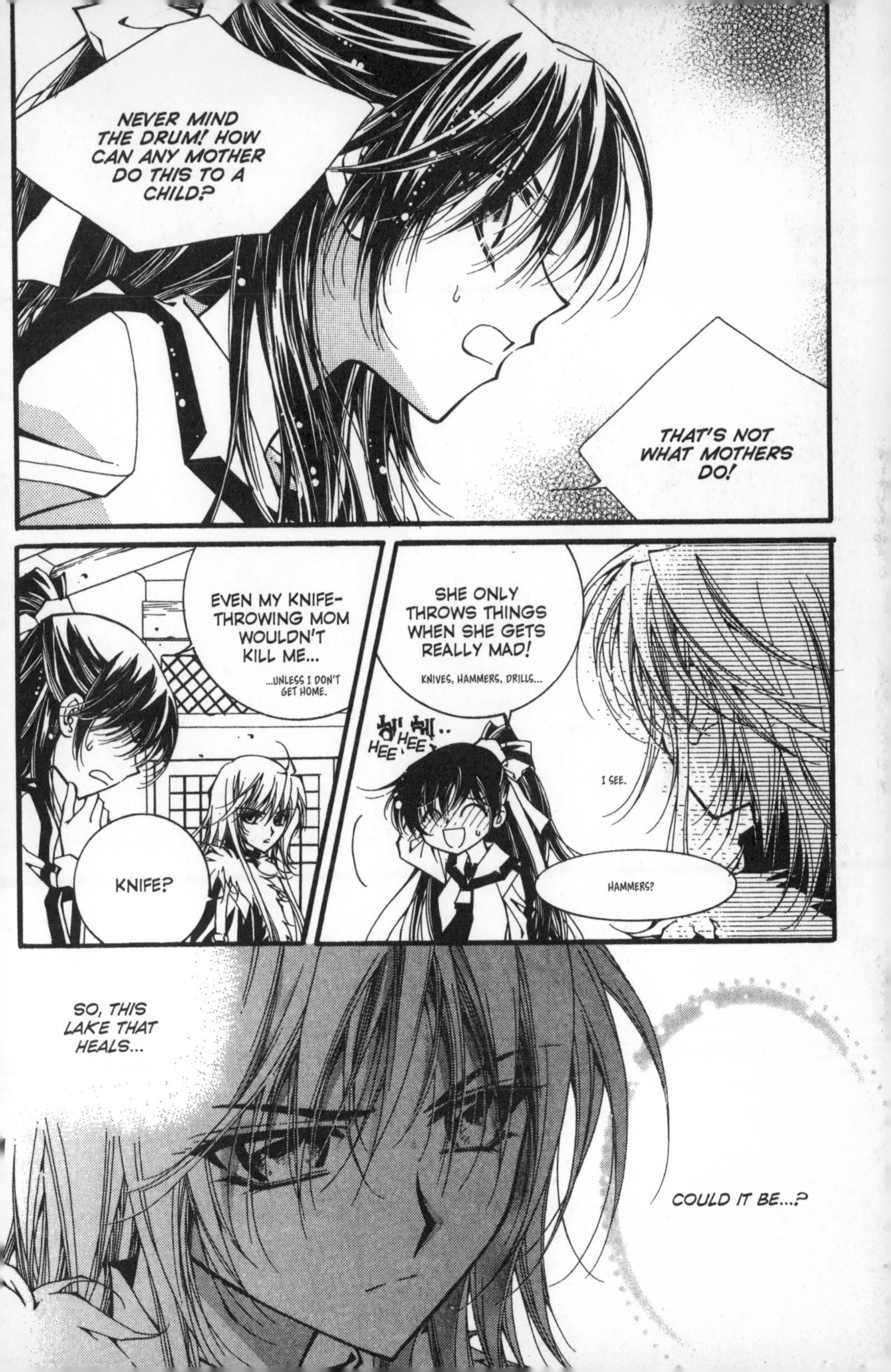
NEVER MIND THE DRUM! HOW CAN ANY MOTHER DO THIS TO A CHILD?
THAT'S NOT WHAT MOTHERS DO!
EVEN MY KNIFE-THROWING MOM WOULDN'T KILL ME...
...UNLESS I DON'T GET HOME.
KNIFE?
SHE ONLY THROWS THINGS WHEN SHE GETS REALLY MAD!
KNIVES, HAMMERS, DRILLS...
헤헤..
HEE HEE
I SEE.
HAMMERS?
SO, THIS LAKE THAT HEALS...
COULD IT BE...?

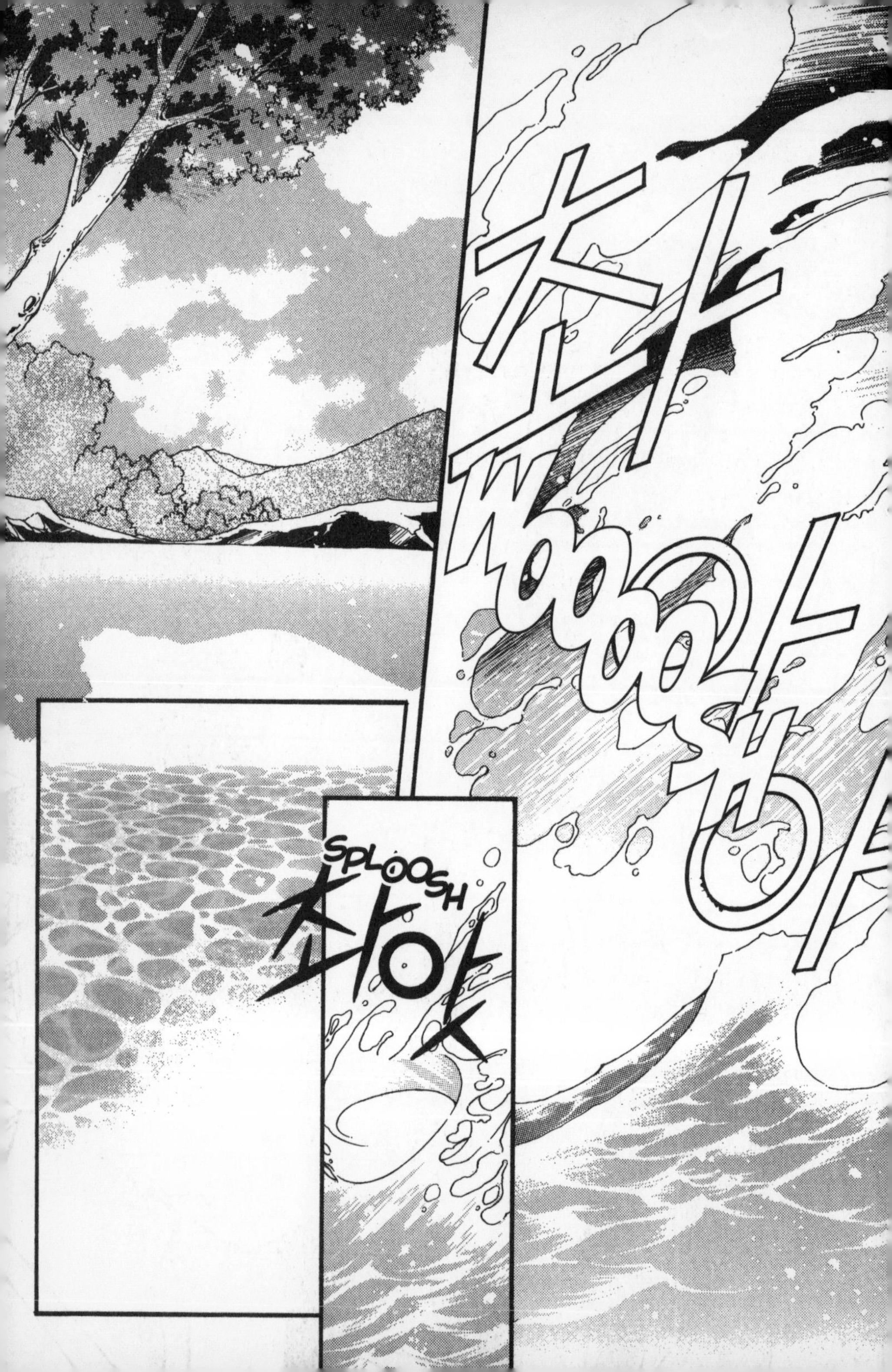
WHOOOOSH
SPLOOSH

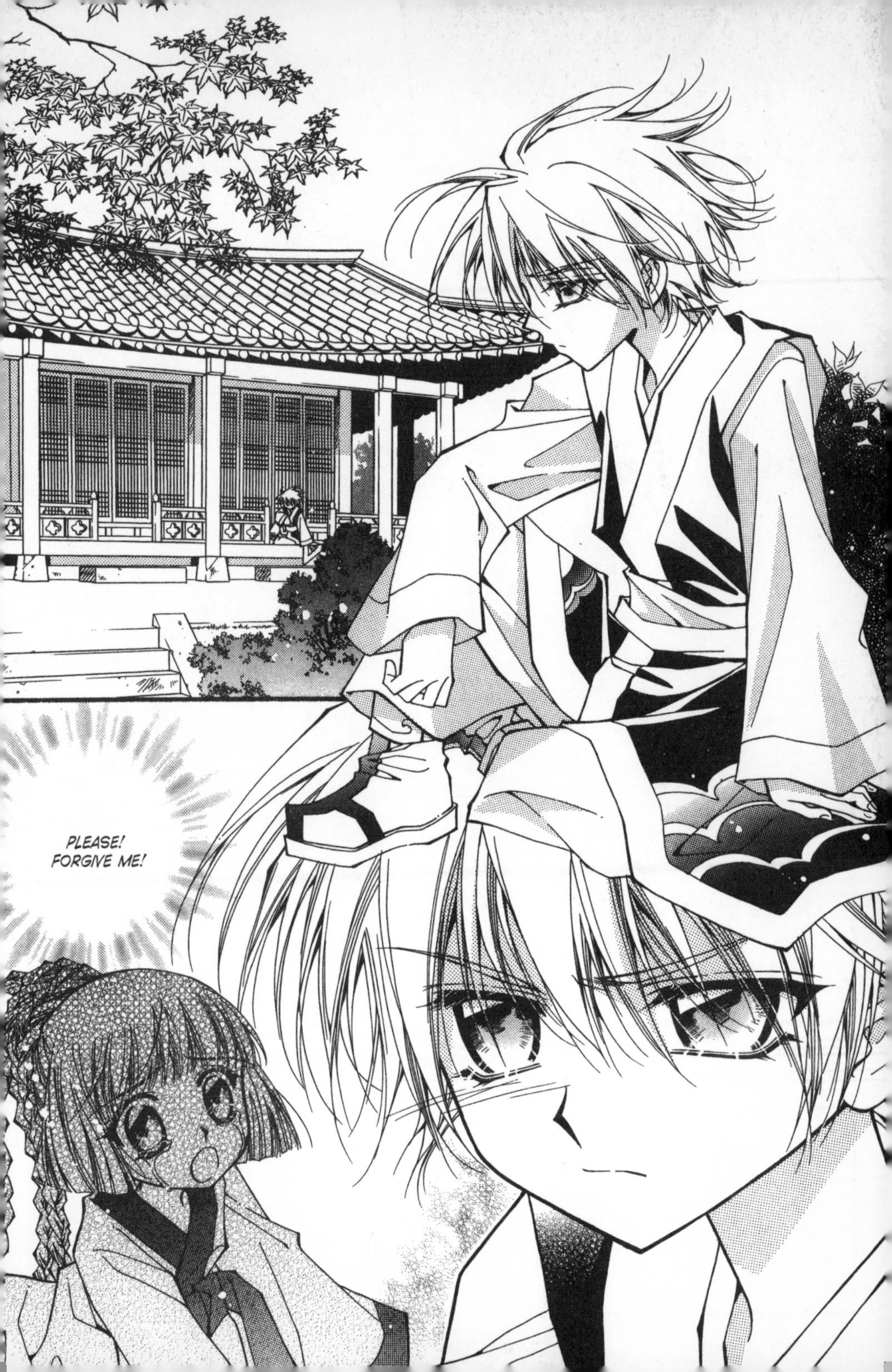
PLEASE! FORGIVE ME!

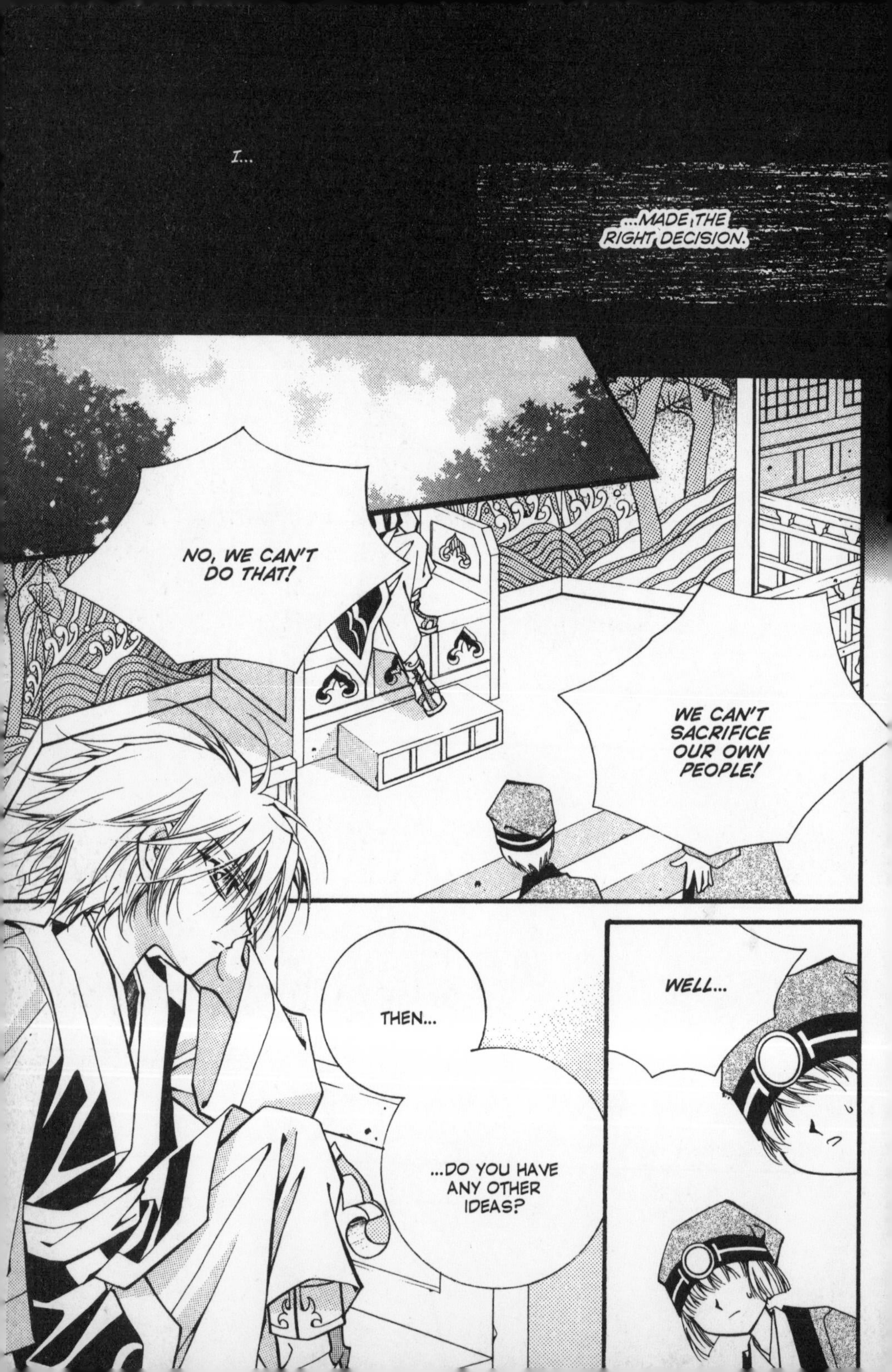
I...
...MADE THE RIGHT DECISION.
NO, WE CAN'T DO THAT!
WE CAN'T SACRIFICE OUR OWN PEOPLE!
THEN...
...DO YOU HAVE ANY OTHER IDEAS?
WELL...

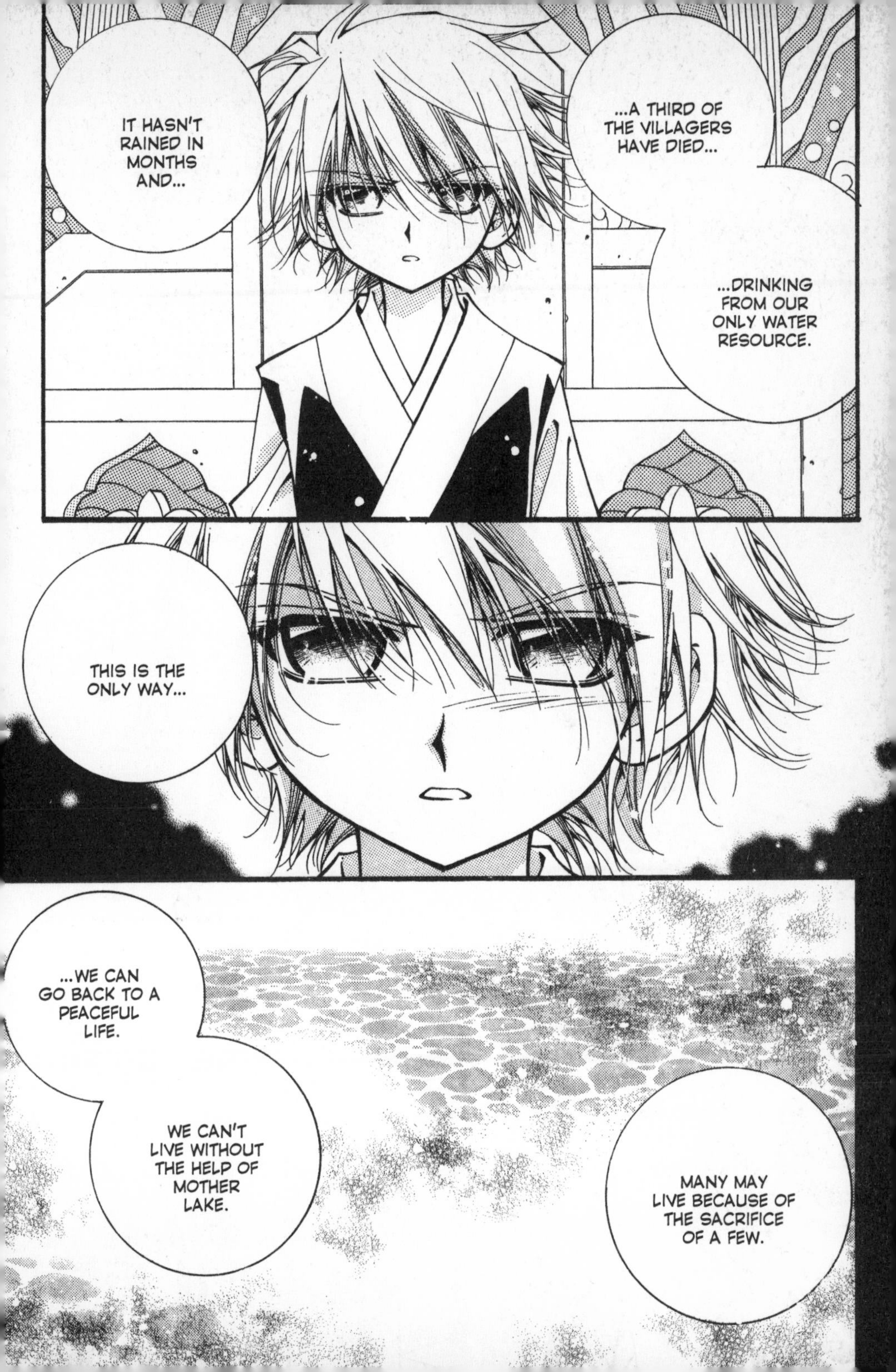
IT HASN'T RAINED IN MONTHS AND...
...A THIRD OF THE VILLAGERS HAVE DIED...
...DRINKING FROM OUR ONLY WATER RESOURCE.
THIS IS THE ONLY WAY...
...WE CAN GO BACK TO A PEACEFUL LIFE.
WE CAN'T LIVE WITHOUT THE HELP OF MOTHER LAKE.
MANY MAY LIVE BECAUSE OF THE SACRIFICE OF A FEW.

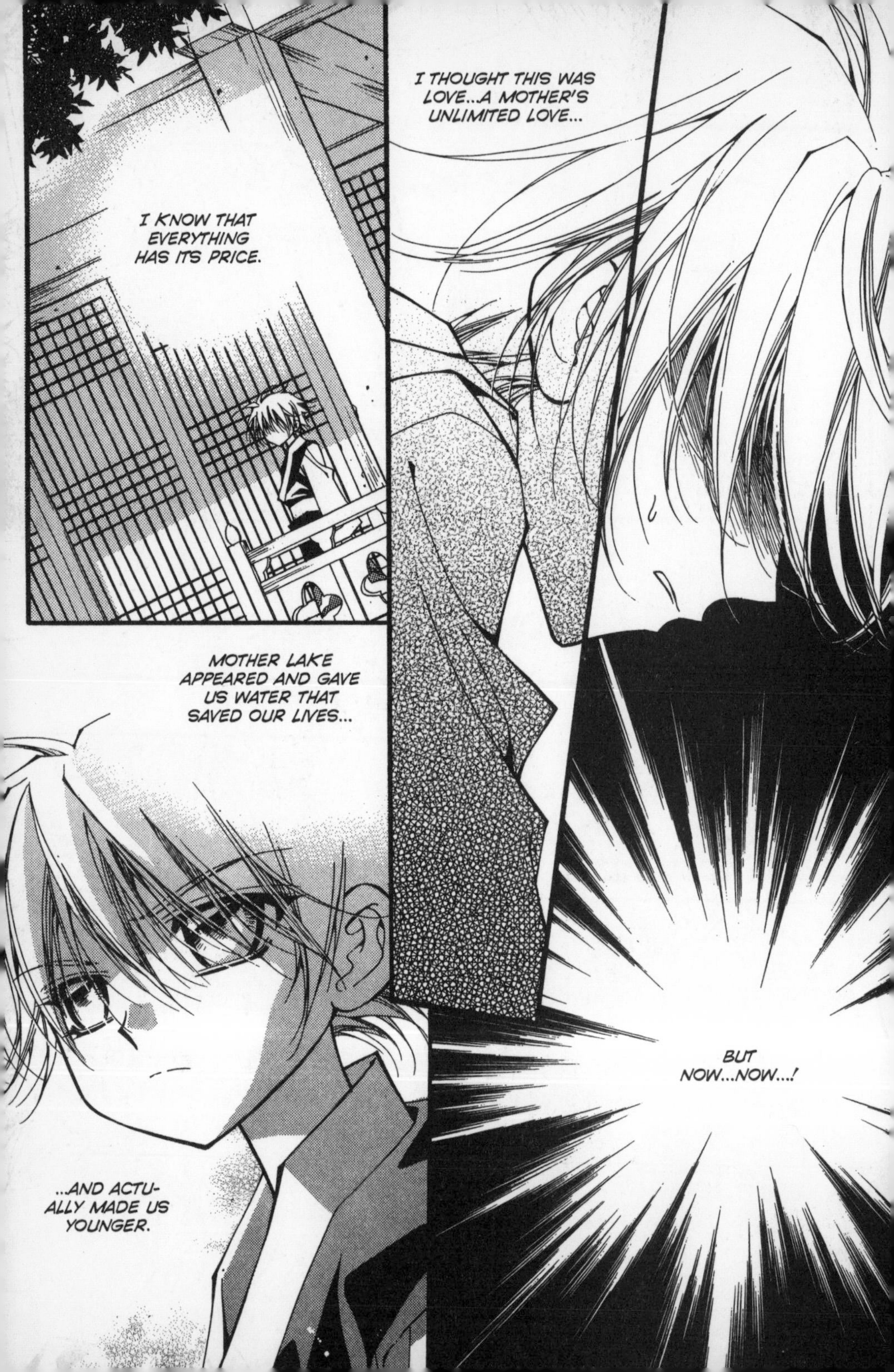
I KNOW THAT EVERYTHING HAS ITS PRICE.
MOTHER LAKE APPEARED AND GAVE US WATER THAT SAVED OUR LIVES...
...AND ACTU-ALLY MADE US YOUNGER.
I THOUGHT THIS WAS LOVE...A MOTHER'S UNLIMITED LOVE...
BUT NOW...NOW...!

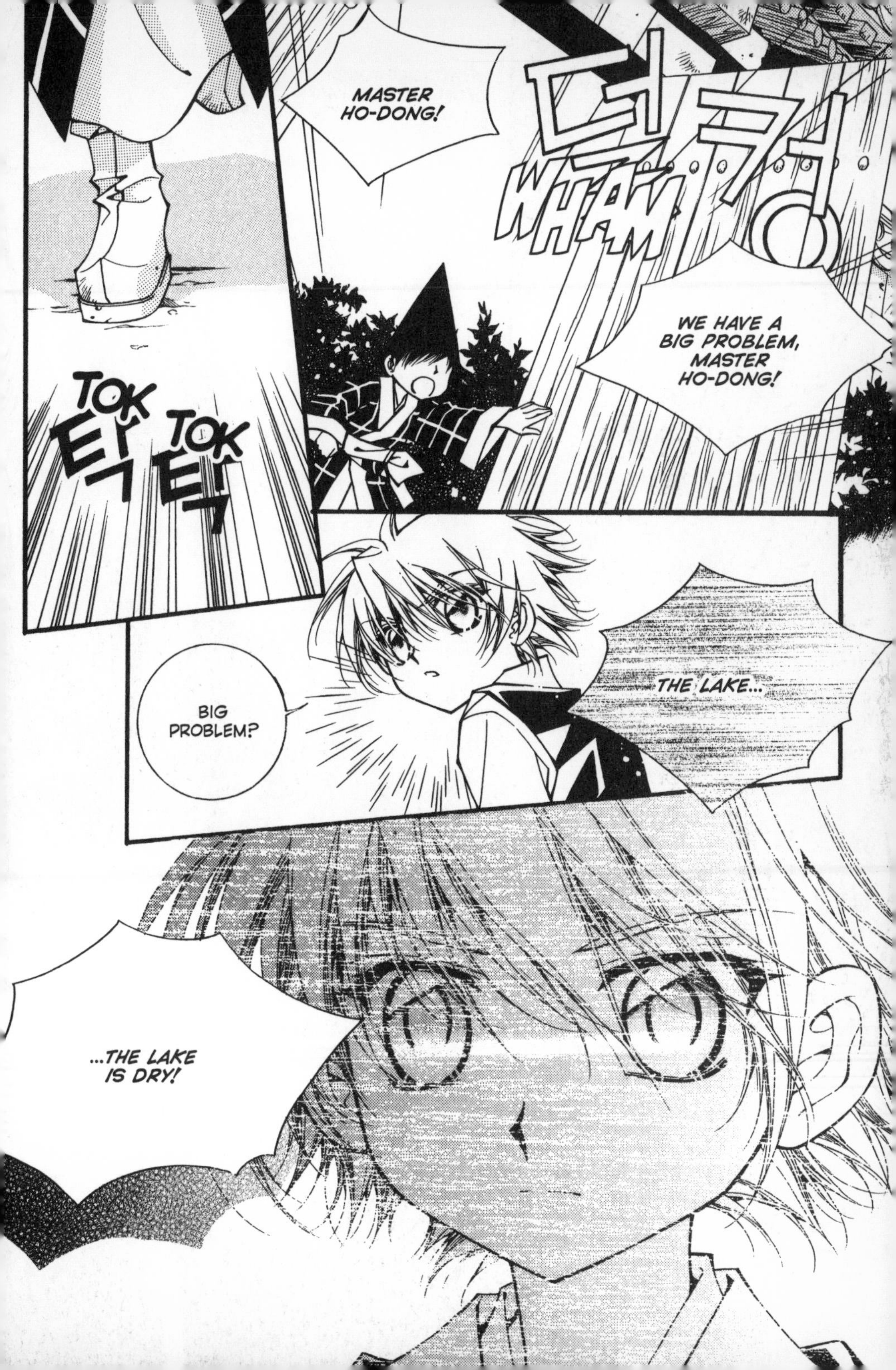
TOK TOK
MASTER HO-DONG!
WHAM
WE HAVE A BIG PROBLEM, MASTER HO-DONG!
BIG PROBLEM?
THE LAKE...
...THE LAKE IS DRY!

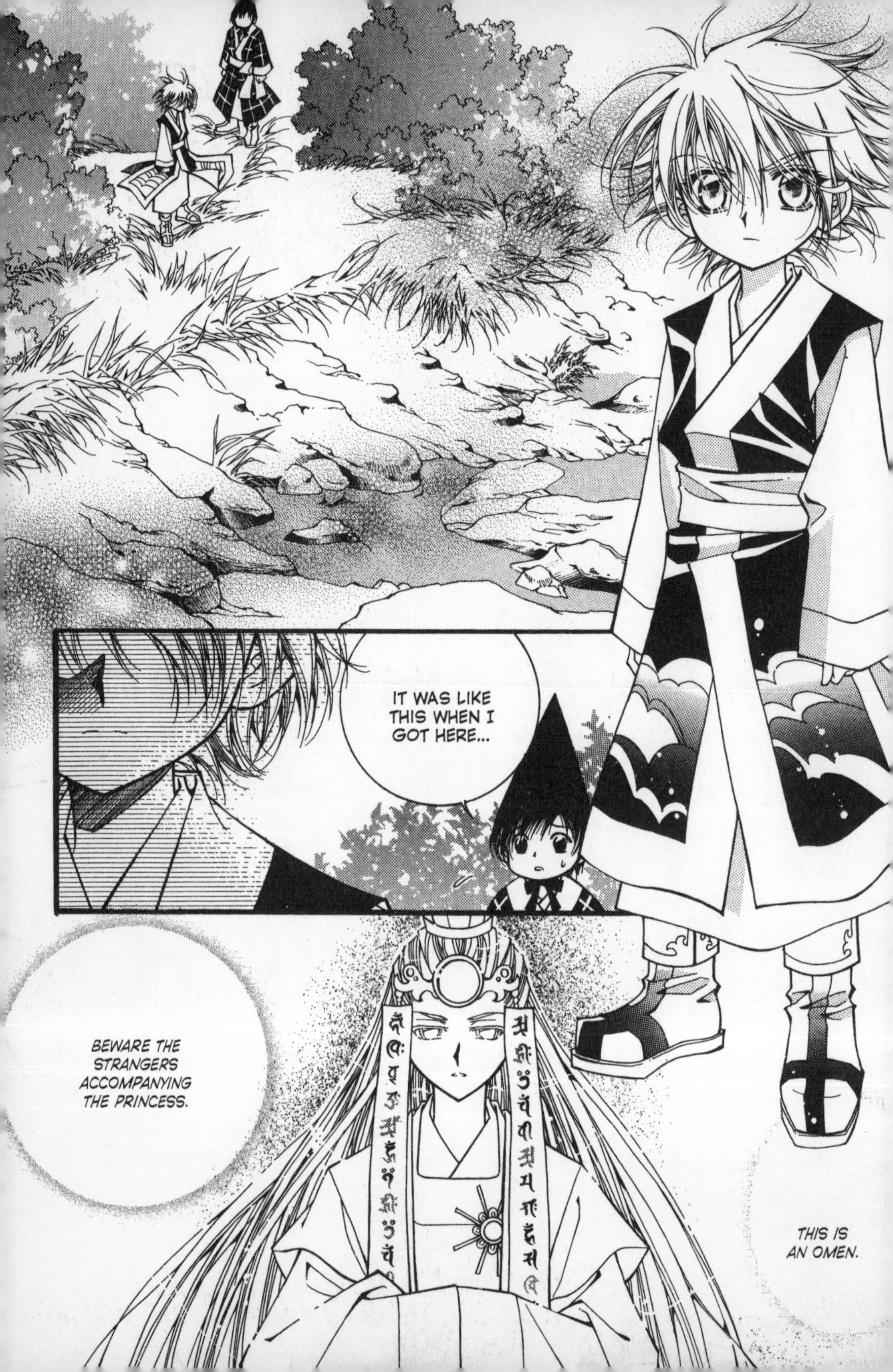
IT WAS LIKE THIS WHEN I GOT HERE...
BEWARE THE STRANGERS ACCOMPANYING THE PRINCESS.
THIS IS AN OMEN.

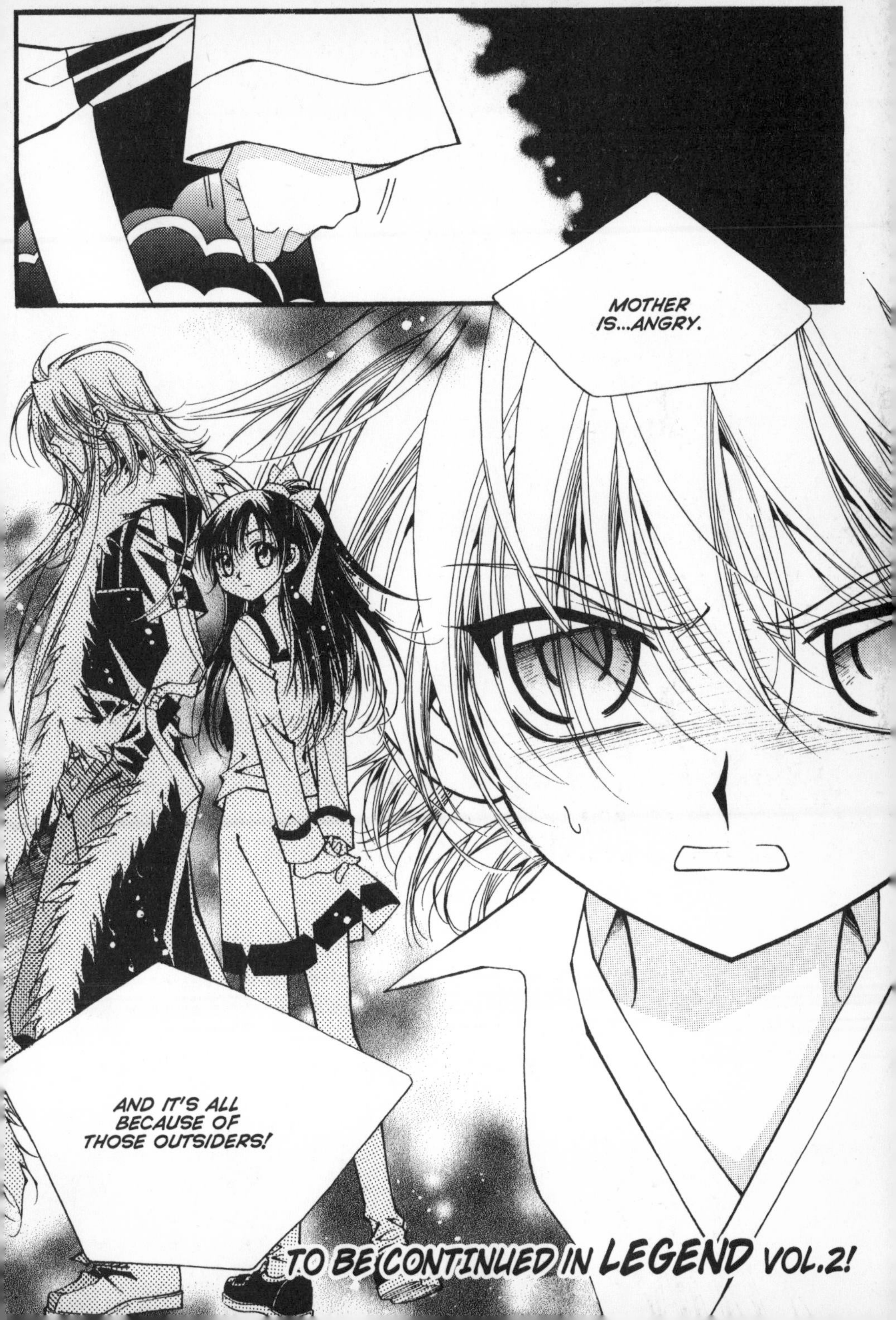
MOTHER IS...ANGRY.
AND IT'S ALL BECAUSE OF THOSE OUTSIDERS!
TO BE CONTINUED IN LEGEND VOL.2!

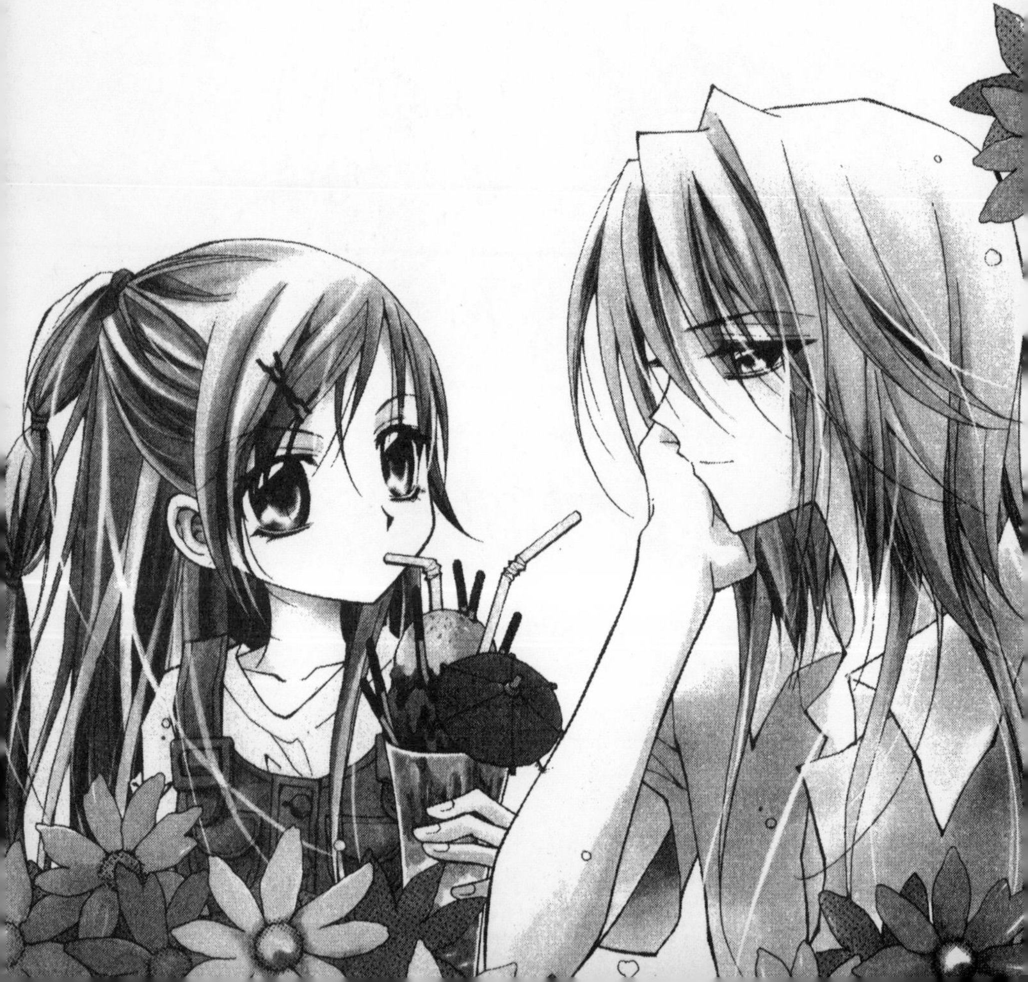

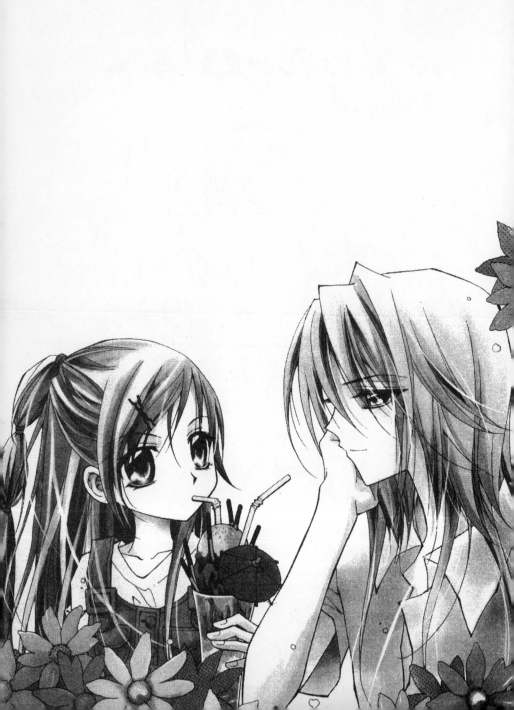

CHOCOLAT

vol.4

JiSang Shin·Geo

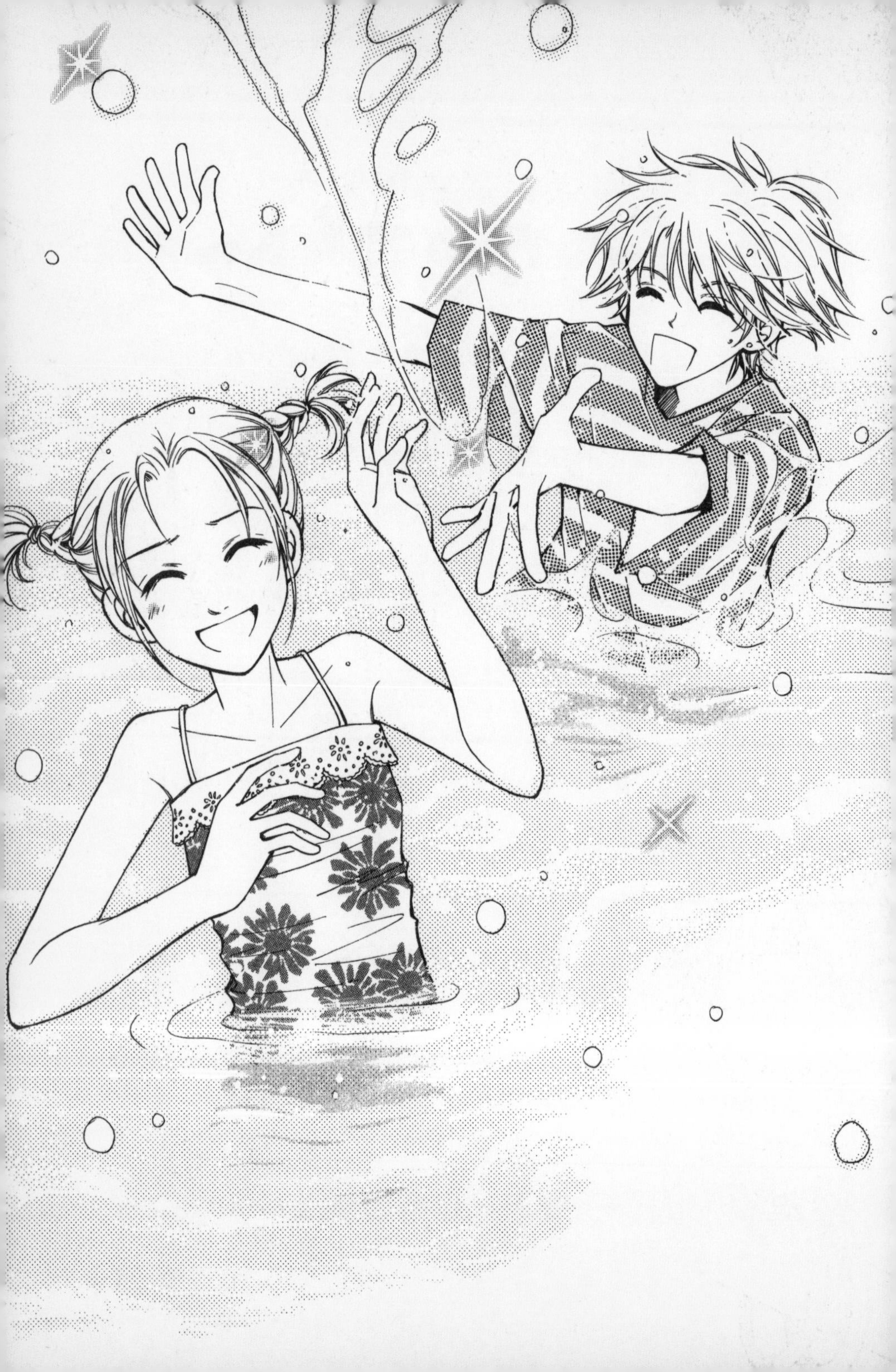

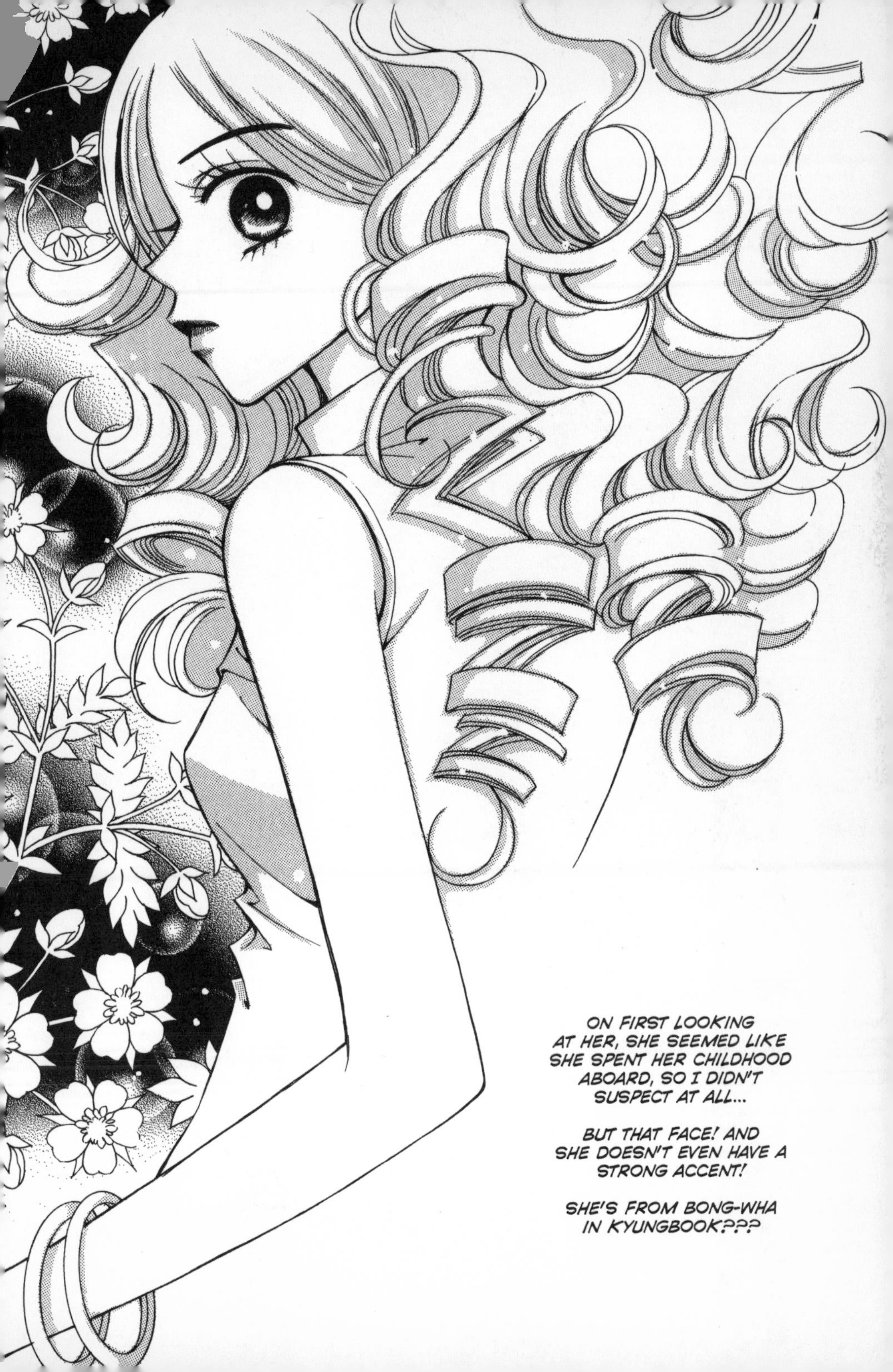
ON FIRST LOOKING AT HER, SHE SEEMED LIKE SHE SPENT HER CHILDHOOD ABOARD, SO I DIDN'T SUSPECT AT ALL...
BUT THAT FACE! AND SHE DOESN'T EVEN HAVE A STRONG ACCENT!
SHE'S FROM BONG-WHA IN KYUNGBOOK???

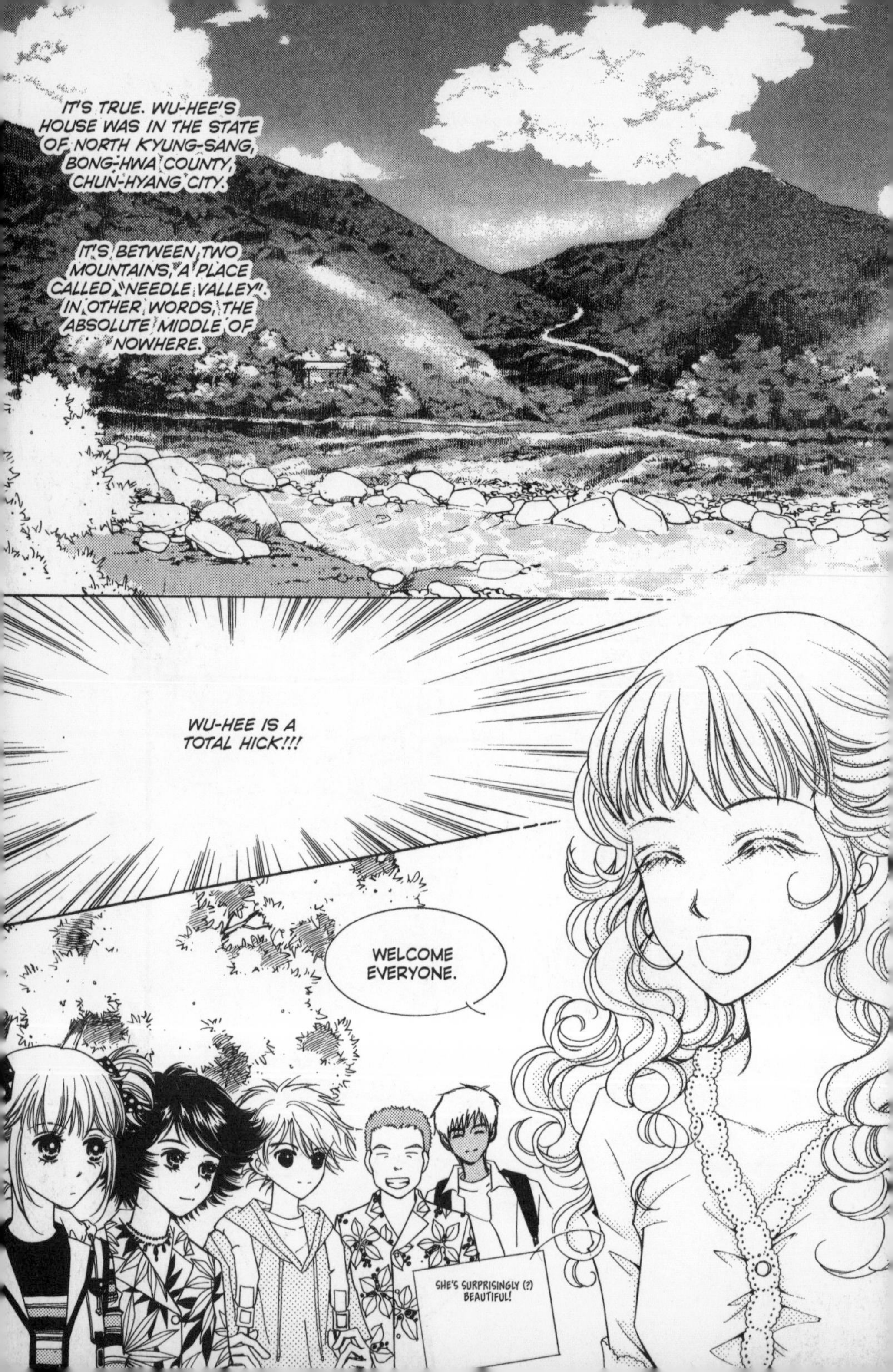
IT'S TRUE. WU-HEE'S HOUSE WAS IN THE STATE OF NORTH KYUNG-SANG, BONG-HWA COUNTY, CHUN-HYANG CITY.
IT'S BETWEEN TWO MOUNTAINS, A PLACE CALLED "NEEDLE VALLEY". IN OTHER WORDS, THE ABSOLUTE MIDDLE OF NOWHERE.
WU-HEE IS A TOTAL HICK!!!
WELCOME EVERYONE.
SHE'S SURPRISINGLY (?) BEAUTIFUL!

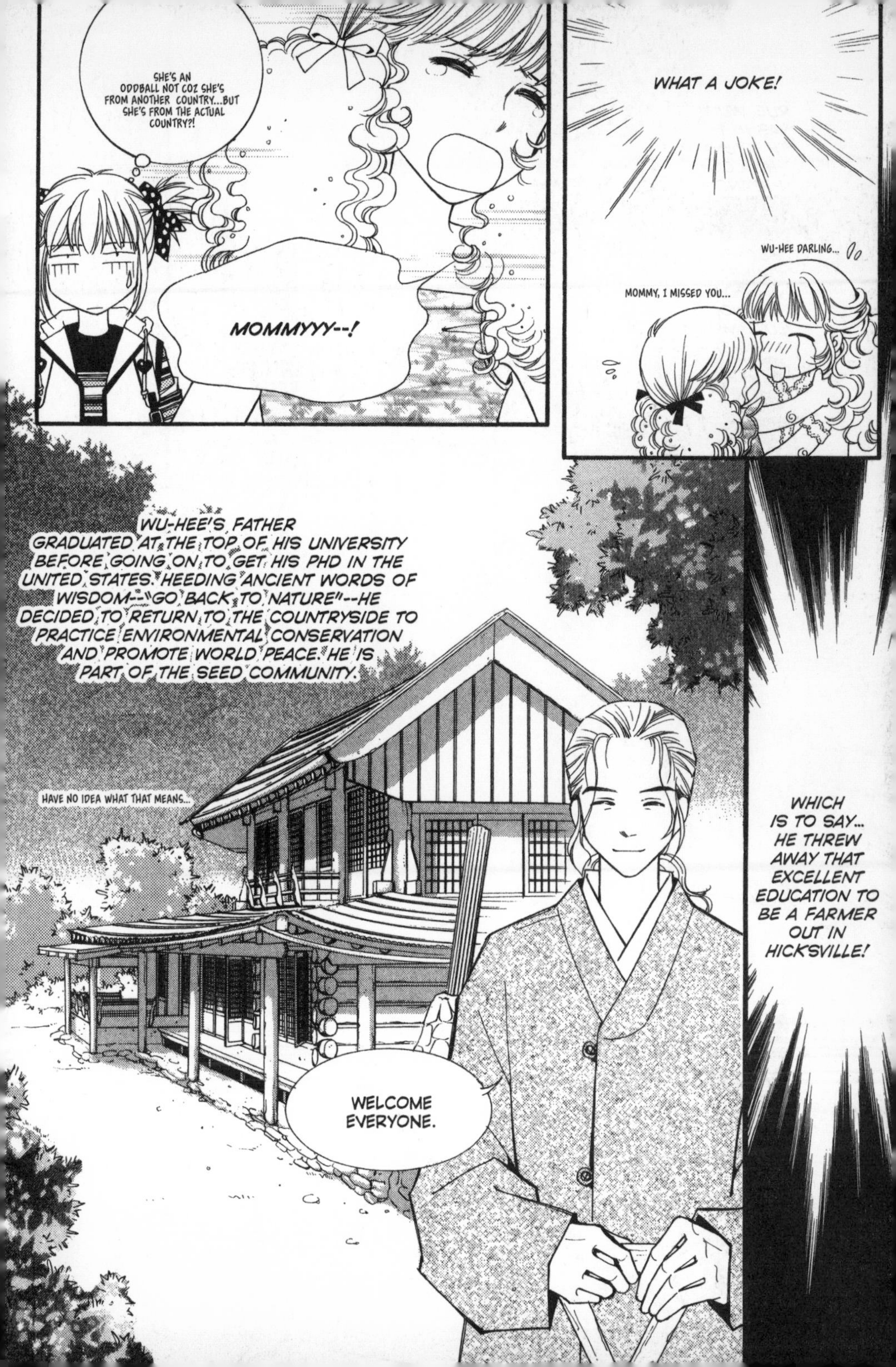
SHE'S AN ODDBALL NOT COZ SHE'S FROM ANOTHER COUNTRY...BUT SHE'S FROM THE ACTUAL COUNTRY?!
MOMMYYY--!
WHAT A JOKE!
WU-HEE DARLING...
MOMMY, I MISSED YOU...
WU-HEE'S FATHER GRADUATED AT THE TOP OF HIS UNIVERSITY BEFORE GOING ON TO GET HIS PHD IN THE UNITED STATES. HEEDING ANCIENT WORDS OF WISDOM--"GO BACK TO NATURE"--HE DECIDED TO RETURN TO THE COUNTRYSIDE TO PRACTICE ENVIRONMENTAL CONSERVATION AND PROMOTE WORLD PEACE. HE IS PART OF THE SEED COMMUNITY.
HAVE NO IDEA WHAT THAT MEANS...
WHICH IS TO SAY... HE THREW AWAY THAT EXCELLENT EDUCATION TO BE A FARMER OUT IN HICKSVILLE!
WELCOME EVERYONE.

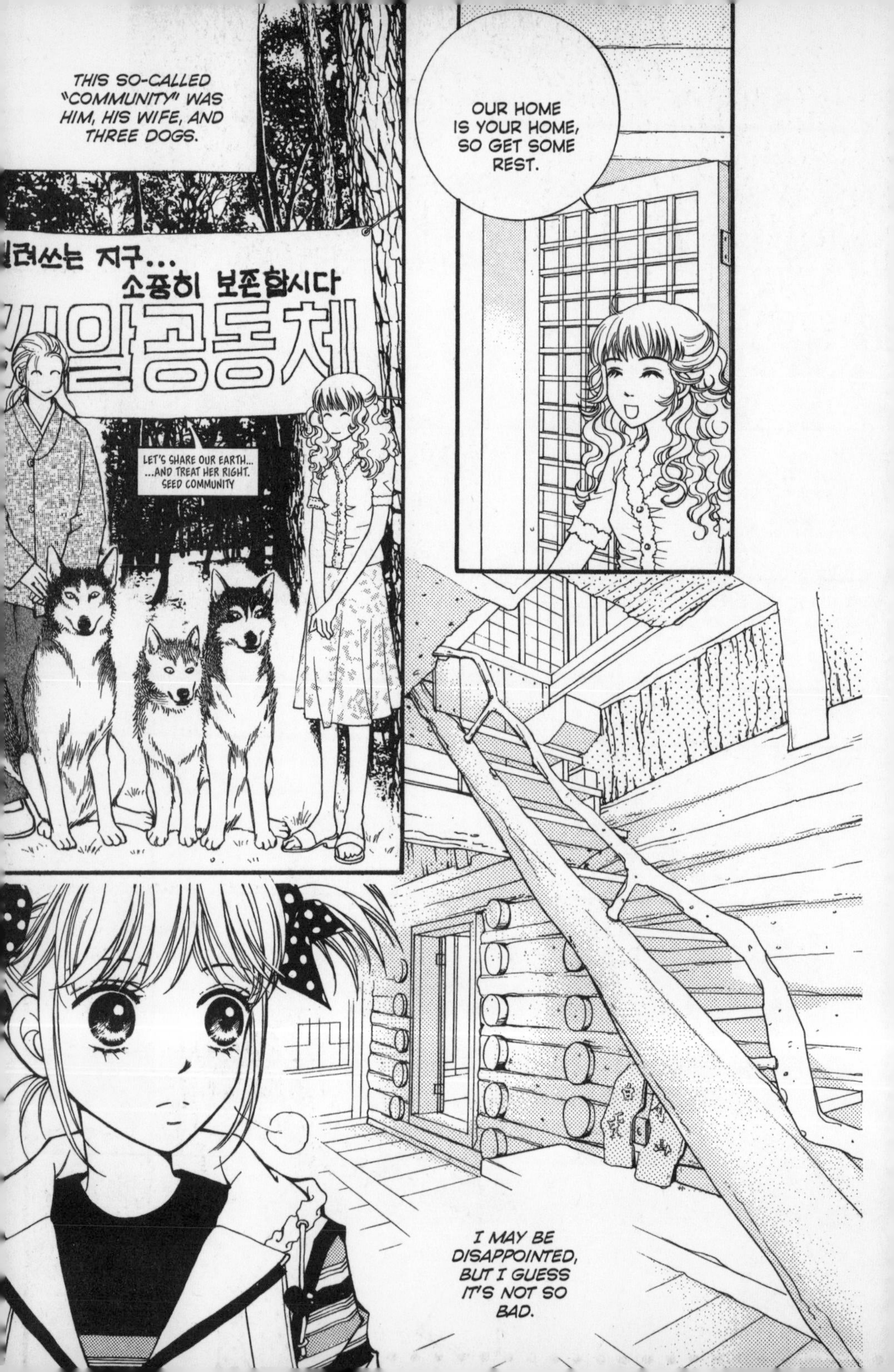
THIS SO-CALLED "COMMUNITY" WAS HIM, HIS WIFE, AND THREE DOGS.
려쓰는 지구...
소중히 보존합시다
알공동체
LET'S SHARE OUR EARTH... ...AND TREAT HER RIGHT. SEED COMMUNITY
OUR HOME IS YOUR HOME, SO GET SOME REST.
I MAY BE DISAPPOINTED, BUT I GUESS IT'S NOT SO BAD.

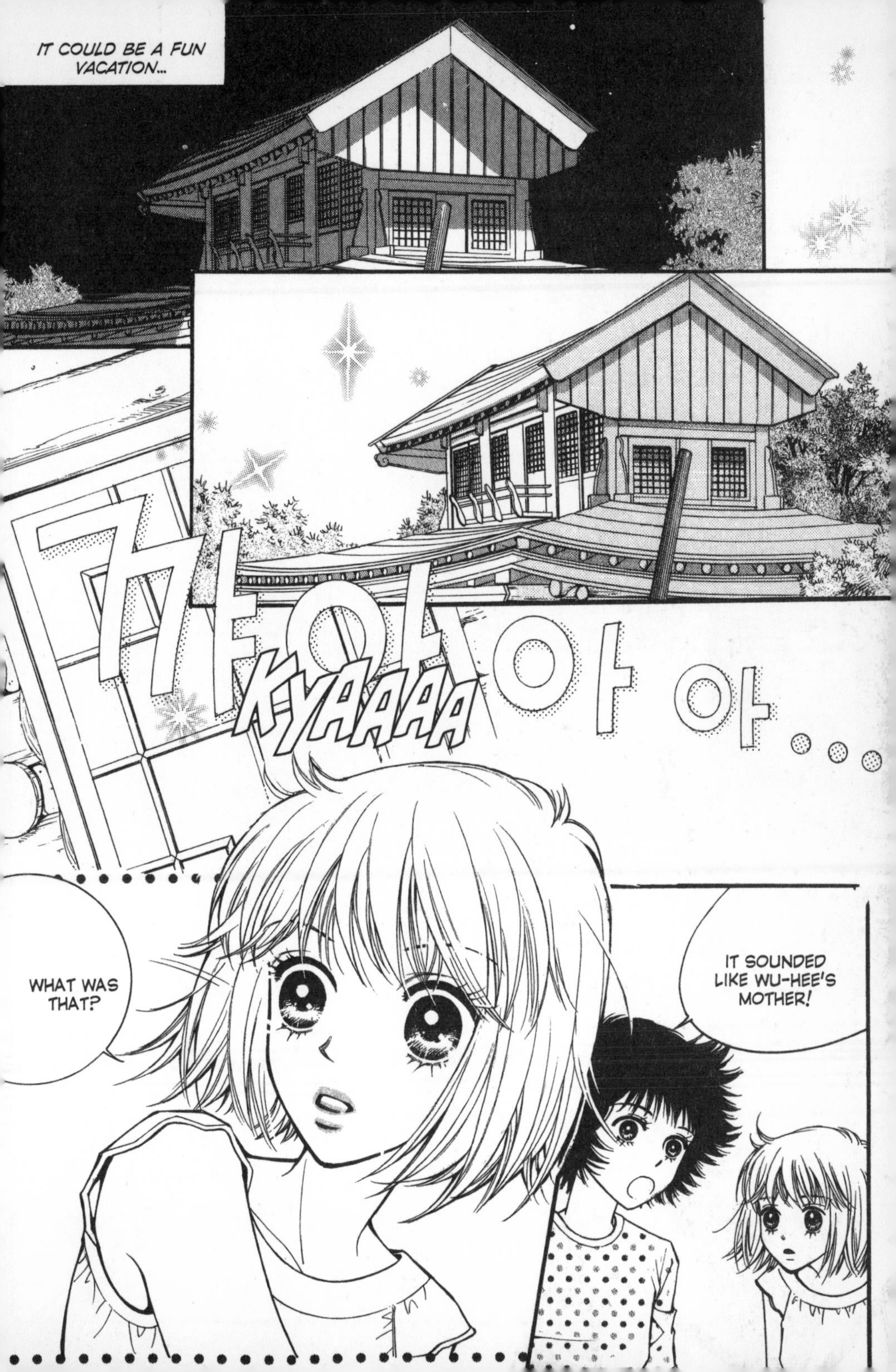
IT COULD BE A FUN VACATION...
KYAAAA
WHAT WAS THAT?
IT SOUNDED LIKE WU-HEE'S MOTHER!

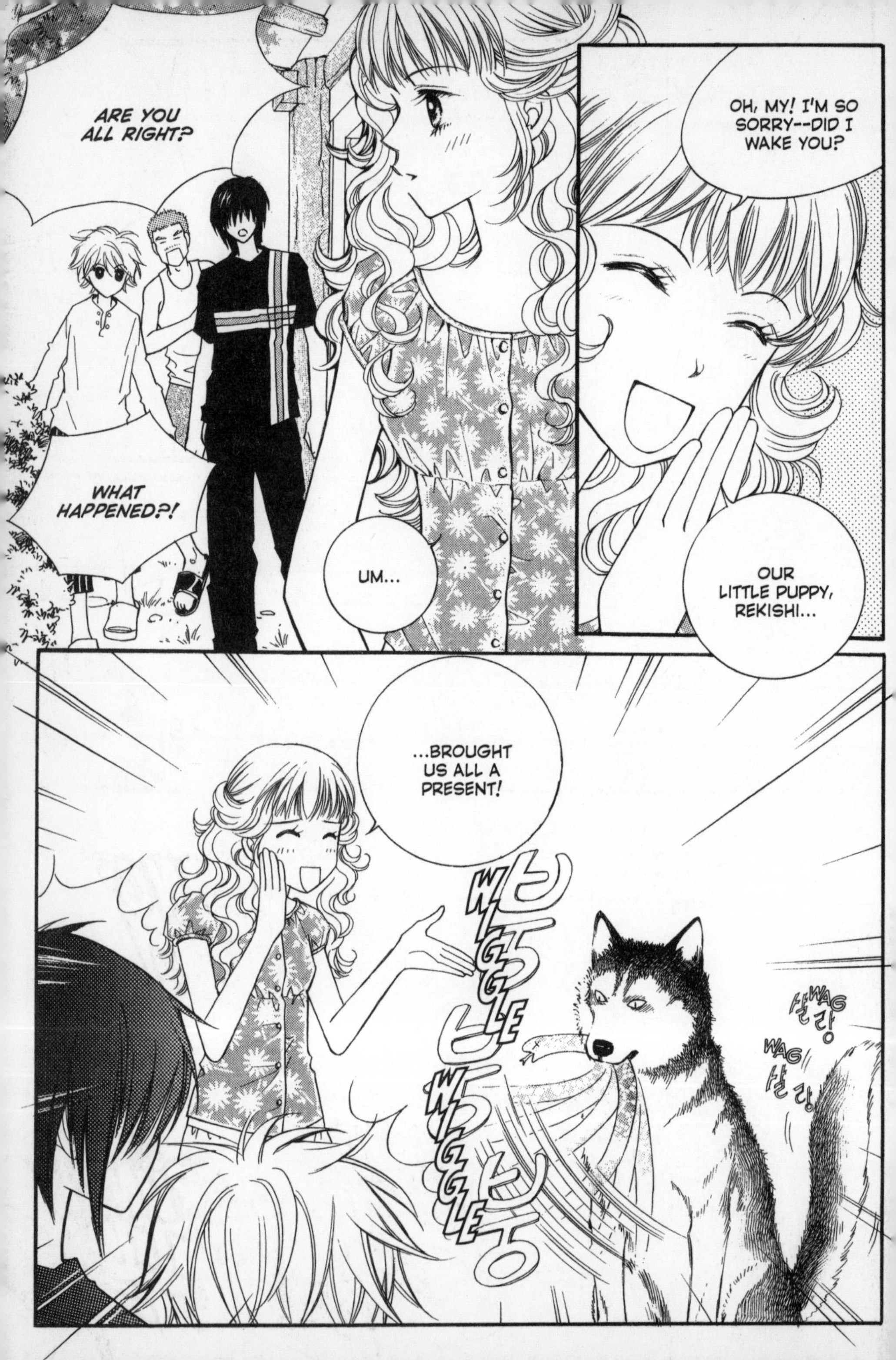
ARE YOU ALL RIGHT?
WHAT HAPPENED?!
UM...
OH, MY! I'M SO SORRY--DID I WAKE YOU?
OUR LITTLE PUPPY, REKISHI...
...BROUGHT US ALL A PRESENT!
WIGGLE
WIGGLE
WAG
WAG

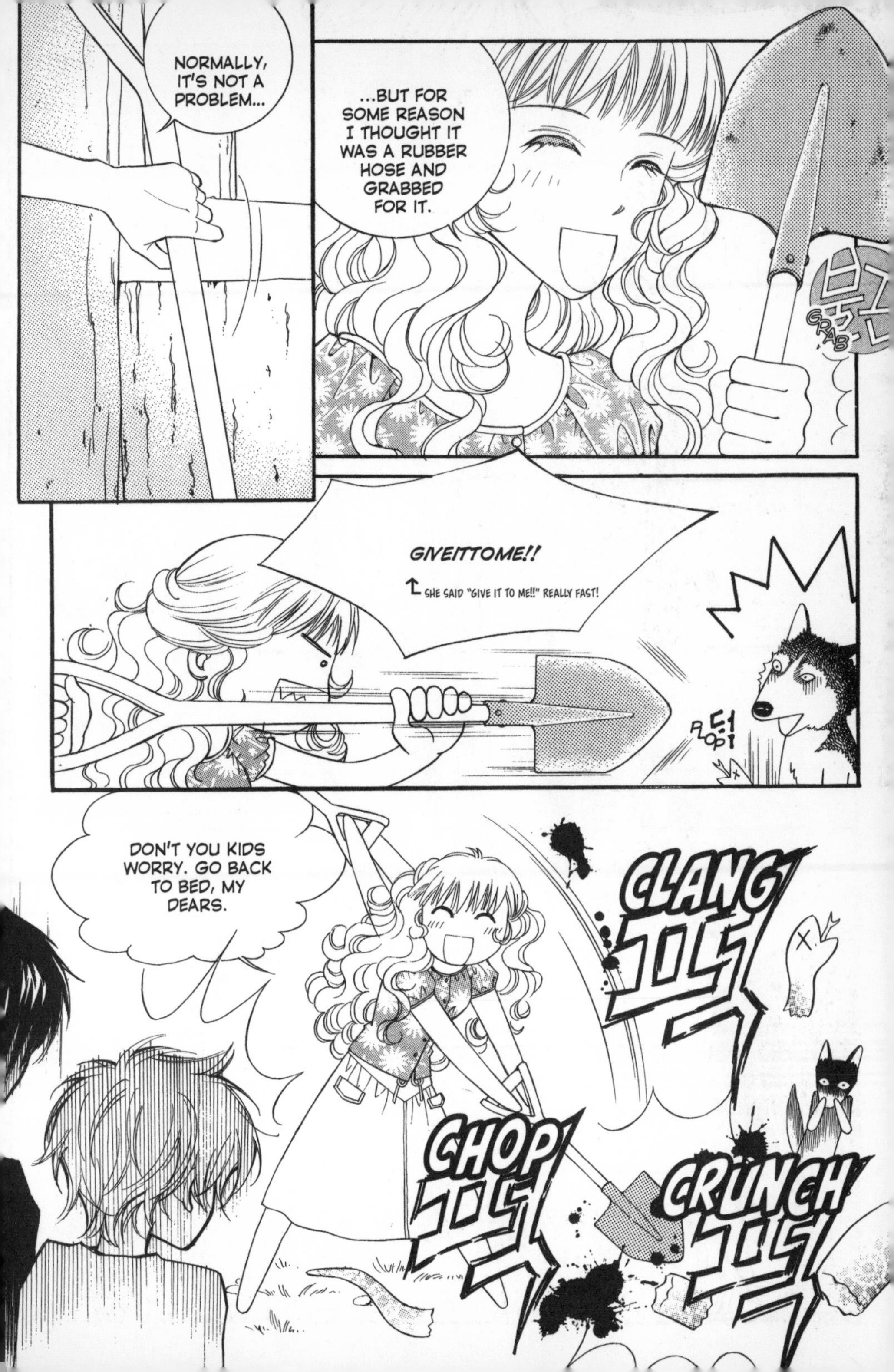
NORMALLY, IT'S NOT A PROBLEM...
...BUT FOR SOME REASON I THOUGHT IT WAS A RUBBER HOSE AND GRABBED FOR IT.
GRAB
GIVEITTOME!!
SHE SAID "GIVE IT TO ME!!" REALLY FAST!
FLOP!
DON'T YOU KIDS WORRY. GO BACK TO BED, MY DEARS.
CLANG
CHOP
CRUNCH

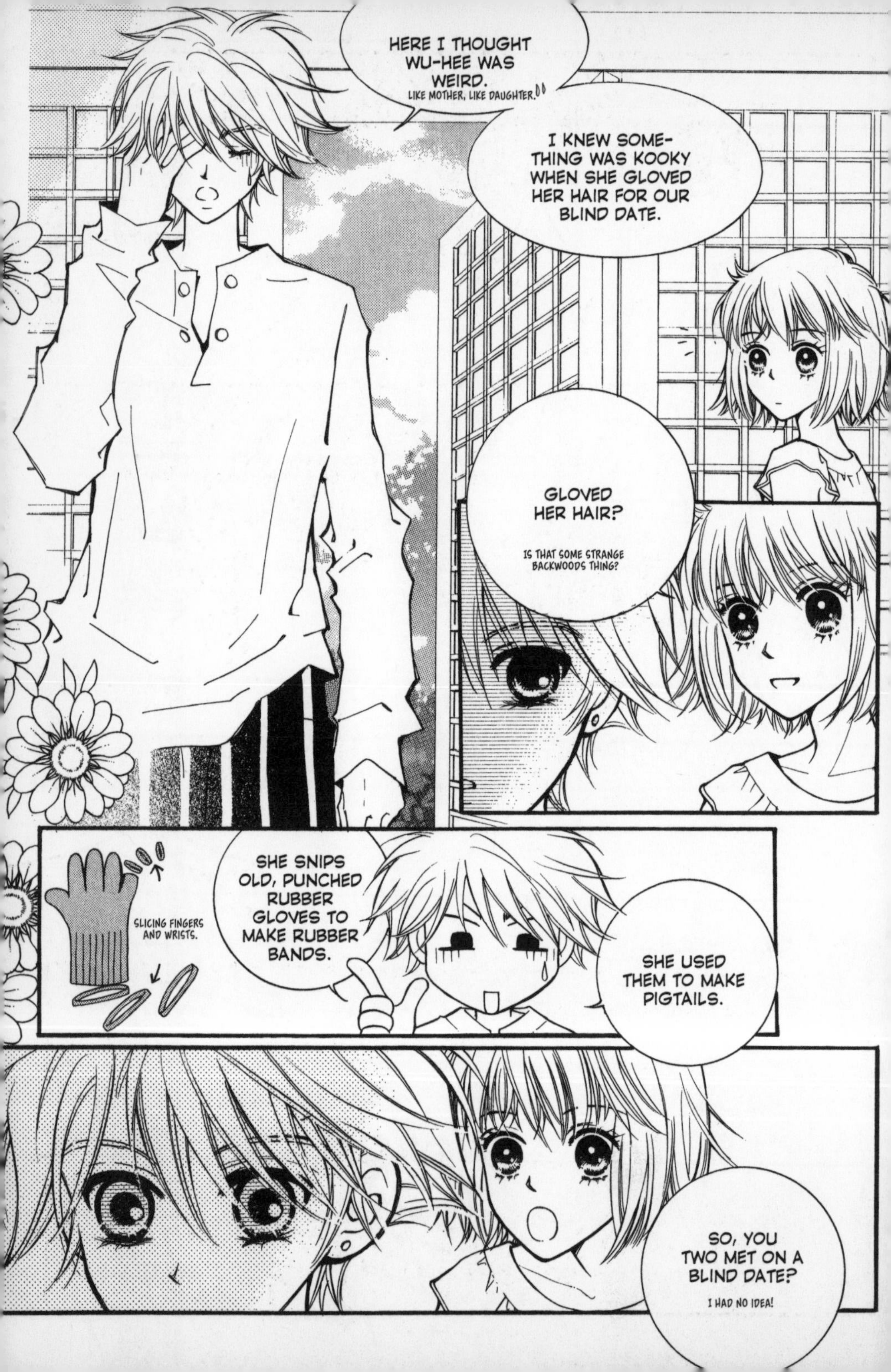
HERE I THOUGHT WU-HEE WAS WEIRD.
LIKE MOTHER, LIKE DAUGHTER.
I KNEW SOME-THING WAS KOOKY WHEN SHE GLOVED HER HAIR FOR OUR BLIND DATE.
GLOVED HER HAIR?
IS THAT SOME STRANGE BACKWOODS THING?
SLICING FINGERS AND WRISTS.
SHE SNIPS OLD, PUNCHED RUBBER GLOVES TO MAKE RUBBER BANDS.
SHE USED THEM TO MAKE PIGTAILS.
SO, YOU TWO MET ON A BLIND DATE?
I HAD NO IDEA!

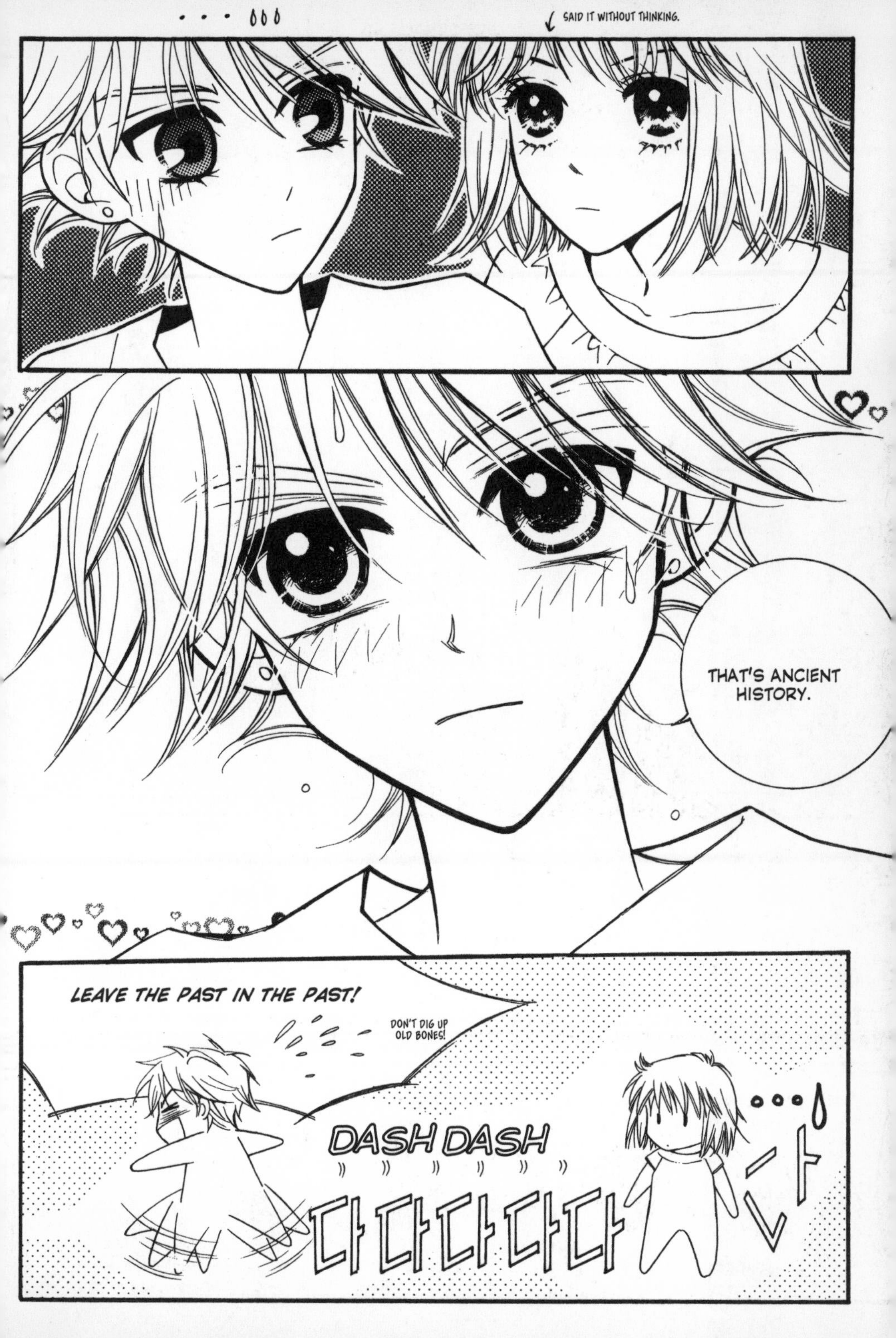
SAID IT WITHOUT THINKING.
THAT'S ANCIENT HISTORY.
LEAVE THE PAST IN THE PAST!
DON'T DIG UP OLD BONES!
DASH DASH

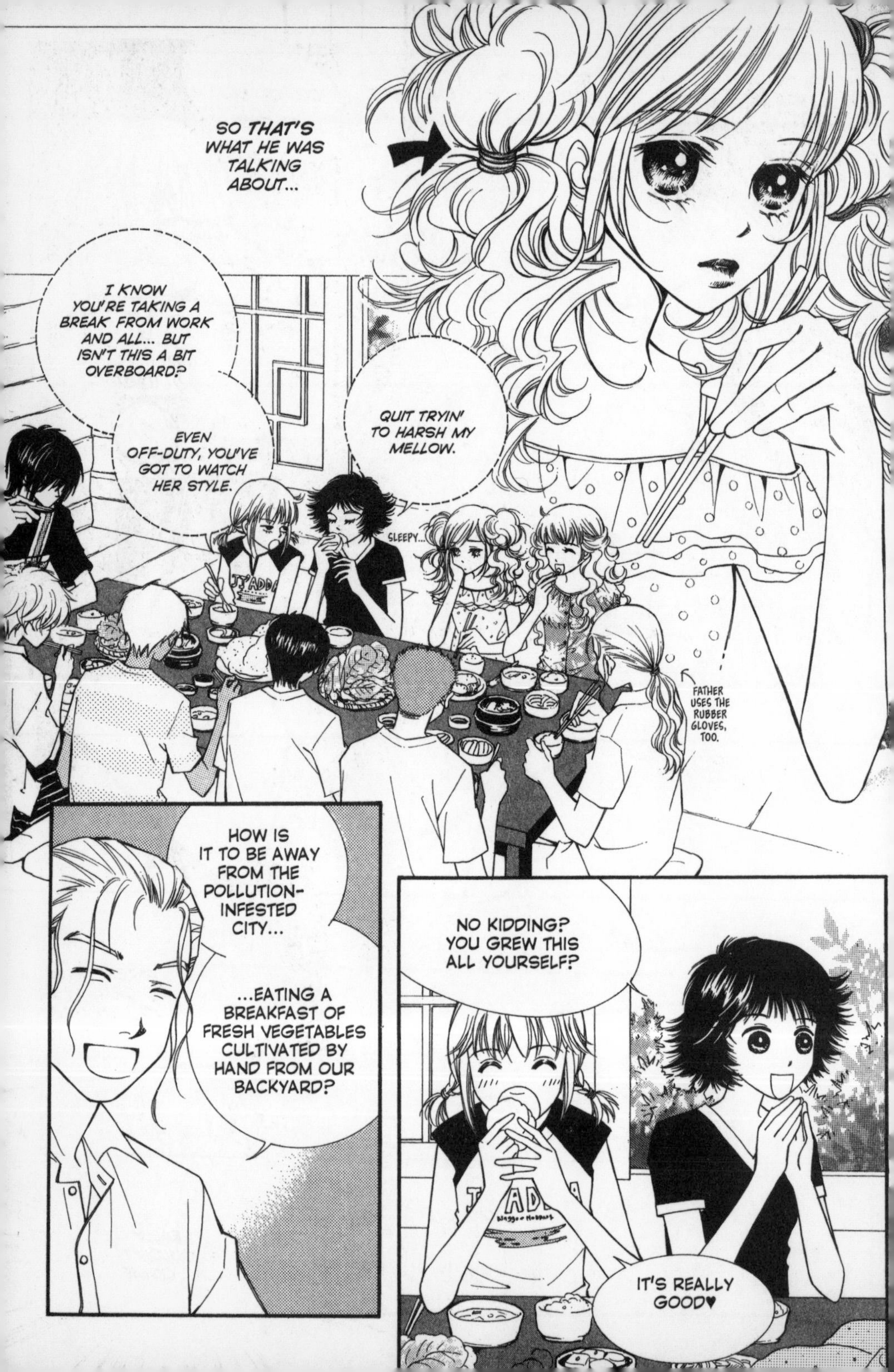
SO THAT'S WHAT HE WAS TALKING ABOUT...
I KNOW YOU'RE TAKING A BREAK FROM WORK AND ALL... BUT ISN'T THIS A BIT OVERBOARD?
EVEN OFF-DUTY, YOU'VE GOT TO WATCH HER STYLE.
QUIT TRYIN' TO HARSH MY MELLOW.
SLEEPY...
FATHER USES THE RUBBER GLOVES, TOO.
HOW IS IT TO BE AWAY FROM THE POLLUTION-INFESTED CITY...
...EATING A BREAKFAST OF FRESH VEGETABLES CULTIVATED BY HAND FROM OUR BACKYARD?
NO KIDDING? YOU GREW THIS ALL YOURSELF?
IT'S REALLY GOOD♥

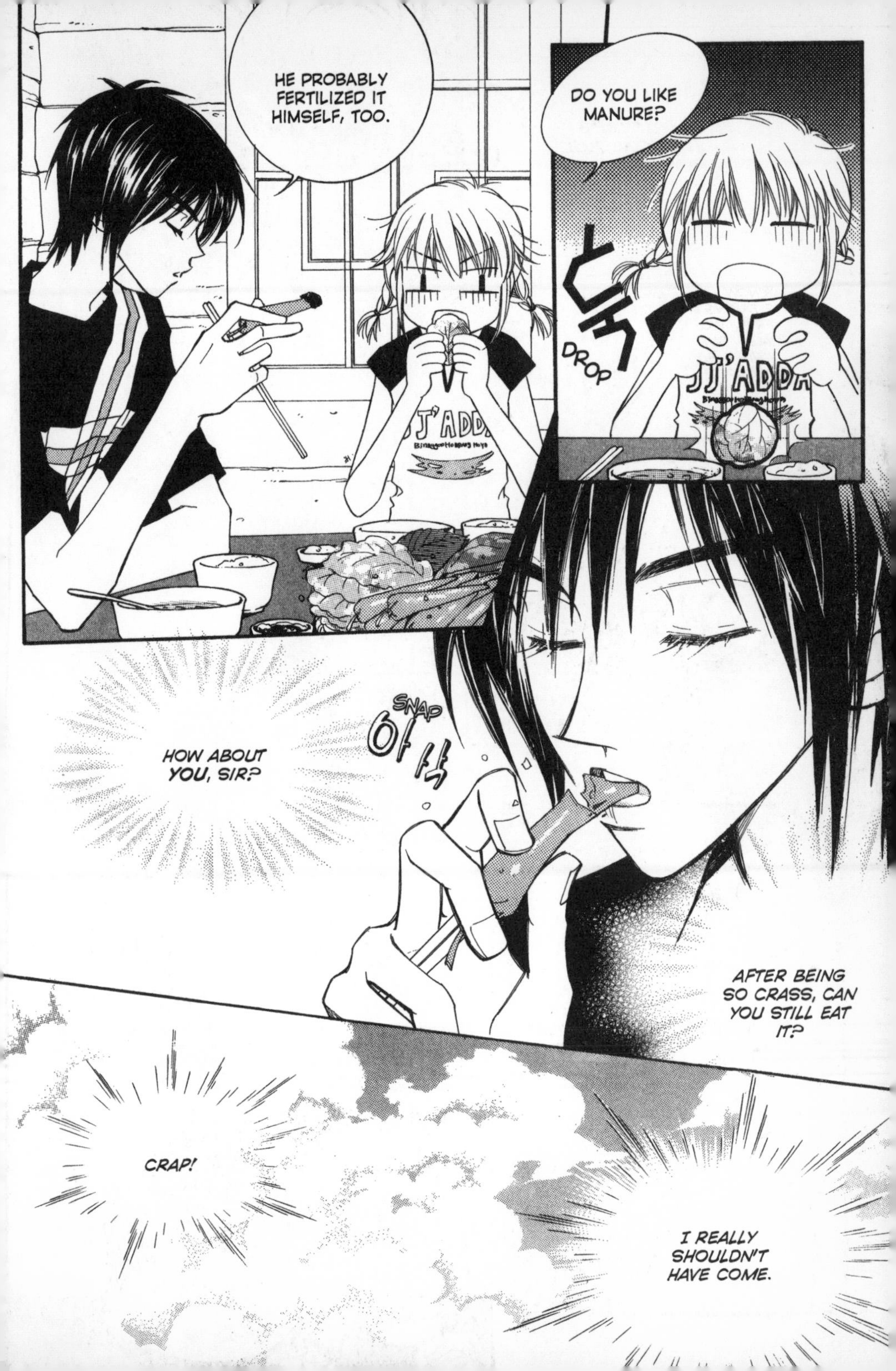
HE PROBABLY FERTILIZED IT HIMSELF, TOO.
DO YOU LIKE MANURE?
DROP
HOW ABOUT YOU, SIR?
SNAP
AFTER BEING SO CRASS, CAN YOU STILL EAT IT?
CRAP!
I REALLY SHOULDN'T HAVE COME.

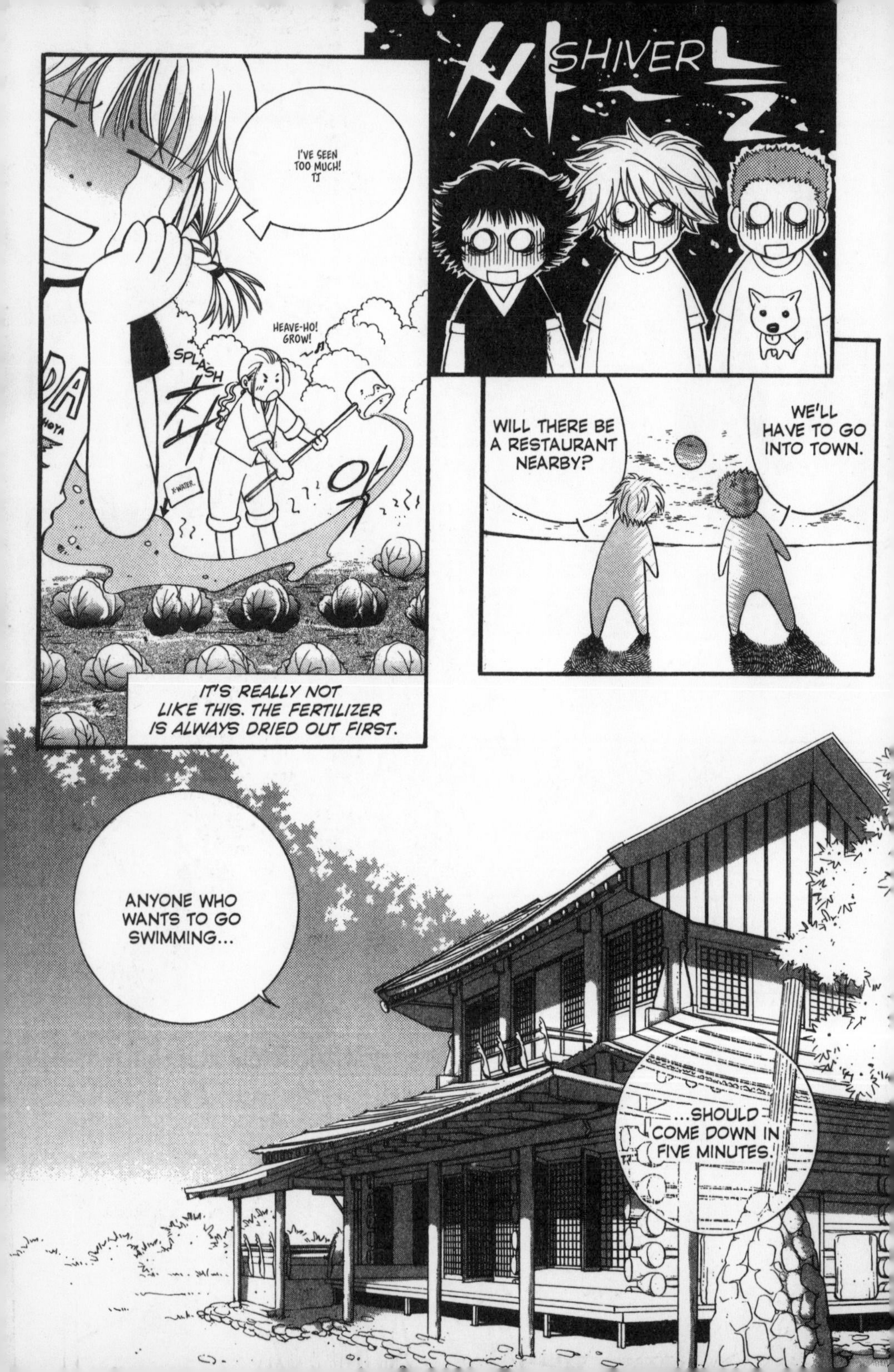
I'VE SEEN TOO MUCH! TJ
HEAVE-HO! GROW!
SPLASH
X-WATER.
IT'S REALLY NOT LIKE THIS. THE FERTILIZER IS ALWAYS DRIED OUT FIRST.
SHIVER
WILL THERE BE A RESTAURANT NEARBY?
WE'LL HAVE TO GO INTO TOWN.
ANYONE WHO WANTS TO GO SWIMMING...
...SHOULD COME DOWN IN FIVE MINUTES.

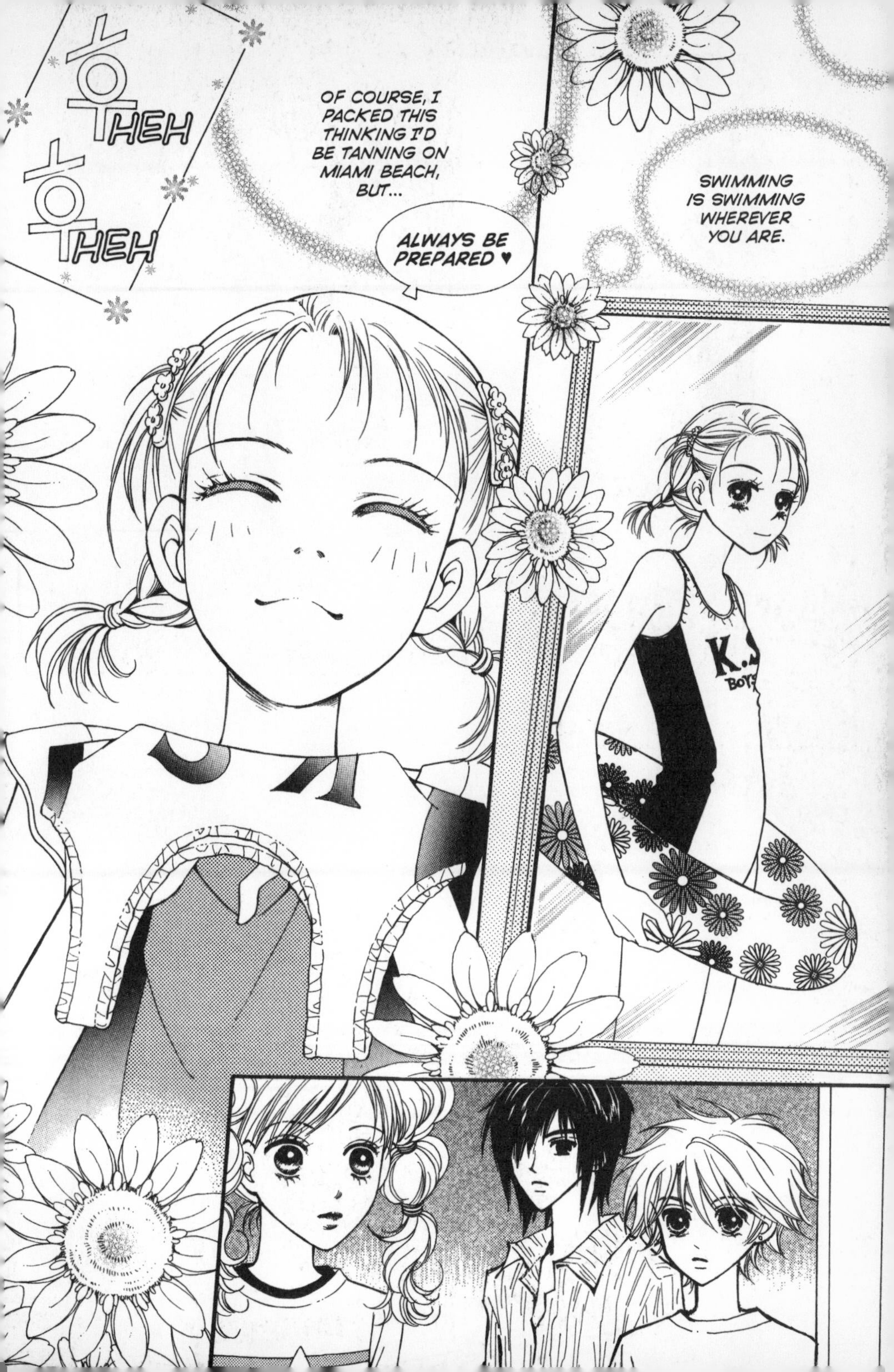

HEH
HEH
OF COURSE, I PACKED THIS THINKING I'D BE TANNING ON MIAMI BEACH, BUT...
ALWAYS BE PREPARED ♥
SWIMMING IS SWIMMING WHEREVER YOU ARE.

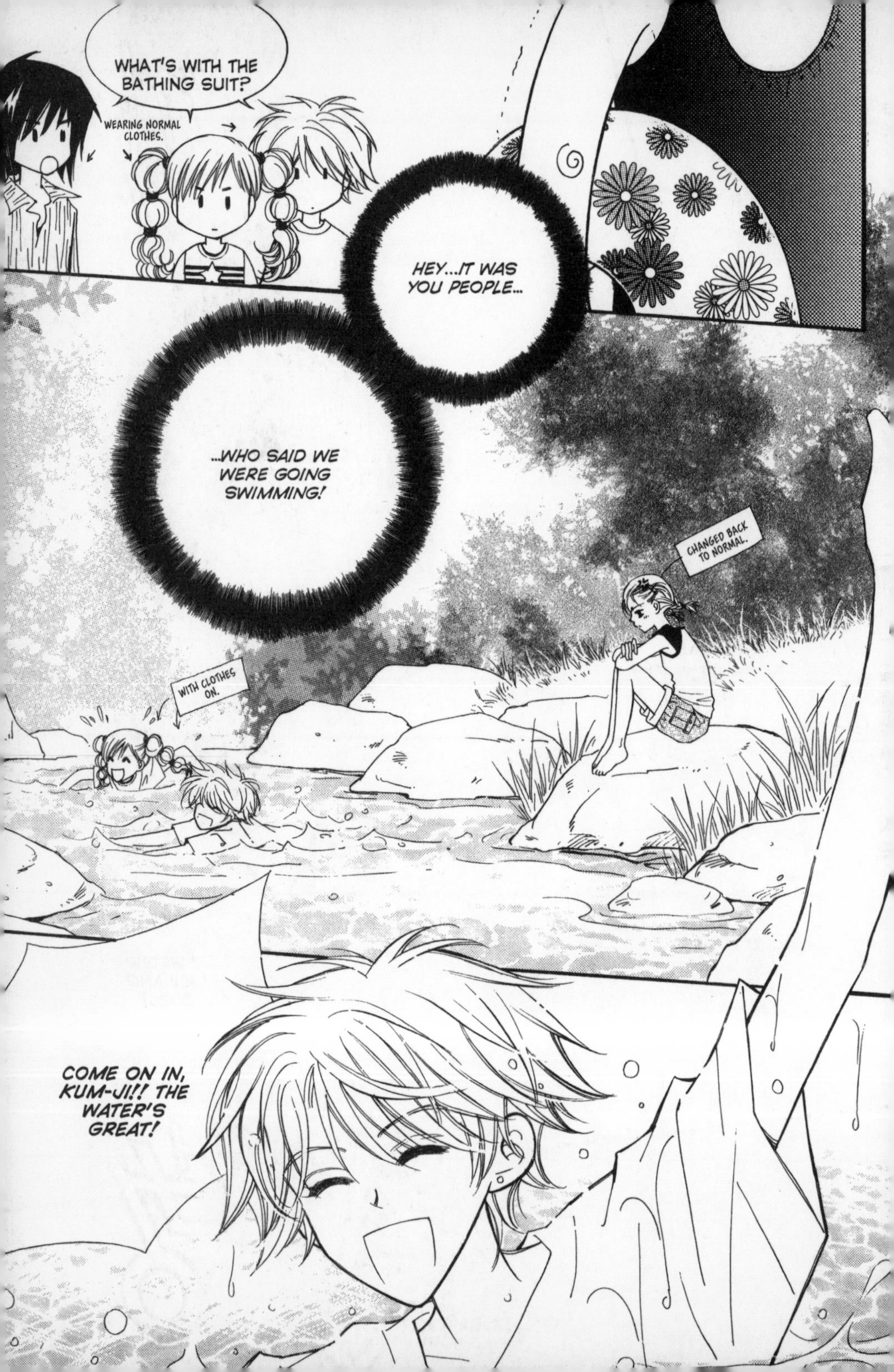
WHAT'S WITH THE BATHING SUIT?
WEARING NORMAL CLOTHES.
HEY...IT WAS YOU PEOPLE...
...WHO SAID WE WERE GOING SWIMMING!
CHANGED BACK TO NORMAL.
WITH CLOTHES ON.
COME ON IN, KUM-JI!! THE WATER'S GREAT!

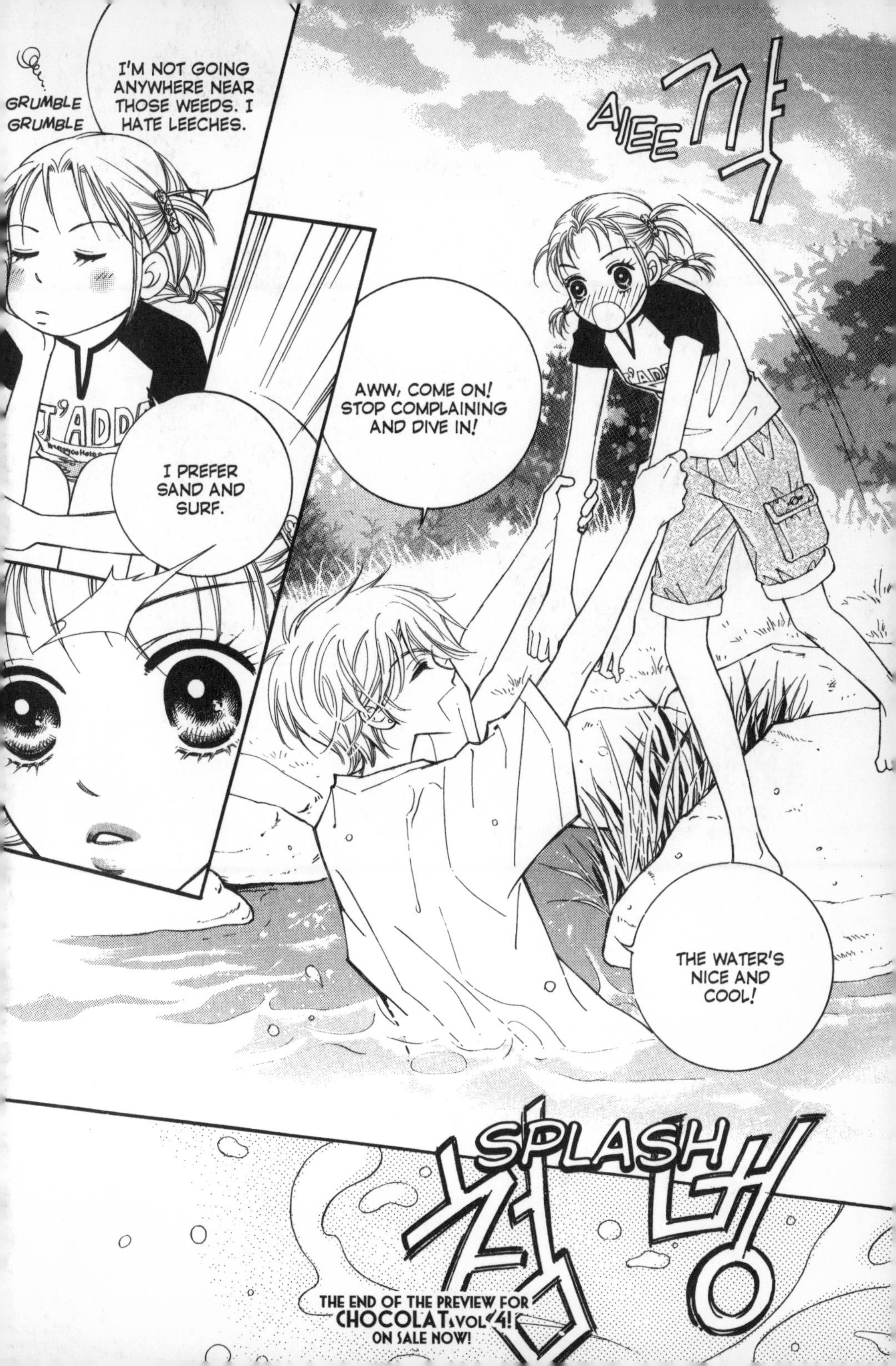
GRUMBLE GRUMBLE
I'M NOT GOING ANYWHERE NEAR THOSE WEEDS. I HATE LEECHES.
AIEE 꺄
AWW, COME ON! STOP COMPLAINING AND DIVE IN!
I PREFER SAND AND SURF.
THE WATER'S NICE AND COOL!
SPLASH 첨벙
THE END OF THE PREVIEW FOR CHOCOLAT, VOL. 4! ON SALE NOW!

Danbi Original

Legend vol.1

Story by Woo SooJung
Art by KARA

Translation HyeYoung Im
English Adaptation J. Torres
Touch-up and Lettering Terri Delgado · Marshall Dillon
Graphic Design EunKyung Kim

ICE Kunion

English Adaptation Editor HyeYoung Im · J. Torres
Managing Editor Marshall Dillon
Marketing Manager Erik Ko
Assistant Editor SoYeon Kim
Senior Editor JuYoun Lee
Editorial Director DongEun Lee
Managing Director Jackie Lee
Publisher and C.E.O. JaeKook Chun

Legend © 2006 Kara · Woo SooJung
First published in Korea in 2004 by SEOUL CULTURAL PUBLISHERS, Inc.
English text translation rights arranged by SEOUL CULTURAL PUBLISHERS, Inc.
English text © 2006 ICE KUNION

Published by ICE Kunion.
SIGONGSA 2F Yeil Bldg. 1619-4, Seocho-dong, Seocho-gu, Seoul, 137-878, Korea

ISBN : 89-527-4612-0

First printing, November 2006
10 9 8 7 6 5 4 3 2 1
Printed in Canada

www.icekunion.com/www.koreanmanhwa.com